❧ *The* ❧
PRESIDENT,
the POPE,
and the
PRIME
MINISTER

❧ *The* ❧
PRESIDENT,
the POPE,
and the
PRIME
MINISTER

THREE WHO CHANGED THE WORLD

JOHN O'SULLIVAN

Since 1947
REGNERY PUBLISHING, INC.
An Eagle Publishing Company • Washington, DC

Cataloging-in-Publication data on file with the Library of Congress

ISBN 978-1-59698-016-7

Published in the United States by
Regnery Publishing, Inc.
One Massachusetts Avenue, NW
Washington, DC 20001
www.regnery.com

First paperback published in 2008
Manufactured in the United States of America

10 9 8 7 6 5 4 3 2 1

Books are available in quantity for promotional or premium use. Write to Director of Special Sales, Regnery Publishing, Inc., One Massachusetts Avenue NW, Washington, DC 20001, for information on discounts and terms or call (202) 216-0600.

To my mother

CONTENTS

᚛᚜

Chapter One: The Indian Summer of Liberaldom
page 1

Chapter Two: The Nightmare Years
page 33

Chapter Three: Did God Guide the Bullets?
page 65

Chapter Four: Be Not Afraid
page 91

Chapter Five: Friends in Need
page 137

Chapter Six: Keeping Hope Alive
page 163

Chapter Seven: Imperial Overstretch
page 197

Chapter Eight: Triumph and Disaster
page 235

Chapter Nine: Checkmate
page 283

Acknowledgments
page 335

Notes
page 337

Index
page 353

CHAPTER ONE

THE INDIAN SUMMER OF LIBERALDOM

As the 1970s began, three talented middle managers worried about their respective institutions, which seemed to be crumbling. Worse, there seemed little they could do about it. All three were, in the jargon of management, on the edge of the boardroom, not at the center of events and decision-making.

Karol Wojtyla was the cardinal-archbishop of Cracow, Poland's second city, in a Church still dominated by an Italian pope and Italian clerical bureaucrats. Margaret Thatcher had just entered the cabinet of Edward Heath's new Conservative government in the middle-ranking position of minister of education. Ronald Reagan was in his second and final term as governor of California.

All three had strong personalities, great abilities, and loyal followings. Two of them had good prospects.

Wojtyla might conceivably rise to become the Catholic primate of Communist Poland and an influential religious leader in an Eastern Europe then adjusting to the permanence of Soviet rule. Thatcher might become Britain's first female chancellor of the exchequer (finance minister in non-medieval language) if her wildest ambitions were realized. She conceded at the time that the post of prime minister would remain beyond the grasp of a woman for many more decades.[1] Both were still rising stars.

At the age of sixty, however, Reagan was probably basking in the warmth of his last hurrah. The Right's favorite had failed in a late bid for the Republican Party's 1968 presidential nomination, and now his successful, more moderate rival, Richard Nixon, was almost certain to run for re-election in 1972. The Californian's presidential prospects looked highly uncertain—his national future perhaps limited to a return to the "mashed potato" circuit of political lecturing. On the verge of receiving his first Social Security check when the 1976 primaries opened, Reagan was already dangerously close to becoming an elder statesman.

All three were plainly at or near the peak of their careers. And those peaks were tantalizingly short of the very top.

It was not hard for any intelligent observer to explain why these three, with such high abilities, had obtained only limited success. All three were handicapped by being too sharp, clear, and definite in an age of increasingly fluid identities and sophisticated doubts. Put simply, Wojtyla was too Catholic, Thatcher too conservative, and Reagan too American.

These qualities might not have been disadvantages in times of greater confidence in Western civilization—or in moments of grave crisis such as 1940 in Britain, or 1941 in America, or in sixteenth-century Rome—when people prefer their leaders to be lions rather than foxes. But 1970 was two years after the revolutionary *annus mirabilis* of 1968. It was a time when historical currents seemed to be smoothly bearing mankind, including the Catholic Church, Britain, and America, in an undeniably liberal and even progressive direction.

Revolutions of every kind—sexual, religious, political, economic, social—were breaking out from the campus to the Vatican to the rice paddies of the Third World. The sexual revolution of the 1960s, now actually being implemented, was liberating gays, lesbians, housewives, unhappy spouses, single parents—and, of course, those who wanted to sleep with them—from closets of either silence or irksome duty. Feminism and the United States Supreme Court had added legal abortion to the growing list of women's rights. The Catholic Church had embarked in the previous decade on the internal revolution of the Second Vatican Council; Catholic liberals were now threading through the dioceses of Western Europe and America, purging the liturgy of traditional hymns and high-sounding language and seeking to reconcile faith with secular forms of "liberation." The welfare revolution, already entrenched in Europe, was now being extended to America by, of all people, Richard Nixon, with his plans for a guaranteed minimum income and affirmative action. As Nixon also conceded ("We're all Keynesians now"), the Keynesian revolution in economics was believed to be the key to steadily rising prosperity guided by government and interrupted hardly at all by recessions. The scientific "Green Revolution," together with government-to-government aid, promised to extend this prosperity to the poor nations of the Third World. The Third World itself, growing in confidence and clout at United Nations forums, gained more recruits when the Portuguese empire in Africa collapsed overnight, replaced by two new independent governments in Angola and Mozambique. That left South Africa and Rhodesia as the last doomed holdouts against the world revolutions of decolonization and racial equality carried out under UN auspices. There and in countries such as Iran and Brazil, where change was resisted by oppressive governments or the military, more violent forms of revolution were employed. These had been encouraged when armed Marxist peasants in black pajamas had won half a victory in Vietnam as the war wound down, or was at least "Vietnamized" and American POWs began returning home. But it was generally agreed among progressive opinion that the Vietnam War had been an immoral mistake never to be repeated. More realistic statesmen in the advanced world saw the wisdom of avoiding violence and upheaval by yielding gracefully to other revolutions. Mao's China came in from the cold and took its permanent seat on the UN Security Council courtesy of the Nixon-Kissinger "opening" to China. Edward Heath's Conservative government in Britain not only offered left-wing labor unions an unprecedented say in determining economic policy, but also surrendered Britain's recently imperial sovereignty to an embryonic united European superpower. Looking further ahead, the West German government was forging links with the East European Communist regimes in a policy of *Ostpolitik* that assumed the two halves of Europe would soon converge in some new blend of planned economy and social democracy. Détente promised the same convergence for the two superpowers, making the threat of nuclear war seem pointless in a world moving inexorably toward a future of peace, love, and bureaucracy.

Driving all these subordinate revolutions was what Walt W. Rostow, the distinguished liberal theorist of economic takeoff, called "the revolution of rising expectations." Mankind the world over wanted a better life, was no longer prepared to live under the old rules and limits, and demanded that governments and social institutions provide a blend of prosperity, welfare, and equality—or yield office to those who would. Politicians of the liberal Left were far more prepared to promise such delights than those of a conservative Right that still tended toward caution and even pessimism. Liberals were also more comfortable with striking attitudes of rebellion from positions of authority—which legitimated that authority in an anti-establishment age. Accordingly, liberals dominated debate and the general direction of policy even when they were out of power. And though they sometimes lost the power of government through election defeats, they and their colleagues almost never lost power in the bureaucracy, the courts, the universities, the media, the charitable sector, and the great cultural institutions. The West—Europe more than America but both to different degrees—was governed by the assumptions of a liberal church just as Christendom had been governed according to the assumptions of the conservative Roman Catholic Church. This new order might have been called Liberaldom.

In those days even the Catholic Church—let alone the Tory and Republican parties—was seeking to soften its image to accommodate a more liberal world, a less deferential congregation, and a less orthodox philosophical climate. Even many traditionalists, political and religious, wanted subtle and ingenious leaders who might divert these new challenges into orthodox channels, rather than stiff-necked reactionaries who might break themselves and their institutions in a futile attempt to resist historical inevitabilities. Wojtyla, Thatcher, and Reagan all embodied such fading virtues as faith, self-reliance, and patriotism—which the modern world seemed to be leaving behind. To use a British political metaphor, if they were "big beasts" in the jungles of politics and religion, that was because they were dinosaurs.

An Orthodox Rebel

Karol Wojtyla was less subject to this suspicion than Reagan and Thatcher, for the simple reason that he was less well known. Except for a brief period in Rome, he had lived his life in a Poland invaded by the Nazis, occupied by the Soviets, and ruled by their Polish Communist satraps. His main intellectual interests had been cultural and philosophical rather than directly political, which was why the Communist authorities had initially regarded him as relatively harmless and even pliable. Wojtyla's fame was also obscured by his modesty. When he was consecrated auxiliary bishop of Cracow in 1958 and full archbishop in 1964, and even when he was made a cardinal three years later, he self-consciously subordinated himself to the great Polish primate Cardinal Stefan Wyszynski. All these things meant that a certain mystery cloaked his views and personality for those outside his diocese and Poland.

As a Catholic bishop under a Communist government, moreover, he was concerned principally with Eastern European issues that Western Europe, America, and the rest of the world knew little about. Indeed, throughout the 1970s most political and religious leaders, betraying the provincialism of the sophisticated, cared less and less about the persecuted Church or the "captive nations" where Christians lived under modern penal laws. While the archbishop of Cracow struggled to ensure that Polish Catholic workers would have a local church on their new housing developments, specifically designed by the Communist authorities to exclude religion, the Church outside Eastern Europe was dealing nervously with a very different set of problems. They included the implementation of Vatican II reforms throughout the Church, the controversy over Catholic teaching on artificial birth control, and the gradual softening of Catholic opposition to Marxism seen both in Vatican diplomacy and in the growing sympathy for a *Marxisant* "liberation theology" in Latin America.

On all of these questions Wojtyla took essentially orthodox positions that theoretically put him at odds with the "progressive" bishops and theologians of Western Europe and the United States. As an academic philosopher, however, he brought a distinctive argumentative approach to them based on "personalism"—the Christian response to liberal individualism that sees the individual not as an isolated actor achieving a mythical self-realization but as someone developing his personality within the social context of friends, family, and work. This philosophical bent, reinforced by his pastoral experience and by his own personality, allowed Wojtyla to express his orthodoxy through subtle, humane, and novel arguments. This combination—*fortiter in re, suaviter in modo*—would be a hallmark of his papacy. It was a superb and effective political strategy—except that it was not a political strategy. It was a sincere reflection of Wojtyla's firm belief that Catholic truth must be presented in terms that were intelligible and sympathetic to modern well-educated laymen as well as to other faiths. Still, its effect in these early days was to soften but not disguise the traditional nature of Wojtyla's Catholicism. That made him a puzzle to progressive churchmen in Rome and elsewhere outside Poland, but it also meant that they cherished hopes that he might perhaps move to their side of the altar rail.

Reform and Resistance

Wojtyla was least at odds with progressive and liberal Catholics in his attitude to the implementation of the Vatican II reforms. It was as a participant in the Council debates that he began to establish a reputation with his episcopal colleagues worldwide. Many of the reforms that emerged from these debates were rooted in Wojtyla's thought and reflected progressive concerns. This was especially true for ecumenism and the declaration on religious freedom.

Wojtyla had always shown the respect for other faiths that later animated his papacy and produced the encyclical *Ut Unum Sint*. When a locally respected Lutheran teacher died in Cracow, the archbishop said a requiem Mass for her and arranged for her Lutheran pastor to attend. Walking into the church that day, Wojtyla went directly over and embraced the pastor "as a brother in Christ." It was a small gesture perhaps, but one very heartening to the Lutheran minority in Cracow, and merely one of many such gestures over the decades. This practical ecumenism was reflected intellectually in the 1959 essay that, as a novice bishop, Wojtyla sent to Rome in preparation for Vatican II. In it he argued for "less emphasis on those things that separate us and searching instead for all that brings us together." His occasional interventions on ecumenism in debates were consistently in tune with this outlook.

Not surprisingly, he was equally firm in his support for the related value of religious freedom. As noted by his distinguished biographer, George Weigel[2] (to whom all writers on John Paul II are indebted beyond possibility of repayment), both religious freedom and ecumenism were logically derived from the "Christian humanism" that Wojtyla developed through prayer, philosophy, and pastoral work. When Christ became Man, He established the high standing of the human being in creation. Every human being has a dignity—and by extension a right to freedom of conscience—that both Church and state are obliged to respect. In a written contribution to the Second Vatican Council debates, Wojtyla made the implications of this individual human dignity unmistakably plain to a gathering that included bishops still attached to the argument that error had no rights: "This civil right is founded not just in a principle of toleration, but in the natural right of every person to be familiar with the truth, which right we must set alongside the Church's right to hand on the truth."[3] From a Catholic standpoint, it would be hard to go further in defense of religious and intellectual liberty than comparing it to the teaching authority of the Church.

Wojtyla was less in tune with progressive Catholics on the Vatican reforms dealing with the government of the Church. He shared the progressives' view that the laity was as important as priests, bishops, and popes in the communion of believers. But he thought the role of Christian laymen was to take the truths of Christianity out to the world where lay people worked—to engage in a dialogue with the world over both Christian and secular truths—rather than, as the progressives argued, to share the responsibility for governing the Church with priests and bishops. Like the progressives, he supported more "authority" for the bishops. But he was critical of their argument that greater authority for the bishops required an increase in their power at the expense of the pope. Secular ideas such as "the separation of powers," he maintained, did not apply to ecclesiastical government because pope and bishops were united in a collegial relationship rather than divided by a struggle for power. Christian truth and the good government of the church would both emerge gradually from debate conducted by the bishops with each other and with the pope rather than from an imitation of government, opposition, and majority rule.

It sounds a somewhat vague and otherworldly view—except for what happened next. (Granted, a bishop might reasonably regard "otherworldly" as a term of praise.) When the Second Vatican Council ended, there began a long debate on what it signified throughout the Church. Liberal Catholics endorsed the Vatican II reforms as a still incomplete agenda for the "democratization" of the Church. "Reactionaries" such as the followers of Archbishop Marcel Lefebvre (who eventually became schismatics) warned that it represented surrender to a hostile and anarchic modernity. Many faithful orthodox Catholics felt uneasy and nervous about this clash of interpretations—and also by some of the liturgical changes introduced by liberal Church bureaucrats—but they sought faithfully to grasp and implement the reforms. Not all these disputes have evaporated even today.

In the Cracow archdiocese, however, the reception of Vatican II was very different. Following his own unworldly prescription for Church government, Wojtyla submitted the Vatican reforms to a long debate by both the laymen and clergy of Cracow. Weigel describes Wojtyla's thinking on this: "The best way to deepen the Council's interpretation . . . was for the archdiocese as a whole to relive the experience of Vatican II through an archdiocesan synod, a mini-Council on the local church level." The synod was established on May 8, 1972, and closed seven years later, when its founder was already pope, on the feast day of St. Stanislaw in 1979. Between those dates the laity and clergy of the diocese studied the texts of the Second Vatican Council and their bishop's commentaries on them in more than five hundred study groups. Eventually they produced three hundred pages of documents covering every aspect of life in the diocese. Long before they reached the stage of proposing changes in church life, however, they had imbibed the teachings of Vatican II more or less intravenously in their study groups. The disputes that roiled Catholic life elsewhere never really emerged in Wojtyla's diocese. And Vatican II was experienced there, in Weigel's words, "as a religious event aimed at strengthening the evangelical and apostolic life of the Church, not as a political struggle over power within the Church bureaucracy."

That success served not only to increase Wojtyla's prestige throughout the Church but also to blind progressives yet again to his essential orthodoxy. As someone who had apparently converted a conservative Polish diocese to Vatican II without protests, he looked like an archbishop they could do business with.

New Issues for an Age-Old Religion

Wojtyla was more clearly at odds with progressives over the question that came to dominate Catholic debate more than any other in the late 1960s and early 1970s: the 1968 papal encyclical *Humanae Vitae* and its continued prohibition of artificial methods of birth control. Shortly after he became pope, Paul VI had asked an established papal commission on family, population, and the birth rate to report on whether the Church should rethink its teaching that artificial methods of birth control were morally inadmissible. The sexual revolution was spreading through Western society. The Pill had been invented in 1961. Young Catholic couples were asking their confessors, in effect, for permission to use it. And many liberal theologians were inclined to argue that its occasional use was permissible in a marriage generally open to the possibility of children. The commission was scheduled to send its report to the pope in 1966. Its members included the young Bishop Wojtyla.

His inclusion was not surprising. The pope admired Wojtyla's sensitivity to the needs of modern lay people. As a priest, philosopher, and bishop, he had always taken a close interest in problems of sexuality, marriage, and the family. While serving as a priest in a university parish, he had recruited young people for what were, in effect, pre-marriage guidance counseling sessions on weekends in the country. (Interestingly, none of the young people who attended these sessions and later married have subsequently divorced.)[4] Wojtyla incorporated what he learned from these sessions, from his philosophical work, and perhaps above all from the confessional itself in several later works, in particular his 1960 treatise *Love and Responsibility*. One quotation from it will establish both the personalist flavor of Wojtyla's thinking on these questions and his anxiety that much sexual unhappiness, if not most, could be traced to male egoism: "[Female frigidity] is usually the result of egoism in the man who, failing to recognize the subjective desires of the woman in intercourse, and the objective laws of the sexual process taking place in her, seeks merely his own satisfaction, sometimes quite brutally."[5]

That anxiety would shape Wojtyla's own contribution—and that of his diocese—to the *Humanae Vitae* controversy. He established a diocesan commission to study the question of birth control. It began meeting six months before the papal commission quietly presented two reports to the pope—a majority report allowing artificial contraception and a minority one upholding traditional Church doctrine. Wojtyla could not attend the commission's final meeting in Rome because the Polish government refused him an exit visa. It is clear, however, that if he had been in attendance, he would have voted with the minority. The memorandum of his diocesan commission—presented two years later to a Pope Paul still agonizing over his choice between the two papal reports—was firmly opposed to any dilution of the traditional view.

Its grounds of opposition, however, were a blend of the traditional and the personalist. Married couples, it argued, had a duty to regulate their families responsibly. Artificial methods of contraception were rejected, however, because they violated the physical integrity of the woman while liberating the man for selfish pursuit of his own pleasure. Instead of promoting mutual love, they tended to objectify one's spouse and to reduce him or her (generally her) to a mere means. They thus contradicted the concept of marital equality. And in attempting to outwit nature, they risked damaging the health of the woman in a way that natural family planning did not.

These arguments arrived on Pope Paul's desk a few months before he issued *Humanae Vitae* and doubtless helped him to confirm the traditional doctrine. Some of those who worked on the diocesan report are convinced that it greatly influenced the encyclical. Weigel is probably right, however, to argue that its influence was relatively superficial and that *Humanae Vitae* lacked "the rich personalist context" of the Cracow document. Even so, an encyclical more influenced by Cracow might have made very little difference in 1968. Wojtyla's emphasis on women's rights in both sex and marriage was certainly in tune with some of the egalitarian arguments of the fledgling feminist movement. But that same movement—and other new movements promoting personal self-realization—wanted women to assume male sexual egoism rather than for men to become sexually chaste. Weigel's ingenious fallback argument that a more positive stress on natural family planning might have appealed to an ecologically minded generation then waking up to the importance of "nature"[6] is logical enough. But the new environmentalists saw man as an enemy of nature rather than as an integral part of it. They were quite happy to employ unnatural methods to reduce his numbers and environmental impact. Besides, they were whoring after strange goddesses, notably Gaia (an anthropomorphic expression of nature fathered by James Lovelock in 1972), and so they were increasingly deaf to Christian concepts of environmental stewardship. It was, after all, 1968.

It is also unfortunately true that the language used by theologians to discuss sex is even more clinically distant from the actual experience than that employed by sexologists. So *Humanae Vitae* was always unlikely to persuade a generation tasting the first forbidden fruits of sexual liberation.

And, in fact, it was widely ignored by many otherwise faithful Catholics in Western Europe and America. Bishops and priests, rather than face an open schism, failed to support the encyclical in either the confessional or the pulpit. An initial exception was Cardinal O'Boyle of Washington, D.C., who sought to discipline priests who had openly dissented. Rome intervened to ensure that there would be neither disciplinary action nor a retraction by the dissidents. There ensued what Father Richard John Neuhaus, a distinguished Catholic theologian and the editor of the journal *First Things*, calls the "Truce of 1968," whereby "rejecting moral doctrines solemnly proclaimed by the Church's teaching authority was, essentially, penalty-free."[7] These internal divisions on birth control still fester today; indeed, they have spread to other issues, such as gay rights.

Whatever the impact of the "Truce of 1968" on the Church, however, it probably had a beneficial effect on the career of Bishop Wojtyla. By lowering the temperature of the *Humanae Vitae* debate, the truce made liberal bishops less likely to reflexively oppose anyone who had defended traditional doctrines—particularly one who, like Wojtyla, had done so with non-traditional arguments.

Not for the first time, nor for the last, Wojtyla found himself in the happy position of the young Melbourne in Robert Bolt's film *Lady Caroline Lamb*. A young Whig, Melbourne is congratulated on his first parliamentary speech by the Tory leader, George Canning.

"A Whig speech, Sir," says Melbourne defensively.

"Whig speech, Tory arguments," replies Canning with complacent shrewdness.

Marxism and the Church

In Wojtyla's case, any complacency on the part of progressive opponents would have been quite unjustified. His arguments, however unconventional, were always in the service of a clear and definite orthodoxy. And when it came to relations between the Church and Communism—the third major development in 1970s Catholic thought—Wojtyla could call on something more powerful than arguments to defend traditional positions: namely, experience.

Relations between the Catholic Church and Communism were a topic on which Wojtyla was undisguisedly swimming against the intellectual tide in both the Church and Western intellectual opinion. As early as the mid-1960s, the idea had arisen in intellectual Catholic circles that Christianity and Marxism were more compatible than Vatican diplomacy under Pius

XII had allowed. Catholic intellectuals and theologians began to advocate a Christian-Marxist dialogue on the grounds that both sets of doctrines sought to ameliorate the lot of the poor through greater social justice and were therefore allied against a liberal capitalism that allegedly created and aggravated poverty. These ideas were exported from Europe and the United States to Latin America, where, in a less democratic climate, they blossomed into the dark flowers of "liberation theology."

Liberation theology sought to justify violence against an unjust state by defining the social order of Latin countries as "latent violence." It was also a form of secular reductionism that transformed sin into capitalist "structures," the Church into the proletariat, salvation into economic "liberation," and Christ into a revolutionary guerrilla. These arguments were bizarrely overreaching, to say the very least, yet they were widely accepted on the international Catholic Left. And in the 1970s many thought they had been given a kind of papal blessing by a new Vatican diplomacy of *Ostpolitik* that sought better treatment for the Church in Eastern Europe by toning down the ideological volume of traditional Catholic anti-Communism.

The first two developments—Christian-Marxist dialogues and liberation theology—were rooted in a simple but profound misunderstanding. Though Marxism and Christianity are both opposed to economic and social injustice, their grounds of opposition are radically different. Christianity is a religion of love, Marxism a doctrine of power. Even when they seem to be engaged in the same cause, they are aiming at quite different results. For instance, both might agree to urge a capitalist employer to raise the wages of his workers and even support a strike against him if he resisted. But the aim of the Marxist would be to weaken the capitalist so that eventually he would be bankrupted, taken over by a monopoly, or forced to hand over his concern to the workers. Such contradictions in the capitalist system as a whole would lead to its collapse and the transfer of power to the proletariat. Strikes were an important tool in effecting that result. Christians, on the other hand, would seek a higher wage as a matter of justice. Once it was granted they would seek to reconcile the workers and the employer and, more generally, to shape an economic system that promoted harmony between different social classes on the basis of such ideas as the living wage. And love, unlike power, embraces all sides. It is more than arguable that Christians would be obliged to counsel *against* a strike that had as its aim the destruction of the employer or his enterprise—and that he would be justified in resisting it on behalf of his shareholders, or his family, or his own legitimate rights. That being so, a member of a Latin American upper or middle class would be still more justified in resisting the violence advocated by liberation theologians who sought to replace his authoritarian society with a still more oppressive totalitarian one.

Wojtyla was never tempted by such ideas, for the good reason that he was actually living in an oppressive totalitarian society. He was constantly battling a Polish government that was seeking to harass the Church and reduce its influence over an overwhelmingly Catholic population. Poland did not suffer the very worst brutalities like those imposed on the Soviet Union and Hungary, but the harassment was relentless and inventive nonetheless. Priests were taxed excessively, and often followed and beaten up; students were denied admission to universities if their parents were churchgoers; permits for the building of churches were withheld when new towns were developed; the state abolished old religious holidays and invented ersatz national ones; and there was a constant ideological campaign of lies in the media designed to weaken religion and reduce it to an expression of patriotic nostalgia.

Wojtyla resisted all these pressures by evading them inventively as much as by challenging them boldly. When the regime refused a permit to build a church—which was equivalent to preventing the creation of a new parish—the archbishop of Cracow would encourage his priests to form what Weigel calls "a parish-without-a-church"[8] by door-to-door evangelization. Once such an invisible parish had been created, he would demand a building permit to accommodate this new reality. Such an agitation enabled the construction of the famous "Ark" church in the workers' suburb of Nowa Huta. Its construction became a cause célèbre and was assisted by pilgrims from the whole of Europe, and the steel figure of a crucified Christ that today dominates the church was forged by the workers in Nowa Huta's Lenin Steelworks. Altogether, the building of the "Ark" church was a major moral defeat for the Communist regime.

On another occasion, a priest hit by a heavy tax bill was advised by his archbishop to report to prison for non-payment. Wojtyla then announced to the parishioners that he would take over the priest's parish duties for the period of his incarceration. The priest was promptly released. Wojtyla's technique of resistance disguised as accommodation was extremely hard for the regime to counter without resorting to outright brutal repression that would lose them the propaganda war. They were baffled by Wojtyla's understated defiance and grew increasingly hostile toward the troublesome priest.

But the extent of oppression and the resistance were not fully appreciated by Catholic churchmen outside Poland. This became clear to Wojtyla at the 1974 synod of bishops in Rome, which discussed, among other questions, the evangelization of the Communist world. Wojtyla was distressed by the failure of Western European and Latin American bishops to grasp the unpleasant "everyday reality" of Marxism, instead regarding it as a "fascinating abstraction."[9] Though appointed "relator," with the task of drafting the final report on which the bishops would vote, he was unable to persuade the various factions to accept an agreed draft. (The task was passed on to a commission.) Liberation theology and Christian-Marxist dialogues were exciting new ideas, blessed by the spirit of the age, which the bishops did not want to dismiss too rashly. Nor, probably, did they wish to give comfort to a capitalist system of which the Church had many criticisms at a moment when it seemed weakened by currency crises, oil price hikes, labor disputes, and the threat of hyper-inflation. Finally, the new Vatican *Ostpolitik* acted as a sort of indulgence, permitting bishops to flirt with the Marxist devil.

Ostpolitik was in reality embarked upon from much more hard-headed motives than ideological fashion. Like the West German government headed by Willy Brandt some years later, the Vatican of Pope Paul VI and Secretary of State Cardinal Agostino Casaroli had concluded that Eastern

Europe was destined to remain Communist for the indefinite future. That being so, the first responsibility of the wider Church was to protect the persecuted Christians of the Soviet bloc and the institutional church serving them. Rome wanted legal agreements with Communist governments that would allow the Vatican to appoint priests and bishops for service in the Eastern bloc. It was a strategy called *salvare il salvabile* (saving what can be saved) and even Pope Paul conceded that it was hardly a "policy of glory."[10] And there was, inevitably, a price to pay for it: consultation with the regimes on episcopal appointments, a diminution of anti-Communist rhetoric, the Vatican's diplomatic distancing from the West, and the halting of clandestine ordinations of priests in the Eastern bloc. In this cautious spirit *Ostpolitik* was pursued—symbolized all too neatly by Cardinal Casaroli donning a normal business suit to visit Poland in 1966 for negotiations with its government over a possible papal visit to mark the millennium of Polish Christianity.

No such visit was permitted. This was doubtless a disappointment to the Polish Catholic hierarchy, but it must also have confirmed their suspicions about the utility of *Ostpolitik*. Three strong doubts, objections even, about the Vatican's policy worried the Polish primate, Cardinal Wyszynski, and his deputy, Wojtyla. In the first place, they feared that the Communists—as technicians of power before all else—might be able to exploit differences of opinion within the Church to their own advantage. That was why Wyszynski sought to monopolize contacts between the Church and the regime—and why Wojtyla firmly and consistently subordinated himself to the primate on every conceivable question. On one occasion, asked by a journalist how many Polish cardinals could ski, Wojtyla replied, "40 percent." As there were only two Polish cardinals at the time, the journalist wondered how that could be. Wojtyla replied, "In Poland, Wyszynski counts for 60 percent."

Their second objection was that the assumption underlying *Ostpolitik* might well be false: the dominance of the Communist regimes in Eastern Europe was neither permanent nor stable. Not only were the subjects of the Soviet empire restive and discontented—there had been rebellions, after all, in East Germany in 1953, in Hungary in 1956, in Czechoslovakia in

1968, and in Poland itself in 1970—but the moral-cum-ideological foundations of the Communist regime were shaky and uncertain. The Communists had originally enjoyed some social support and even ideological respectability, and they still did outside Poland. As time went on, however, they increasingly depended, in the words of Norman Davies, the most distinguished foreign historian of the country, "on policemen rather than . . . philosophers" to remain in power.[11] Both Wyszynski and Wojtyla knew this from an "everyday reality" that the Vatican had never experienced. The Polish Church was able to call upon the loyalty of virtually the entire Polish nation—including the workers and excluding only the apparatchiks. That amounted to a highly unstable situation. It was not precisely replicated in other Communist satellites. In all of them, however, under its concrete façade Communist power was fragile, unstable, and kept in place only by domestic repression and popular fear of Soviet intervention.

Their third objection was that there were better strategies against Communist power than *Ostpolitik*, even if Communism proved permanent. Wyszynski's approach was one of firm political resistance in defense of the Church's rights and independence even under a Communist regime. Such a strategy was essential to prevent a manipulative government eroding Catholic rights over time. Wojtyla's approach was somewhat different—complementary rather than opposed—because it relied on the firmness of Wyszynski in the background. It is rightly described by Weigel as "cultural resistance" rather than strictly political resistance. It consisted of using all the legal avenues of expression—small magazines, theaters, universities, the pulpit, church organizations—to encourage a debate that, even when it seemed to be entirely cultural or religious, inevitably had political undertones. It meant reaching out to many social groups, even such left-wing dissidents as Adam Michnik, and drawing them into a common debate with Catholic intellectuals and the Church. It meant ignoring the Communist government rather than opposing it in order to build what would now be called an alternative "civil society." And it baffled the Communists because the debates conducted by this civil society were more exciting and realistic than those of the totalitarian state, even though the latter theoretically disposed of all the power.

Wojtyla's style of resistance began to influence the wider Polish Church. Poland's bishops became more outspoken—and in his distinctive way. A 1978 joint pastoral letter that declared "the spirit of freedom is the proper climate for the full development of the person" clearly bears the marks of Wojtyla's personalist Catholicism. His influence now began to spread from Poland to next-door Czechoslovakia. The Czech Church, persecuted more harshly than Poland's, was suffering from a shortage of priests, owing in part to the Vatican's *Ostpolitik* prohibition on the ordination of new priests by "underground" bishops. Wojtyla now began ordaining new priests for service in Czechoslovakia. He did so with the explicit permission of the Czech bishop who would be the priest's superior but without consulting the Vatican. He assumed—according to an interview he gave to Weigel many years later—that the Vatican may have turned a blind eye because it welcomed his actions as a kind of "safety valve."

Another guess may also be hazarded: Wojtyla was a Pole. There was an indulgence toward Poles on the topic of Communism in the Vatican then and later. It was understood that their anti-Communism was especially deep and that their courage had carved out a unique degree of religious freedom in the Communist world. That indulgence would not change the Vatican's mind on *Ostpolitik*, but it would excuse some degree of Polish resistance to it. By the same token, however, a Polish bishop would be viewed with greater reserve, if not suspicion, when it came to selecting the person who would be ultimately responsible for that and all other Vatican policies: the next pope.

Wojtyla was a coming cardinal by the mid-1970s. He led a new kind of cultural resistance to Communism in Poland. He was seen abroad as an impressively intellectual Church leader. Pope Paul had an admiring fondness for him and, as a mark of special favor, had invited him to give the 1976 Lenten retreat for the pope and the Roman Curia—a Lenten sacrifice in itself as it required from him no fewer than twenty-two sermons delivered in Italian over one week. He had impressed his influential listeners with a characteristic blend of sophisticated philosophy and theological orthodoxy. Yet the papacy looked to be beyond his reach. However silver his tongue and however fresh his philosophical arguments, he was still a

Polish traditionalist in a modernizing Church—too Catholic, in other words, to be pope.

~~え や~~

Three years before Wojtyla delivered his Lenten sermons, Dirk Gleysteen, a middle-ranking U.S. diplomat, had a very good lunch at the Connaught Hotel in London on May 22, 1973.[12] He would have enjoyed the food anyway; the Connaught, then as now, housed two of London's best restaurants. But he probably enjoyed the conversation much more than he expected because his lunch companion, the secretary of state for education and science, the Right Honorable Margaret Thatcher, despite having a public reputation as rather a starchy schoolmarm, was flagrantly indiscreet about her colleagues in the Heath government.

The conversation began with some conventional throat-clearing on Thatcher's part. "Parties don't win elections," she told the diplomat, "governments lose them." She forecast (wrongly) that food prices and housing would be the main issues in the next general election and (rightly) that her own responsibility of education would not. She had a low opinion of her Labour opposite number, Roy Hattersley ("no spine"), and a high one of her junior minister, Norman St. John-Stevas ("not very good at administration but lively, full of ideas, and making a useful contribution"). And she made the modest boast that the recent round of public spending cuts had not hurt education because she had persuaded the cabinet to reject the Treasury's initial program.

Gleysteen would have realized at this early stage that, as many others have since learned, Thatcher was exceptionally frank even for a British minister talking to a friendly diplomat. But she had scarcely begun. She went on to express high praise for social services secretary Sir Keith Joseph ("brilliant, versatile, and full of further promise") and for the former home secretary Reginald Maudling ("one of the best minds in the party"). Other judgments were more qualified: she clearly respected Geoffrey Howe, a senior minister in charge of price control, even though he was "too willing to compromise" and might not get over this "weakness"; Environment

Secretary Peter Walker was a "good politician" but lacked "the kind of first-class mind needed at the top"; junior minister David Howell was very able indeed but "always talking in phrases no one could understand." She was positively damning about others. Paul Channon and Christopher Chattaway she dismissed as "lightweights," and she remarked crisply of the telegenic Michael Heseltine that he "had everything it took in politics except brains."

Not all these judgments have stood the test of time. Maudling was dropped from Thatcher's own Shadow Cabinet a few years later largely because of his ineffectiveness. Walker, Channon, Howell, Howe, and Heseltine all served in senior positions in her governments with varying degrees of distinction. The latter two lit the fuse of her downfall eighteen years later—though it is fair to add that Heseltine never achieved the premiership in part because many Tories felt he lacked an intellectual anchor.

To Gleysteen, however, these frank judgments must have seemed pure gold. He rushed back to the embassy and sent the ambassador a memorandum repeating them. Few diplomatic lunches pay such lively dividends. But the U.S. ambassador, Walter Annenberg, also recognized that they were gold—with all the dangerous properties of that substance to blind. He sat on the memorandum for a full month, and when he finally sent it to Washington on June 25, 1973, he prefaced it with a character study of Thatcher and her political prospects that set her comments in perspective.

Annenberg's study was friendly, shrewd, and relatively conventional. It struck notes that endured throughout Thatcher's career. And it underestimated her. She was, wrote Annenberg, a very real political asset to the government, a strong supporter of Heath, and a "workhorse" who carried weight within Tory councils, but it was most doubtful that she could realistically expect to lead her party. He summed her up:

> Mrs. Thatcher is an almost archetypical, slightly to the right-of-center Tory whose views are strongly influenced by her own middle-class background and experience. A well-educated, intelligent, and even sophisticated woman herself, Mrs. Thatcher

shares with others in her party a certain anti-intellectual bias. Her views on her party colleagues are interesting but should be read with the above in mind.[13]

In a phrase: too conservative.

Annenberg and other friendly observers were not foolishly wrong here, but they had not quite grasped the complicated cocktail of Thatcher's political personality and how it might be suited to the changing circumstances of Britain. It was a cocktail with three ingredients.

The first was Thatcherism—though it was not called that until well into Thatcher's time as prime minister. Thatcherism is a combination of economic liberty, traditional conservative and Christian values, British patriotism, and a strong attachment to the United States and other like-minded countries in the English-speaking world. In her intellectual life—her occasional lectures, her reading, her participation in seminars—she has been extremely consistent in her attachment to these ideas.

The first major occasion on which she was invited to give an account of her own brand of Toryism was at the Conservative Conference of 1968, when she delivered the Conservative Political Center (CPC) lecture.[14] This was a prestigious lecture in Tory circles and an occasion when the speaker was expected to rise above day-to-day politics and wax philosophical. Thatcher's invitation was a sign that her star was rising. Much would ride on her performance.

Read today, the lecture—"What's Wrong with Politics?"—is an almost uncanny forecast of what the Thatcher governments sought and sometimes achieved more than a decade later. It has its topical references, to be sure, but even these she used to make characteristically Thatcherite points. To the then fashionable panacea of "participation," for instance, she argued that "the way to get...participation is not for people to take part in more and more government decisions but to make government reduce the area of decision over which it presides and consequently leave the citizen to 'participate'...by making more of his own decisions." Elsewhere the lecture attacked government prices and incomes control, argued that the way to control inflation was for government to exercise fiscal and monetary restraint and to promote competition, suggested tax incentives for private health and education, and criticized the notion of "consensus" as an excuse for avoiding hard decisions. Anyone who treated the lecture as a guide to future decisions by a Thatcher government would have been right nine times out of ten.

Not that she clung to these verities in a blind way. Thatcher loved a good argument and the play of ideas. She once urged a group of Tory journalists on the *Daily Telegraph* to write the kind of satirically anti-socialist pamphlets that Colm Brogan (later *National Review*'s London correspondent) had written in the 1940s and that had lifted her morale when she was a young candidate.[15] Far from being the "anti-intellectual" woman depicted by Annenberg, she was a perpetual student who sought further enlightenment from a series of academic gurus—including F. A. Hayek and Milton Friedman in economics and Robert Conquest, Hugh Thomas, and Norman Stone in foreign policy. She had been an early groupie of the influential Institute of Economic Affairs established by Ralph Harris and Arthur Seldon to promote free market ideas in the 1950s. These tutorials served to deepen and broaden her instinctive commitment to Thatcherite ideas rather than to change them significantly. It must also be said that the economic history of Britain from 1945 to 1979 did nothing to undermine her views.

At the time, however, her CPC lecture was only a modest success. It was noticed less for what it suggested about her fundamental ideas than for a passage in which she placed two statements on economic policy by Labour governments alongside two Tory statements and pointed out that they were "almost indistinguishable." That ruffled the feathers of former ministers who had produced the Tory statements, but it also exemplified the second ingredient in the Thatcher cocktail: outspokenness. In private she almost invariably said what she thought, as the Gleysteen memorandum demonstrated; in public, she was only slightly less candid, frequently departing from the agreed party line if she disagreed with it and even if she were actually carrying it out in government. During her premiership, Andrew Alexander, the *Daily Mail*'s acerbic parliamentary sketch-writer, once described her as the "Leader of the Opposition" because of her habit of publicly disowning policies that had been forced on her by the Tory "wets."[16]

The third ingredient might at first seem incompatible with the first two: political prudence. From her arrival in Parliament in 1959 until her resignation in 1990, Thatcher never took on a fight unless she thought she could win it. Until the two Tory election defeats of 1972, that meant supporting the party vigorously (she was a party "workhorse," as Annenberg wrote), sticking to her specific front-bench responsibilities, and not engaging in any doomed rebellion against policies she disliked. Once a feasible rebellion became possible against Heath's leadership in 1974, she promptly joined it. As Tory leader and then as prime minister, she transferred that prudence to decisions on governing—for instance, she surrendered to the 1981 miners' strike because she thought she couldn't win it and began quietly preparing to defeat the miners in the "Scargill insurrection" of 1984–1985.[17]

The Rise of an Iron Lady

How was it possible to combine the outspoken expression of firm Thatcherite views with loyalty to a party and government that at times embraced very different ideas? The general answer is that until New Labour both major British political parties exercised a very wide ideological tolerance. Heath was in many ways a natural autocrat, but he was reasonably relaxed about the expression of different views provided that such dissent did not spill over into the voting lobbies or into an orchestrated cabinet rebellion. As she climbed the ladder, Mrs. Thatcher kept to those rules.

Her front-bench career began in 1961, when she became a very junior minister at the pensions ministry in the Macmillan government. She rose steadily through a succession of minor front-bench posts in government and opposition until the 1966 Labour landslide. In those years she could have endorsed the flat earth theory without anyone much caring; junior front-bench spokesmen are the pond life of Westminster. Her promotion by Ted Heath to serious front-bench positions after 1966 was doubly lucky; it coincided with the Tory Party's drift to the right on policy. Her CPC lecture neatly anticipated the coming orthodoxy—tax cuts, no incomes policy, reducing government intervention in industry—that was adopted in full in the 1970 general election manifesto. When the Tories won a solid victory, Thatcher was appointed to the middle-ranking cabinet position of secretary of state for education and science.

At this stage Thatcher was seen as a Heath clone. The irreverent male chauvinists on the Tory benches used to refer to the new education secretary as "Ted with tits." But Ted himself knew better—or at least he knew himself better. A natural corporatist who had adopted the free market as a managerial technique rather than as a governing philosophy, Heath exiled the two cabinet colleagues most committed to it to non-economic ministries. Thatcher went to the Department of Education and Science, Sir Keith Joseph to the Department of Social Services.

Thatcher performed competently at the DES but left its left-leaning ethos fundamentally unchanged. As she concedes in her memoirs, she failed in particular to halt or even obstruct the drive toward closing down the selective schools favored by the party's middle-class supporters in the country. Such a radical policy shift, certain to be bitterly opposed by the educationist establishment, would have required the full backing of the prime minister. It took her fifteen months to get Heath even to attend a meeting to discuss the principles of education. His growing dislike was indicated by the consolatory minute from one of the Downing Street civil servants setting up the meeting: "I doubt it would be practicable to exclude her from the discussion, but you might perhaps like to bring in a number of non-officials to liven things up." The meeting proved to be a pointless rehash of the department's conventional policy mix of more spending and specific educational initiatives, such as raising the school graduation age. Overall, the best that could be said about Thatcher's stewardship of education was said by Annenberg: "Believing strongly that educational policy is not an issue on which her party could expect to gain political advantage, she has concentrated...on making sure that it does not become a disadvantage."

But the DES had one advantage that accrued to Thatcher personally. When Heath performed his famous "U-turn" during 1971 and 1972— nationalizing Rolls-Royce; imposing control of incomes, prices, and dividends; abandoning his attempt to reform the labor unions; subsidizing "lame duck" industries; and embarking on a massive expansion of the money supply to stimulate growth—Thatcher was out of the loop. So was Sir Keith Joseph. They prudently stayed out of the loop. They neither resigned nor tried to organize cabinet opposition to the new corporate Toryism that was so little different from socialism that a Marxist group urged its members to vote Tory. Indeed, Thatcher was praised ("held in high esteem in the party... has kept us out of trouble") and recommended for cabinet promotion by the chief whip, Francis Pym, in a secret memorandum to the prime minister. She might have been embarrassed by the offer of an economic ministry that would have required her to administer a near-socialist policy, thus ensuring that she would never be heard of again. But fate intervened in the form of a crisis over incomes policy and an early election called to resolve it.

Not enough Marxists voted Conservative in the spring election of 1974. Nor enough voters of any kind. Before he could offer Thatcher a job, Heath lost his own in a narrow election defeat and the Tories went into opposition. As no party enjoyed a parliamentary majority, everyone knew that a second election would follow very soon. But Heath took his defeat as an instruction from history to move the Tories further left in pursuit of an all-party Government of National Unity. It was then that Sir Keith, supported by Thatcher, broke with Heath (or rather with his policy, as both remained uncomfortably in the Shadow Cabinet), established a new think tank, the Centre for Policy Studies, to advance their common agenda of economic freedom, and launched a series of major speeches repudiating the U-turn policies to which Heath was now indissolubly attached.

It was bold; yet it was prescient too. Most Tories had never been comfortable with Heath's corporatist socialism, and now it had provoked both a crisis and an election defeat. If he lost the next election, he would have to be replaced, almost certainly by a more conventional Conservative. When the defeat duly occurred in the fall election of 1974, Sir Keith let it be known that he would stand against Heath when a leadership contest could be held. Thatcher was the only member of the Shadow Cabinet to endorse him.[18]

Sir Keith was everything that Thatcher had said of him in the conversation with Gleysteen—"brilliant, versatile, and full of further promise."

But he was also highly strung and full of self-doubt. When he came under a viciously ludicrous attack as a supposed advocate of eugenics, it distressed him and his family more than he expected. He came to the conclusion that he was not leadership material and withdrew. Thatcher announced, with his backing, that she would stand in his stead.

Not even her natural supporters believed she was likely to win. At a meeting of sympathetic journalists, the *Daily Telegraph*'s Frank Johnson asked her what she would do after the leadership election.

"I shall be leader of the Conservative Party," she replied.

"No, I mean, *really*," said Johnson, slightly nettled at being treated like part of a public press conference.

"Frank," she responded. "I would not run for this job if I did not really think I could win it."[19]

Others shared Johnson's skepticism, including Dirk Gleysteen's colleagues at the U.S. embassy and the U.S. State Department. Thatcher was, after all, a mere middle-ranking opposition spokesman, internationally unknown, taking on a former prime minister. Nonetheless, on February 4, 1975, Brent Scowcroft at the White House received a memorandum from George S. Springsteen at State informing him that Heath had been "unexpectedly defeated" as opposition leader on the first ballot. But, it was "doubtful that Mrs. Thatcher will win on the second ballot," a week later. A more likely victor was "popular Willie Whitelaw," a more centrist figure whose last position in government had been secretary of state for energy.[20]

One week later, however, Springsteen had to inform General Scowcroft that Thatcher had soundly defeated four other candidates, including Willie Whitelaw, to capture the leadership of the Conservative Party. Her victory was as unexpected as popular Willie's "poor showing"—Thatcher got about twice as many votes as her opponent. That merely established her acceptability to the Tory Party, however, not to Britain as a whole. Springsteen added to his list of predictions by pointing out that "to win a future election she will have to move an appreciable distance from her position on the right wing of her party."[21]

She was, in the now familiar term, "too conservative."

~≈e ℈~

One of the very few Americans who might have disputed that judgment was the former governor of California and the hero of the Republican Right, Ronald Reagan. Governor Reagan and Mrs. Thatcher had not met each other at this point, but they had heard of each other. Thatcher's husband, Denis, had returned home from a meeting of the Institute of Directors in 1969 singing the praises of the Californian governor who had given them a stirring defense of capitalism of a kind then rare in British politics. Reagan in turn had been told of a bright new Tory star by Justin Dart, one of the members of his "kitchen cabinet." When Reagan visited Britain two months after Thatcher's elevation to the Tory leadership, he arranged through Dart to meet her.

The meeting lasted well over its scheduled time. That was good judgment on Thatcher's part—especially since the Labour government had hardly rolled out the red carpet for a very conservative politician with little apparent chance of higher office—but it also reflected their discovery of a common outlook. When Reagan left, they had agreed to keep in regular touch. Reagan's office sent her his columns and radio commentaries, which she undoubtedly read. Thatcher also promised to see Reagan on a future visit to the U.S. But the most significant result of that first meeting was Reagan's bread-and-butter letter sent to the British politician on April 30, 1975.

"I've chosen a dark day to write a belated thank-you," he began. "The news has just arrived of Saigon's surrender and somehow the shadows seem to have lengthened." For the people of Vietnam and Cambodia, who faced oppression and genocide, the shadows had indeed lengthened. Thatcher undoubtedly felt the same sadness as Reagan; she was to make the famous "Iron Lady" speech, denouncing Soviet expansionism, shortly afterward. But the fall of Saigon, though tragic, was also the most important of several major developments that were to add credibility to Thatcher's bid for Downing Street and propel Reagan into the presidency.

For in early 1975 Reagan was at a crossroads. His second term as California governor had ended at the beginning of the year with plaudits even from opponents. His record was summed up by *Newsweek*, not a particularly friendly source, as "on balance successful years running the nation's largest state—a passage in which he balanced a deep-red budget, held down employment by the state, pared the welfare rolls, and in other ways demonstrated his competence to govern."[22] This success had revived the presidential prospects that had looked bleak earlier in the decade. On leaving office, he had therefore signed up to write a newspaper column, to deliver a daily radio address, and to tour America giving speeches.[23] He was a political celebrity, well regarded by the Republican establishment and adored by conservatives. But the political way forward was blocked with an immense obstacle thrown in his way by the Watergate crisis.

Before Watergate, Reagan could assume that if he ran in 1976, he would be the strongest conservative candidate in a field of newcomers. Watergate demolished that assumption when Gerald Ford became president after Nixon's resignation. A moderate conservative already holding the presidency would be the man to beat in 1976. That was a much more formidable task—especially in a Republican Party that placed a high premium on loyalty. Reagan plainly wanted to run but he needed to feel that a presidential bid would not be doomed in advance.

Ford came to Reagan's rescue. He weakened his own support among conservatives by committing what sports commentators call an "unforced error." He appointed Nelson Rockefeller, whom Sun Belt conservatives distrusted as a liberal panjandrum from the Eastern establishment, to be his vice president. This provoked a massive protest. Conservatives felt betrayed—or, worse, about to be betrayed. Reagan was the beneficiary of this outrage.

He was still uncertain, however, and he needed a plausible justification for running against a Republican president. The policies pursued by the Ford administration gave him this pretext. Three of the most common and deeply felt themes in Reagan's columns and broadcasts then and later were opposition to détente as a version of appeasement, support for America's free market system as the most efficient means of creating prosperity, and a corresponding anxiety about the growth of government and government regulation. The Ford administration sinned somewhat on the latter two grounds—Reagan was worried in particular about the spread of government regulation that had continued under Nixon and Ford. But it was its foreign policy of détente, led by Secretary of State Henry Kissinger, above all that motivated him. (It was as unfortunate for President Ford as it was manna to rightist conspiracy theorists that Dr. Kissinger had been the foreign policy adviser to Rockefeller when he ran for the presidency in 1968.)

Reagan and Kissinger were not opposed on foreign policy across the board. Reagan's column on the fall of Saigon echoed the arguments that the secretary of state had made to congressmen, urging approval of promised military supplies to the Thieu regime, before its final collapse. Both men were concerned that America's betrayal of its South Vietnamese ally would weaken American alliances around the globe as well as stain the national honor.[24] But détente revealed two sharp differences between them. The lesser difference was Reagan's judgment that the compromises of détente were generally lopsided. The Soviet Union usually got the better of the bargain, especially on arms control.

The more significant difference was an almost spiritual one. Threading through all Reagan's writings was a deep belief in the virtue of America and the recuperative powers of its free people. His view of Soviet Communism was the precise opposite: Communism was a "form of insanity—a temporary aberration" that would one day disappear from the earth because it was contrary to human nature.[25] He consequently regarded détente as a policy that gave undeserved respectability to the Soviet Union, helping to prop it up morally, weakening the resistance of anti-Soviet dissidents, even lending credence to the idea that the U.S. and the USSR were more or less indistinguishable superpowers. Reagan favored a policy of ideological resistance to Soviet goals rather than accommodation.

This was utopian nonsense to the foreign policy establishment, which increasingly saw the Soviet Union as a stable, successful, and therefore permanent presence in the world. In addition to being a member in good standing of that establishment, Kissinger believed that the best a presidency weakened by Watergate and the loss of Vietnam could do was to hold the line by making trade deals conditional upon Soviet good behavior until domestic American opinion was prepared to back stronger measures. It must be said that the secretary of state had cooperated slightly in his own caricaturing as a second Metternich upholding a new order.

The stage was set for a contrast between Reagan, advocating an "American" policy of spreading freedom and human rights, and the Kissinger-Ford administration devoted to a "European" defense of amoral stability. Even those liberal members of the foreign policy establishment critical of Kissinger felt that Reagan was simply "too American"—i.e., too naïve, too superficial, too moralistic. This view spread quickly through America's political and cultural elites. To be sure, there were influential new dissidents from establishment liberalism, neo-conservatives like Norman Podhoretz and Irving Kristol, who sympathized with Reagan's criticism of détente. But they were disposed to identify Ambassador Daniel Patrick Moynihan, then upholding American values at the United Nations, rather than a California Republican as their champion. Surely, however, the American people would likely warm to a candidate whom the elites saw as "too American"?

Reagan decided to see. In July 1975 he gave Nevada senator Paul Laxalt permission to set up a "Citizens for Reagan" exploratory committee. All the signs were good—the polls, the money—and Reagan prepared to launch his campaign in November 1975. Even late in the day Ford could have avoided a primary challenge, but he made a second unforced error. Realizing that Rockefeller was so unpopular with GOP conservatives that he threatened Ford's own re-election, the president dropped him from the ticket. This decision came fewer than three weeks before Reagan's announcement. If Ford had invited Reagan to be his running mate at that point, the Californian would have found it hard to refuse. The Ford-Reagan ticket would have almost certainly triumphed the following year. But Ford had never treated Reagan seriously. No soundings were taken, and Reagan went ahead with his announcement.[26]

The announcement was made on November 20, 1975, not, as most accounts claim, at midday at the National Press Club in Washington but several hours before in a signed article by Reagan in the London *Daily Telegraph*.[27] This modest world scoop revealed some embarrassment on Reagan's part that he would be challenging a president of his own party, but he asserted he was responding to popular demand. People he had met on his cross-country tours had urged him to stand so that voters would have a clear-cut choice "between the opposing theories of centralization and diffusion of power." He also denounced the growth of government regulation. But he did not mention Ford in these contexts. Reagan might have been aiming at the Democrats in control of Congress; the reader was left to distribute the blame himself. Ford's name came up only as a president who lacked full political legitimacy. Because he had been appointed without going through the national nominating process, argued the challenger, the president should not really benefit from "the usual traditions of incumbency."

All the same, incumbency won the nomination for Ford. The primary campaign divided neatly into three segments. From New Hampshire onward Ford won all the primaries until North Carolina. Reagan stopped him there, with the help of Senator Jesse Helms and his local organization, and then caught up with a series of victories, including Texas. Then in early June Ford won the first two of the three major primaries in New Jersey, Wisconsin, and California. When the candidates arrived at the Kansas City convention, Ford had a slight edge in numbers but Reagan was the favorite of the mainly conservative delegates. On a free vote Reagan would probably have won in a landslide. As president and candidate of the GOP establishment, however, Ford was able to call in favors and exert pressures that delivered him victory. Even so, it was tantalizingly close: Ford won the nomination by 1,187 votes to 1,070.

That should have been the end of Reagan's political career—a creditable end, as, if he had won, he would have been the first candidate in ninety-two years to wrest the nomination from a sitting president. But it was an end nonetheless.[28] Reagan himself believed it was the end; *Newsweek* reported that he and Nancy laughed at the following day's breakfast when Laxalt obliquely suggested that he might have a second chance: "These are strange times. Anything could happen."[29] Laxalt proved to be an instant prophet.

That evening, after Ford had delivered his acceptance speech, he invited Reagan onto the stage and, in an unusual move, asked him to say a few words. Reagan apparently extemporized a speech, calling to mind a radio script on which he had been working. He had been asked to write a letter for a time capsule due to be opened in 2076 on the occasion of America's Tricentennial. In writing it, he had suddenly realized that the readers of the letter would know whether this generation of Americans had met the challenges of nuclear war and state encroachment on personal freedom. He asked his Republican audience that night:

> Will they look back in appreciation and say, "Thank God for those people in 1976 who headed off that loss of freedom, who kept us now a hundred years later free, who kept our world from nuclear destruction"? And if we fail, they probably won't get to read the letter at all because it spoke of individual freedom, and they won't be allowed to talk of that or read of it.

On the printed page these words are not particularly eloquent; in the hall they were electrifying. Delegates were made horribly aware, at some subliminal level, that they had chosen the wrong man. The man who had just spoken was not simply an able politician, a talented actor, or a principled conservative (though he seemed to be all of those). He was the embodiment of something. He had connected 1776 to their deliberations and to the future of America like an American Edmund Burke. More than Burke, however, Reagan embodied what he preached. He was the archetypical American.

Was that, however, "too American"?

If the delegates at Kansas City had been asked that question, they would have laughed it to scorn. He was not too American for them. He was almost certainly their future leader (though they could not quite see how). Besides, how could anyone be too American?

They were just about to find out.

CHAPTER TWO

The Nightmare Years

Ford *was clearly the GOP's second-best candidate.* But he fought a strong campaign and narrowly lost the 1976 election to James Earl Carter, a Southern governor, Georgia peanut farmer, and former naval officer who had served on a nuclear submarine. If Carter had been designed to win over the conservative suburbanites of the Midwest and the New South, he would have looked just like his résumé. But his administration had a very different character from the start. It was an expression not of the New South's moderate conservatism but of the McGovernization of the Democratic Party. This transformation had begun with the student rebellions over Vietnam; had continued with the Pyrrhic defeat of Eugene McCarthy at the 1968 convention; had developed further with the nomination of the students' candidate, George McGovern, for the doomed campaign against Nixon in 1972; and had been consolidated by the gradual surrender of party regulars and blue-collar unions to the middle-class radicals who now controlled the party machine. These radicals, ten years older and sometimes wiser, now began to take over the U.S. government. And as time went by, Carter looked more and more like his administration.

In 1977 that seemed to be an advantage—or at least a necessity. The Carter administration was an almost self-conscious attempt to adjust U.S. foreign and domestic, and especially economic, policy to the currents of history. If these historical currents had seemed to be bearing mankind and America in a liberal and optimistic direction in the early 1970s, they had become markedly darker since then—and this deterioration was far from reaching its end.

The Decline of the West?

After a long period in which crime rates had steadily declined in most industrial countries, they began rising in the 1960s and accelerated sharply in the 1970s. A victimization survey conducted by the U.S. Justice Department found that in 1973, one family in every four had suffered a rape, robbery, assault, burglary, larceny, or auto theft that year—and that in large cities the figure was one in every three families.[1] Other indicators of social regress in the United States and elsewhere were a growing underclass, an alarming rise in sexually transmitted diseases, greater segregation by geography as parents fled bad inner-city schools and court-ordered municipal busing, and rising figures for divorce, illegitimacy, drug abuse, and many other ills.[2] These varied nationally but, with rare exceptions (usually Japan or Switzerland), they showed the same pattern throughout the West, severely disappointing those who had believed such problems would be mitigated by the numerous costly government programs recently established to combat them

Four problems eclipsed all the rest, however, because they had an impact, direct or indirect, on everyone: the rise of terrorism, the collapse of South Vietnam in 1975, OPEC's quadrupling of oil prices in 1973, and the growing power and strategic reach of the Soviet Union.

The modern epidemic of terrorism had scarcely begun in 1970. That year, a secular Arab terrorist group seized four airplanes, landed three of them on Dawson's Field in Jordan, and threatened to murder the passengers unless their governments agreed to demands that included releasing terrorists from prison. Not only did Britain, West Germany, and Switzerland surrender to these demands, but they also put pressure on Israel to release terrorists whom the Israelis knew would immediately set about murdering more of their citizens—and not for the last time. In almost every terrorist crisis, European governments ignored and evaded their common institutions of anti-terrorist intelligence to reach quiet deals with the terrorists—usually on the latter's terms.[3]

Fed in this way, terrorism grew steadily. By the decade's end, the victims of terrorism included Egypt's Anwar Sadat, Lord Louis Mountbatten, Aldo Moro (a leading Italian Christian Democrat), the West German banker Jurgen Ponto; the prime ministers of Jordan and Spain; U.S. ambassadors to Guatemala, Sudan, Cyprus, and Lebanon; and countless ordinary people who simply happened to be standing nearby when a bomb went off. To give some idea of the carnage inflicted by terrorism, Irish Republican terrorists alone murdered 944 people between 1969 and 1975, mainly in Northern Ireland but also on the British mainland.[4]

North Vietnam's conquest of the South had an impact on world opinion far beyond its intrinsic importance. It was commonly said at the time that the world's most technologically advanced military power had been defeated by a small guerrilla army whose soldiers could survive for a week on a sockful of rice. The dramatic photographs of U.S. helicopters lifting off the Saigon embassy with desperate Vietnamese clinging to their undercarriages both dramatized the defeat and underscored America's betrayal of its allies. In reality the betrayal was truer than the defeat. America had not been defeated on the battlefield and South Vietnamese ground forces had themselves defeated a full-scale North Vietnamese invasion in 1972 when they still enjoyed U.S. air support. Not only did the United States withhold such support in 1975, but Congress also refused to supply even the ammunition and military supplies that it had promised when the American forces left. For some perverse psychological motive, the American establishment acted as if the United States would not be genuinely free of involvement in Vietnam until its allies were conquered and occupied. Sirik Matak, a former Cambodian prime minister, refused an offer of asylum from the American ambassador (remaining in Phnom Penh to be murdered viciously by the Khmer Rouge) in a letter that said, "I cannot, alas, leave in such a cowardly fashion. As for you, and in particular, for your great country, I never believed for a moment that you would have this sentiment of abandoning a people which has chosen liberty." It was worse than that. In the final hours America switched sides.

The price of this betrayal was unforeseen and psychologically complex. Waves of "boat people" fled North Vietnam's oppressive rule in large numbers, some perishing on the high seas, others murdered by pirates, still others creating a refugee crisis in Asia. In Cambodia, 1.7 million were killed or starved to death in the internal genocide of the Khmer Rouge. Rather than concluding that such atrocities bore out the justice of its original intervention in Indo-China, the United States found itself hostage to the so-called "Vietnam Syndrome": a deep aversion to foreign involvement of almost any kind on the part of both liberal elites and popular opinion. This hobbled American foreign policy in countless ways, so that the popular image of America became one of a "helpless giant." America's allies became nervous and America's enemies were emboldened. The USSR increased its assistance to Marxist guerrilla groups in Central America and established a second Cuba in Nicaragua. Cuba itself stationed troops in a dozen African countries; in particular, Cubans helped defend Angola's Marxist government against an attack from UNITA rebels backed by South Africa. Above all, the myth of the invincible Marxist guerrilla took hold of the popular mind both in the Third World and in the West.

Also taking hold of the popular mind was the power of oil. OPEC's quadrupling of oil prices had both mythical power and practical impact. It brought about a massive transfer of wealth from the industrial West to the oil-producing Middle East, imposed a worldwide recession, and stimulated a massive increase in inflation when Western countries sought to head off the recession by expanding the money supply. As David Frum points out, this OPEC-induced inflation came on top of the mild inflation to which even the United States had become accustomed. In the fiscal year ending in July 1975, inflation exceeded 11 percent in France and Japan, topped 17 percent in Italy, and reached 26 percent in Britain.[5] Although mild inflation was commonly regarded as a preferred alternative to high unemployment, hyper-inflation on this scale was particularly unsettling because it substantially raised unemployment. The resulting two-headed economic monster, known as "stagflation," stalked the West for almost a decade. And conventional Keynesian remedies—control of incomes and prices, manipulating fiscal policy, "jawboning" unions, business, and consumers to show restraint—either proved ineffective or made matters worse.

The mythical effects of the price hike were perhaps more damaging than stagflation. One myth was the fear on the part of Western governments (and hope on the part of anti-Western radicals) that OPEC was merely the first of a series of raw material cartels organized by the Third World. Such cartels would raise raw material prices permanently, transfer wealth on a massive scale from "North" to "South" (terms that began to challenge "East" and "West" in political jargon), and severely reduce Western standards of living. In vain did economically literate commentators such as Norman Macrae of *The Economist* point out that raising raw material prices by political fiat would reduce demand, stimulate supply, provide incentives to switch to alternative technologies, and thereby result in the long-term collapse of oil prices. His entirely accurate 1974 forecasts that many OPEC countries would face a financial crisis in a decade when oil revenues fell below their projected levels were widely ridiculed.[6]

European governments did their best to make the nightmare come true by rushing to Iran, Saudi Arabia, and other OPEC members with offers amounting to a joint producer-consumer cartel that would have "managed" shortages indefinitely. Luckily these came to nothing, but the UN took up the same idea more ambitiously and began to promote the concept of a New World Economic Order that would institutionalize similar arrangements in other commodities. Though the U.S. government, under Ford and Kissinger, was skeptical, the American people were open to such ideas: the national high school debate topic for 1976 was "Resolved: An International Organization ought to allocate all scarce resources."[7]

This resolution neatly linked the fear of Third World cartels with another myth, already in existence but sleeping until kissed by OPEC: that the world was running out of raw materials and therefore faced a future of inevitable shortages and falling standards of living. In truth it was topsy-turvy logic to imagine that a cartel would produce a natural shortage. If there had been any economic link at all, the shortage would have produced or at least facilitated the cartel. There was no such link in OPEC's case, but once this paranoia was released, it rapidly became the conventional wisdom. A Davos-style group of concerned businessmen and economists, who called themselves the Club of Rome, had published a book called *The Limits to Growth* in 1972. They forecast that the prices of raw materials would rise exponentially until they produced another depression, which could be alleviated only by rationing. It was nonsense, what statisticians call "naïve extrapolation"—even nonsense on stilts, as it extrapolated on the basis of price increases that were themselves distorted upward by the West's own inflationary policies.[8] But nonsense that appealed to the anti-market prejudices of intellectuals was hard to demystify. Before long, respected economists who should have known better, such as the late Professor Robert Lekachman of NYU, were pontificating grandly: "The era of growth is over and the era of limits is upon us. It means the whole politics of the country has changed." In fact, it was the other way around: the whole politics of the United States was changing in the direction of controls by the mid-1970s. As controls were progressively introduced, above all controls over oil and gas, lo and behold—the era of limits descended upon us.

Another sleeping monster beginning to stir in the middle and late 1970s was the Soviet threat. In 1973, the heyday of optimism about superpower convergence, nobody paid much attention to a British intelligence report that Leonid Brezhnev had told a meeting of Communist leaders in Prague that, as a result of détente, "a decisive shift in the correlation of forces will be such that come 1985 we will be able to extend our will wherever we need to." (Reagan even complained in one of several radio commentaries on the Brezhnev speech that a report of it in the *Boston Globe*, despite its obvious news value, had been reprinted only in *National Review* four years later.)[9]

By the middle and late 1970s, however, the signs of this shift in the correlation of forces seemed to be everywhere. The Soviets were planting highly accurate SS-20 missiles in Eastern Europe within easy target range of Western capitals. These placed a question mark over the reliability of the U.S. nuclear umbrella. As the Warsaw Pact enjoyed a massive prepon-

derance in conventional forces, the Red Army was now "a specter threatening Europe" (in the words of Raymond Aron, paraphrasing Marx). But
the Soviet threat was not confined to the central theater of the Cold War
in Europe. A Soviet world-class navy had been built and was now shad-
owing the U.S. Sixth Fleet in the Mediterranean. Both the American naval
base at Cam Ranh Bay in Vietnam and the old British imperial port of
Aden in the Persian Gulf now hosted Soviet ships. A retreating West was
being followed by an advancing East. Suddenly, Brezhnev's forecast seemed
not boastful but prophetic.

Even taken singly, these four threats looked formidable. Taken together,
they provoked increasing alarm, initially on the political right, over time
across the spectrum. They seemed to reinforce each other. Terrorism, for
example, was believed to be covertly financed and sponsored by the Soviet
Union and its allies. That was an additional reason for fighting it. The oil-
producing countries were often friendly to Palestinian terrorist groups
(even after Carlos the Jackal, leading such a group, had kidnapped OPEC
ministers briefly in Vienna). The West wanted OPEC governments to continue recycling petrodollars into Western investments to avoid a recession.
This was a strong reason for not fighting terrorism too fiercely—in fact, a
strong reason for appeasing it—and hoping that it would strike one's
neighbor rather than oneself.[10] David Frum added up the results: "Between
January 1972 and January 1974 European police forces apprehended fifty
suspected Arab terrorists. Of those fifty only seven ever saw the inside of
a prison. Thirty-six were released in response to threats, direct or
implied."[11] Those thirty-six included the murderers of the Israeli athletes
at the 1972 Munich Olympics.

If the Soviets were covertly assisting terrorists, they were openly backing left-wing guerrillas in coups and revolutionary wars and loudly supporting the Third World's plans for international economic redistribution
at the United Nations. Cuban regulars in Angola, local guerrillas in
Nicaragua, and East German military advisers in Ethiopia were all trained,
transported, and supplied by the Soviets for Third World interventions. But
the long-running crisis of stagflation in Europe, coupled with the Vietnam
Syndrome in America, made governments reluctant to allocate the defense

spending necessary to counter such subversions. The Soviet–Third World alliance meanwhile meant that the anti-Western side could usually count on a majority vote in the UN General Assembly on issues from Rhodesia to the Law of the Sea to the "Zionism is racism" resolution. The UN also developed the habit of designating left-wing guerrilla groups as "the sole legitimate representative" of colonized peoples, thus obstructing the West from directing its military and financial support to more accommodating clients. Indeed, whatever the crisis, the West always seemed to face an obstacle to responding effectively.

Giving In to Despair

The cumulative effect of all these developments was to quickly alter the psychological climate of Western opinion from optimism to despair. All the revolutions that had seemed harbingers of a freer, more prosperous, and more harmonious world in 1970 now took on a different and more threatening aspect. Sexual freedom had produced family breakdown and herpes (AIDS came later). Keynesian economics had spurred inflation. Economic growth had run up against environmental limits. Decolonization had been followed by hostile dictatorships in the former colonies. Western defeat at Suez in 1956 and the West's retreat from the Gulf had led by degrees to OPEC. Détente had accelerated the Soviet threat. Left-wing guerrillas were advancing, hardly impeded, throughout the Third World. The future seemed likely to be more radical than liberal. As Leo Labedz, the Anglo-Polish editor of *Survey*, mordantly observed of this change of sentiment: "The revolution of rising expectations was replaced by the expectation of rising revolutions."[12]

Literature, publishing, films, criticism, journalism, and popular culture all hinted or proclaimed "the end of civilization as we know it." Books appeared with titles suggesting apocalypse in one sphere after another: in politics, *The Twilight of Authority*, *The Collapse of Democracy*, and *The Death of British Democracy*; in ecology, Paul Ehrlich's *The Population Bomb*; in economics, *The Crash of 1979*; in religion, Hal Lindsey's *The Late Great Planet Earth* (the most widely read religious book of the 1970s).[13] There were varieties of apocalypse, of course. The connoisseur of despair could choose between environmentalist doomsdayism (The Club of Rome, the movie *Soylent Green*, the book *The Population Bomb*) and the more traditional religious end-time (Hal Lindsey's books, *The Omen*— a Gregory Peck movie about the birth of the Antichrist—and the growing numbers of televangelists). On the whole, religious apocalypticism looks better in retrospect. It was less easy to disprove. The Antichrist never arrived, but his nonexistence was never conclusively demonstrated either. Paul Ehrlich's predictions of billions dying in a worldwide famine, however, were the exact opposite of the vast agricultural surpluses that actually materialized. Within a decade we were lamenting the "beef mountains" and "wine lakes" created by the European Union's agricultural subsidies. The second ice age also failed to materialize. But the failure of these scientific and economic prophecies never dented the reputation of the prophets or reduced the popular appetite for catastrophe.

Even more significant than these self-conscious expressions of angst in media and popular culture was the spread of a general sensibility of despair. The most mundane topics seemed to elicit these lines from Yeats:

> Things fall apart; the center cannot hold;
> Mere anarchy is loosed upon the world,
> The blood-dimmed tide is loosed, and everywhere
> The ceremony of innocence is drowned;
> The best lack all conviction, while the worst
> Are full of passionate intensity.[14]

At first it was literary magazines and opinion weeklies where Yeats popped up to lend significance to an argument that the world was running out of oil (or copper, or food, or whatever). Soon, however, his lines were staple filling for op-ed articles in middle-market tabloids on anything from Middle East terrorism to the increase in "unofficial" strikes in Great Britain. Eventually, they became a sort of Muzak that, instead of making the point more vivid, wrapped it in an aural cotton wool that rendered it heavy, soft, and forgettable. Had the quotation been a pop record, it would have made a fortune in royalties for the Yeats estate.

Cyril Connolly was still alive when his world-weary epigram hit the mass market in the 1970s. In 1949, he had written: "It is closing-time in the gardens of the West and from now on an artist will be judged only by the resonance of his solitude or the quality of his despair."

At that time Colm Brogan, Thatcher's favorite satirist, had likened this kind of thing to the emotions felt by an adolescent on losing his religious faith "in between intervals of playing the saxophone." And in fact it was closing time only for *Horizon*, the London literary magazine Connolly had founded and steered through the rapids of wartime censorship and post-war austerity to its death that year. The gardens of the West flowered quite luxuriantly for the next twenty years. As the 1970s arrived and wore on, however, they began to look like Brighton or Coney Island on a bank or federal holiday—overgrown, untidy, unkempt, and overcrowded. Gas lines, hijackings, rising mortgages, anti-Vietnam demonstrations, rumors of famine, and other indications of a local apocalypse began to proliferate.

But these internal threats were minor compared to the external night-mares: notably, the Marxist guerrilla lurking in the undergrowth. *Exiles*, a John Osborne play about expatriates exchanging bitchy gossip on a lux-urious Caribbean island, ended with the sudden invasion of black guerril-las who, for no particular reason of plot, promptly gunned down the rest of the cast. *Queimada!,* an anti-imperialist parable about Vietnam set in the eighteenth-century Caribbean, ended happily with the murder of a counter-revolutionary soldier of fortune (Marlon Brando in his best lan-guid English aristocrat style) by the leader of the black revolution. When *The Battle of Algiers*—a brilliant Marxist account of the struggle for con-trol of the city between the French army and left-wing Algerian terrorists— was shown in a north London cinema in the 1970s, an audience of students cheered the final political triumph of the terrorists.[15]

The sardonic French novelist Jean Raspail took one step further into nightmare when instead of Marxist guerrillas advancing through the Third World he imagined the entire Third World invading Europe.[16] His power-ful poetic satire, *The Camp of the Saints*, described a successful landing on the Côte d'Azur by a Third World armada of starving Asiatic hordes bent on conquest, occupation, and the death of the West. The West fell victim not only to these invaders but also to their two domestic allies: the left-wing coalition of revolutionary, Marxist, nihilist, anti-racist, and anti-colonial movements—or "the Beast"—and the West's own humanitarian sentiments. The liberal West simply could not bring itself to fire on an impoverished and miserable mob.[17] If that were truly so, the Third World would eventually break into and trample the once secret gardens of the West, in a scene that would resemble the Dunkirk evacuation as described by a horrified upper-class Guards officer: "My dear, the noise. And the *people*."

These nightmares reflected a widespread sense of helplessness in the face of gathering storms. There was accordingly a burst of relief and rejoicing when, almost uniquely, Israel struck back in the Entebbe crisis, rescued its citizens and other passengers held in the Ugandan airport, killed the hijackers who had kidnapped them, humiliated the murderous comedian-dictator, Idi Amin, who had aided the hijacking, and returned home with only one life tragically lost—that of the young commando leading the rescue, Jonathan Netanyahu.[18] Though their citizens rejoiced at this almost miraculous evidence that civilization was not helpless before terror, Western governments were more circumspect and remained shiftily silent. Kurt Waldheim, the UN secretary-general, even condemned the rescue as a violation of Ugandan sovereignty.[19] So when the immediate crisis had passed and the rejoicing evaporated, ordinary Westerners felt more helpless than ever. Colin Welch, the British journalist and wit, expressed a common sentiment when he argued in the London *Daily Telegraph* that the Israelis and the West were mortally threatened by the same enemies but the Israelis "know it. We don't." And the longer that governments signaled that they would not or could not take effective action against the threats mounting against the West, the more the public mood turned from mere helplessness to bitter frustration. Peter Finch, as Howard Beale, the "mad prophet of the airwaves" in the superb 1976 satire on television news, *Network*, tapped into this public mood when he goaded his viewers into opening their windows and shouting into the street: "I'm mad as hell and I'm not gonna take it any more!"

A Post-American Administration

That was the mood of the American people in the mid-1970s, but it was definitely not the mood of the U.S. administration. The Carter administration was a post-American administration before the concept of post-Americanism had been invented. Its younger members, such as Anthony Lake, director of policy planning at the State Department, had been radicalized by the Vietnam War. Its older establishment representatives, such as Secretary of State Cyrus Vance, had effectively internalized the radical critique of their own former "Cold War liberalism." There were other factions, representing more traditional and Democratic views and constituencies within the administration: Zbigniew Brzezinski at the National Security Council, Harold Brown at Defense. Occasionally they won important battles, such as the decision to back a moderate increase in defense spending in Carter's later years. But the president himself, though superficially a moderate Southern Democrat, was increasingly disposed to support the radical forces rather than the liberal ones—let alone the "Cold War liberal" ones, in his administration.

That was not recognized for some time, because Carter's radicalism had roots in religion that most Washington insiders did not share and could hardly recognize. He was a serious Christian, a Southern Baptist brought up under Jim Crow, who realized as an adult that the political status quo of his youth had been structurally sinful. He was therefore more open than most to the secular argument advanced by 1960s radicals that the United States was a nation deeply implicated in a structurally sinful international status quo. Domestically, the Watergate crisis had revealed corruption, lying, illegal wiretapping, the criminal misuse of government agencies (including intelligence and law enforcement agencies), and other crimes at the heart of the U.S. government. Democrats had to admit, albeit quietly, that "it didn't start with Watergate." Those things, not Jeffersonian democracy, were "The System." From this high-minded standpoint, America's international role looked even more sinister: supporting right-wing dictators around the globe; interfering in foreign elections to prevent the election of pro-Communist parties; trying (and failing) to assassinate Fidel Castro; seeking to suppress popular revolutionary movements such as the

Vietcong; and ignoring the human rights of those oppressed by such U.S. allies as General Pinochet, South Africa, or the shah of Iran. In the 1970s, another charge had been added to the indictment: the United States was also a frivolously wasteful power in its economic and environmental policies. Its exploitation of the world's scarce natural resources was selfish and unsustainable both because we used those resources to support a wasteful lifestyle and because they were now running out. All these evils were sustained by an international economic and political system with the United States at its center. Carter's campaign claim that he wanted an American government "as good as the American people" was widely seen as a response to Watergate. It was in fact a comprehensive prescription for public policy.

Carter's motto was also, at least in the eyes of its practitioners, something more than the pursuit of political virtue. It was a hard-headed accommodation of large historical trends that might be diverted but could not really be stopped. Vietnam showed that oppressed peoples in the Third World would never submit to being governed permanently by either foreigners or kleptocrats. Both decolonization and the spread of radical nationalist or socialist governments were simply a matter of time. The only question for America was whether to be for or against them. And to side with oppressed people meant changing sides, in many cases, as their oppressors were our friends and allies.

An unending series of terrorist atrocities from Israel to Uruguay similarly showed that there was no purely military solution to terrorism. Because the terrorist would always get through, like the bomber in the 1930s,[20] the best solution was to siphon off his support by proposing political changes such as land reform and "human rights." These reforms would meet the legitimate popular aspirations he was exploiting and isolate him politically. A similar logic dictated a more cooperative relationship with poorer countries. We could no longer oppose outright such ideas as the New World International Order (NWIO) which was designed by the UN to share the world's wealth more equitably (and thus less to the benefit of the United States). These proposals arose from the clash between shrinking world resources and growing demands for global justice.

Something like an NWIO was inevitable. Americans had to come to terms with that fact, change their lifestyle, and tighten their belts voluntarily— or accept the imposition of economic controls by government. Economic controls would probably be necessary anyway in order to conquer the omnipresent inflation.

And there was, finally, the Soviet threat. This looked real enough, and in a sense it was—the Soviet navy, the Red Army, and the SS-20s all existed. According to the Carter outlook, however, these were politically a symptom of the Soviets' strategic insecurity rather than a bid for strategic dominance. This insecurity would only be encouraged by any U.S. policy of strategic competition. It could best be averted by arms control negotiations that demonstrated the United States' willingness to surrender any weapons systems that gave it a strategic advantage. By gaining the Soviets' trust, we would help them to disarm. Otherwise, the United States and the USSR would be "apes on a treadmill," as Paul Warnke, Carter's arms control director and chief Strategic Arms Limitation Talks (SALT) negotiator, put it in an influential 1975 article in *Foreign Policy* magazine. "We can be the first off the treadmill," wrote Warnke. "That's the only victory the arms race has to offer."

In general the Carter policy held that the United States should demonstrate through its words and actions that it understood and supported the aspirations of the Third World. In the future Washington would be the linchpin of global justice and human rights. In adopting this new stance, the United States, under Carter, would be acting prudently and sensibly as well as morally. It would be assisting historical forces that were more or less bound to prevail, while simultaneously undermining the Soviet Union by switching from military to ideological and even moral competition in world politics, not wasting its substance backing the dictators and corrupt right-wingers doomed by history. Instead of resisting the global trends that struck most Americans and Western Europeans as threatening, the Carter administration would embrace and exploit them.

Despite its diverse and even contradictory origins—the Baptist religion, 1960s radicalism, a left-wing foreign policy "realism"—the Carter foreign policy held together intellectually. It also had one signal success: its stress on supporting human rights succeeded in embarrassing the Soviet Union. In particular, Carter's exploitation of the Helsinki process granting civil and political rights to dissidents in Eastern Europe gave the latter real, if limited, help in their struggles with the Communist governments. Both Reagan and Margaret Thatcher attacked the Helsinki Final Act on the grounds, themselves valid, that it formalized Soviet control of Eastern Europe. Karol Wojtyla was of two minds about it, disliking its confirmation of Yalta but also grasping how dissidents might exploit its provisions on rights. This ambivalence reflected both his distinctive policy of "cultural resistance," which might have been designed for Helsinki, and his skepticism over the *Ostpolitik* of Cardinal Casaroli, who had chaired the thirty-five-nation conference at which Helsinki was signed. But then, Casaroli, Reagan, Thatcher, and the Kremlin itself were probably all taken aback by the extent to which Helsinki helped to subvert Soviet rule. Carter himself may have been pleasantly surprised. If anyone really saw its liberating potential in advance, it was probably two Poles: Wojtyla in Cracow and Brzezinski in the White House.

That one success aside, Carter's overall approach had two great flaws. The first was that it failed on almost everything except Helsinki. The second was that it was deeply at variance with U.S. interests, with the efficiency of the U.S. economy, with rooted American values, and above all with the confident, patriotic, "can-do" spirit of American life. Carter's desire for a government that was "as good as the American people," noted above, betrayed a conviction that the United States had been either a hypocritically imperialist power or mistakenly on the wrong side of history— or something of both—until his presidency. Most Americans believed, not without evidence, that the United States had been one of the most generous great powers in history.

Carter accepted Leonid Brezhnev's assurances, sealed with a kiss, that the Soviet Union was now essentially a pacifistic power eager to end the Cold War and thus a trustworthy partner in arms control negotiations. Most Americans, then in the grip of the Vietnam Syndrome, hoped that was the case, but their flinty skepticism, Yankee or Jacksonian according to taste, made them doubt that policy should be based on such hopes as long as Soviet surrogates were rampaging around Africa and Latin America. Carter felt—he would have said "recognized"—that the American way of life, combining freedom with prosperity, was no longer possible in a world where shortages of raw materials made controls essential and rationing perhaps morally obligatory. Above all, Carter had concluded that the American people should maturely accept a narrowing of their hopes and horizons in an interdependent world where other nations, international bodies, and the facts of economic life would increasingly constrict America's options. Most Americans, on the other hand, still thought that the free enterprise system would deliver the goods unless government obstructed it, and still believed, with Ronald Reagan, that "you ain't seen nothing yet."

Carter's beliefs were not anti-American; he was a patriot who had served in the military. Nor were they "un-American," as that word had acquired a special meaning in the postwar years. But they might fairly be described as "post-American," as they assumed that the "American century" had come to a premature end, that America was losing its preeminent role in global politics as other nations caught up, and that American values would have be reshaped to conform to these new realities.

Prescriptions for Failure

If Carter had been a solitary calculating machine like Richard Nixon, his moralizing pessimism might not have mattered. But he was by nature a missionary who felt the need to communicate the uncomfortable new truths of post-Americanism to a nation lost in complacency. If the policies rooted in post-Americanism had then succeeded, the American people would have gradually seen and imitated his wisdom. But the policies failed. And the combination of missionary zeal and practical failure destroyed the Carter presidency. Three episodes in particular stand out in that long decline.

In his first year in office, the president said in a commencement address at Notre Dame University, "We are now free of that inordinate fear of Communism which once led us to embrace any dictator who joined us in our fear." This simple sentence performed three tasks: it exonerated the

Soviets ("inordinate fear"), it indicted the United States for backing dictators without due cause, and it announced a new hostility toward such now unrespectable allies. Carter duly followed his own prescriptions. In order to win Soviet goodwill and tempt the ape off the treadmill, he abandoned both the B-1 bomber program and the neutron bomb after persuading his close allies, British prime minister Jim Callaghan and West German chancellor Helmut Schmidt, to spend scarce political capital on supporting the latter highly controversial proposal. He urged the human rights reforms on the shah of Iran that helped to bring about the shah's downfall and replacement by Ayatollah Khomeini. But Carter raised little objection to the Soviet Union airlifting East Germans and Cubans to help a far more murderous pro-Marxist Ethiopian government in its war with Somalia or to the USSR's continuing installation of missiles in Eastern Europe aimed at Western capitals. It sometimes seemed that Carter had replaced our "inordinate fear of Communism" with the principle that Washington could pursue American values only if they conflicted with U.S. interests. Unfortunately for the president, his memorable phrase ensured that people were paying unusual attention to such niceties. And his foreign policy soon became associated with passivity and retreat.

The second episode occurred in his third year of office. It was an attempt to revive his presidency that, given Carter's luck, soon became known as the "malaise" speech. In July 1979 oil prices were again raised by OPEC and gas lines reappeared in the United States. Carter had already given five major presidential addresses on energy and the energy crisis. His analysis had always been fundamentally pessimistic, assuming continued oil and natural gas shortages and high prices, and his proposals had therefore stressed energy conservation, rationing, and the extension of price controls. It was no different on this occasion: the practical proposals in his speech were oil import quotas and such trivialities as voluntary weekend closings of gas stations. He plainly needed something more powerful. He decided to shroud the practicalities in a high spiritual appeal. Having summoned a series of national leaders to Camp David for consultations on the way forward for America, Carter adopted the analysis of his pollster, Patrick Caddell, that America was in the grip of a "malaise" that explained its other problems. Carter duly delivered a speech suggesting that America suffered from something far worse than an energy crisis—namely, a crisis of the national soul: "We can see this crisis in the growing doubt about the meaning of our own lives and in the loss of a unity of purpose for our nation." It was a sermon rather than a speech, heavy with calls for repentance, sacrifice, and renewal, and all in all gloomy rather than inspiring. Despite that, it was initially well received. People appreciated that Carter was being honest, but the president had not managed to establish any real connection between the spiritual crisis and the actual practical problems faced by Americans—let alone his solutions to them. Those solutions in practice made matters worse: price controls on natural gas, for instance, created and prolonged shortages rather than removing them. And within a short time the energy situation and Carter's polling numbers were as bad as ever. Though Carter had never used the word "malaise"—it had been leaked to the press from Caddell's memo—his "malaise" speech nonetheless came to be a symbol of the administration's high-minded and sickly incompetence in domestic and economic policy.

The third episode was the president's handling of the crisis that ensued when the U.S. embassy in Tehran was seized and sixty-six Americans, mainly U.S. diplomats, were taken as hostages by Iranian "students" supported by the new revolutionary Islamic government under Khomeini.[21] American policy went through three stages. In the first stage, it sought to demonstrate that the United States was no longer an evil hegemon hostile to Third World revolutions. It would not overreact. Secretary of State Cyrus Vance explained this to the American people in terms that eventually became wearisome: "Most Americans recognize that we cannot alone dictate events. This recognition is not a sign of America's decline. It is a sign of growing American maturity in a complex world."[22]

When this "maturity" failed to persuade Tehran to free the hostages, the administration issued vague threats. Given Carter's general reputation, however, these threats were not believed by Tehran. Khomeini took to openly mocking the president. But the third stage was the worst of all: virtually forced to react by popular pressure, Carter attempted a rescue mission in April 1980 that had to be aborted when some of the helicopters were grounded in the desert by sand in the machinery.[23] Then, adding to the disaster, one helicopter crashed and eight American servicemen were killed. It is hard today to grasp just how severe a blow to American prestige—and to America's friends around the world—the fiasco of Desert One was. Antonio Martino, later Italy's defense minister in the Iraq war, was at the time a leading economist in Rome and a public figure well known for his pro-American views. He remembers getting telephone calls that morning from left-wing friends, genuinely commiserating with him on the humiliating collapse of America as a great power.[24] To friends and enemies alike, Carter's foreign policy increasingly seemed to be one of active helplessness.

Propelled by these crises and by ever-worsening economic statistics, the Carter administration careened toward defeat in an atmosphere of growing national anxiety. It was not alone. The later 1970s were years of crisis and setback in every region of the world. The Four Horsemen of the Apocalypse did a victory lap around Africa, where there were wars, civil wars, revolutions, and famines in Angola, Mozambique, Rhodesia (now Zimbabwe), Ethiopia, South-West Africa (now Namibia), and the Horn of Africa. In Asia, China invaded Vietnam, Vietnam invaded Cambodia, and Cambodia's Marxist government killed off an estimated one-fifth of its own people. In Europe, Italy was being attacked internally by Red Brigade terrorists who routinely murdered judges; Germany, still divided, had its own terrorist threat in the form of the Baader-Meinhof gang, who murdered industrialists; and Britain was suffering from inflation, unemployment, strikes, and a government that seemed increasingly helpless in dealing with them. Throughout the world a spirit of anarchy had taken hold, and it was producing pessimism and gloom among ordinary citizens.

More than the Carter administration was collapsing. An entire structure of power and ideas—Liberaldom—was beginning to crumble. Steven Hayward, in the fine first volume of his *The Age of Reagan*, describes it as the "fall of the old liberal order," that had hegemony in the West from 1964 to 1980.[25] From a British or European perspective, the dominant ideology would be called "social democracy" and its dominance would begin in 1945 with the election of the postwar Labour government, or even earlier with the postwar social planning of Churchill's wartime coalition. If we think that the Soviet half of Europe should be included in this collapse (which seems more reasonable after 1989 than in 1979), we should call it the decline of statism. But however it should be described, this collapse began to accelerate in the second half of the 1970s. And the faster the decline, the more Wojtyla, Thatcher, and Reagan seemed to be vindicated. From the invasion of Afghanistan, to the "misery index" of inflation and unemployment, to the social ills that seemed to have been spawned or accelerated by the "permissive society," events now came to their aid in a peculiarly direct and dramatic way. The threats they had warned against were shown to be real dangers. The solutions they had espoused looked sensible. The personal qualities they possessed—courage, firmness, and optimism—seemed to be exactly those needed as antidotes to a prevailing sense of despair and helplessness. Wojtyla no longer seemed too Catholic, nor Thatcher too conservative, nor Reagan too American. They were just what the doctor ordered to cure malaise.

The first event was a death. Pope Paul VI died on August 6, 1978, and was buried in St. Peter's Basilica in Rome six days later. The pope had died an unhappy man, feeling that his stewardship of the Church had been a failure. This was not an entirely fair judgment: Paul had left behind a record of considerable administrative, liturgical, and ecumenical reform. But it was not wholly false. The Church had continued to be divided by bitter disputes between theological liberals and conservatives over the legacy of Vatican II. Almost directly political quarrels broke out among churchmen over such matters as "liberation theology." In Western Europe and America there was a perceptible crisis of faith as congregations dwindled, theologians promoted doctrines hard to distinguish from heresy, seminaries emptied, priests left the church (often to get married), nuns transformed themselves from brides of Christ into political activists, and the Catholic faithful increasingly ignored moral teachings they found onerous.

Paul VI was not directly responsible for these developments, which arose from profound cultural changes in Western society: a growing public secularism, a kind of operational agnosticism in social theory, and above all the sexual revolution. But the pope's tentative and nervous public personality failed to inspire the faithful to resist them. The impression that the Vatican gave in those years alternated between drift and a feeble opposition to the spirit of the age that did little to halt it. This is too harsh a judgment on Paul VI personally, yet it seems to have been close to the pope's own regretful verdict.

The cardinals, accordingly, were in an anxious mood when they gathered in Rome to elect a new pope. In addition to the Church's own distinctive troubles, they had to be worried by the worldwide secular trends. *Ostpolitik* may have looked more necessary in light of the Soviet Union's political advance. But the advance of an avowedly atheist superpower was bound to be highly disturbing to the Church for both spiritual and practical reasons. The sexual revolution had produced rising illegitimacy and divorce rates, greater incidence of child abuse, and the growing acceptability of "non-traditional" families. It was clearly not a revolution that could be successfully appeased by something as modest as granting permission for Catholic couples to use contraceptives. It was more elemental than that. What was needed was a pope who could deal with such elemental challenges.

Wojtyla arrived in Rome with a growing international reputation that fell just short of being *papabile* (suitable for the papacy). He had experience dealing with Communism in the East, an orthodox but imaginative approach to the sexual questions that dominated Catholic debate in the West, and an inspiring personality that gave hope to the faithful, including even the cardinals. But though the cardinals had grasped that the Church needed a leader in a new mold, from a background bolder and fresher than that of Paul VI, a diplomat from a distinguished Italian family that had given long service to the Vatican, they shrank from the radical step of a non-Italian. After four ballots, they elected Cardinal Albino Luciani of Venice, who took the name Pope John Paul I.

It has become conventional to dismiss John Paul I as a good, simple man out of his depth in the papacy, who was physically crushed by its demands. That may well be unfair. As a cardinal in Venice he had been a very popular local figure. He had written a charming book of letters to historical figures he liked, including Mark Twain and G. K. Chesterton. His few acts as pope—such as refusing a formal coronation and inviting children to chat in audiences—showed both a simplicity of temperament and a sure touch for public relations. He was described to me by a shrewd Italian political observer at the time as someone who had made Catholicism popular with ordinary Italians again. He had written a stern letter to the Jesuits urging greater orthodoxy, which was unsent at his death but subsequently signed and sent by his successor. The physical illness that killed him, heart disease, was well advanced at the time of his election. But we will never know what achievements Pope John Paul I had in him, as God called him home only thirty-three days after his election.

The cardinals reassembled in a chastened and curious mood to elect a second new pope. They recalled the slightly eerie fact that the traditional method of informing the world that a new pope had been elected—namely, puffs of white smoke from the Vatican chimney—had not functioned properly in Luciani's case. Cardinal Joseph Ratzinger asked the new conclave the question that was already in all their hearts: "What is God's will for us at this moment? We were convinced that the election [of John Paul I] was made in correspondence with the will of God, not simply in a human way...and if one month after being elected in accordance with the will of God, he died, God has something to say to us." His statement encouraged, indeed created, what Ratzinger called "the possibility of doing something new."[26] When an apparent deadlock occurred between the two leading Italian candidates, the possibility of something new pointed to a non-Italian.

Wojtyla was only one of many non-Italians now considered papabile. He was not seen as papabile by all, even by some who knew him well. When his name was suggested by Vienna's Cardinal Koenig, Wyszynski, the primate of Poland, said, "No, he's too young, too unknown. He could never be pope." But Wojtyla's unique mixture of qualities recommended him to the dominant coalition of moderate cardinals worried that the

Church was going astray: his novel method of outmaneuvering Communism seemed wise to Western Europeans suddenly reawakened to the Communist threat, his doctrinal orthodoxy attracted cardinals from the growing Asian and African branches of the church, and his pastoral experience recommended him to all.

After several inconclusive votes in the conclave, Wojtyla suddenly realized that he might be elected. Weeping, he sought solace from Wyszynski, who said, "You must accept. For Poland."[27] He was chosen by the conclave on the eighth ballot on October 16, 1978. To loud applause from the conclave he took the name of John Paul II. The new pope immediately broke tradition by declining to greet the cardinals seated, as their superior. "I greet my brothers standing," he declared.

He then went out onto the balcony to address the crowd of Romans still distressed that their popular favorite, John Paul I, had been taken from them. He reassured them in fluent Italian, "We are all still grieved after the death of our most beloved John Paul I. And now the eminent cardinals have called a new bishop to Rome. They have called him from a far country: far, but always near through the communion of faith and in the Christian tradition."[28] In that far country, the news was not officially released for some hours while the Communist authorities worked out a proper Marxist response. It spread rapidly anyway through the ringing of church bells and the joyous shouts of believers and Polish patriots. Even the first secretary of the Communist party, Stanislaw Kania, one of the first to hear the news, emitted a remarkably non-Communist ejaculation: "Holy Mother of God."[29]

It may not have been a pious ejaculation.

One evening in the late summer of 1978, Frank Johnson, later editor of the London *Spectator* and then holding down one of the most coveted posts in British political journalism as parliamentary sketch-writer of the *Daily Telegraph*, was having his hair cut in north London. He asked his Turkish Cypriot barber if the television could be turned on so that he could listen to Labour prime minister Jim Callaghan announce the date of the general election.

"Frank," said the barber, "Callaghan's not going to call a general election."

Drawing on his full authority as a member of the parliamentary press gallery, Johnson assured the barber that Callaghan would indeed call an election. It was common knowledge in the Westminster village. The barber repeated his denial, saying that Callaghan knew he would lose an election, so why call one until it was legally necessary?

They turned on the television. Callaghan announced that no election would be held until the following year.

Once he had recovered his dignity, Johnson set to thinking. The barber had not only been right, he concluded, but more right than either of them knew. Polls must have shown that Labour's electoral prospects for that fall were really dreadful, because its prior electoral strategy had almost required an early election.

By 1978 Labour had recovered from its 1975–76 slough of despond, when the rate of inflation had risen above 20 percent, the International Monetary Fund had sent in its accountants to see if Britain's financial prospects justified a loan, and a Labour government had introduced a budget that cut welfare spending by more than the Tories had ever dared propose. It had recovered from these humiliations by combining policies from left and right. Its right-wing policy was Friedmanite monetarism: curbing the money supply in order to bring down inflation. (Callaghan's son-in-law, Peter Jay, Britain's ambassador to Washington and an admirer of Milton Friedman, had convinced the prime minister that extra spending would not reduce unemployment but increase it. Callaghan announced this abandonment of Keynesianism to an astonished and horrified annual Labour conference.)[30] Its left-wing policy was price and wage control under which the labor unions agreed to restrain their wage demands in return for a say over government policy in general. This left-right syncretism was justified with the argument that, by restraining demands for higher wages, the labor unions ensured that their members would not price themselves out of jobs. Monetarism would thereby gradually reduce inflation without causing excessive unemployment. And some of the economic indicators were now turning favorable for Labour.

Even so, Labour's "social contract" with the unions looked indispensable. It was a fig leaf distinguishing Labour's monetarism from the Tory variety and enabling Chancellor Denis Healey to argue that Labour's monetarism was a civilized alternative to Thatcher's "sado-monetarism." It reminded the voters that the failure of Heath's Tory government either to control the unions or to make friends of them had led to massive national strikes and the shutdown of the "three-day week." And it fed the nervous suspicion of middle-of-the-road voters that the Tories might be "extreme" on labor unions and thus provoke social conflict and more industrial shutdowns.

The Tories were hardly less nervous. In the four years since her election, Thatcher had built up an international reputation, especially in the United States, as a tough but competent right-wing leader. She had made a favorable impression on foreign leaders in several overseas trips, beginning with a 1975 United States visit, when she had substantive conversations with Ford and Kissinger. (She did not see her new friend in California on the trip as promised; they met again in London in 1978.) In her first overseas outing, she made such a popular impact that civil servants had to answer complaints from Labour ministers that she was getting too much diplomatic help. This reflected in part the widespread expectation, shared by British diplomats in the United States, that she was likely to become the first female leader of a major Western democracy. But it also reflected her professionalism and her dynamism. She worked hard at knowing about foreign policy and international economics and at putting across her views on them forcefully. Her official welcome also owed something, it must be said, to the perception in the mid-1970s that Britain was economically at rock bottom and badly needed a savior. In a meeting with the president in 1975 to prepare for Thatcher's visit, Kissinger said, "Britain is a tragedy—it has sunk to begging, borrowing, and stealing until North Sea oil comes in." Brits could only sorrowfully agree with him.

Domestically, through these years, Thatcher skillfully united her fractious party around a set of policies that were robustly conservative and positive in tone. They stressed the economic revival of Britain through tax cuts and enterprise rather than through harsh cuts in spending. She presented herself as a bold and optimistic leader who, in contrast to the "exhausted volcanoes" on the Labour front bench, was determined to halt and reverse the economic decline of Britain. On most issues, notably taxation, she had won public opinion over with a combination of effective speeches and an advertising campaign so imaginative that Senator Bill Brock, then chairman of the Republican National Committee, imported it without alteration to the United States.[31] It showed Britain as a runner who is initially ahead of his rivals but who is loaded up with weights, representing taxation and regulation, at the end of every lap until eventually he loses his lead and staggers in last. The largest weight that the Tory Party had to bear, however, was still the labor union problem.

Union reform was an item on the Tory agenda. But the proposed reforms were cautious, incremental, and directed toward protecting the rights of union members rather than restricting the rights of the unions themselves. Some leading Tories were quietly defeatist. They believed that a Conservative government could never win against a miners' strike, such as had twice vanquished Heath's government, and wanted to maintain Labour's corporatist cooperation with labor unions under themselves. Even Thatcher, though firmly committed to bringing unions under the rule of law, thought that a pre-election row with the unions was the one issue that might cost her victory.

That was why Johnson and other shrewd observers had been convinced that Callaghan would call an early election. The compact between Callaghan's government and the union leaders was beginning to break down. As always happens with prices and incomes control, the dam eventually burst. Ordinary trade unionists, fed up with modest pay increases in a time of higher prices and angered because some unions seemed to be treated favorably, were demanding wage increases above the agreed government-union formula. Their bosses were finding it difficult to hold the line. That was why the political punditocracy had assumed Callaghan would get the election over early.

Sure enough, at the 1978 annual Labour conference, two years after Callaghan had horrified the delegates by embracing monetarism, the unions horrified Labour ministers by rejecting voluntary wage restraint. Labour's principal electoral card had been snatched from them by its own natural supporters. They no longer had a clear advantage over Thatcher on the labor union question. And it was about to get much worse.

Only weeks later, in the winter of 1978–79, a series of strikes, official and unofficial, in support of wage hikes above the official limit spread over Britain. When some workers resisted calls to leave work or delivered goods to blockaded factories, "flying pickets" (union militants from other businesses) turned up to enforce solidarity. As "the winter of discontent" wore on, heart patients were turned away from hospitals by striking ambulance workers, the dead went unburied in Liverpool owing to a strike by gravediggers, mountains of rubbish piled up in Leicester Square, one of the main tourist destinations in central London, and food supplies ran low in parts of the country. Britain seemed on the edge of being ungovernable. This was far worse than the three-day week of Heath's day, and it effectively replaced that memory in the electorate's mind.

Callaghan himself made matters worse, first by being photographed on the beach in sunny Guadeloupe (where he was attending a summit conference) as the country ground to a halt, second by downplaying the seriousness of the situation on his return. "Crisis? What Crisis?" screeched the tabloid headlines. Callaghan never said those words, any more than Carter had used the term "malaise," but they seemed to sum up his message and the complacent timidity of the government in the face of mayhem by its union allies. The union issue switched sides. In a Gallup poll 84 percent of Britons agreed that the unions had too much power. Thatcher's robust conservatism suddenly looked just right.

Events now slipped completely out of Labour's control. Callaghan's government lost a parliamentary motion of no confidence by a single vote—the first such government loss for more than fifty years. An election had to be called. Thatcher and the Tories fought a cool and controlled campaign on a radical manifesto that now seemed commonsensical. The winter of discontent gave them a solid majority of forty-four seats, almost certainly higher than they would have enjoyed if Callaghan had called the election for the previous October. And Thatcher entered Downing Street as prime minister on Friday, May 4, 1979.

On the steps she recited the famous prayer of St. Francis of Assisi, given to her by playwright and occasional speechwriter Ronnie Millar: "Where there is error, may we bring truth. Where there is doubt, may we bring faith. And where there is despair, may we bring hope." Ronnie's dramatic skill had deserted him on this occasion. The prayer did not strike quite the right note, however; it was overly pious for such a practical politician. And as she later reflected ruefully, error, doubt, and despair were so firmly entrenched in British society after the winter of discontent that overcoming them would not be possible "without a measure of discord."

She couldn't guess the half of it.

Ronald Reagan telephoned Downing Street that Friday to congratulate his friend on her election. He wasn't put through. The Downing Street switchboard, usually impeccably efficient, knew nothing of their friendship and, when so many important congratulations were flooding in, did not think that a former California governor quite made the grade. The mistake was discovered, however, and the following day Reagan and the new prime minister exchanged compliments and hopes. Three weeks later he used his column to express his pleasure at her success: "It's been my privilege to meet and have two lengthy audiences with Mrs. Thatcher and I've been rooting for her to become prime minister since our first meeting.... If anyone can remind England of [her] greatness... it will be the prime minister the English press has already nicknamed 'Maggie.'"[32]

Reagan was principally writing columns and radio talks between the 1976 election and the summer of 1979. That suited him just fine. He later remarked that he developed his political views (and educated himself out of the Democratic and into the Republican Party) mainly by writing and so having to think his way through problems. Several aides testify that they

can recall him losing his temper only when he was interrupted while trying to finish a column or speech. His radio talks were ways of both keeping himself before the voters and developing the arguments that he would
later put before the American people.

That second aim was more principled and intellectual than political. A
typical Reagan column was almost never partisan or even explicitly conservative. It almost never attacked Carter or other Democrats and rarely
even mentioned them. It selected a topic, say, arms control, provided some
recent information about it, say, the Carter administration's latest proposal
in the Strategic Arms Limitation Talks, produced evidence or expert testimony to suggest that the administration's proposals were mistaken, and
finally reached some wider conclusion or moral. Reagan's language was
simple and direct. So were his arguments, but they were not, as liberal critics then and later argued, inadequate or half-formed.

John Gross, the distinguished literary critic, had not then coined the epigram that "complexity is the first refuge of the scoundrel." In a discussion
of the Vietnam War, however, Reagan grasped Gross's underlying point:
the liberal elevation of complexity was not a virtue when inevitable and
was a vice when voluntary. "The fetish of complexity," he said, "the trick
of making hard decisions harder to make—the art, finally, of rationalizing
the non-decision, have made a ruin of American foreign policy."[33] Reagan's
columns and radio talks deconstructed this and other liberal intellectual
fetishes on a weekly basis. Though Carter was rarely mentioned, his policies were logically examined and found wanting in clear terms and in the
most amiable tone of voice. And over time Reagan articulated an entire
conservative political philosophy without ever descending into partisan-
ship.

Reagan's principal theme, threaded through four years of broadcasts
and countless topics, was a defense of America. He defended America's
postwar foreign policy on the grounds that it was a bulwark against totalitarianism, America's free enterprise system on the grounds that it was
more productive than government regulation, and America's traditional
values on the grounds that they were both more decent and more realistic
than countercultural values. As the Carter administration, infatuated with

post-American complexities, was skeptical about all these propositions, it was on these issues that Reagan was most critical of the Carter record—though sometimes in original ways that diverged from standard conservative themes. Reagan was very hostile toward Carter's appeasement of the Soviet Union, for instance, but less because he feared Soviet power than because he felt Carter was not taking advantage of Soviet weakness.[34] He cited the testimony of an exiled Vladimir Bukovsky that his fellow dissidents still in the Soviet Union were openly speaking out against the system even at the cost of brutality and imprisonment. He concluded that "a little less détente with the politburo and a little more encouragement to the dissenters might be worth a lot of armored divisions."[35]

Reagan devoted innumerable columns, often very witty ones, to the absurdities of state regulation and intervention. Needless to say, he was scathing about Carter's "malaise" speech and its pessimism about America's future, saying that "people who talk about an age of limits are really talking about their own limitations, not America's." He threw in the occasional sentimental story—for instance, about the rescue of refugees at sea by U.S. sailors—that illustrated American virtue in a sentimental way that cooler political heads would have foolishly avoided or done badly. While Reagan was converting listeners, his political aides were building up a national political organization—a laborious but not difficult task as he was plainly the GOP's front-runner. They set about winning over constituencies that had been absent in 1976: in particular Republican Party regulars loyal to Ford and neo-conservative intellectuals who would have preferred Moynihan but who were disappointed with his loyalty toward a national Democratic Party they had abandoned and now regarded as hopeless.

As with Thatcher and the winter of discontent, however, events proved to be Reagan's most persuasive recruiting sergeant. The Soviet invasion of Afghanistan made Carter look foolish and Reagan prophetic. The long Tehran hostage crisis made his reputation for toughness seem desirable. The "misery index" that added inflation to unemployment—Carter's own preferred test four years earlier—rose from 12.6 percent then to more than 20 percent in 1980 and confirmed Reagan's commonsense economics. At almost every turn in 1980 the news sounded like Republican Party propaganda. After a shaky start, Reagan coasted to victory in the Republican primaries and was a clear but not certain favorite for the presidential election. He was no longer "too American." After four years of post-Americanism, the voters wanted a patriot in primary colors.

There was one main obstacle blocking his way: the public fear that he might be a danger to peace in a nuclear age. Reagan put this fear to flight with his answer to a question on the unrelated topic of national health insurance in a debate watched by an estimated one hundred million people. When Carter accused him of opposing Medicare as an example of his general extremism, Reagan smiled, shook his head, and said, "There you go again." It was The Perfect Squelch. With that one remark, Reagan convinced Americans that he was a fundamentally relaxed and easygoing guy who could be trusted with the nuclear football. He won the election easily, helped the GOP to win the Senate on his coattails, and took office on January 20, 1981.

Within half an hour of his taking the oath of office, the plane returning the U.S. hostages took off from Tehran. The ayatollahs had clearly not drawn the same message as the American voters from "There you go again."

In the short space of twenty-six months, pope, president, and prime minister had all conquered the doubts of their peers and countrymen and entered the highest office open to each of them. It had been an immense struggle to reach those summits. Considered coolly, however, they had not climbed a peak so much as entered a boxing ring. And the bruisers lurking in the opposite corners looked like a very formidable crew indeed.

CHAPTER THREE

DID GOD GUIDE
THE BULLETS?

～⁑～

I f *life were a supernatural thriller,* the next plot twists would have been expected. Twenty-six months separated the elections of John Paul II and Ronald Reagan, and Margaret Thatcher began her premiership roughly in between. Fewer than three months (to be precise, seventy days) separated Reagan's election and the attempt on his life by John Hinckley on March 30, 1981. John Paul II narrowly survived an attempted assassination a mere forty-three days later, on May 13. And three years later Thatcher escaped unharmed when an IRA bomb intended to kill her exploded in the Grand Hotel in Brighton on October 12, 1984, killing five people and wounding many others, including her close friend and ally Norman Tebbit.

There is an almost cinematic neatness about this series of crimes. In *The Omen* or *The Exorcist* they would be readily explained as the forces of Satan seeking to destroy the apostles of hope before they could do too much good (though a more formulaic film director than God would have insisted that Satan move his attempt on Thatcher's life up to 1981). This slightly eerie impression is reinforced by the extraordinary narrowness of the escape of all three intended victims. At least two of those intended victims believed that God had intervened to preserve their lives, and guided their later actions by the light of that belief.

Assassinations have sometimes altered the course of history; the First World War arose from one. On these occasions, it was the failure of assassination that may have altered history.

A Close Call at St. Peter's

On May 13, 1981, John Paul was struck by two bullets fired by Mehmet Ali Agca, a Turkish professional assassin and terrorist, as the pope passed by him on a circuit of St. Peter's Square at 5:13 in the afternoon.[1] Agca had been waiting in the second row of pilgrims behind wooden barriers. He was only twenty feet away from the pope when he fired his Browning 9 mm semi-automatic pistol. His aim was true. Agca hit the pope twice, once in the abdomen and once on the elbow, and the pope immediately fell backward into the arms of his secretary, Monsignor Stanislaw Dziwisz. Though Agca was promptly seized by nearby pilgrims and handed over to the police, he must have felt that he had succeeded in his murderous aim.

Nor was he entirely wrong. The pope was in mortal peril. He was rushed by ambulance to the Gemelli hospital, four miles away. By the time he arrived his blood pressure was falling and his pulse was weak. His secretary administered last rites in the operating theater as the medical staff cut away the pope's clothes to discover the nature of his wounds.

Dr. Francesco Crucitti, one of the Gemelli's chief surgeons, was at another hospital when he learned of the attack. He rushed to the Gemelli, which had been designated as the venue for any medical emergency involving the pope; a suite was kept in permanent readiness. Speeding over to the hospital (talking his way past traffic police), he discovered on arrival that the inside of the pope's abdomen was awash in blood. Six pints of it had to be suctioned out so that the surgeon could find the source of the bleeding. When it had been stanched and blood transfusions given, the surgeon set about dealing with the pope's actual wounds. These were multiple: blast wounds from the bullet in his abdomen, a perforated colon, and five wounds in his small intestine. It took five hours of surgery to close these wounds and to remove the damaged parts of his intestine. Only after midnight, more than seven hours after Agca had struck, was the pope's condition satisfactory enough for a hopeful bulletin to be issued.

Yet John Paul had been extraordinarily lucky. Agca's bullet missed his abdominal artery, his spinal column, and every major nerve cluster when it passed through his body. It did so by a millimeter or two. It was probably deflected from its original course by striking the pope's finger (which was broken), thus missing the vital organs that it otherwise would have damaged. The result of the bullet's diversion was that the pope was not killed on the spot, did not bleed to death in the ambulance, and did not suffer serious paralysis—all of which would have happened if the bullet had taken a slightly different course and probably even its original course. Both the pope's doctors and his secretary (into whose arms he had fallen when the bullet struck) agreed that this was "miraculous."

The pope himself put the same point more fully a few years later: "One hand fired and another hand guided the bullet."[2]

In their vivid account of the attempted assassination of John Paul II, Carl Bernstein and Marco Politi remark in passing of the bullet's trajectory: "Like the bullet that almost killed Ronald Reagan, it had passed a few millimeters from the central aorta."[3]

In fact, the attempted assassination of Reagan on March 30, 1981, came even closer to success than Agca's shooting of the pope. We are inclined to believe the opposite because of the behavior of both men immediately following the attacks. The pope did not lose consciousness immediately. But he told Dziwisz that he had been shot in the stomach, closed his eyes, and promptly began to pray, repeating "Mary, my mother, Mary, my mother." Though he was plainly in great pain, he remained more or less conscious on the ambulance journey. But he lost consciousness as he arrived at the hospital and had to be carried in. Our memory of these events, however, is colored by the photograph of the pope falling back into the monsignor's arms in an unnerving imitation of the *Pieta*. It is an image of someone brought face-to-face with death in the space of a moment.

Reagan, on the other hand, did not at first realize that he had been shot.[4] When John Hinckley began shooting, Jerry Parr, the White House security chief, and another agent, Ray Shaddick, pushed the president downward into his official limousine with an unceremonious shove, jumped in on top of him, and ordered the driver to leave at once for the White House. Sitting up, Reagan felt a sharp pain in his side and complained of Parr's roughness, saying, "I think you've broken one of my ribs." A moment later he started coughing up bright red blood. He was obviously in great pain. Parr instructed the driver to change course for the emergency room of nearby George Washington Hospital. He also felt around the president's ribs and back but could find no obvious sign of injury.

Ten minutes after being shot, Reagan arrived at the hospital entrance not only in great pain but also having trouble breathing. Still, he got out of the car, stood up, and told Parr, "I'll walk in." He walked about twenty yards through the entrance to the emergency room and then buckled to the floor. Parr and Shaddick carried him farther while nurses and doctors cut off his clothes. When Reagan said that he couldn't breathe, doctors made an incision in his throat and inserted a breathing tube. His blood pressure had fallen to half its normal level. Blood was flooding into his lung. Reagan finally passed out. As the doctors were struggling to drain the blood and reinflate the lung, a nurse, Kathy Paul, and a doctor, Wesley Price, noticed a thin slit under the president's left armpit.[5]

Reagan regained consciousness enough to hear the nurse say: "Uh-oh, he's been shot." He realized himself for the first time what had happened and, as he told Morris, remembered the crouching figure he had seen through the car door. He recalled his thoughts later:

> I focused on that tiled ceiling and prayed. But I realized that I couldn't ask for God's help while at the same time I felt hatred for the mixed-up young man who had shot me. Isn't that the meaning of the lost sheep? We are all God's children and there-

fore equally beloved by Him. I began to pray for his soul and that he would find his way back into the fold.[6]

About an hour after Reagan was shot, the bullet was removed from his body by Dr. Benjamin Aaron, the chief of thoracic surgery at the hospital. But the president's troubles were only beginning. Though the bullet had not killed Reagan, it had inflicted serious internal damage on him. He had lost half the blood in his body, he had a collapsed lung, and he was kept alive only by constant transfusions. In this weakened state he was placed under anesthesia and underwent an operation lasting nearly three hours. When he regained consciousness an hour later—about five hours after being shot—he suffered serious chest pains and was given morphine and put on a respirator. Throughout most of that night he was in pain alleviated somewhat by further doses of morphine.

Three days later the president still had a fever of 103 degrees and was spitting up small amounts of blood. Doctors considered a second operation to remove damaged lung tissue. They were worried that he was developing pneumonia over the weekend of April 4 and 5, and prescribed stronger doses of antibiotics. One week after the shooting he was well enough to see visitors, including Speaker of the House Tip O'Neill, bringing the best wishes of the now distinctly loyal opposition. But Reagan's guests were shocked at how ill he looked. After thirteen days in the hospital the president had lost a dozen pounds. He returned home to the White House on April 11, 1981, cheerful in a red sweater and waving to the crowd, and walked fifty yards to the elevator. But he fell into a chair exhausted once he was upstairs. It was not until nearly three weeks after Hinckley's attack that Reagan was really able to perform any of his normal tasks, such as calling congressmen to solicit their votes. Very soon afterward, he achieved one of the most remarkable legislative victories ever by getting a majority Democratic House of Representatives to pass the tax cut program that launched Reaganomics. But that achievement was a triumph over adversity rather than a display of effortless superiority.

Why is our impression of the attempted assassination of Reagan and its medical aftermath very different from this grim Calvary? At the time official spokesmen gave falsely cheery accounts of the president's state of health. The doctors went along. "The president's vital signs were absolutely rock solid through this whole thing," said the dean of clinical affairs at GW. "He was at no time in any serious danger." These assurances were not strictly true, but they were justified by the need to reassure an anxious nation. What is interesting is that they were so readily believed by the media and the public in an atmosphere of post-Watergate skepticism. Later biographers from Edmund Morris to Richard Reeves have corrected these false accounts in detail and incontrovertibly. But their more accurate reports have never really changed a public view that is now firmly entrenched.

The reason is Reagan himself. Not only did he walk unaided from the car into the GW emergency room, but he also kept up the steady string of reassuring jokes that have since passed into legend. At the time and in retrospect it was an astounding performance. He had been shot, had lost a large amount of blood, and was experiencing acute chest pains from a collapsed lung when he forced himself to get up out of the car and walk into the hospital. He awoke at one point to find a nurse holding his hand. "Does Nancy know about us?" he asked. "I hope you guys are all Republicans," he told the doctors just before the operation. ("Mr. President, today we're all Republicans," replied the doctor.) When his wife arrived, he said, "Honey, I forgot to duck." Even though he was barely conscious, his main concern was to reassure both the country and those around him that all was well. Then he overcame his own reasonable anger at the assassin so he could pray for him.

These were acts of great nobility. As Daniel Patrick Moynihan, quoting Hemingway, said in the Senate that day, they showed "grace under pressure." They had a powerful political impact. David Broder in the *Washington Post* predicted two days later, "As long as people remember the hospitalized president joshing his doctors—and they will remember—no critic will be able to portray Reagan as a cruel or callow or heartless man." He was right: Reagan's political invulnerability lasted five years, until Iran-Contra. The most long-lasting effect of Reagan's bravery, however, is that today we find it hard to grasp just how close to death he came.

Hinckley's bullet was a .22-caliber slug intended to explode in Reagan's body. But when it hit the presidential limousine's bulletproof surface, it was shaped by the impact into a small, flat disc. In that form it had ricocheted through the hairline crack in the limousine door and entered Reagan's body under his arm as he was being flung into the limo. If the bullet had been its original shape, it would have passed quickly through his body, wreaking maximum damage and probably killing him even if it had not exploded. But as a flat disc, it turned over slowly in the president's flesh, meeting maximum resistance, hit a rib, was diverted, and rolled slowly toward his heart, halting about an inch away from it. Even then his life was at risk. The doctors did not know he had been shot and the almost invisible wound might have escaped their notice longer than it did.

Like John Paul, Reagan came within an inch of death. Unlike the pope, he did not fall back into Parr's arms, but walked into the hospital and started cracking jokes. We have been misled by that gallantry ever since. But the reality is that both men almost died and each had the same explanation for his survival: "One hand fired and another hand guided the bullet."

In the early morning of October 12, 1984, Margaret Thatcher was in the prime ministerial suite of the Grand Hotel, Brighton, completing her speech for the annual Tory conference later that day. Her speechwriting sessions were always Stakhanovite occasions at which several speechwriters labored over ever-changing texts sometimes for days and invariably late into the night. On this occasion Thatcher, the speechwriters, and her close ally Norman Tebbit (a former journalist with a talent for the stiletto phrase) had been working through an evening broken only by her visit to the annual Conservative Agents Ball. They wrapped up the final version of the speech at about 2:40 in the morning. The speechwriters departed for their beds. The rewritten passages were handed to the secretaries across the hall to type up. The prime minister briefly used the bathroom. She returned to the suite to deal with official government business, still in a ball gown, with Robin Butler, the cabinet secretary. They discussed a memo on the forthcoming Liverpool Garden Festival.

At 2:54 a.m., as Butler was putting away the papers, they heard a "loud thud" followed by the sound of falling masonry. They both knew instantly that it was a bomb but had no idea where it had exploded.[7] They guessed it was a car bomb. In fact, the bomb had exploded in the Grand Hotel itself, placed there three weeks before by IRA terrorists pretending to be tourists and detonated by a sophisticated timing device. Neither the main room nor the bedroom of the prime ministerial suite suffered anything worse than shattered glass. Denis Thatcher, who had been asleep in the bedroom, emerged to see if his wife was safe and then returned to dress. Others now entered the suite to check that the Thatchers had suffered no injury—ministers, their wives, detectives, civil servants, and aides. Included among these was Mrs. Cynthia Crawford ("Crawfie"), who traveled with the prime minister, advised her on clothes, and had become an indispensable helpmeet. No one was allowed to leave the hotel until the police were sure that the exits were neither blocked nor booby-trapped. So Crawfie packed a vanity case of overnight clothes for the Thatchers, Butler put away government papers, and the secretaries said exactly the right thing to the prime minister: "It's all right, PM, the speech is perfectly safe." Then, at 3:10 a.m., only sixteen minutes after the bombing, the detectives guided the prime ministerial party through the shattered hotel to a waiting car.

"The air was full of thick cement dust," recalled Thatcher in her memoirs. "It was in my mouth and it covered my clothes as I clambered over discarded belongings and broken furniture towards the back entrance of the hotel."[8]

Thatcher did not find out until later that five people had died in the blast, including her friends Anthony Berry, a Tory MP, and Roberta Wakeham, the wife of minister John Wakeham, who was himself severely hurt. Nor did she know that among those still trapped in the rubble and suffering terrible pain from major injuries were Norman Tebbit and his wife, Margaret, who was permanently paralyzed after that night.

Thatcher and her little party went first to the Brighton police station, where an impromptu cabinet committee meeting was held. She decided very firmly that she would deliver her speech later that morning, as planned, unless the conference hall had also been attacked. After changing from her gown to a business suit, she spoke briefly to the press about not surrendering to terrorism and, accompanied by Denis and Crawfie, drove to Lewes police college to rest and think.

In fact, she could think of only one thing to do: "Crawfie and I knelt by the sides of our beds and prayed for some time in silence."[9]

The rest of her day was a combination of sleepwalking dutifully through her prime ministerial tasks, visiting the injured, and encountering odd little coincidences that made it all slightly less terrible. She went to the Royal Sussex County Hospital and discovered that the consultant in charge was a former Tory MP, Tony Trafford, who knew most of the injured well and was striving to save them with everything he had. When she heard that John Wakeham, still unconscious, was in danger of losing both his legs, she spent hours on the phone tracking down a world-class specialist in the treatment of crush injuries from El Salvador. He turned out to be visiting the Royal Sussex. And when she went to address the Tory conference that morning, she was surprised to see almost the entire cabinet and many ordinary delegates resplendent in new suits and smart dresses. Marks and Spencer had opened their stores in Brighton early that morning and dressed anyone who had lost their belongings in the Grand Hotel bombing from top to toe in free outfits.

Thatcher's speech was perhaps not her finest performance from a technical standpoint. It had been rewritten in haste just before delivery. She had to speak from a paper text rather than from the Autocue that she had learned about from Ronald Reagan, which she preferred. And she ad-libbed a good deal, which, because of the strain of the previous nine hours, did not produce her most brilliant lines. But it was remarkable that the speech was being delivered at all—a point she underlined in one sentence: "[T]he fact that we are gathered here now, shocked but composed and determined, is a sign not only that this attack has failed, but that all attempts to destroy democracy by terrorism will fail."

The truth was she was the best guarantee that the promise would be kept. But she was more shocked than she appeared. After a weekend spent recovering at Chequers, she gave an interview to Channel Four in which she was asked what had been the worst of the experience for her. Her reply was uncharacteristically introspective:

> I think in church Sunday morning. It was a lovely morning. We have not had many lovely days. And the sun was just coming through the stained glass windows and falling on some flowers right across the church and it just occurred to me that this was the day I was meant not to see, and then all of a sudden, I thought, "There are some of my dearest friends who are not seeing this day!" and had you been able to see the previous Sunday what would happen during the coming week, you could not have endured it, you just could not have endured it. So it is as well we cannot see into the future.

Yet she had survived unscathed. Unlike Reagan and the pope, she had not taken a bullet, had not been rushed to the hospital, had not struggled against a series of injuries and secondary infections. In fact, she had not suffered a scratch and, whatever her private distress at the sufferings of friends and colleagues, she sailed through the day after with a kind of pent-up calm and efficiency.

All the same, she had had a phenomenally narrow escape. She was not an inch or two inches from death; she was exactly two rooms from death. And she had been saved by the structure of the Grand Hotel.

The hotel was divided vertically in four parts. Thick supporting walls separated each of the four vertical quarters while thinner walls and ceilings divided each quarter into rooms and floors. A bomb placed in one of these vertical quarters would do enormous damage, but the thick walls ensured that the blast would be directed upward and downward much more than sideways. Patrick Magee, the main IRA bomber, placed his device in a room in one of the two central quarters. (Photographs of the Grand Hotel taken the next day show a structure like a mouth with several central front teeth missing.) Its main impact was to collapse most of the rooms within that vertical structure into one another. Those killed and injured were in rooms above or below the bomb. Many of them were maimed not by the bomb blast itself but by the "falling masonry" that Thatcher and Butler heard immediately following the bomb. They found themselves falling down a shaft with the floor sinking below them and the roof cascading in on top of them. It took half a day to dig some of them out.

Those staying in rooms in the other three vertical structures were in much less danger. That is why, for instance, the convivial crowd in the bar suffered only shock and falling plaster when the bomb went off. They were not directly below the explosion and afterward walked out into the street generally unharmed but looking like ghosts, covered in powdered plaster. Anyone in a room directly abutting the collapsed quarter, however, was at some risk—and anyone in a nearby room on the same floor as the bomb was at very serious risk indeed.

Thatcher was three floors below the bomb. Her bathroom directly abutted the vertical quarter that housed the bomb. It was badly wrecked when the bomb exploded and later it too collapsed into rubble. She had been in that bathroom only six or seven minutes prior to the explosion. If the bomb had detonated then, she would have been injured, perhaps seriously, perhaps disfigured by flying glass. But she was two rooms distant from the collapsing quarter when it mattered.

That margin was enough to save her from even a scratch.

Of the three attempted assassinations, that against the pope conforms most closely to the cinematic thriller ideal because it remains something of a mystery. We know beyond any doubt that Reagan's would-be assassin was a lone gunman (insane by most standards) who hoped his crime would attract the admiration of a Hollywood film star. The IRA claimed responsibility for the bombing of the Grand Hotel right away. Patrick Magee, its main perpetrator, was sentenced to thirty-five years' imprisonment for the crime a few years later.[10] But it has so far proved impossible to dispel all controversy over who or what was behind the attack on the pope.

It is universally accepted that the man who pulled the trigger was Mehmet Ali Agca. He was grabbed immediately by tourists and handed over to the police. Within a short time he was tried and found guilty by an Italian court. Agca admitted his guilt and sought forgiveness from John Paul. Whatever else Agca was, however, he was not a lone gunman. He had traveled around Europe in the months before the attack, staying in expensive hotels. He was obviously receiving financial support and protection. Those facts alone amount to a strong case that Agca was the instrument of a conspiracy. If so, who were the conspirators?

One theory—which sounds more believable in today's world of al Qaeda terrorism—is that the pope's attacker was acting on behalf of a radical Islamist organization. He had denounced the pope three years before as a "Commander of the Crusades" in a letter to a Turkish newspaper. He had even threatened to kill John Paul when the pope visited Istanbul.

But this argument looks like a case of imposing our current anxieties on the recent past. Agca emerged in the Turkish underground as a thug working for the highly nationalistic, semi-fascist, and not particularly Islamic Grey Wolves. (His first murder was of a liberal Turkish journalist.) He escaped from prison with suspicious ease in a Turkey whose army and intelligence services were then hostile to Islamism. And the contradictory accounts of his motives he gave in the years following his arrest in 1981 suggested that he was either a fantasist or was deliberately sowing confusion about his contacts.

Between his escape and the attempt on the pope's life, moreover, Agca moved easily around Western Europe, apparently flush with cash—as did other terrorists like Carlos the Jackal in those days. Yet this terrorist tourism took place before there were large and self-consciously Muslim diasporas across the Continent. At that time the Middle Eastern terrorist organizations that might have given him aid and sanctuary were secular, often Marxist, and allied to Soviet bloc regimes, the kind of terrorism depicted in Stephen Spielberg's film *Munich*. Within this terrorist network, groups that seem ideologically incompatible to us, such as the Red Brigades and the Grey Wolves, sometimes received money, guns, and training from the same Soviet bloc intelligence agencies.

In 1981, therefore, it is much more likely that Agca was working for a secular terrorist group than for a religious one. It is also possible, even likely, that he may not even have known who his real employers were.

At the time his most likely employer—the terrorist godfather of last resort—was the Kremlin. By 1981 John Paul had already awakened anti-Communist hopes throughout Eastern Europe, most notably through his support of Poland's Solidarity trade union. The Soviet Politburo, much better informed than Western intelligence agencies about the fragility of its evil empire, knew that the pope was a serious threat. In particular, some minutes of the Politburo meetings smuggled out after the collapse of Communism show that Yuri Andropov, who headed the KGB, held the absurd and even naïve belief that the pope's election was part of a Western intelligence plot to destabilize Soviet rule. So the Politburo had a clear motive for ordering his death. They may even have felt justified in doing so: it was tit-for-tat in an intelligence war.

But motive is only one guide to solving a crime. And asking *cui bono*—who benefits from it?—is a notoriously dangerous guide to guilt. Other questions must be asked as well, notably: if the Soviets ordered the pope's death, how did they carry it out?

In the 1980s circumstantial evidence emerged to support a theory that the Bulgarian intelligence service, acting for the Soviets, had hired Agca to kill the pope, positioned him for the attack, but failed to spirit him away after the shooting because the crowd seized him. If this is true, Agca is a fortunate man, as he would probably have been killed himself as soon as his employers got him safely out of the way. Dead assassins finger no plotters.

A case was brought. But an Italian court in 1986 acquitted a Bulgarian airline employee and suspected intelligence agent, Sergei Antonov, of complicity in any such plot. His alibi was that he was in his office, not St. Peter's Square, when the pope was shot. With that acquittal, the trail went cold.

Besides, most of the interested parties were uninterested in establishing whether the Soviets had ordered a papal assassination. The pope himself preferred to consider that the devil himself was behind it; anyone else was merely his intermediary.[11] When Thomas P. Melady, U.S. ambassador to the Vatican, presented his credentials to the pope in 1989, he asked whether John Paul would welcome a U.S. investigation into the supposed plot. "No, not now," replied the pope. Cardinal Casaroli later explained to the ambassador that since 1987 the pope had been in private communication with Mikhail Gorbachev, who had raised the possibility of a papal visit to the USSR. John Paul was asking the Soviet leader to carry out reforms establishing freedom of religion and human rights so that such a visit might be possible. He did not want to spoil this cautious Vatican diplomacy by raking up a grave scandal that principally involved Gorbachev's late predecessor Leonid Brezhnev.[12]

Western governments were even more reluctant to indict the Kremlin. Some intelligence agencies suspected a Soviet role but their political masters did not want to prove one, as that would make negotiations with the USSR impossible. Leading Italians feared that if the Soviets were shown to have carried out such a crime in Italy, it would have meant an almost irreparable diplomatic breach between the two countries. One of the most important figures in the governing Christian Democratic Party, Giulio Andreotti, both prime minister and foreign minister at various times, vigorously denied any Soviet connection. Andreotti also seems to have persuaded the pope that there was no Bulgarian involvement in the attack. Based on these assurances, John Paul subsequently exonerated Bulgaria during a visit there.

But the story refused to die. In 1991 there was a flurry of interest when Agca gave an interview from prison in which he seemed to suggest that Palestinian terrorists acting on behalf of the Soviets had helped him. Visiting Gorbachev around that time in Moscow, Andreotti raised the matter. He was obviously worried that he had been wrong in his strong denials of Soviet involvement a decade earlier. He said to Gorbachev:

> At a time when they accused the Soviet Union and Bulgaria [of involvement in the anti-papal conspiracy], I took a very firm stance. I kept saying that the information from the trial gave no proofs of such participation. Today the discussions are inflamed

again. I would like to ask you, in case you get some new data, to inform me promptly. I have found myself in a very difficult situation now, because I took a vigorous stance at the time when the campaign of political disinformation was being spread and speculations were used in order to block the process of overcoming the Cold War.

Gorbachev replied that no one had told him anything new about the attempted assassination. Andreotti then referred to Agca's new claims and ended on a note of worried pleading:

> He [Agca] gives concrete information which he surely did not know and could not know. This means that someone had told him this. Someone is feeding him. Some mess is going on around him. That is why I implore you, if you get some information, to share it with me.[13]

Gorbachev agreed to do so.

Andreotti had clearly come to suspect that he might have been misled about Soviet involvement in the attempted assassination, and, contrary to his earlier assurances to the pope, the Soviets might have been guilty. Fearing he might look like a Soviet apologist or, worse, a dupe if definite proof of such involvement emerged, Andreotti wanted a definite claim of innocence from Gorbachev. (That year the Soviet leader did deny Soviet complicity.)

Next to trigger interest in Agca was the Italian parliament's Mitrokhin Commission. Vasili Mitrokhin, a former KGB archivist, defected to the West in 1992. His revelations of extensive Soviet penetration of Italy prompted the establishment of a parliamentary commission that determined that its first inquiry would be into whether a Soviet conspiracy was behind the attempt to kill the pope. The commission looked at three sorts of evidence.

It drew, first, on evidence supplied by the French anti-terrorist judge (known popularly as "the Sheriff") Jean-Louis Bruguiere, who had been conducting a long inquiry into the 1970s terrorist Carlos the Jackal.

Bruguiere told the commission that testimony from the terrorist Abu Nidal and others in the Soviet-connected terror network implicated Russian military intelligence, the GRU, in a plot ordered by Brezhnev and the Politburo to assassinate John Paul. The commission also examined the files of the Stasi, the East German intelligence service. These showed that the Stasi had launched a propaganda campaign to whitewash the Soviet Union and Bulgaria against suspicion so soon after the attempted assassination that it must almost certainly have had advance warning. (Much of the wild Internet speculation on the assassination may well derive from this campaign.) And finally, the commission subjected photographs showing a man near Agca in the crowd in St. Peter's Square to advanced computer recognition techniques. These identified him as Sergei Antonov, the suspected Bulgarian agent acquitted by an Italian court. Agca had already identified Antonov from photographs back in 1981, provided accurate details about him and his life, and claimed that they had entered the square together. The photographs showed that Antonov was not in his office when the pope was shot, but in the square, which undermined not only his alibi but also his denial of knowing Agca.[14]

The Mitrokhin Commission concluded from these different strands that the Soviet Union was responsible for the attempted assassination "beyond all reasonable doubt." The report was treated as a serious one by Italian magistrates who had been investigating the case independently. While disagreeing with some of its conclusions, one magistrate, Ferdinando Imposimato, cited additional evidence of a Bulgarian link: for instance, Agca and Carlos the Jackal, who was protected by KGB and the Stasi, stayed at the same hotel in Sofia at the same time.[15] From a legal standpoint, none of this evidence can overturn Antonov's 1986 acquittal. But it serves to establish the guilt of the Bulgarian intelligence services, certainly on the criterion of a preponderance of evidence, perhaps even by the stricter test of beyond a reasonable doubt, as the Italians claim.

Does it also establish, however, the guilt of Brezhnev, Andropov, and the Politburo? Could the Bulgarians not have acted independently? Might not the "Becket" theory—that they heard a frustrated Brezhnev or Andropov exclaim, "Will no one rid me of this turbulent pope?" and decided to do him a favor—explain the origins of such a foolishly wicked scheme?[16]

It is a tempting explanation but a wholly implausible one. The Bulgarians would never have dared embark on such an enormity without explicit Soviet instruction. We can say that with certainty because Bulgarian intelligence sought Soviet permission for their assassination of the émigré Bulgarian writer Georgi Markov in London. (The Soviets not only agreed; they supplied the poison for the umbrella used to stab Markov.) If the Bulgarians had to seek Soviet permission to murder a brave but minor dissident writer who was of no interest to Moscow, they would certainly have needed it to assassinate a major international figure like the pope. In his final book, *Memory and Identity*, John Paul II seemed to be inching toward that conclusion.

That said, there will never be a "smoking gun" to indict Brezhnev, Andropov, or the rest of the Politburo. The full Politburo archives were never opened to researchers (though some documents were smuggled out). Under Putin they will surely remain closed indefinitely. In any event, decisions of such dark magnitude are rarely put down on paper. Lesser decisions were shrouded by the Soviets in euphemisms. The Politburo decision to invade Afghanistan (so sensitive that it had to be handwritten rather than entrusted to typists) is headed—rough translation—"Concerning the matter of A." It records only that the Politburo accepts the advice of Andropov, Dmitriy Ustinov, and others, empowers them to act on it, and also to make any such corrections as may be required. Only the most experienced researcher would grasp its significance.

If even the decision to invade another country—which the Kremlin could scarcely deny since its troops landed in the country shortly afterward—has to be wrapped in this bureaucratic bafflegab, one can only imagine the secrecy it would employ to conceal its instructions to murder a pope. We are unlikely to see even such a nebulous document about this sinister event. And with the veterans and heirs of this KGB tradition now running Russia again, the chances of the Kremlin telling the final truth about Soviet complicity in the attempted assassination shrink still further.

Besides, in the end the assassination attempt failed. Faith and hope proved mightier than either the sword or the assassin's bullet. John Paul II, though commanding no divisions, went on to help defeat the evil empire anyway.

Providence and Practicality

Did the attempts on the lives of John Paul, Reagan, and Thatcher perhaps advance this result? Were they spared by God for the great purpose of bringing about the largely peaceful collapse of the Soviet Union? And did God's hand therefore, as John Paul believed, "guide" the bullets and the bomb those crucial inches and feet from their intended targets?

Orthodox Christian believers (and adherents of other religions) believe along with the late pope that God's providence plays a role in history. He has a plan for us, with which we may refuse to cooperate, but which we cannot wholly frustrate. That plan is unknowable, however, except in the broadest outline (God hopes for our salvation), and it is realized in history through human agency. The best that a human being, whether pope or layman, can do to cooperate with God in advancing His plan is to pray for His grace and guidance in following what seems to be the most decent and virtuous course of action in any particular case. Trying to second-guess God in planning a global strategy is pointless vanity.

There are obvious problems with this providential theory of history. The Holocaust, for example, has prompted both Christians and Jews to ask how God's plan can encompass the murder of millions of innocents. The Lisbon earthquake provoked Voltaire to ask how God could allow the impersonal evil of nature to deliver the same tragic result. Christian theodicy has answers to these questions that may or may not satisfy anguished hearts. But they are not questions that the historian can fruitfully consider because they are religious, not historical, questions.

Just as the scientist seeking truths of nature must examine only natural phenomena, so the historian seeking truths about the human past has to limit himself to investigating human actions. The assumption that all events can be explained by either natural law or human agency may not reflect his ultimate metaphysical beliefs. The off-duty historian might be anything from an agnostic to an Anabaptist. But miracles are beyond his professional capacity. If a bullet went in a certain direction, he must assume that it was because the laws of physics pushed it in that direction. And if he encounters events that seem to have no natural explanation or even to run counter to the laws of nature, he must candidly admit that he doesn't know why and how they happened.

In the light of these naturalistic assumptions, John Paul, Reagan, and Thatcher were very lucky people indeed. Their narrow but accidental survival meant that the Soviet leaders were very unlucky people: three unusually strong-minded opponents remained in place to keep up their pressure on a crumbling economy and a weakening despotism. If the attempted murder of the pope began as an instruction from the Politburo, then it both reflected Soviet weakness and, insofar as it was thought to be a Soviet conspiracy, intensified that weakness. All in all, the survival of pope, president, and prime minister were happy accidents that perhaps acted as modest catalysts in the process that ended the Cold War on Western terms.

What the historian may legitimately conclude and what the survivor of an attempted murder may believe are two very different things. And what the survivor believes may then give rise to historical actions of the first importance. So what did Reagan, Thatcher, and the pope believe about their survival?

John Paul and Reagan have told us very plainly: they believed that God had spared them for some great purpose. John Paul seems to have believed in particular that his devotion to Our Lady of Fatima had helped spare his life. A young pilgrim in St. Peter's Square held up an image of the Virgin Mary, and the pope, leaning forward to see it better just at the moment Agca fired, may have ensured that the bullet missed the exact point on his body where it was aimed. Agca launched his attack, moreover, on the anniversary of Our Lady's appearance in Fatima, Portugal. On the following anniversary the pope went to Fatima to give thanks to God and Mary for his deliverance. While there he expressed the view that "in the designs of Providence there are no mere coincidences."[17]

Yet the pope's gratitude to Our Lady of Fatima may not have greatly affected his policies or Vatican diplomacy. Long before May 1981 John Paul believed that in his life, and in all human lives, there were "no mere coincidences." His survival may have given him a more dramatic sense of that truth, but it did not change his conviction. In John Paul, moreover, there were strong elements of the Christian mystic. His sense of the designs of Providence was almost certainly emotionally felt as much as it was rationally accepted even before he was attacked. His policies toward the Soviet Union—his call for religious freedom and human rights in the Eastern bloc, his support for Solidarity in Poland—were set in place two years before the Agca attack, and were not significantly altered for another six years. Then the pope's reason for adopting a softer approach was that Gorbachev— whom John Paul sometimes called "a providential man" to his friends—was dismantling the repressive apparatus of state atheism in the Soviet Union with his policies of *glasnost* and *perestroika*. In the interests of "reconciliation," John Paul would have sought better relations with the Soviet Union at any point when it was willing to extend greater freedom to believers.

It is unlikely therefore that Agca's attack on John Paul caused a major change in the pope's outlook or in Vatican policy. Its failure, of course, meant that John Paul's powerful support for religious and other freedoms in the Soviet bloc not only continued but was reinforced by his near-martyr status.

Thatcher's narrow escape, in contrast, had little direct impact on history. The Brighton bombing occurred five years into her premiership, when the government's policies on almost all issues were firmly set and were even bearing fruit. American missiles were being installed in Europe, the Falklands War had been won, the British economy was recovering fast from the recession of the early 1980s, the "peace movement" had been successfully seen off, and inflation had been brought under control. The Anglo-Irish agreement was still being negotiated between London and Dublin, but the only effect of the Brighton bomb was a paradoxical one: it impelled the British government to toughen its negotiating stance temporarily to show that the bomb had had no effect. It had even less effect on British policy toward the Soviet Union. Two months after Brighton, Thatcher held a meeting at Chequers with Mikhail Gorbachev, then tipped as the likely successor to the ailing Soviet leader Konstantin Chernenko. She pronounced Gorbachev a man she could "do business with," recommended him as such to Reagan, and began a new course in East-West relations.[18]

Thatcher was then at the height of her powers as a self-confident national leader making an impact on the world stage. But her self-confidence was a very matter-of-fact one rooted in hard work, mastery of detail, experience, and firm conviction. When a teacher at school had suggested she was lucky to win a prize, the young Margaret Thatcher replied indignantly, "I wasn't lucky. I deserved it."[19] And in her memoirs she confesses to feeling on the eve of the 1979 election that, like the great Chatham, she could save Britain and that no one else could.[20] But that was as much a judgment on her peers and opponents as on herself.

Her self-confidence, though it sometimes bordered on arrogance, coexisted with real humility. She knew that she was bright and worked hard and so "deserved" to succeed, but she was also aware of her deficiencies and unafraid to admit ignorance or to take instruction from those with the knowledge or skills she lacked. When preparing for a major meeting with someone like Gorbachev, Prime Minister Thatcher would summon a seminar of Kremlinologists to brief her. When she realized that she was a poor television performer, she asked a television producer, Gordon Reece (and on one occasion Sir Lawrence Olivier), for advice on improving her appearance, voice, and acting skills.[21] (Reece became one of her most important advisers.) She has never stopped improving herself. To the end of her premiership there was a small measure of insecurity in the clever provincial scholarship girl moving in the great world. It was simply conquered daily by hard work and great dedication.

But her survival at Brighton did not seem to change her. As far as others can judge, it gave her no greater sense of historical destiny, no messianic conviction, no feeling that God had spared her for great things. When I directly asked her if, like Reagan and the pope, she believed that God had spared her that day for some great purpose, she said simply, "No." She seemed to think that it would be vainglorious to believe so. This should not surprise us. Her religious upbringing, which shaped her throughout her premiership, was a very practical Methodist one. It encouraged good works more than introspection and concern for others before oneself. Her first actions after the bombing reflected this: she prayed, she visited the injured to see how she could help them, and she got on with work. She believed that government policy should reflect the moral commonsense of a Christian culture (and famously differed with the liberal Anglican bishops on what that implied). But she thought more in terms of trying to do what the God of her (much underlined) Methodist catechism wanted rather than in terms of God having a special purpose for her. And there was a personal factor. Several of her closest friends and advisers—notably her leadership campaign manager, Airey Neave—had been murdered by the IRA. That alone would have deterred her from dwelling too much on her survival as an example of providence in history.

Unlike the pope, Thatcher was not vividly aware that God had intervened to save her for a purpose; like him, however, she maintained her existing political intentions.

Reagan, however, was changed within moments of his shooting. As he told his official biographer, almost his first thought on hearing he had been shot, immediately following a natural surge of anger at the mental image of a crouching John Hinckley firing at him, was to pray for his young assailant. Nor did he forget this prayer when the imminent prospect of death and judgment had passed.

It is well known that John Paul personally forgave Agca soon after his recovery. The pope later received Agca's mother in an audience. And when he died in 2005, Agca's brother issued a statement that the entire family was grieving for a pope who had befriended them all. It is less well known that Reagan forgave Hinckley and sought to do so in person. Dr. Roger Peele, head of psychiatry at St. Elizabeth's Hospital in Washington, where Hinckley was detained for treatment, revealed in 2004 that the president had approached him twenty-one years before asking for a private meeting with his would-be assassin.[22] Reagan added, however, that "he only wanted to do what was in Mr. Hinckley's best interests." Peele advised against such a meeting and the president accepted his decision.[23]

When Reagan himself was still in the hospital, he told his daughter Maureen that God had spared his life for a purpose. When he returned to the White House on April 11, 1981, he wrote in his journal that night: "Whatever happens now I owe my life to God and will try to serve Him in every way I can." Four days later, he asked staffer Michael Deaver to arrange a meeting with a senior cleric. Deaver invited New York's Cardinal Cooke to the White House. After a meeting in the private quarters upstairs, the weakened president told the cardinal, "I have decided that whatever time I have left is left for Him."[24] And in public, the president said exactly the same thing in more Reaganesque terms: "Whatever time I have left belongs to the Big Fella Upstairs."[25]

In terms of policy, that did not mean any great change of direction. Reagan had only just arrived in the White House when he was shot. Very few policies had been established firmly enough to be altered. And the policies that were pursued after the shooting, in particular the domestic tax cut program and the defense buildup, had been clearly foreshadowed both in the campaign and in the four years of radio broadcasts and speeches in which Reagan had laid out his basic philosophy of governing. These went ahead unchanged.

The first effect of Reagan's heroic survival was his greater clout with Congress. That brought him not only a standing ovation when he addressed both Houses two weeks after leaving the hospital but also the defection of sixty-three Democrats to support his Program of Economic Recovery. It passed the Democrat-controlled House by a margin of 253 to 176. A much more important effect, however, was Reagan's greater determination to pursue the policies he favored and, no less vital, to articulate the moral arguments behind them against all opposition, including that of the opposition party, the government bureaucracy, and even some within his own party. He thought he knew the great purpose for which God had spared him. It was to hasten the collapse of Communism. He had always opposed it and had criticized the Western policies that propped it up. Now, however, he began to speak of its imminent demise as both a practical reality and an indisputably worthwhile goal.

That did not mean, as many critics and the Soviets themselves speculated, war or nuclear confrontation with Moscow. Reagan intended to compete the Soviets into bankruptcy until they were ready to make the compromises that signaled a genuine peace. But he began by offering them a chance to avoid that competition. He drafted a personal letter to Leonid Brezhnev and sent it over to the State Department for approval. It coupled a lifting of the grain embargo (which Reagan had promised in the campaign) with a personal appeal to Brezhnev to join him in shaping a lasting peace in which ordinary people on both sides of the Iron Curtain could raise their families without fear. Secretary of State Al Haig and his colleagues thought this too conciliatory, even naïve, and responded with a draft that contained stern criticisms of the long Soviet military buildup. Drafts went back and forth until Reagan, encouraged by Deaver, insisted on sending his personal plea for peace alongside the State Department version.[26]

Brenzhev responded with a reply from Agitprop Central blaming the United States for the Cold War in terms that Reagan later described as "icy." Even Anatoly Dobrynin, the Soviet ambassador, wrote in his memoirs that the official Soviet reply was a "standard polemical" response that "underestimated the psychological aspects" of Reagan's original letter.[27] With that response the Soviets threw away an opportunity to end the Cold War on terms acceptable to them—and confirmed Reagan's view that the Soviets would have to be brought to the point of defeat before they would consider compromise.

From that point onward, Reagan carried out the strategy of economic and military competition intensified by rhetorical honesty. Secretary of Defense Caspar Weinberger's military buildup was the most visible expression of that strategy. But Reagan's rhetorical honesty about the nature of Communism and the Soviet Union was almost as important—and excited plenty of opposition among liberals in the United States and Europe. Reagan's prediction in his 1982 Westminster speech to the British parliament that Communism was destined to be shortly "on the ash-heap of history," and his description of the Soviet Union as "an evil empire" in his 1983 speech to the National Association of Evangelicals struck conventional diplomats as pointless provocations with no constructive purpose. Almost the entire transatlantic liberal establishment denounced him as a dangerous Cold Warrior who was risking real war.

We now know that those speeches had a vital effect in weakening Soviet morale and encouraging dissidents throughout the Soviet bloc. At the time, however, Reagan seemed intellectually isolated. Henry Steele Commager, a distinguished presidential historian who claimed to have read every presidential address, called the "evil empire" speech the "worst" in history. The Soviets called it "lunatic anti-Communism." Allies were silent or condemned "megaphone diplomacy." But Reagan ploughed on with this defiant truth-telling. He believed that he had been spared by God for some great purpose that surely did not include sugarcoating the truth about totalitarianism. When poor deluded John Hinckley pulled the trigger that day, he inflicted a mortal wound on the Soviet Union.

Like all the events in his life, the attempted assassination became for Reagan the basis for a good anecdote. He would sometimes direct visitors to the Oval Office away from their grievances with his gripping account of how March 30, 1981, looked from the wrong end of a gun. On one such occasion in 1982, he began this story at the door just as his aides were trying to hurry out some conservative activists after a "stroking" session about taxes. Halfway into the corridor, the Reaganauts all seemed moved by his minute-by-minute account of a recent near-tragedy. When Reagan finished, one of them spoke up sympathetically.

"Yes, Mr. President, that was a terrible day, a terrible day. When I heard the news, all I could think of was—*this means that George Bush is going to be president.*"

Everybody froze as the ruthless implications of this remark sank in. The activists looked at their shoes, the aides at their boss.

Reagan let the suspense hang in the air for a moment. Then he laughed. That allowed everybody else to laugh as well.[28]

"What makes God laugh?" goes an old joke. "People making plans." With God making the plans, Reagan could afford to laugh.

CHAPTER FOUR

BE NOT AFRAID

~≈℘ ℘≈~

J ust ten days after Jimmy Carter's inauguration in 1977, Richard V. Allen, a former senior adviser to President Nixon and an influential figure in the growing conservative wing of the foreign policy establishment, had signed on to work for Ronald Reagan. He hadn't intended to do so. It was the first occasion that Allen and Reagan had met alone, and Allen was uncertain both about Reagan's prospects and about the seriousness of his foreign policy commitment.

At the end of the meeting, as Allen got up to leave, Reagan said something that, as Allen wrote later, "literally changed my life."[1] Reagan offered Allen his theory of the Cold War. He acknowledged that many people thought his views simplistic but said, "My theory of the Cold War is that we win and they lose."

Allen replied, "Well, Governor, I don't know if you if you ever intend to run again for president of the United States, but if you do, please count me in."

Two years later, in June 1979, now the Californian's chief foreign policy adviser, Allen broke off an intense discussion with Reagan so that they could watch the news coverage of the pope's first visit to Poland. Both men were astounded by the scenes shown on the television screen. John Paul was walking among vast, enthusiastic crowds who greeted him not only as their pontiff but also as their national savior. The pope proclaimed not only religious but also patriotic and political hope. His message was "Let Your Spirit come down and renew the face of the land—this land." The regime's representatives, apart from a ceremonial welcome at the airport, had all but disappeared. Security and organization for the pope's visit were provided by thousands of Catholic volunteers. At that moment—and for the duration of his visit—the pope was the effective government of Poland.

Allen, a Catholic, was deeply moved. But he was almost as impressed by Reagan's reaction. The future president was gripped by the scenes on television. He watched them intently without speaking. As he did so, his eyes teared up. Allen left the meeting convinced that Reagan, like himself, had seen the papal visit as a first, massive crack in the impressive façade of Soviet power.

A Threat from Rome

To do the Soviets justice, they had grasped this risk immediately after the pope's election. Andropov telephoned the KGB resident in Warsaw to ask how he could have allowed a citizen of a Communist country to be elected pope. The resident bravely shifted responsibility to the KGB man in Rome.[2] Andropov promptly commissioned an analysis of the implications of a Polish pope. Reflecting the Soviets' espionage paranoia, the study concluded that the election had been organized by a German–American conspiracy in which the key players were Poles, namely Zbigniew Brzezinski, Carter's national security adviser, and the Polish American Cardinal John Krol of Philadelphia.[3] As Weigel observes, this absurd conspiracy theory nonetheless gave birth to an accurate threat analysis: a Polish pope would destabilize Poland and undermine Soviet rule throughout Eastern Europe. Another, more cool-headed study, prepared for the Communist Party's Central Committee by Oleg Bogomolov, the head of a Soviet economic think tank, not only confirmed this conclusion but also accurately predicted the nature of that threat: the new pope would probably wage a campaign for human rights and religious freedom in the Soviet bloc. This was a very serious threat requiring counter-measures such as a rapprochement with the Ukrainian and Lithuanian Catholic churches and a hint that Vatican-inspired trouble would meet with further Soviet repression of Eastern bloc churches.

These hard-headed analyses almost certainly represented the majority view in the Soviet and Eastern European Communist leaderships, but they were not universally accepted throughout the Soviet intelligentsia. The Poles were especially reluctant to accept them since they implied an ideological crackdown that would have gone completely against the grain of Polish popular opinion. Some commentators even gave way to wishful thinking, arguing that a pope from a Communist country would inevitably leaven the anti-Communism of the Church.

As late as April 1980, Edward Gierek, the Polish Communist leader, told Vadim Zagladin, a senior member of the Communist Party's International Department, "It is good that Wojtyla has left for Rome. Here, in Poland, he would be a disaster. He would create great difficulties for us. In Rome, he is less dangerous. Moreover, to some extent he can even be useful there. After all, he has 'exported' a lot of ideas and considerations inspired by socialism."

Gierek went on to speculate more perceptively that the way to handle the pope was to appeal to his Slavic sympathies.[4] Gorbachev would attempt to do so much later.[5] But evidence mounted very quickly in the late 1970s and early 1980s that the pope was a threat to the Soviet empire for which no amount of Slavophilia could compensate.

Most of the evidence was provided quite readily by the pope himself. Immediately after his election, when the cardinals were paying him homage, he had embraced the elderly Cardinal Frantisek Tomasek of Prague, saying, "We are standing very close to one another and will stand closer still because now the responsibility for you is being transferred to me." In his visit to Assisi only one month into his papacy, John Paul declared of the Church behind the Iron Curtain, "It is not a church of silence any more because it speaks with my voice." On the thirtieth anniversary of the UN Declaration of Human Rights one month later, he said, "Freedom of religion for everyone and for all people must be respected by everyone everywhere." He cited the Declaration in a letter of support to the persecuted Ukrainian Catholic Church a few months later. And he made human rights a central theme of his first encyclical, *Redemptor Hominis,* released less than six months into his papacy.

John Paul's criticism of Communism was oblique rather than direct, as it had been when he developed the strategy of cultural resistance in Cracow. As Bogomolov had forecast, it focused in particular upon the defense of religious liberty throughout the world—a stance to which the Soviets could hardly object in public. But his statements of support for this liberty were addressed more often than not to Church leaders behind the Iron Curtain. Soviet leaders could not miss the dangerous significance of passages like this in *Redemptor Hominis*: "It is therefore difficult...to accept a position that gives only atheism the right of citizenship in public and social life while believers are barely tolerated...or are even entirely deprived of the rights of citizenship."[6] All of this was unsettling for the leaders of an officially atheist state that penalized believers in major and minor ways.

The situation was sufficiently serious for Andrei Gromyko, the USSR's foreign minister, to pay a personal call to the Vatican in January 1979 to judge for himself the pope's intentions. He may also have calculated that his relationship with Cardinal Casaroli, the intellectual architect of the Vatican's *Ostpolitik*, would help him to sway the pope toward an accommodationist policy early in his papacy. In his account of his meeting with the pope and Casaroli,[7] Gromyko begins with the usual Soviet overtures in favor of world peace designed to coincide with some Vatican positions. Within a short time, however, John Paul introduced a new topic, as Gromyko later recalled:

> The pope moved on to the issue of religious belief. "It is possible that the obstacles to freedom of religion have not been removed everywhere." He paused. "According to some sources, something of this sort may be happening in the USSR."
> This kind of accusation was nothing new to us. I replied, "Not all rumors deserve attention. The West spreads all kind

of misinformation about the state of the church in the Soviet Union, but the truth is that from the first day of its existence the Soviet state has guaranteed freedom of religious belief... We have religious people, but that doesn't create problems either for themselves or for Soviet society."

The pope and Casaroli listened thoughtfully. Then the pope said, "That's more or less what we thought."

This passage is either a pack of barefaced lies, as Weigel believes, or an unintentionally hilarious literal-minded report by a stranger to irony who happens to be dealing with two diplomats who have a highly developed sense of it. In neither case can the account be taken at face value. If that is so, then the pope's sign-off line—"That's more or less what we thought"—takes on an entirely different meaning. It becomes an ironic acceptance that the Soviets have no intention of respecting the human and religious rights of their peoples and must therefore be either confronted or outmaneuvered.

This papal determination created a painful dilemma for the Soviets. All their instincts, confirmed by the several studies they ordered, suggested that the pope was a threat to their system. He confirmed it daily. But their Polish colleagues faced an overwhelming national demand for a papal visit. They had survived the refusal to admit Paul VI to Poland to celebrate the Polish Christian millennium in 1966. But John Paul was a *Polish* pope. It is even conceivable that some in the Politburo were secretly proud of his election. So the Poles argued that they would be taking the lesser political risk by accepting a papal visit to Poland in 1979.

Even in Poland, however, there were divided counsels. Communists at a local level sensed that it might produce an uncontrollable situation for the regime. Senior officials thought they could manage the visit and perhaps even gain some political credit by associating themselves with a national hero. The popular pressure for a visit was unremitting. And when the pope himself intervened in the debate by saying publicly that he had a "duty" to take part in the anniversary celebrations of St. Stanislaw's martyrdom, it had become impossible for Warsaw to say no.

Still, the Soviets might have tried to exercise a veto. Telephone lines between Moscow and Warsaw buzzed incessantly. The debate was ended in a conversation between Gierek and Brezhnev himself in which the Soviet leader gave the Poles a blunt and realistic warning: "Take my advice, don't give [the pope] any reception. It will only cause trouble."

Unfortunately for the Soviets, the Polish Communist regime had reached a stage of political decay at which it was willing to make concessions that undermined its long-term authority in order to survive an immediate crisis. Ten years later the Soviets would find themselves in exactly the same position. Indeed, they had already reached an intermediate stage: they were not prepared to order Gierek to cancel the visit, as they once would have done.

The discussion ended with Brezhnev admitting defeat, saying to Gierek, "Well, do as you wish. But be careful you don't regret it later."[8]

"It Is Not a True Theology"

In fact, they would regret it sooner rather than later. Negotiations between the Vatican and Warsaw were tortuous and long-winded. But they produced a timetable that enabled the pope to visit six cities in Poland over nine days, from June 2 in Warsaw to June 10 in Cracow.

In the fast-forward operation of memory, John Paul goes almost directly from his election in October 1978 to his arrival in Warsaw in June 1979. In reality he threw himself into a marathon of activity that, in the intervening eight months, saw his diplomatic offensive for religious liberty in the Soviet bloc, his mediation of the Beagle Channel dispute between Argentina and Chile, his beginning of what became four years of addresses on "the theology of the body," and his visit to Mexico for an episcopal conference on liberation theology. With the exception of his successful mediation of the Beagle Channel dispute (which revived an old tradition of Vatican diplomacy between Catholic countries in conflict), these all concerned matters of deep interest to him.

John Paul's diplomacy of religious liberty is discussed throughout this book. His "theology of the body," developed in 129 addresses over four years, expanded on the attempt he had begun as a member of Paul VI's commission on marriage and sexuality to move beyond the Church's traditional rules-based view of sexuality toward one influenced by Christian personalism. It was a sophisticated intellectual attempt to base sexual relations in an ethic of mutual self-giving rooted in unifying the sexes within marriage. In particular it opposed the sexual revolution as one that treated people, especially women, as objects to be used. Yet despite its modernist philosophical clothing and its affinity with certain feminist ideas, this is the aspect of John Paul's thought with which liberal Westerners, including liberal Catholics, were most uncomfortable. They were largely uninterested in the theological arguments and were baffled by the Church's failure or inability to take advantage of technical advances in the control of fertility.

After the Cold War this liberal suspicion meant that Western states and institutions such as the European Union gradually found themselves opposing the Vatican in international debates on reproductive and other sexual "rights." In the 1970s and 1980s, however, they largely ignored John Paul's quite original justifications for a Christian approach to sexuality as merely the kind of things popes had to say at a time when he was saying and doing very unusual things in other areas.

That was not the case with liberation theology or Christian-Marxist dialogues. Many Western elites, again including liberal Catholics, were actively sympathetic to the argument that the Church should reject a view of Christianity as an "otherworldly" religion of personal salvation in favor of a "social gospel" of collective social reform and even revolution. This reflected a number of understandable political opinions: a reasonable suspicion of the military regimes in Latin America, an admirable sympathy for the poor and downtrodden, a partly accurate insight that the Catholic Church was losing ground in the Latin world, and an utter misunderstanding of the economic structure of Latin American countries as "market economies" (when in fact they were examples of what was later called "crony capitalism"). With some of these opinions the pope and orthodox Catholics could and did sympathize. But the First World's sympathy for liberation theology also rested on a generally agnostic view of religion and on the particular assumption that the Latin American poor could not possibly place eternal salvation above a higher standard of living (achieved, if necessary, by revolutionary violence) on their scale of values. This condescension toward the poor the pope very definitely did not share.

John Paul's visit to Puebla, Mexico, where he addressed the conference of Latin American bishops, was the first great pilgrimage of his papacy. It

was also his first great test. The Latin American church had many problems: it was discredited in the eyes of many faithful Catholics because of
its association with dictatorial and oligarchic regimes; it was losing believers, especially among the poor, to the growing congregations of evangelical Protestants; and it was divided between supporters and opponents of
liberation theology. In retrospect the rise of evangelical and Pentecostal
Protestantism was the greatest of these challenges. These churches, then
very small, offered the poor a religion of both salvation and social justice,
treating them as moral agents who could reform their own lives as well as
improve the social order. They transformed bad Catholics into good
Protestants and produced what David Martin, the Anglican sociologist and
author of *Tongues of Fire*,[9] called a "buried intelligentsia" of the poor
themselves. These were able peasants who, having discovered their religious vocation as pastors, went on to give their neighbors social and political leadership as well. Partly as a result of their example, Protestant
workers tended to be more industrious, Protestant husbands more faithful, and Protestant villages safer, more prosperous, and better kept than
nominally Catholic ones. Finally, these new Protestant sects provided a
tempting haven for Catholics repelled by both the institutional Church's
links with oppressive Latin regimes and the semi-materialistic gospel of the
liberation theologians. They thus revealed that liberation theology, far
from being a religion designed for the poor, was actually driving poor
Catholics into forms of Protestantism that delivered greater social justice
precisely because they were "otherworldly."

Neither the seriousness nor the nature of this challenge was realized for
almost another decade. Yet the pope, in addressing the topical division
between liberation theologians and their opponents, managed also to
address the main concerns fueling this new Hispanic Reformation. He did
so in two powerful speeches. The second of these was a speech to half a
million Mexican Indians in the town of Cuilapan. It was a lament for the
social distress of Indians working a rich land for poor returns, a stern
rebuke to the unjust policies that had so reduced them, and a call for economic justice. As he had told the persecuted Eastern European church in
Assisi, he told the Indians that he wanted "to be your voice, the voice of

those who cannot speak or are silenced." He said that the Indian agricultural worker "has the right to be respected and not to be deprived, with maneuvers which are sometimes tantamount to real spoliation of the little that he has." He also called for "bold changes" and "urgent reforms."[10]

If John Paul had given no other speech on this trip, the Cuilapan address would have been interpreted as a strong endorsement of liberation theology in light disguise. But it followed both in time and in logic a firm rejection of the liberation theologians' main tenets in his address to Catholic bishops at Puebla. The pope was unusually nervous about this speech, because he knew that many of the bishops were attracted to liberation theology—which, like most heresies, was less an outright falsehood than a perversion of the truth. It began with Christian love for the poor but very soon became a quest for power over the rich, to whose spiritual welfare it seemed indifferent at best. John Paul sent out signals in advance that he felt this transformation devalued the full truth of a Christian message addressed by Christ to rich and poor alike. Even before he arrived in Mexico, he had told journalists on his plane, "It is not a true theology. It distorts the true sense of the gospel. It leads those who have given themselves to God away from the true role that the Church has assigned for them." In his first Mass in the cathedral of Mexico City, he warned that "those who have launched into the adventurous and Utopian construction of a so-called Church of the future" were not being faithful to the Church. And when he finally met the bishops at Puebla, he told them, "You are spiritual guides, not social leaders, not political executives, or functionaries of a secular state."

The remainder of the Puebla sermon was a systematic deconstruction of liberation theology as theology. It was, he argued, a reductionist doctrine that sought to equate the Kingdom of God with "a mere changing of structures." In contrast, the Gospels clearly showed "that Jesus does not accept the position of those who mixed the things of God with merely political attitudes. He unequivocally rejects recourse to violence. He opens his message of conversion to everyone." True liberation was therefore to be found in the "transforming, peacemaking, pardoning, and reconciling love" offered by Christ and his Church. From his theological studies, his pastoral work, and not least his experience of living under Marxism, John Paul had developed in these two speeches a Christian message that not only unmasked the casuistries of liberation theology but also addressed the concerns of Catholics straying into a revived evangelical Protestantism. In effect, he demolished the false choice between social justice and personal salvation. He pointed out that social justice would be most securely achieved by the reconciling love of Christ's truth. In this spirit, he urged the rich and powerful to carry out the economic and political reforms that were more readily in their gift. But he did not treat the poor as mere objects of charity. He treated them as morally responsible actors who, by seeking God's truth and living Christian lives, would contribute to their own worldly improvement (and to the betterment of society) as well as to their ultimate salvation.

Liberation theology would continue to be a source of division in the Church for some time, resurfacing dramatically in John Paul's 1983 visit to Nicaragua. The challenge of evangelical Protestantism would grow in the next two decades as well. But on his first pilgrimage, the pope had passed his first great test. He had given a full theological answer to both challenges. As he learned afterwards, the Latin American bishops had received his critique of liberation theology well. And the popular response of Mexicans to his visit had been one of overwhelming love and enthusiasm. As he left Mexico City for Rome, millions of Mexicans held up mirrors to the sun, reflecting its rays in the direction of the departing plane—more than a million points of light.

It was a hard reception to follow.

The Itinerant Son Returns

Five months later, however, on Saturday, June 2, an even more enthusiastic crowd waited to greet John Paul when he walked down the stairway from his Alitalia jet at Warsaw airport, kissed the ground of his native Poland, and—watched by the entire world, including Ronald Reagan in California—began shaking the foundations of the Soviet empire.

The nation to which John Paul returned that day was in what even the Communists suspected might be a pre-revolutionary situation, though their Marxism obliged them to call it by harsher names. Three years before, the towns of Radom and Ursus had witnessed uprisings that were brutally suppressed. A Workers Defense Committee (KOR) had been established that same year, bringing together workers and dissident intellectuals from different strands of opinion, including former Communists, united at first only by their opposition to the regime. The regime had first imprisoned and then released some of these activists, intending to demonstrate compassion but in fact betraying uncertainty and encouraging its opponents. As a result the dissidents of KOR were gradually extending their range of contacts to encompass the whole of Polish society, including the Church, at a time when Cardinal Wojtyla was seeking contacts among secular dissidents as part of his policy of building "cultural resistance" to the regime.

Wojtyla had then appeared in the Warsaw apartment of Bogdan Cywinski, a Catholic intellectual with ties to KOR, to meet some of its members, including Jacek Kuron, Antoni Macierewicz, Jan Jozef Lipski, and Piotr Naimski. Naimski, then a Ph.D. student in biochemistry at the Polish Academy of Sciences (later minister for energy in the democratic Polish government), remembers that the cardinal was very open in his support for KOR's activities. (Since the secret police were outside, the regime would have reached much the same conclusion.) Even so, the general analysis of the meeting was largely pessimistic. Cywinski described the political situation as "stable bad" in that the workers were more willing to take action to improve their conditions but the regime was still strong enough to resist serious change. The different forces of opposition, only just beginning to unite, had no real sense of their own numbers.[11]

Vladimir Bukovsky, the Soviet dissident, had pointed to their real strength a few years before at a press conference in Switzerland following his release from the Gulag and expulsion from the USSR. He was asked, "How many political prisoners are there today in the Soviet Union?" He replied, "Two hundred and eighty million." He went on to explain that the very jailers in the Gulag and the officers in the KGB were political prisoners. The more each man realized that the person next to him felt like a prisoner too, the stronger the resistance grew and the weaker the despotism became. What was needed was for people to recognize how they and others all felt. In faraway California Ronald Reagan read Bukovsky's argument and endorsed it in a radio broadcast sent over the airwaves in the same month that the pope visited Poland.[12] And what the pope's visit achieved was that exact revelation. It revealed to the Poles that they were an entire nation of dissidents on which the Communist government rested as a sort of dull and irritating façade. The Poles were "We" and the Communist government was "Them."

This revelation took countless forms in the nine days of John Paul's visit. It was first seen in the easy way that the pope himself took control of the visit and ran it without reference to the authorities. As Naimski saw it, "he met the Polish state and party leaders like [President Henryk] Jablonski and Gierek, exchanged a few official courtesies, and then simply elbowed them aside, almost as if saying, 'It's my show, boys, so I'll take over now.'"[13] At the Belvedere Palace the pope had surprised Gierek by making clear, albeit in diplomatic language, that the Communist Party's willingness to grant the Catholic Church a larger protected role in Polish society had been overtaken by events and his own papacy. The Polish Church now intended to exert a larger influence over the economic and social life of the people.[14] It would not be confined to a purely pastoral role.

The remainder of the pope's pilgrimage illustrated his point. The people were already in the camp of the Church. They greeted the pope with flowers, singing, and love. The Masses and sermons were joyous occasions as well as solemn ones. John Paul's pilgrimage was treated as a fiesta by the Polish nation. And the authorities were largely invisible throughout (though they had made careful preparations beforehand to shape and limit its impact). Catholic volunteers provided the stewards and security. The pope himself ensured that the crowds and congregations never became unruly or rebellious by his natural authority and use of humor. On one occasion, when some young men hoisted a twelve-foot cross and others in the crowd held up small crosses in an electrifying moment that looked like it might become a mass political demonstration or even a riot, the pope defused the situation, first with jokes, then with reflection and with what one observer called "something deeper."[15]

"It's late, my friends," he ended. "Let's go home quietly."

The crowd did so. Throughout the entire nine days, John Paul led an extraordinary demonstration of mass public dignity.

Another revelation for the Poles was the sheer size of the crowds. For the Masses and the sermons there were rarely fewer than one million of the faithful and sometimes as many as three million. John Paul's final address in his old diocese of Cracow was attended by a crowd estimated to be the largest gathering of Poles in history. Between such events the pope traveled along roads lined with cheering and even weeping crowds. These crowds were not composed only of old people and nuns, as the camera shots of Poland's state television sought to suggest. Young people were present in large numbers on all these occasions, and also enjoyed their own special events. On three nights running in Cracow, a vast array of youngsters kept John Paul from his bed by singing outside his residence—and insisting he join in their songs. (That may have contributed to the sore throat that plagued him toward the end of his visit.)

These crowds were not political rallies, moreover, but church congregations. The pope never strayed from the role of Christian pilgrim during his visit. Political ideas—Poland's right to independence, the Poles' need for liberty, the injustice of the Yalta division of Europe—could be glimpsed between the lines in his addresses. These worried the regime and annoyed the Soviets. But the pontiff's main themes were always those of spiritual and cultural renewal, Poland's special closeness to God, and the transforming power of Christ's love. The congregations responded in kind, those in Victory Square chanting: "We want God, we want God, we want God in the family, we want God in the schools, we want God in books."

In an officially atheist state, this affirmation of faith was both a patriotic declaration and an act of political subversion. On the sidelines were political activists taking advantage of the sanctuary offered by the pope's visit to deliver their own message. Naimski's group of dissidents had published an English-language version of their underground magazine, *Voice*, that they distributed to the crowd at Victory Square. It was really directed at the foreign journalists accompanying the pope so they would get a sense of the subterranean resistance then enjoying an open-air vacation courtesy of the pontiff.[16]

Even without the assistance of *Voice*, however, the international media was bound to give extensive coverage to a trip that offered a feast for photojournalism and color-writing, with events ranging from the Roman pontiff surrounded by guitar-playing young people to the Christian penitent kneeling at Auschwitz, "this Golgotha of the contemporary world." In doing so, the media ensured that coverage would break free of the sanitized censorship of the official press in Poland and Eastern Europe and be witnessed by their peoples. During the visit Radio Free Europe's Polish service ran thirteen hours of coverage each day. Other stations such as the BBC World Service, the Voice of America, and Deutsche Welle broadcast extensive coverage. Pilgrims from other Eastern European states, despite sly attempts to obstruct their journeys, returned to describe the visit to their fellow believers. And the unsettling effect that had transformed Poland in nine days began to spread inexorably to the rest of the evil empire.

What exactly was that effect? A Polish miner summed it up when he was asked why anyone should wish to be a Christian in a Communist state: "To praise the Mother of God and to spite those bastards."[17] Both aims were present in the crowds that attended John Paul's Masses and cheered his motorcades. The pope's moral leadership ensured that Christian love restrained the (perfectly understandable) desire to "spite those bastards" and averted anything like a riot. Nonetheless, the crowds fully realized their presence was an act of defiance. Thirteen million Poles—one-third of the nation—saw the pope in person (and millions more watched the television coverage). They no longer felt the suspicion of their neighbors that had previously divided them. They no longer felt the need to lie. They now knew that the Polish nation was united in its affirmation of Catholicism ("to praise the Mother of God") and defiance of the Communists ("to spite those bastards"). To quote Weigel's judgment, the pope had in nine days "begun to exorcise the fear, the anomie, and the sense of hopelessness that had previously kept the 'we' of society from coalescing." He had given Poles the intoxicating gifts of hope and fellowship.

When John Paul's plane left for Rome, the regime breathed a sigh of relief. The visit had given them many moments of anxiety, but it had ended without riot or open rebellion. Maybe it had even been a useful release of tensions that might otherwise have burst forth more dangerously. As the year went on in relative calm, they began to relax and congratulate themselves on a shrewd handling of a difficult problem.

They did not realize that their relationship to the pope was rather like that of the condemned man to the skilled executioner in the Arabian tale. The executioner, famous for his brilliance in decapitating prisoners, began with a dazzling display of thrusts and parries with a scimitar about his victim's head. The condemned man scoffed that he was unharmed by all this showmanship. The executioner smiled knowingly.

"Nod your head," he said.

Almost exactly one month before the pope arrived in Warsaw, Margaret Thatcher crossed the threshold of 10 Downing Street as Britain's first woman prime minister. Her first three years in office were dominated by domestic concerns: trade union reform, the fight against inflation, the steel strike, and curbing public expenditure. Only five weeks after the election she and her finance minister, Geoffrey Howe, launched an ambitious and controversial economic program with a budget that cut the standard rate of tax to 30 percent and the top rate to 60 percent (from 98 percent). It was permanent controversy on the domestic front thereafter. In those early days she made only two major forays into foreign policy, and both were only remotely connected to the Cold War. They were her settlement of the long-running Rhodesia problem and her repeated and eventually successful attempt to secure a budgetary rebate from the European Community (later the European Union) to compensate Britain for its disproportionate contribution to the collective budget.

Both were diplomatic successes; neither entirely fulfilled the new prime minister's hopes. The Lancaster House agreement that transformed white-ruled Rhodesia into (briefly) democratic Zimbabwe under the Marxist Robert Mugabe was a reluctant concession by Thatcher to the reality that only a comprehensive settlement endorsed by all parties would be internationally accepted. Her success in getting the EU to disgorge two-thirds of Britain's overpayment via a rebate that continued until 2005 initially displeased her because it was one-third less than she had demanded. But since it was also one-third more than Germany and France would ideally have conceded, it subsequently became a triumph about which she boasted at regular intervals. Both deals, even if inadequate, finally settled problems that had bedeviled British politics for fifteen and eight years respectively. They were early signs that this prime minister was an activist who wanted to solve problems and build achievements.

There was an early financial sign, moreover, that suggested even then that fighting the Cold War was very high in her priorities. At a time when Geoffrey Howe, as chancellor of the exchequer, was desperately seeking to cut spending in order to cut taxes, Thatcher insisted that defense spending should rise by 3 percent annually in line with Britain's pledge to NATO. Given that Britain already spent substantially more on defense than any other European member of NATO, this was a bold step. It indicated that, despite Britain's manifest economic difficulties, the new Tory government seriously intended a new course in foreign and defense policy.

The Soviets evidently thought so. They had been fascinated by Thatcher ever since her "Iron Lady" speech in 1976. Their interest was not entirely favorable. When a Soviet Communist Party (CPSU) delegation visited Britain that year at the invitation of the Labour Party, its members were invited to watch prime minister's question time from the visitors' gallery. Thatcher took the occasion to criticize Callaghan for the Labour Party's unusual willingness, symbolized by the party-to-party invitation, to treat the Soviet Communists as a legitimate political party. Some Conservative back-benchers, including Winston Churchill (grandson of the wartime prime minister), called for the Soviet visitors to be ejected from the gallery. One member of that delegation was Anatoly Chernyaev, deputy head of the CPSU International Department, who kept a diary charting the changing opinions of the Soviet elite and their contacts with foreign visitors. He described the parliamentary scene in his entry for November 7, 1976, as follows: "The grandson of Churchill...together with Margaret Thatcher—she is a beautiful lady, but a bitch—and others obstructed the discussion on the usual agenda."[18]

Now the Soviets wanted to see the beautiful bitch up close.

They gave permission for the prime ministerial plane to stop over in Moscow for refueling on the way to the G-7 Tokyo summit in June 1979. To Thatcher's surprise, when she disembarked for an expected short delay, she found that an elaborate feast had been laid out for her and that half the Politburo was in attendance. Indeed, Alexei Kosygin, the Soviet prime minister, had left a conference of Communist prime ministers to meet her. The topic of defense was briefly discussed. But Thatcher quickly raised what was then the topical plight of the Vietnamese "boat people." These wretched victims of Communism were fleeing Vietnam in small boats by the hundreds of thousands. Some were drowning at sea, some were murdered by pirates, and some made it safely to friendly ports, in particular Hong Kong, where they languished in refugee camps. In addition to being a humanitarian disaster, these poor people were also a political problem for the West. Vietnam was a Soviet client state. Thatcher asked if Kosygin could not use Moscow's influence with Hanoi to treat its citizens better and to stem the outflow. She describes Kosygin's reaction in her memoirs:

> His words were translated to me: "W-e-ll," he said (or the Russian equivalent), "they are all drug-takers or criminals. . . ." He got no further. "What?" I asked. "One million of them? Is Communism so bad that a million have to take drugs or steal to live?" He immediately dropped the subject.

It was a minor exchange, but it could not have been reassuring to the Soviets. It suggested that Thatcher, as she later reflected, would be an outspoken presence on the international stage challenging their lies.[19]

Her presence at the Tokyo summit of the G-7, however, was more notable for her challenge to the entrenched errors of the West. In retrospect the 1979 Tokyo summit marked the beginning of the end for the economic policies of the 1970s—in particular, the policies of solving the energy crisis by controls on the price of oil, combating OPEC's induced recession with "easy money," and relying on "locomotive" economies such as West Germany to drag the world toward prosperity. These had all produced perverse results, such as gas lines and stagflation, and even some center-left governments were reconsidering them. To her slight surprise, Thatcher found herself allied with West German chancellor Helmut Schmidt, an economically robust social democrat, against the French, Italian, and even U.S. governments. It was, she wrote later, "the nearest we ever came to an Anglo-German entente." Both agreed that the price mechanism was the best method of encouraging energy conservation. Neither approved of the coordinated reflation of demand that previous summits had agreed upon. Each backed the other in a joint determination not to be bounced by summitry into policies they disliked. Accordingly, the once-standard plea for coordinated reflation disappeared from the communiqué. If the advanced industrial world had not yet decided on a new economic course, it had at least ceased to promote the old corporatist one.[20]

By implication this was a rebuff for President Carter, whose interventionist policies were the ones being sidelined (including by himself). At Tokyo he was meeting Thatcher for the first time as prime minister. They got on moderately well then and later. In her memoirs she gave him a mixed verdict. She thought him clever, sincere, deeply religious, and—a sure mark of approval from Thatcher—possessing a clear grasp of science and the scientific method. She praised him as a good friend to Britain and to herself. Though she felt bound to give whatever support she could to the leader of the Atlantic alliance, she was out of sympathy with Carter's broad economic and foreign policies, especially his apparent tolerance of Soviet expansionism. Above all, as a passionate admirer herself of America and its gung-ho spirit, she sensed that the president's general outlook, stressing limits to growth and a national "malaise," was alien to the optimistic American imagination.[21]

The opinion polls in the United States seemed to support her skepticism. They suggested that the president would very likely lose the nomination of his own Democratic Party to the young lion of liberalism, Senator Edward Kennedy. In 1976 Carter had caught the spirit of the age. Three years later it looked like an age drawing to its close. But it was still unclear who might replace him—and with what political philosophy.

One curiosity about the Tokyo summit is that it paid surprisingly little attention to the pope's visit to Poland, even though it was then reverberating powerfully throughout Eastern Europe. Most of the leaders assembled, notably the Germans, assumed that *Ostpolitik* still represented the future of Vatican-Soviet relations. Religion was seen as a declining social force rather than as a shaker of regimes. The *New York Times* accurately reflected the views of the international establishment, including the Tokyo participants, when it editorially reassured its readers earlier that month: "As much as the visit of Pope John Paul II to Poland must reinvigorate and reinspire the Roman Catholic Church in Poland, it does not threaten the political order of the nation or of Eastern Europe."[22] Soviet rule was seen as a permanent fact; the pope merely a transient phenomenon.

Plotting against the Pope

Back in London three months later, Thatcher and her government colleagues did have a pressing interest in the pope: namely, his forthcoming visit to Ireland in October 1979 on his way to the United States. It was vital to the British government that the pope refrain from saying anything that might give aid and comfort to the terrorists of the Provisional IRA. Terrorist violence was rampant in Ulster and had touched the prime minister personally. Two weeks before she entered Downing Street, Airey Neave, her close friend and adviser, had been murdered by a bomb planted by INLA (a breakaway Irish Republican terrorist group) in the House of Commons parking lot. Four months later, in early August 1979, Lord Mountbatten (the most senior British commander in the Pacific war—supreme Allied commander, Southeast Asia—and a hero to Thatcher) was killed on his yacht off the coast of Sligo, along with two relatives and a local boy crewing the boat, by an IRA bomb. That same day eighteen British soldiers died at Warrenpoint in Northern Ireland in a double IRA bombing. The Irish "Troubles" seemed to be accelerating.

But if British ministers had any fears about what the pope might say, these proved groundless. Thirty miles from the North–South border at a massive public meeting in Drogheda attended by many people from Northern Ireland, John Paul delivered one of his most eloquent denunciations of violence. Addressing terrorists and their sympathizers on both sides of the sectarian divide, but presumably expecting to be heard mainly by Catholics, including those nationalist priests who had harbored IRA fugitives, he said powerfully, "On my knees I beg you to turn away from the paths of violence and to return to the ways of peace ... violence destroys the work of justice.... Further violence in Ireland will only drag down to ruin the land you claim to love and the values you claim to cherish."

This appeal did not end the strife; the IRA hunger strikes were only two years ahead, and thousands more innocent lives were to be taken in Northern Ireland. But the pope's words detached the Catholic Church from any possible accusation of sympathy for IRA terrorism in Ireland and removed one potential obstacle to the growing influence of Roman Catholicism in England. John Paul had not directly intended these political benefits to flow from an essentially pastoral message. As would happen frequently with the new pope, however, such benefits flowed all the same.

John Paul's next stop, his first pilgrimage to America, was even more of a popular triumph. *Time* magazine hailed him as "John Paul—Superstar." He addressed vast enthusiastic crowds of the faithful in open-air Masses. He was greeted everywhere with love and respect even by non-Catholic Americans. And politicians from New York mayor Edward Koch to President Carter lined up to meet and greet him. It was an astounding conversion of the "Protestant America" that fifty-one years before had joked that Catholic Al Smith, after his defeat in the presidential election, had sent Pope Pius XI a one-word telegram: "Unpack."

The political focus of the papal visit was John Paul's address to the United Nations on October 2, 1979. It continued the themes that had inspired his first year as pope—his stresses on human rights and in particular on religious liberty. For this particular audience, he added the thought that peace itself ultimately depended upon respect for these human liberties embodied in just political structures. What he said contained implicit rebukes for both West and East. Yet the main brunt of his criticism was on structures that condemned the religious believer to a second-class existence—"to see compromised ... his professional career ... and to lose even the possibility of educating his children freely"—and that was unmistakably a powerful attack on the Soviet bloc.

Witnessing the scene, Daniel Patrick Moynihan, then U.S. ambassador to the UN and himself a formidable critic of totalitarianism, thought the speech had hit home. The Soviet bloc delegates, he said, "knew exactly what he was talking about and, for once in that chamber, looked fearful rather than bored."[23] It was yet another warning for them: this pope had a message that resonated well beyond the frontiers of Poland.

The Soviet leaders, less complacent than their Polish colleagues, took prompt action. Six weeks after the pope's UN speech, the CPSU Central Committee secretariat approved a document with the characteristically long-winded title "Decision to Work against the Policies of the Vatican in Relation to Socialist States." Most of its six points urged various Communist organizations in both halves of Europe to run more efficient agit-prop campaigns against the Church while researching the Church's own political activities. But it also contained some fascinating and slightly mysterious instructions. The foreign ministry, for instance, was to "enter into contact with those groups in the Catholic Church engaged in work for peace" and to explain to them "the policies of the Soviet Union in favor of world peace." The KGB was urged to use "special channels," as well as the publications it controlled, to "show that the leadership of the new pope, John Paul II, is dangerous to the Catholic Church." And there was what Weigel calls the "ominous" proposal that the KGB should "improve the quality of the struggle against the new Eastern European policies of the Vatican." The document was drafted by one future leader of the Soviet Union, Yuri Andropov, then head of the KGB, and his deputy, Viktor Chebrikov, and signed by two others: Konstantin Chernenko and Mikhail Gorbachev. It was a major state document that was meant to halt and reverse the pope's impact on the Soviet world.[24]

The policy's impact is hard to assess when so many other developments were occurring. Of course, the campaign it outlined ultimately failed. But it may have enjoyed some successes during the general Soviet retreat. Surely the rise of the "peace" and "anti-nuclear" movements of the 1980s in Europe and America, in which left-wing Catholic activists were prominent, owed something to these instructions. One would also like to know more about the "special channels" mentioned. John Paul was certainly subject to an unusual level of criticism from within the Church for a pope who was unusually popular outside it. And whether the "quality of the struggle" improved would be easier to gauge if we knew the nature of the struggle. Weigel points out the eerie coincidence that Mehmet Ali Agca escaped from a Turkish prison in unexplained circumstances, threatening to murder the pope, only two weeks after the Soviet document was endorsed and distributed. Nothing in the document suggests assassination. But the dull prose of the Soviet bureaucracy covered a multitude of sins.

The overall interest of the document, however, is that it shows the Soviet leaders not only recognized a real threat in John Paul II in late 1979 but still had sufficient self-confidence to plan opposing and defeating that threat in a (relatively) straightforward way.

One month after the Soviet document was approved, Thatcher followed in the pope's footsteps to America for her first visit as prime minister. This was intended to be a businesslike occasion at the White House, concerned with NATO, Rhodesia, and Northern Ireland, rather than one built around grand public appearances. But she was arriving shortly after the seizure of American hostages in the Tehran embassy. Both the United States and Carter personally wanted reassurance and help from allies, and she was the first foreign leader to arrive since the hostages had been seized.

Oddly, her first instinct—she was still a novice uncertain in foreign affairs—was not to mention the hostage seizure in her public statements. But her two more experienced advisers, Foreign Secretary Lord Carrington and Frank Cooper of the Ministry of Defense, prevailed on her to do so since America was not really interested in any other topic.[25] Once she had overcome her doubts, as so often with Thatcher, she then spoke with clarion force. On the White House lawn, she said, "At times like this you are entitled to look to your friends for support. We are your friends, we do support you. Let there be no doubt about that."

Britain's ambassador to Washington, Sir Nicholas Henderson, later described these words as "like a trumpet blast of cheer to a government and people badly in need of reassurance."[26] Thatcher became a popular figure in the United States from that moment, and the remainder of her visit was a string of successes. She gave a well-received address to Congress. With the benefit of questions twice weekly in the Commons, she had no difficulty in answering questions from congressmen with a bravura confidence. Her biographer reports that more than one invited her to accept the Republican nomination for president.[27] And in New York she gave a powerful address to the Foreign Policy Association warning against the well-armed ambitions of the Soviet Union: "The threat is not only to our security in Europe but also, both directly and by proxy, in the Third World."

Ten days later, the Soviet Union invaded Afghanistan. The "Christmas Invasion" that disillusioned and undermined Carter confirmed and strengthened Thatcher. Her view of Soviet reality had been borne out by the Soviets themselves. Her confidence in her own judgment was naturally growing. But she was not yet a dominant figure able to call the shots either at home or abroad. She had not followed up her strong words of support for America over the hostage crisis, for instance, by freezing Iran's assets in London because she had been advised that such a move would be damaging to London as a financial center and arguably illegal. She faced similar difficulties now.

Three days after the invasion, Carter telephoned her at Chequers, determined to take a stronger anti-Soviet line. They agreed that the Afghan invasion was a serious attempt by the Soviets to upset the Cold War balance of power in their favor. It justified serious counter-measures and, if necessary, sacrifices by the West. For once Carter's measures were tough. They included recalling the U.S. ambassador from Moscow, covertly aiding the Afghan resistance, and promulgating the "Carter doctrine" that any attempt by an external power to gain control of the Persian Gulf region would be regarded as an attack on the vital interests of the United States. As with Iran, Thatcher wanted to give as much support as possible to the United States. She decided that Britain would impose economic sanctions on the USSR—not renewing the Anglo-Soviet credit agreement, curtailing technology transfers, etc.—and exploit Britain's Commonwealth links to direct the non-aligned Third World against the invasion.

These steps were useful but modest; she was not able to deliver on two more significant promises. Britain's athletes, unlike America's, refused government pleas to boycott the 1980 Moscow Olympics. And the British prime minister was unable to persuade other Western Europeans, particularly West Germany, to risk the trade and economic benefits of détente over a faraway country like Afghanistan. This was a division—the United States and Britain on one side, the rest of Western Europe on the other—that was to recur in future years.

For the moment, however, Thatcher was relatively undaunted by it. One year before the election of Ronald Reagan, she sensed that America and the West were at least beginning to wake up to the Soviet threat and even, if hesitantly, to respond to it. If so, she felt, then ultimate victory was certain.

This conviction was briefly shaken by the fiasco of Desert One in April 1980. "I felt America's wound as if it were Britain's own," she wrote in her memoirs, "and in a sense it was, for anyone who exposed American weakness increased ours."[28] She was given the chance to demolish any such impression when she faced her first life-or-death decision less than one week later.

On April 30, 1980, six Iranian terrorists seized the Iranian embassy in London, taking twenty-six people hostage and demanding the release of political prisoners in Iran. Right from the start Thatcher insisted that terrorism had to be defeated and seen to be defeated. She placed the day-to-day handling of the crisis in the safe hands of her deputy prime minister, Willie Whitelaw, agreeing with him that if the terrorists started shooting hostages, then the Special Air Service (SAS) commandos on standby were to be sent in. For six days the Iranian embassy crisis dragged on in the usual way, with long-running negotiations over various possible outcomes. The terrorists gradually released six hostages, and most observers assumed that the affair would end in the usual messy compromise. Then on Sunday, May 6, as the prime minister was returning to London from Chequers by car, the gunmen executed a hostage, dumping his body outside the embassy door. Whitelaw asked Thatcher for permission to send in the SAS.

"Yes, go in," she told him.

A camera crew was on permanent duty opposite the embassy. That Sunday was a British bank holiday weekend; the entire nation was on a short vacation. The SAS moved in at prime time. Television stations everywhere broke into their regular programming with a live broadcast. Most of Britain and half the world were suddenly captivated by the sight of black-clad SAS soldiers descending the front of the embassy on ropes, throwing percussion grenades through the windows, and leaping in after them. Luckily for the SAS, the terrorists were not watching television.

The SAS rescued nineteen of the remaining twenty hostages (the gunmen murdered another hostage during the raid). Five terrorists were killed and the other captured. There were no police or SAS casualties. It had been an overwhelming success.

After hearing the good news, a relieved Thatcher went to the SAS barracks to get a full report from their commander, Peter de la Billiere. Together they watched the television news report of the rescue; the rescuers added their own commentary. One of them turned to Thatcher and said, "We never thought you'd let us do it."

Exactly one year and two days after arriving in Downing Street, the Iron Lady had drawn blood.

Two months after the SAS rescue in London, the Polish government finally nodded its head. On July 2, 1980, it announced massive increases in the price of foodstuffs such as beef, pork, and poultry. This provoked a rash of strikes beginning with the railroad workers of Lublin. These workers were a traditionally privileged group because they controlled the strategic railroad links to the Soviet Union. Gierek, on vacation in the Crimea, was summoned by a worried Brezhnev to his own Crimean villa to discuss the growing crisis. Gierek affected nonchalance even though he must have been aware of the potential dangers, as price increases had provoked earlier government crises. Neither he nor his defense minister, General Wojciech Jaruzelski, whom the Soviets increasingly saw as their man in Warsaw, believed the use of military force to drive strikers back to work was prudent—or perhaps necessary. They would settle the Lublin strike with the "sausage" with which in the past they had stuffed the mouths of such key workers. Gierek's public attitude was not unlike Callaghan's in the winter of discontent twenty months before: "Crisis? What crisis?"[29]

For a few days this detachment seemed sensible. The Lublin strike was settled in the usual way. But the strikers' original demands had gone well beyond "sausage." They sought the legalization of a right to strike, new elections to the official trade union, and talks with government authorities. These essentially political demands were now taken up by people angry at the government-mandated price increases in other industries and other parts of Poland. The strikes spread to more than 150 enterprises. An industrial crisis was becoming a political one.

One important center of potential resistance, however, remained quiescent. The Lenin naval shipyard in Gdansk on the Baltic coast had been the main arena of the 1970 riots that brought down Polish Communist leader Wladyslaw Gomulka. Police had shot forty-five workers at that time. There was an understandable reluctance to provoke another such outcome. The shipyard workers remained aloof from the growing strike movement.

Then, on August 7, 1980, the shipyard management dismissed a crane operator, Anna Walentynowicz, for stealing. She had been collecting the stumps of old candles to melt them down into a new candle for a memorial to the murdered workers of 1970. This dishonest and politically motivated dismissal stirred demands for a strike that the management, like Gierek, then sought to head off with a pay raise. But on August 14 an unemployed electrician, Lech Walesa, climbed the perimeter fence into his old workplace, addressed the workers, persuaded them to reject the offer, and then led them in an "occupation strike." Over the next four days the strikers barricaded themselves into the shipyard, locked out the security forces, discussed and rejected several more offers from the shipyard management, and issued an escalating series of strike demands that included the Lublin program—that is, political demands: free trade unions, the release of political prisoners, an easing of censorship, and the erection of Anna Walentynowicz's memorial to the dead of 1970.

After that the collapse of Communist authority and its replacement by that of the new Solidarity trade union occurred at the pace of a speeded-up silent movie:

⁜ On August 17, the authorities, hoping to lower tensions, agreed to the celebration of an open-air Mass in the shipyard by Father Henryk Jankowski, Walesa's own pastor. Four thousand strikers attended and another two thousand of their friends and families participated from outside the gates. A large wooden cross, made by shipyard carpenters, was blessed by Jankowski and erected by a shipyard gate as an interim memorial to the workers who had been shot down by the regime in 1970.

⁜ On August 18, the workers' demands in negotiations with management—broadcast live over loudspeakers in the shipyard—began to fan anti-Communist defiance across Poland. Dissidents in KOR and other organizations passed along information that the state-controlled media suppressed. Sympathy strikes stopped factories across the country.

⁜ On August 20, the pope gave two prayers for Poland at his general audience, commending the Polish Church to the special care of Our Lady. Briefed by his secretary, Father Dziwisz, who had just returned from a "vacation" in Poland, he also sent a letter to the Polish primate, Cardinal Wyszynski.

⁜ On August 21, the local Catholic bishop for Gdansk traveled to Warsaw to brief Wyszynski and the secretariat of the Polish bishops' conference. He assured them that Walesa genuinely represented the shipyard workers.

⁜ On August 22, a group of intellectuals under the leadership of Tadeusz Mazowiecki, editor of the Catholic magazine *Link*, and including the historian Bronislaw Geremek arrived in the Lenin shipyard at the strikers' request to act as advisers in negotiations.

⁜ On August 23, the pope's letter to Wyszynski was published. It asked the Polish bishops to help the nation "in its difficult struggle for daily bread, for social justice, and the safeguarding of its inviolable rights to its own life and development." These words were immediately seen to be an endorsement of Walesa and the strike. That same evening the Communist government agreed to enter into direct negotiations with the Inter-factory

Strike Committee representing workers from along the Baltic coast. But the crisis was not yet over. The intense negotiations would last a week. And outside events continued to influence their progress.

✣ On August 25, Brezhner reported to the Politburo about the situation in Poland. The Politburo commission on Poland was established: Suslov (chair), Gromyko, Andropov, Ustinov, Chernenko, etc., etc.

✣ On August 26, Wyszynski delivered a major sermon which, while it defended the principle of "free association," was nonetheless seen by everyone as guidance to the strikers that they should not insist on immediately establishing an independent trade union. Probably inspired by the cardinal's fear of Soviet intervention, the sermon was promptly seized on by the regime and its more accommodating passages repeatedly broadcast over state television. But Wyszynski, who had shown an unsure touch throughout the crisis, was losing his authority. Though the strikers, particularly Walesa himself, continued to manifest their loyalty to the Church and to Our Lady, they and their intellectual supporters simply ignored the sermon—and waited for Rome to speak.

✣ On August 27, the pope used his general audience, broadcast over Vatican radio and heard in Gdansk and throughout Poland, to issue a gentle disavowal of Wyszynski. He placed the problems of Poland in the lap of Our Lady of Czestochowa, whose feast the previous day had been the occasion of Wyszynski's sermon, but said pointedly that they could only be solved by "bringing peace and justice to our country." *Roma locuta est, causa est finita.*

Later that day in Warsaw, the Polish bishops gathered in emergency session and issued a long document that explicitly endorsed the "right to independence both of organizations representing the workers and of organizations of self-government." The Gdansk strikers now enjoyed the full formal blessing of the Polish Church.

✣ On August 31, the government capitulated and signed the Gdansk accords establishing the first independent trade union behind the Iron Curtain. Walesa signed for the strikers with an outsized pen—a souvenir of the pope's visit to Poland—bearing a picture of John Paul II. Solidarity had been born. A week later, Gierek resigned.

The Gdansk strike itself had been an almost textbook implementation of the pope's theory of cultural resistance. The pope's visit before the strike made the people aware that they were a united Catholic nation and need not be divided by Communist-enforced fear and lies. That gave them the necessary moral courage and willingness to work together. The strike itself then drew together very different social groups—shipyard workers, dissident intellectuals (both Catholic and secular), the Church, workers in other industries—who used their different talents in what was now a wider cause than one shipyard strike. By their self-discipline, the reasonableness of their demands, and their self-identification with the Church and Poland, the strikers won public support at home and abroad. By disavowing violence, they presented the government with the painful choice of either using violence (thus risking bloody resistance) or compromising with Solidarity on unfavorable terms. And within a short time they won a great and peaceful victory.

It helped, of course, that the head of the largest world religion was in their corner. But the strikers and the Polish people were the main protagonists. And having tasted freedom, they wanted more.

Strikes spread across Poland, variations on the Gdansk agreement were demanded elsewhere, and other independent unions were set up. In mid-September delegates from thirty-five new and independent unions met in Gdansk and adopted Solidarity as the name of their new national union. But Solidarity was really much more than a federation of labor unions. It was a movement for democracy and national independence. And because the delegates to Solidarity had been elected, it had more moral authority than the legal institutions of the Communist state.

Moral authority is no mere theoretical advantage; organizations that possess it find that their orders are obeyed and their wishes respected.

Bodies that lack moral authority have to rely on the use or threat of force. Over the next fifteen months, this disparity in true authority meant that Solidarity was repeatedly able to defeat the legalistic and political obstacles that the Polish Communists put in its way. First they dragged their feet on granting Solidarity legal registration with the courts; a one-hour national strike forced them to reconsider. Next the judge registering Solidarity arbitrarily added to its statutes (drawn up democratically by the delegates from the different unions) a clause recognizing the leading role of the Communist Party in government. Solidarity threatened a full-scale national strike if the offending provision were not removed. The Polish Supreme Court duly overruled the earlier court in a compromise heavily weighted in Solidarity's favor.[30] Even the state-controlled media moved toward fairer reporting of news that involved Solidarity.

The Church, under John Paul's leadership, had for the moment cast aside any prudential reservations. The Polish bishops intervened in the registration crisis to urge that the Gdansk accords be fully implemented. And in a meeting with Warsaw's Solidarity leader, Zbigniew Bujak, Cardinal Wyszynski, despite his continuing anxiety about Soviet intervention, said, "I am with you."

After Solidarity's victory in court and a celebratory drink with Wyszynski, Walesa and his colleagues went off to a cabaret, where a popular song caught the mood of the times: "Let Poland Be Poland."

The View from the Kremlin

They were not singing it in Moscow. The advance of Solidarity in Poland and the apparent inability of the Polish Communists to halt it had created a crisis for the Soviets. They saw clearly that unless this train of events were reversed, Poland would soon cease to be a Communist country. After an interval it would then either leave the Warsaw Pact or become a highly unreliable member of it. In either case Solidarity was undermining the USSR's strategic position in the Cold War. They held a series of alarmed meetings—with themselves, with other Warsaw Pact governments, and with the errant Polish Communists—over the next few months. And their conclusions were brutal.

Before the ink was even dry on the Gdansk accords, the Soviets were discussing how to reverse them. A document titled "Theses for Conversation with Representatives of the Polish Leadership," with the highest secret classification and marked "Personally to Comrades Brezhnev, Andropov, Gromyko, Rakhmanin," was approved by the Politburo on September 3, 1980. It is unclear who actually talked to the Poles, but there is an inscription at the top of the paper: "For the KGB: to send, in encoded form, to the point of destination." A few excerpts will reveal the document's flavor:

> [The Gdansk Agreement] is a very high political and economic price for the "settlement" you have achieved. Of course, we understand in what conditions you had to take this difficult decision. The agreement practically means legalization of the anti-socialist opposition....
>
> Now, your task is to prepare a counter-offensive, and to win back the lost positions in the working class, among the people.... To make efforts to restrict the activity and influence of the so-called "self-governed" trade unions in the masses.... To actively infiltrate the so-called "self-governed" trade unions with the people loyal to the part.... To take greater care of the army, paying particular attention to the military and political training of the personnel.... To use the opportunities of involving the military commanders into work in the party and in the economy.
>
> In these conditions, you should clearly indicate the limits of the allowed. You should say openly that the law forbids any statements against socialism.[31]

At a Politburo meeting on October 29, 1980, there was general agreement that a "counter-revolution" was taking place in Poland and that it had to be reversed. Brezhnev himself complained that Walesa was being honored by local tributes across Poland and that the authorities were doing nothing to stop this outrage: "Not even television is standing up to these anti-socialist elements." Gromyko said simply, "We must not lose Poland."

Andropov, Ustinov, and others agreed. But what was to be done? Politburo members would have liked the Poles to introduce martial law. But even their favorite, General Jaruzelski, seemed to think that the army might not fire on the workers. They had already issued firm instructions to the Poles. Their conclusion now was revealingly vague: they would have to do so again, but this time more sternly.

A new Politburo member, Mikhail Gorbachev, expressed the general view: "We should speak openly and firmly with our Polish friends. Up till now they haven't taken the necessary steps. They're in a sort of defensive position, and they can't hold it for long—they might end up being overthrown themselves."[32]

So they decided to tell the Poles to take action.

Their opportunity came two days later when Stanislaw Kania, who had replaced Gierek as head of the Polish Communist Party, and Prime Minister Jozef Pinkowski arrived in Moscow for talks. The Polish comrades asked for more time to deal with the crisis, but promised that they would indeed take action. They even talked, vaguely, of ceasing to yield to anti-socialist elements and normalizing the situation. As November wore on, however, the situation in Poland showed no sign of returning to socialist "normality."

What made the Polish troubles so traumatic was that in addition to threatening the Soviet Union's strategic position, they also upset a world political picture that was otherwise quite favorable to Moscow. In particular, Central America and Western Europe were showing signs of moving away from a close reliance on the United States.

Since well before 1980, the Soviet Union had been investing modestly in the cause of Central and Latin American revolution. Numerous secret Soviet documents (copied and brought to the West by Vladimir Bukovsky in the early period of openness after the fall of Communism) show that the Soviet Union funded, trained, and supplied Central American left-wing terrorists, generally through the agency of the CPSU International Department, from as early as 1974.[33] On January 29 of that year, for instance, a memo from the International Department to the Central Committee summarized recent requests for military training from several Latin American

Communist parties (including the Nicaraguan party) and advised that they be granted. The next day the Central Committee secretariat ordered Soviet military intelligence, the GRU, to arrange the training.[34]

This assistance to the Nicaraguan left was a long shot in 1974. Five years later, largely owing to the follies of the Carter administration when it sought the overthrow of the corrupt Nicaraguan dictator Anastasio Somoza—with no idea of who might replace him—the investment paid off. The Sandinista guerrilla forces found a vacuum in Managua and seized power on July 17, 1979. Given its partial responsibility for this upset, the Carter administration was anxious to deceive itself about the new rulers; Warren Christopher, then deputy secretary of state, told Congress that the Sandinistas were "generally moderate and pluralistic." To keep getting U.S. aid, the Sandinistas were content to play along with this charade for a while. Moderates were invited to join the Sandinista junta. But Humberto Ortega, a junta member and brother of the new president, had said candidly, "We wanted to copy in a mechanical way the model that we knew, which was Cuba, and we identified with it." That was the new reality of Nicaragua.[35]

Four thousand Cuban advisers arrived in Nicaragua over the next year. But the real experts in transforming a shaky mixed-left regime into a reliable proletarian dictatorship were farther away. A Sandinista delegation arrived in Moscow in March 1980, seven months after seizing power, to sign an agreement with the Soviet Union. Two senior officials, K. Brutents and P. Smolsky, revealed the Sandinistas' true plans in a secret memo to the Central Committee on March 14:

> The SFNL [Sandinista Front of National Liberation] is the ruling political organization. The leadership of the SFNL considers it essential to establish a Marxist-Leninist party on the basis of the front, with the aim of building socialism in Nicaragua. At present, for tactical reasons and in view of the existing political situation in the Central American region, the leadership of the SFNL prefers to make no public statements about this ultimate goal.

> We believe it would be possible to accept the offer made by
> the leadership of the SFNL, and suggest signing a plan of con-
> tacts between the CPSU and the SFNL for 1980–1981 during
> the delegation's visit to Moscow.[36]

Five days later, an agreement to this effect was signed in Moscow by Boris Ponomarev on behalf of the Central Committee and by Henri Ruiz for the Sandinistas. As many as one hundred Sandinista activists were scheduled to receive "special training" in Moscow annually under the agreement. By December of that year, the Sandinista newspaper, *Barricada*, was being printed on free supplies of Soviet paper. On Christmas Day 1980 the Soviets allocated 10,000 foreign currency rubles for the creation of a Marxist-Leninist youth movement in Nicaragua—"the sole" such movement, it specified. One week later KGB head Andropov sought permission in a top-secret memo to place a senior operative in the Soviet embassy in Managua for the protection of Soviet institutions and citizens. It was granted three weeks later.[37] For the rest of that decade a Communist regime in light green camouflage governed the Central American state.

El Salvador was a slightly different case. Because a rightist government was in power, Soviet efforts were devoted to assisting the left-wing FMLN movement to overthrow it. Such support had been provided for many years, but it was stepped up after the Sandinista victory in Nicaragua showed what was possible. Thus, an August 1980 resolution of the Central Committee, proposed by Anatoly Chernyaev and signed by, among others, Mikhail Gorbachev, agreed to provide six months of military training for thirty Salvadoran Communists in Moscow and then to pay for their return to El Salvador. The nature of that training was laid out in detail in the initial request from the general secretary of the El Salvador Communist Party, one Shafik Jandal: "Six comrades for army intelligence; eight comrades to be trained as commanders of guerrilla units; five comrades to be trained as commanders of artillery; five comrades for training as commanders of sabotage units; and six comrades for training in communications"—these last presumably being the most deadly of all.

Another top-secret resolution from that period, also signed by Gorbachev, agreed to deliver "a consignment of sixty to eighty tons of Western-manufactured firearms and ammunition from Hanoi to Havana, to be passed on to our Salvadoran friends via Cuban comrades." Aeroflot would deliver the armaments and the Soviet state budget would bear the expenses "as gratis aid to foreign countries." The resolution notes that "F. Castro and S. Jandal" had already agreed to these arrangements.[38] In other words, there was an established route whereby Moscow could arrange for weapons, apparently from the West, to be transferred via Cuba to Communist guerrillas in Central America under the guise of foreign aid. This network helped to sustain a losing civil war in El Salvador for a decade.

Within a short time, for quite modest sums of money, the Soviet Union had been able to help install and entrench a reliable ally in America's backyard, to undermine U.S. allies in the region by providing arms and military training to left-wing guerrilla movements there, and generally to cause problems for the United States where no serious problems had existed before. And in late 1980 these Soviet subversions were at their peak.

The Soviets also had reason to be moderately satisfied with their diplomacy toward Western Europe. Détente and *Ostpolitik*, though increasingly criticized in America, were still the consensus of the European establishment. As Thatcher found to her cost, these orthodoxies had even survived the invasion of Afghanistan. Carter's sudden toughness on the issue served mainly to remind European leaders of his previous flip-flops, as when he had persuaded them to spend political capital on supporting the neutron bomb only to abandon it himself without warning. And now an even worse specter was threatening Europe: the specter of a Ronald Reagan presidency.

Reagan was such a bogeyman to the social democratic Left that dominated European politics in the 1970s that much of Soviet diplomacy in 1980 consisted largely of nodding in agreement to European fears. A procession of foreign visitors trooped through Vadim Zagladin's office in the CPSU International Department complaining about the prospect of this cowboy in the White House. Karsten Voigt, a rising foreign policy star of the West German Social Democratic Party (SPD), visited Moscow at the invitation of the Committee of Youth Organizations and met Zagladin in October 1980. Voigt admitted that it had not been easy for the West Germans to cooperate with the Carter administration, but said, "Perhaps even this level of cooperation will be jeopardized if the new man comes to the White House."[39] Earlier that year an expert adviser to the SPD had compared both Carter and Reagan unfavorably to Brezhnev, who, he said, was trusted absolutely by Helmut Schmidt and French president Valery Giscard d'Estaing. Their trust restrained Carter from attempting to destroy "the bridges of détente" within Europe. Even so, the expert had no doubt who was the lesser of the two evils: "If we completely abandon Carter, Reagan is going to win the elections. That surely will not make anything better."[40] Soviet leaders had always dreamed of separating Western Europe from the United States. Now it seemed to be happening naturally.

So it was infuriating that these excellent world prospects were being spoiled by Solidarity in Poland. It tilted the international "correlation of forces" in the wrong direction. It threatened the Soviet claim that socialism was historically inevitable. Something had to be done about it. Yes, something. But what?

On December 5, 1980, the Kremlin held a meeting of the Warsaw Pact political leaderships in Moscow to settle the question. It was preceded by all the usual signs of a Soviet crackdown: troop maneuvers, erection of field hospitals on the Polish border, attacks on Polish "counter-revolutionaries" in the controlled press of the satellite countries, and demands for normalization from other Warsaw Pact leaders. A military plan was already prepared for the Politburo's signature: Soviet, Czech, and East German divisions were to move into Poland over two days. Martial law was to be declared. The leadership of Solidarity was to be rounded up, court-martialed, and shot. It was set to begin on Monday, December 8, 1980, and if the invasion met with as little resistance as the 1968 invasion of Czechoslovakia, it would all be over in a few days.

All these things became known in the West. The U.S. government had the plans in minute detail from several sources, notably satellite reconnaissance and a senior Polish staff officer, Colonel Ryszard Kuklinski, who was the liaison officer to the Soviet commander in chief of the Warsaw Pact and was also spying for the West. Even before the immediate crisis, Washington had begun to orchestrate a strong diplomatic response to a Soviet invasion—officially warning the USSR of "grave consequences," taking NATO to a higher level of defense readiness, leaking that the United States would sell China advanced weaponry in response, and generally making it clear that the Soviets would suffer much worse than over Afghanistan if they invaded.[41] But the plans gave Washington another weapon. Over the weekend before the expected invasion, Brzezinski, himself Polish, who had been running administration policy on Poland (and keeping President-elect Reagan informed on it), took more direct action to halt the invasion. He told various dignitaries, including India's Indira Gandhi, who was hosting Brezhnev that week, that the United States would have to take strong measures in response to the invasion he feared was about to happen. He contacted the pope, whom he had known as a friend since meeting him in Boston in 1976, and told him of the Soviet plans. He also contacted Solidarity representatives in London, who in turn telephoned their colleagues in Poland with the news that the Soviets would be invading by about breakfast time.

At his flat in Warsaw, Solidarity activist Piotr Naimski got the news and telephoned his friend Antoni Macierewicz. They discussed it for a while, decided that there was nothing much they could do about it at that stage, and went back to sleep.[42]

They could afford to slumber that year. At the Warsaw Pact meeting in Moscow on Friday, December 5, the assembled Communist leaders did not decide to invade. Brzezinski's diplomatic signaling may have succeeded in getting through to them that they would pay a heavy practical price if they invaded. They would also risk losing the West European goodwill they had cultivated in the previous decade. Poland's general secretary Stanislaw Kania had argued that Polish soldiers and civilians might resist and transform the invasion into a battle. Making the world forget an uncontested invasion on the 1968 Czech model was one thing; persuading it to overlook a bloody suppression on the 1956 Hungarian precedent would be quite another.[43]

That is the conventional historical view of the 1980 Polish crisis. Yet there is a plausible alternative explanation for all these events, namely that the Soviets never intended to invade Poland in the first place, neither in 1980 nor later in the 1981 crisis. On that argument, all the preparations for an invasion, including military plans that might leak and maneuvers that could be seen from space, were designed to ramp up anxiety abroad so that when the Polish army imposed martial law, the reaction in Western Europe and the world would be relief that the Soviets had not invaded rather than outrage that the Polish Communists had effectively done so.

That was certainly the calculation in late 1981. If it was also the calculation in 1980, then the Polish Communists would have been aware from the start that the Soviets intended Warsaw to impose a military solution. They would therefore have been complicit in the bluff of a Soviet intervention rather than threatened by it. Archive accounts of the meetings between the Polish and Soviet leaderships to resolve the crisis show them discussing what the Poles should do—for instance, infiltrate Solidarity—rather than what the Soviets will do. Later in 1981 at the famous meeting in the railway carriage in Brest, little or nothing is said about Soviet intervention. Andropov's report to the Politburo suggests it revolved almost entirely around when and how the Poles would introduce martial law. The report includes the following of what the Soviets said:

> As for the martial law [we said], you could have introduced it long ago. What does introduction of a martial law means? It would only help you to break the offensive of the counter-revolutionaries, of various troublemakers, to stop the strikes, the anarchy of economy, once and for all. The draft document about introduction of the martial law is prepared, with our comrades' help, and now you should sign these documents.
>
> After our explanation, comrades Kania and Jaruzelski said they would read and sign this document on 11 April.[44]

In later meetings, as we shall see, the Politburo dismissed the idea of Soviet intervention out of hand, even when the Poles requested it! Such an interpretation would still represent a weakening of the Politburo's will—and of its ability to get its orders obeyed. It would mean that the Soviets shrank from the direct intervention they would have carried out twenty years before. It would also mean that they had taken more than a year to compel a reluctant Polish leadership to enforce martial law on their own. What is more, throughout that year they were continually telling themselves that the Poles were finally ready to act, only to find a month or two later that they had to read them the riot act yet again. By any standards that represented a weakening of power and will.

At a Politburo meeting at the end of 1980, the Soviets continued to take refuge in wishful thinking. They contented themselves with the reflection that their Polish comrades now fully recognized the seriousness of the Solidarity problem and were finally determined to do something about it. "They got the charge of energy they needed," observed Gromyko, the perennial hard-liner, not hitherto known for his sunny optimism.[45] Things would now be different.

In fact, the problem remained on the table. The Brezhnev doctrine had been, if not abandoned, then mothballed. For the first time the Soviets had drawn back from settling a question of power by force and relied instead on hoping against hope.

A High-Stakes Bluff

A few weeks later, Walesa, instead of being quietly shot, was making a triumphal tour of Rome. The world had become fascinated with Solidarity and the seeming paradox of a labor union striking against Communism. Photographs had gone around the world showing the pre-Christmas ceremony outside the Gdansk shipyard (attended by the Polish president, the episcopal successor to Archbishop Wojtyla, and hundreds of thousands of people) at which three steel crosses and three anchors had been erected as the official monument to the workers shot down by the government in 1970. Solidarity had graduated from an industrial to a political to a media phenomenon. It was a household name worldwide.

In Rome, Walesa was fêted like a pop star by the Italian political class, including Communists. He gave an interview to Oriana Fallaci in which he told that devout agnostic that nothing could have happened "without the Church." He was granted a public and private audience with the pope. "The son has come to see his father," he said when he and a Solidarity delegation were received in the Vatican.[46] The pope responded by describing Solidarity's efforts as "directed toward...the common good" and expressing "a right that is recognized and confirmed by the law of nations." The two men then went inside for a private conversation.

The following day John Paul wrote a letter to Brezhnev in which, employing the most delicate diplomatic language, he respectfully warned against a Soviet invasion of Poland—"the preoccupation of Europe," he said, that would be contrary to détente, the principle of non-intervention, the Helsinki accords signed by the Soviets, and much else.[47]

All this was bad enough for Moscow. Then, a few days later, the Soviet Politburo received an alarming report that the situation in Poland itself, far from being normalized, as the Polish leadership kept promising, was in fact deteriorating hourly. Solidarity, backed by the bishops, was becoming the dominant social force in Poland. It had four times the membership of the Communist Party. It was extending into the countryside by establishing an organization for private farmers, Rural Solidarity. Its influence over the mass media was accelerating. It was advancing an ever more ambitious economic and political program, such as the five-day work week. In short, its moral authority was morphing into political authority. Politburo members were horrified at the failure of Kania to halt this continuing erosion of Communist power and continued to demand action.

Yet the pope's letter to Brezhnev had not really been necessary. The Soviets had shrunk from intervening in Poland the month before, and the costs of an invasion had not changed. If intervention was ruled out, then the only other course was to pressure the Polish Communists, especially Kania and Jaruzelski, into imposing martial law apparently of their own accord. This the Politburo now set out to do. They kept the *threat* of Soviet intervention on the table in order to pressure Kania and Jaruzelski—just as Jaruzelski later kept it on the table in order to justify and strengthen his imposition of martial law—but it was merely an extraordinarily successful bluff.

Over the next year all the main players in this power game maneuvered around this bluff. The Soviets manipulated it to make anything short of a Soviet invasion seem like a blessing. The Polish Communists exploited it to impose martial law, which was far from a blessing. Walesa and the pope did their best to advance the Solidarity and Gdansk accords within the limits imposed by it. The Solidarity radicals decided to ignore the bluff in pushing for their maximum demands. Wyszynski and his successor as primate, Cardinal Glemp, tried to cut back on the demands of Solidarity in order to avert it. Thatcher, in London, telephoning her NATO colleagues to avoid the disarray that happened after Afghanistan, forged agreement on anti-Soviet sanctions in case they carried it out. And the Reagan administration began to prepare the covert operations—using the CIA, the American labor movement, the Polish American community, and the Church—that would keep Solidarity alive after the bluff had proved to be a genuine threat after all.

As in the August 1980 crisis, events moved quickly once the protagonists had decided what to do. On this occasion, however, the Politburo rather than Solidarity was in the driver's seat.

* On March 4, 1981, Kania and Jaruzelski were summoned to a Politburo meeting in Moscow. After they had been satisfactorily browbeaten, a joint communiqué to the press stated that the defense of Communism in any one country was a matter for "the entire socialist community," which was "indissoluble." The Brezhnev doctrine had been disinterred.

* On March 27, to protest the police beating of Solidarity leaders at Bydgoszcz, millions of workers brought Poland to a halt with a four-hour general strike. A full general strike was called for March 31. Soviet naval and troop maneuvers began around Poland's borders.

* On March 28, the pope, through Cardinal Wyszynski, appealed to Solidarity leaders for restraint, the pope urging that the government abide by the Gdansk accords, Wyszynski urging Solidarity to call off the general strike.

❖ On March 30, Reagan addressed the AFL-CIO building unions and took the opportunity to support Solidarity: "The Polish workers stand as sentinels on behalf of universal human principles." As he left the hotel where the conference was being held, the president was shot by John Hinckley. That same day Solidarity reached a compromise agreement with the regime. The general strike was called off. Several members of Solidarity's national leadership resigned, complaining of a sell-out by Walesa.

❖ On April 3, Kania and Jaruzelski were flown to Brest for a six-hour secret meeting with Andropov and Soviet defense minister Ustinov in a railway carriage. Again, they were browbeaten and presented with an undated declaration of martial law for their signature. They wriggled out of signing it with a reluctant promise to sign it later.[48]

❖ On May 13, the pope was shot by Mehmet Ali Agca in Rome.

❖ In early August the United States was given the detailed plans for the imposition of martial law in Poland, including Polish leaflets printed in Moscow appealing for calm, by Colonel Kuklinski. Reagan passed on this information to the pope.

❖ On September 5, the first Solidarity Congress, hosting 896 delegates representing more than nine million members, was held in Gdansk. Its radical members had the bit between their teeth and were uninterested in caution or compromise. The conference called for major reforms of Polish society, including free elections. Walesa was re-elected national leader but captured only 55 percent of the vote.

❖ On October 18, Kania resigned under pressure from the Soviets and was replaced by Jaruzelski (who now held all the levers of power). Calling to congratulate the general, Brezhnev urged that there be no delay in taking firm measures against counter-revolution.

❖ On November 4, Jaruzelski held a meeting with Walesa and Cardinal Glemp at which he proposed a Front of National

Accord to provide a forum for dialogue on Poland's growing problems. This idea was accepted by Glemp, but found favor neither with Brezhnev (who objected to Solidarity's inclusion) nor with Walesa (who saw that Solidarity would be swamped by the Communist unions and their allies). It got nowhere.

The crisis accelerated. The economy was deteriorating rapidly, the currency losing its value hourly. Wildcat strikes not supported by Solidarity spread across the country. In Rome, the pope told a delegation of Polish intellectuals associated with Solidarity that Communism was ultimately finished. The Poles had recovered their dignity and sense of worth and would not easily relinquish them again. Still, the Soviets could have some unpleasant surprises up their sleeves. The meeting broke up early when the Polish guests sensed, along with the pope, that something was about to happen at home and returned to Poland.

On November 28, the Polish Communists introduced a law to give the government emergency powers, including the power to ban strikes. Solidarity condemned the legislation as an attempt to reverse the Gdansk accords—Cardinal Glemp sent a letter to Jaruzelski saying much the same thing—and threatened a general strike if the legislation passed.

The penultimate act of the drama was the most ironic. On December 10, the Soviet Politburo held an emergency session to discuss a request from Jaruzelski. He was invoking the Brezhnev doctrine: would the other socialist countries, including the USSR, send forces if his attempt to impose martial law ran into trouble? Unanimously the Politburo rejected the suggestion. Andropov said, "We can't risk it." Andrei Gromyko added, "There cannot be any military invention in Poland." Mikhail Suslov explained, "We are carrying out a great work for peace and we shouldn't change now. World opinion won't understand us."[49]

World opinion was the least of it. The Soviet Union could not afford the economic sanctions that invading Poland would invite. Its own economy was failing, its military budget absorbed the lion's share of investment, and its client states' demands were insatiable. The contradictions of détente were suddenly pinching.

Andropov went so far as to say that Poland could go rather than destroy détente: "We are not going to send troops to Poland. This is a right position, and we must follow it to the end. I do not know what will happen to Poland. But even if Poland is under Solidarity's power, it is one thing; whereas if all the capitalist countries go against the Soviet Union, it would be very hard for us. They already have the relevant agreement about various economic and political sanctions against us."[50]

For a decade (and arguably much longer) the Soviets had been exporting world revolution on Western credits. If those credits were suddenly withdrawn, it would be hard-pressed to satisfy its own domestic economic demands. Other socialist countries would have to save themselves—including Poland.

General Viktor Kulikov, the Warsaw Pact commander, was dispatched to Poland to explain that there was no prospect of Soviet intervention. Jaruzelski was expected to save socialism with Polish resources.[51] He proved to be a good Communist soldier.

On December 11 and 12 the Solidarity national commission met in Gdansk. Its debates revolved around that summer's agenda of radical democratic reforms—to the irritation of Walesa, who had realized for some time that repression was more likely than reform. Toward midnight some of the delegates who tried to use the phones or the telex found that they were not operating. At three minutes to midnight on December 12, 1981, all private telephones in Poland were cut off. Almost all the Solidarity delegates in Gdansk, conveniently located in the same hotels, were quickly arrested, along with four thousand other people. Roadblocks were set up. Tanks emerged from military camps and drove to strategic points on the streets of Warsaw. Martial law had been declared.

On this occasion the U.S. government had not informed Solidarity in advance. Maybe it didn't know—after all, this was one coup not signaled in advance by Soviet maneuvers. Or maybe, as Naimski speculates, Washington thought martial law was bound to succeed in the short term and wished to avoid the loss of life that a warning might have provoked. Resistance erupted anyway, but it was quickly suppressed. Only the miners of the Piast mine near Katowice held out for any length of time. They barri-

caded themselves in their mine and repelled an assault of security police at
the cost of thirteen lives (nine miners, four security police), giving up only
at Christmas.[52] Otherwise, normality, Soviet-style, returned to Poland.

The pope was informed by the Polish ambassador to Italy that "temporary emergency measures" had been imposed an hour after the phone
lines were cut. He could not get through to his bishops, so he used his
broadcast audiences to speak directly to Poland over the next few weeks.
His message was that Poland had the right to be itself. He wrote directly
to Jaruzelski to ask for an end to "the shedding of Polish blood." And in
his 1982 New Year message for the World Day of Peace, he attacked "the
false peace of totalitarian regimes"[53] then reigning in Poland.

That kind of peace suited the Politburo very well. But they knew that
the pope had disrupted such a peace only two years before. He might do
so again. They had gained a brief respite, at best. Next time, moreover,
trouble might be less localized than the Polish crisis. In addition to the
problems besetting the Soviet economy, the West was showing signs of
recovery. Reagan had begun a massive military buildup. Thatcher's monetarist experiment was turning the corner. NATO was threatening to install
missiles in Europe to match the SS-20s.

On May 8, 1982, Chernyaev confided to his diary: "No! There will be
no war in the foreseeable future. But there will be a major propagandist,
and particularly economic, offensive which will put us and the whole
socialist world in a situation of crisis. This means we must urgently, fundamentally, change everything from top to bottom. Otherwise, we cannot
avoid a 'Russian Poland' within about ten years."

Perestroika and *glasnost* had been, no, not born, but conceived—and
conceived by that celebrated mother of invention, necessity.

CHAPTER FIVE

FRIENDS IN NEED

❦

"**Y**ou know, we all ought to go dancing again." Mrs. Thatcher was on a high. Her speech had gone well and had been met with loud and genuine applause. She had been cheered in the streets of New York when her limousine was recognized. Her discussions in Washington with the new president and his colleagues had gone outstandingly well. And though a VC-10 was waiting at the airport to whisk her back to London, she felt like going out on the town.

Some of the responsibility for her high spirits rested with Sir Nicholas Henderson, the British ambassador in Washington, who toward the end of an embassy dinner for Ronald and Nancy Reagan the previous night had invited the prime minister to dance. As he whirled her around the floor, she told him that she really enjoyed dancing. It was one of the few frivolous things that she had learned at Oxford. "It was with some difficulty," Henderson wrote later, "that Denis finally managed to extract her." Now she wanted to dance all night, which, given her ability to function well on four hours' sleep, might have been a very long time. Denis put his foot down on her dancing pumps and she returned to London.[1]

Most of Thatcher's high spirits, however, came from President Reagan and the reception he had laid for her. She was the first major foreign leader to be invited to Washington by the newly elected Reagan in 1981.[2] Henderson had arranged this prized early invitation through one of Reagan's trusted Californians, Edwin Meese. It had happened at a party given by Kay Graham, the *Washington Post*'s owner, the previous December and sounds like classic Washington social politics. But on this occasion Henderson was pushing on an open door. The Thatcherites and the Reaganauts, not to mention their principals, had begun to establish warm relations on Reagan's 1975 and 1978 trips to London, and when Reagan won the presidential election, Richard Allen, shortly to be appointed Reagan's first national security adviser, made sure Thatcher's congratulatory telegram was the first one given to the president-elect. Reagan happily read it to supporters in California.[3]

So Reagan was more than content for Thatcher to be his first important visitor. Even though they would be on formal terms for some time yet—"Dear Mr. President," "Dear Madam Prime Minister"—they knew that they were ideologically compatible, they had already established cordial relations, and they wanted to continue getting on well.[4]

That first visit occurred in late February 1981 when both leaders were advancing bold new economic programs. These differed on important details—Thatcher gave priority to controlling spending over tax cuts, Reagan the reverse—but they shared a broad philosophical agreement in favor of personal tax cuts to encourage enterprise, controlling spending (except for defense spending) to limit the size of government, reducing inflation through monetary policy, and reversing national decline.

Where a difficulty might have arisen was that Reagan was then merely proposing his "Reaganomics" program, whereas Thatcher was almost two years into her policy—and February 1981 was the nadir of the severe recession that attended the first stage of her "monetarist" experiment.[5] Seeking to avoid contamination, Reagan's top officials, notably Treasury Secretary Donald Regan and OMB director David Stockman, publicly dissociated the administration from her economic policies, in particular for raising indirect taxes, during the visit. Stockman attacked her for being insufficiently radical, saying bluntly that "what has been implemented has failed." That dismissal reflected a wider Washington and media consensus.[6]

In contrast, however, Reagan went to great lengths to associate himself with the British prime minister both in words and deeds.

His welcoming ceremony on the White House lawn was a lavish one with full military honors. Having given his guest a formal state dinner at the White House that evening, the president broke protocol to attend the return dinner at the British embassy the following night. He invited the Thatchers to have tea with him and Nancy in the Oval Room of the White House on their final morning in Washington.[7] In his three speeches during the visit, Reagan paid Thatcher a series of extravagant compliments, ending with the key assurance that in meeting their current economic difficulties they would both be "home safe and soon enough."[8]

The political implications were clear: where Reagan's staff saw a need to distance him and the administration from Thatcher's difficulties, he saw a need to give her the strong public backing she needed to survive them. He was risking political capital on her behalf. That was a more solid commitment than any number of diplomatic compliments.

This protectiveness went in two directions. Later in the year, at the Ottawa summit, where Reagan was both making his G-7 debut and recovering from Hinckley's gunshot, Thatcher gave him support he badly needed by speaking out strongly in favor of his economic strategy to a conference that was still largely skeptical. She also ensured that the communiqué reflected their economic views rather than the statist solutions of their host, Canada's Pierre Trudeau. Later that year Thatcher joined Reagan in torpedoing any idea of placing the IMF and the World Bank under UN control at a UN summit in Mexico that had been billed as the start of a "North–South dialogue." That brought to an effective end the 1970s campaign by Third World countries for a "new world economic order" built around such ideas as directed investment and controlled raw material prices. Thereafter Thatcher consistently gave Reagan loyal backing at G-7 meetings. "When there were disagreements between the seven," Reagan said after leaving office, "we found we were always on the same side."[9]

That support was personal as much as political. Reagan's aides talk of Thatcher "mothering" their boss on public occasions. As might be expected, French president Francois Mitterrand, who also made his G-7 debut at Ottawa, saw this chemistry rather differently, telling his aide Jacques Attali, "Mrs. Thatcher, who can be so tough when she talks to her European partners, is like a little girl of eight years old when she talks to the president of the United States. You have to cock your ears to hear her, she's really so touching."[10] Thatcher's affinity for Reagan led her domestic critics to argue that she was too subservient to the American president and neglected Britain's interests accordingly. "When President Reagan says, 'Jump,'" alleged Labour's Denis Healey, "Mrs. Thatcher asks, 'How high?'"

Yet though Thatcher was always supportive of Reagan and the United States in public, she argued her and Britain's corner with all the formidable force at her command in private. She did not win every argument, but she won far more arguments in Washington than any other British prime minister would have. Her influence with Reagan was so well known within the administration that when there was an internal dispute, the faction closest to Thatcher's view would often seek her intervention to win the argument.

This happened on NATO's so-called "dual track" policy of negotiating with the Soviets to remove their intermediate nuclear missiles while deploying missiles in five European countries as a counterweight. Thatcher wanted the missiles not only as a deterrent but also as a sign of America's commitment to Europe. When the State Department alerted her that some in the administration wanted to derail this plan, Thatcher raised the issue with Reagan. He agreed, apparently without much argument, to endorse the "dual track" arrangement.[11]

Getting Reagan's agreement on other issues was not always so easy. Sometimes Thatcher had to fight hard, pulling no rhetorical punches, to gain her point. Nor was she any respecter of rank in these exchanges. Reagan's shrewd and influential assistant secretary of defense, Richard Perle— generally on her side but sometimes against her—recalled later, "She never approached the conversations she had . . . with American officials and with the president from a position of supplication or inferiority. Quite the contrary."[12]

Thatcher was able to use forceful tactics, occasionally rough ones, for a simple but important reason: Reagan didn't mind. He liked her, admired her abilities, was prepared to tolerate strong expressions of disagreement within the context of overall support, and was even amused by her occasional outbursts. One time when she was thundering disagreement down the phone line from London, he held up the telephone so that the rest of his meeting could hear and said, "Isn't she wonderful?"

But their partnership, however close, ultimately depended on each partner being able to deliver. While Thatcher was prime minister, she was almost invariably able to deliver. When the two governments differed—as they were shortly to do over the proposed Soviet gas pipeline to Europe—it was because Thatcher herself was hostile to U.S. policy. But how long would she be able to determine British policy, or even remain in office, if the British economy continued to spiral downward into recession?

The White House, with the apparent exception of Reagan himself, continued to worry about this. In July 1981, the American ambassador to the Court of St. James's, John J. Louis Jr., sent over his first major dispatch on British politics. It was extremely gloomy. Richard Allen summarized its contents in a covering note to the president: "Thatcher has lost her grip on the political rudder," and since the Labour Party was anti-American, "some political turbulence is likely with adverse effect on the country's reliability as a U.S. ally."[13]

Maybe the ambassador had been shocked, ten years in advance of American C-SPAN viewers, by the rowdiness of the House of Commons at prime minister's question time. In fact, his alarm was understandable, if exaggerated. Both the political and economic situations in Britain were at their lowest point—which meant that they were, in the inelegant phrase, "bottoming out." That September Thatcher reshuffled her ministers to give herself and her monetarist supporters a clear majority in the cabinet and effectively uncontested control of economic policy. Her dominance was ratified by the overwhelming support of the Tory annual party conference in October at which the "wets" had hoped to defeat her. And the following month the economic statistics showed that the economy had stopped shrinking and begun to rebound. "The fundamentals" had turned in Thatcher's favor.

But it did not feel that way at the time—or for many months thereafter. As late as March 1982 Thatcher's political fortunes had apparently improved hardly at all. She was still one of the most unpopular prime ministers in the history of opinion polls. Unemployment remained stubbornly above the three million mark. And, not surprisingly, her Tory Party was performing poorly. It was level-pegging in the opinion polls with both Labour and the newborn centrist Social Democratic Party (SDP) which the Tories saw as a potentially greater threat than Labour in their conservative heartland. On March 25, 1982, the Tories suffered the latest of several by-election defeats when they lost a Glasgow constituency to Roy Jenkins, a former Labour finance minister and one of the SDP's most distinguished recruits. In terms of political psychology rather than economics, that was the lowest point for Thatcher. Her survival was far from certain. The last thing she needed now was a war.

One week later forty Argentine scrap metal dealers landed on the remote island of South Georgia, hitherto unknown to history, and triggered a war between Britain and Argentina over the Falkland Islands.

Although Thatcher didn't know it yet, or for some months ahead, indeed she was "home safe and soon enough."

War Clouds

The Falkland Islands were described by Sir Denis Thatcher, memorably and accurately, as "miles and miles of bugger all." Lying three hundred miles off the Argentine coast, they had been a British possession several times, going back and forth between France, Spain, Britain, and Argentina in the seventeenth, eighteenth, and nineteenth centuries, until 1833 when Captain Silas Duncan of the USS *Lexington* sacked the Argentine colony while seeking restitution for American property seized by its governor. That left the islands open to a final and decisive British naval coup. Britain had occupied the islands continuously ever since and planted 1,800 settlers there. Argentina had nursed a nationalist grievance equally as long. The ensuing dispute was, quite literally, a profitless one. As Sir Denis observed, there were no resources in the Falklands (or the Malvinas, as Argentina called them) to make them worth possessing, let alone fighting for, on economic grounds. Argentina wanted them as a matter of national pride; Britain felt compelled to retain them as a matter of national obligation to the islanders.[14]

In the decade that led to war, a stately diplomatic minuet was danced around this dispute by four players. Argentines of all political stripes wanted to establish national sovereignty over the Malvinas. The British Foreign Office, seeing the Falklands as an obstacle to better relations and trade with Latin America, was happy to transfer them to Argentina. The Falkland Islanders (also known as "kelpers") were determined that the islands should remain British (while also hoping for better economic ties with nearby Argentina). And the British government hoped to stumble across a formula that would please Argentina without selling out the kelpers.

The Foreign Office duly came up with "lease-back"—i.e., granting sovereignty over the islands to Argentina, which would then lease them back to British administration for, say, ninety-nine years. This was an imaginative compromise that Argentina was prepared to discuss seriously. But the Foreign Office signally failed either to sell it to the kelpers or to persuade successive governments and MPs that the wishes of 1,800 people should no longer be "paramount." So negotiations dragged on under the permanent threat of the kelpers' veto. Argentina grew increasingly frustrated at the failure of negotiations, and the British government devoted itself to more important matters, notably a defense review that cut back the Royal Navy, sold some of its few remaining aircraft carriers, threatened to axe two amphibious warfare ships, *Fearless* and *Intrepid*, and generally removed the navy from the business of transporting and landing troops far from home under fire. Among the ships axed by Defense Secretary John Nott was a humble ice patrol ship, HMS *Endurance*, which was equipped with two Wasp helicopters for anti-submarine warfare and was stationed in the Falkland Islands. It was scheduled to be withdrawn from the South Atlantic no later than October 1982.

All of this was noticed in two other capital cities. In Washington there was some NATO-conscious disquiet about Nott's apparent running-down of the Royal Navy. The chance to do something about it arose when Thatcher, eager to keep the British nuclear deterrent state-of-the-art, decided to cancel Britain's purchase of the Trident C-4 missile and replace it with the more advanced D-5 version. This was a big expense at a bad time for Thatcher. Attentive to his friend's interests, Reagan instructed American defense negotiators to be generous to the Brits. They complied, but they also sought an assurance that Britain reserve its savings on the deal for defense. In particular, they wanted *Intrepid* and *Fearless* to be saved from the breaker's yard. Delighted with the overall arrangement, announced by Thatcher in the Commons on March 11, 1982, the British government agreed to save the two ships.[15] "Without these ships," wrote Max Hastings and Simon Jenkins in their superb book *The Battle for the Falklands*, "an armed landing in the Falklands would have been literally unthinkable."[16]

HMS *Endurance*, however, received no reprieve. In Buenos Aires its prospective withdrawal was taken as a sign that the British were progressively reducing their commitment to the Malvinas. At the same time, given the resistance of the kelpers, negotiations might drag on eternally. But what if a bold military stroke won the islands for Argentina? Surely the British, eager to be rid of them in any event, would acquiesce in such a fait accompli. After all, the whole world had accepted India's seizure of Goa two decades before.

This line of reasoning was very attractive to the shaky military junta then ruling Argentina. The recovery of the Malvinas would surely revive its popularity and strengthen its precarious hold on power. Operation Goa was approved. The junta set the date for the naval invasion between July and October 1982, safely after the departure of *Endurance*.[17]

Then events began to dictate themselves. An Argentine scrap metal merchant had applied to the British embassy in Buenos Aires for permission to clear a derelict site of old barges and scrap iron at Leith whaling station on the island of South Georgia. Permission was granted, forty or so workers landed at the station, and the Argentine flag was raised. This may have been a case of misplaced patriotism by the workers or an attempt by the Argentine navy to assert a creeping covert sovereignty over the Malvinas to help justify an invasion. But the flag-raising was noticed by scientists from the British Antarctic Survey base down the coast and reported back to the Falklands governor and thence to London.

On March 20, 1982, Thatcher was told and agreed with Carrington to send *Endurance* from the Falklands' capital, Port Stanley, to South Georgia with a complement of two dozen Marines. Carrington organized a diplomatic protest to Buenos Aires; Thatcher ordered up a cabinet paper on military options in the South Atlantic. A debate began in Whitehall on when and how to strengthen the Falklands' defenses. One week later, on March 28, Thatcher and Carrington, journeying by plane to Brussels, reviewed the latest intelligence and ordered three nuclear submarines to the Falklands to deter any rash Argentine action.

Two navies were now spurred into action by the scrap metal men. In Buenos Aires the junta reacted to the dispatch of the *Endurance* to South Georgia with alarm. Had London gotten wind of Argentine plans? If so, Buenos Aires would have to act before the British could beef up the Malvinas' defenses. Realistically, that meant moving up the invasion from the fall to ASAP. On Friday, March 26, two days before Thatcher ordered the submarines to the South Atlantic, the junta—General Leopoldo Galtieri, Admiral Jorge Anaya, and air force brigadier Lami Dozo—made the decision to invade the Falklands.[18] Naval leave was cancelled. Stores and equipment were moved to the port nearest the Falklands. The British embassy was informed that negotiations over the South Georgia incident were now closed. And two Argentine missile corvettes left joint naval maneuvers being conducted with the Uruguayans and sailed south. By Wednesday, March 31, a full Argentine fleet was at sea only forty-eight hours' sailing time from Port Stanley.

In London, meanwhile, First Sea Lord Sir Henry Leach (number two in the navy hierarchy) saw in the arrival of the scrap metal men and the dispatch of the submarines a prospect of winning two major battles: one in the South Atlantic, the other in Whitehall. He had bitterly opposed Nott's 1981 defense review with its reduction of the navy's global role. Now, reviewing the latest intelligence of Argentina's naval moves, Leach realized that he might reverse his Whitehall defeat by winning a war over the Falklands. The Argentine navy was large and well equipped and the Falklands were eight thousand miles from home. If they were seized and had to be retaken, that could only be done by the kind of massive amphibious task force that Nott's defense review would soon make impossible. To sharpen this internal dispute further, the list of Britain's military options in the Falklands that Nott's defense staff drew up at Thatcher's request concluded gloomily that there was "no certainty" that even such a force would succeed. Leach set about proving Nott wrong. Five days before the Falklands were actually seized, two days before the Thatcher government decided to regain them by force, Leach and his staff set about constructing a task force that would be able to do the job.[19]

First, however, the politicians had to give the go-ahead. By the evening of Wednesday, March 31, they were desperate enough to consider almost anything. Thatcher convened a meeting of all the senior foreign and defense people, both politicians and civil servants, in her Commons office. The intelligence was now undeniable: the Argentines were moving to invade the Falklands later that week. It seemed that nothing could be done to stop them. The Marines already there were too small a force to fight off such an invasion, the submarines would arrive at least a week late, and Nott's military options suggested that a British defeat could probably not be reversed. To Thatcher this was unacceptable: "I could not believe it: these were our people, our islands. I said instantly, 'If they are invaded, we have got to get them back.'"[20]

But the mood of the entire meeting was more pessimistic and seemingly more practical. Then Leach arrived halfway through. Though clad in the impressive full dress uniform of a First Sea Lord, he had been held up by a House of Commons policeman until his identity could be established.[21]

Now he came to the prime minister's aid like the ghost of Nelson. She asked him what could be done. With the benefit of his preparations, Leach was able to assure her that within forty-eight hours he could put together a task force of destroyers, frigates, landing craft, and supply vessels, led by two aircraft carriers, that could retake the Falklands. But how would he react to such a force, she pressed him, if he were the admiral in charge of the Argentine fleet? He confidently replied, "I would return to harbor immediately."[22]

Steeled by Leach's confidence, the meeting decided to assemble the task force; cooled by Nott's caution, they deferred a decision on whether to dispatch it.

There were several attempts through third-party channels to prevail upon the Argentines to call off the invasion at the last minute. Late on Thursday night, in response to an appeal from Thatcher, Reagan promised to contact Buenos Aires and urge the junta not to take military measures. He added, "We will do what we can to assist you here."[23] He was as good as his word. He spoke to Galtieri, who seemed to be drunk, for more than an hour on the telephone. But the general had deliberately avoided the call until it was too late to cancel hostilities. At a late Downing Street meeting, ministers decided to dispatch the task force, Nott no longer skeptical. From the naval operations room in the Ministry of Defense, Leach issued the order: "The task force is to be made ready and sailed." In Port Stanley, Rex Hunt, the Falklands' governor, sounding a little like Denis Thatcher, called in the commanders of the two Marine detachments at his disposal and gave them the bad news: "It seems as if the buggers mean it."[24]

The Royal Marines fought bravely. They killed two Argentine commandos in an advance party in a sniper battle for Government House. They hit a landing craft with the main Argentine fleet with the unorthodox use of a British anti-tank gun. The twenty-three men on South Georgia held off a naval and helicopter attack for four hours at the cost of four Argentine dead and one wounded British NCO. But the odds were overwhelming, and by mid-morning Hunt declared a surrender. He was promptly flown to Montevideo by the victorious Argentines. The Marines, before also being repatriated, were photographed face-down on the ground. The photographs appeared in the London newspapers hours later, adding a final painful twist of the knife to the growing sense that Britain had suffered a shameful humiliation. An entire nation was suddenly shouting: "We're mad as hell and we're not gonna take it any more!"

The Iron Lady's True Mettle

When Thatcher spoke in a special Saturday session of the House of Commons to debate the Falklands on April 3, she was facing a political crisis that had very personal overtones. The mood of the entire nation, more than reflected in the debate, was one of humiliation and outraged national pride. In the quarter century since Suez, the British had endured a series of imperial retreats and economic failures. Their successes, such as the Malayan and Borneo campaigns, had somehow never registered on the national consciousness. And instead of developing an accurate assessment of themselves as an important middle-ranking power with above-average diplomatic and cultural influence, they felt themselves to be far weaker than they really were.

But this—*this*—was too much. To be treated with such contempt by a Latin American dictatorship, to have decent British kelpers kneeling before a foreign conqueror, to have a legal territorial possession simply grabbed— these were intolerable. They simply could not be allowed to stand. People who had never heard of the Falklands were passionate in their conviction that "our people, our islands" had to be returned to Britain. Even Labour's foreign policy herbivores called for an expeditionary force to reclaim them. The British saw in the Falklands a symbol of the accumulated defeats of the postwar world. Some of them also glimpsed a chance to wipe the slate clean.

Any prime minister facing the Commons on the morrow of a Port Stanley defeat would have had a hard time. For Thatcher, however, the defeat was worse and the challenge greater. Her entire political appeal was that she was a different sort of politician. She had been elected to reverse Britain's decline, not to explain it smoothly away like virtually every other political leader. The "winter of discontent" had symbolized that decline domestically. It had helped to elect her and to justify her tough economic policies. Now the loss of the Falklands symbolized Britain's military and diplomatic decline with equal sharpness. She could not really be blamed for that loss, even though she had made some mistakes. It was the result of the accumulated diplomatic, intelligence, military, and political failures of several governments. She had taken prompt action once the threat looked real. And she was one of the few leading British politicians who would have gratefully accepted Leach's confident advice. But now she had to demonstrate that she had the toughness, stamina, and judgment needed to reverse the defeat and recover the lost islands. Did she have these qualities?

This question was put to her dramatically in the course of a bitter and sometimes rowdy debate. Enoch Powell, the maverick Tory former minister, whose brilliance she admired but whose judgment she doubted, fixed her with his trademark piercing gaze across the chamber and said with heavy deliberation:

> The prime minister, shortly after she came into office, received a soubriquet as the "Iron Lady." It arose in the context of remarks she made about defense against the Soviet Union and its allies; but there was no reason to suppose that the Right Honorable Lady did not welcome and, indeed, take pride in that description. In the next week or two this House, the nation, and the Right Honorable Lady herself will learn of what metal she is made.[25]

Thatcher was seen to nod when this question was asked.

She began to show the necessary steel at once with her announcement of the task force in the debate, her creation of an effective and loyal war cabinet—and her acceptance of the resignations of Carrington and two other Foreign Office ministers to satisfy the popular desire for scapegoats. But she knew, as she wrote in her memoirs, that those cheering the task force were not all cheering the same thing. Some saw it as a merely "diplomatic armada" that would never fight but would draw Argentina back into negotiations. They included members of her own cabinet, including her new foreign secretary and potential rival, the drenchingly "wet" Francis Pym. She herself felt that the Argentines would not give up their "ill-gotten gains" without a fight.[26] Still, she had to spend the weeks between the debate and the arrival of the task force at the Falklands in ensuring that a series of negotiations neither ratified Argentina's seizure nor cast Britain as bent on conflict. It required delicate political skills as well as forceful ones.

Her first success occurred in New York, at the United Nations, before the invasion had even begun. Britain's ambassador to the UN, Anthony Parsons, obtained the nine votes he needed to summon the Security Council on Thursday, April 1. Informing the council of the imminent Argentine assault, he invited and obtained a call from the president of the council (a Zairian) for both sides to "show restraint." Invasion would now put Argentina in the wrong. On the following day, when the Falklands had fallen, Parsons succeeded in constructing a majority in favor of a Security Council resolution (UNSCR 502) demanding an immediate and unconditional withdrawal by the Argentines from the Falklands. This was a remarkable achievement by Parsons, especially given the strong anticolonialist sentiment prevailing at Turtle Bay, and it gave Britain a strong moral and diplomatic advantage throughout the conflict. It was not achieved without friends, however. Parsons wooed the Commonwealth countries to good effect. President Mitterrand telephoned Thatcher to pledge his support—something for which she was always grateful—and France's diplomats at the UN duly pressed their traditional allies there to vote for UNSCR 502. Even then Parsons was one vote short. Knowing that Jordan intended to vote against, he asked the prime minister to intercede directly with King Hussein. When Thatcher telephoned, King Hussein began the conversation with, "What can I do for you, Prime Minister?" It was more than a conversational habit. The king really meant it. Parsons won the vote.

If UN support was helpful, American backing was vital. Without U.S. cooperation on arms supplies, intelligence, and the use of American facilities on Ascension Island, Britain might have been unable to win the Falklands War—or, at best, would have done so at a much higher cost in lives and money. But the British were haunted throughout by the memory of Suez and the fear of being let down by a Washington bent on keeping Latin America friendly. Thatcher was less subject to these anxieties than anyone else, partly because she had international law on her side, unlike Eden at Suez, and partly because she trusted Reagan to back a major NATO ally like Britain over a recent and dubious friend like the Argentine junta.[27] Even so, the course of the three sets of mediation—controlled in turn by Secretary of State Al Haig, the UN secretary-general, and the Peruvian foreign minister—gave her a few bad moments. And the balancing act that was U.S. policy for the first half of the war caused her some frustrations.

It need not have done so. Reagan, Haig, and Defense Secretary Caspar Weinberger were resolved to support Britain openly if it came to actual hostilities and covertly until then. They also hoped, Haig in particular, to avoid hostilities by diplomatic mediation of the dispute either under Haig's direct control or through intermediaries like the Peruvians. U.S. policy was therefore Janus-faced. While Haig was striking the neutral diplomatic pose of a mediator, Weinberger's Pentagon was giving the British everything they asked for. The private supply of resources was more important than the public mediation.

As Geoffrey Smith points out: "Only three days after the Argentine invasion, a small coordinating committee was set up within the Pentagon under the chairmanship of Dov Zakheim, Richard Perle's special assistant, to cut through the normal bureaucratic procedures." In these early days the committee decided to allow the British to use the American base on Ascension Island, to supply them with American aircraft fuel there, to fly in fuel and other supplies for them, to permit them to obtain other military hardware in the United States, and to make special arrangements for later payment.

Weinberger was the moving spirit behind this massive support, which seemed to increase all the time. It grew to include equipment for instant runways, the latest Sidewinder missile, anti-submarine devices, and some weapons that were in short supply for U.S. forces. Since the Zakheim committee worked with the White House, the Joint Chiefs, and the State Department, the extent of this aid was clearly known to Reagan, even if it did not carry his signature. "Cap proposed, the president approved," said one of the principals on the National Security Planning Group.[28] And Cap proposed a great deal.

In the case of intelligence cooperation, U.S. assistance did carry the president's signature. Regular intelligence cooperation between Britain and the

United States is extremely close. Signals intelligence is automatically exchanged between America's National Security Agency and Britain's GCHQ worldwide electronic eavesdropping system. A CIA man sits in at the Downing Street meetings of the Joint Intelligence Committee; a British diplomat fulfils a similar role in Washington—indeed, more than one diplomat. Lawrence Eagleburger told Smith later, "You were so much in our intelligence breeches anyway that had we decided to turn it off, we would have had to send every Brit home from Washington to accomplish it." But the United States went beyond merely maintaining existing close relations. Because there was little U.S. intelligence covering the South Atlantic, a satellite was moved down from the North Atlantic to help British operations there. The final decision to give the British this full cooperation was approved by Reagan himself. It was a clear and probably deliberate signal of which side the United States was on.[29]

If anyone had cause for grievance, it was the Argentines. They were taking part in a public mediation process managed by a power that was privately supplying their enemy with the sinews of war. Haig was uneasy about this and believed that Weinberger had pushed the arming of the British right up to the proper limits—and beyond.[30] It forced him to give assurances to the Argentines that were disingenuous at best. On April 13, for instance, he assured the Argentine foreign minister, "Since the outset of the crisis, the United States has not granted British requests that would go beyond the scope of our customary patterns of cooperation."[31] This was before the satellite was moved down the Atlantic. Even so, Haig's statement sits uncomfortably alongside the help that the Pentagon and intelligence services had been giving to Britain almost from the start.

Haig's mediation was an honest attempt to reach a fair settlement—though both belligerents believed otherwise at different times. It was built around three central ideas: an Argentine withdrawal from the islands, followed by some form of joint or neutral interim administration, while negotiations over long-term sovereignty were conducted. Various sweeteners and conditions—UN administration, a time limit on the sovereignty negotiations—were added or subtracted from time to time. It was generally believed that the mediators had six weeks to arrange a deal—the time that it would take the task force to reach the Falklands and begin fighting. (In fact, as we shall see, the onset of battle spurred some serious last-minute attempts at a settlement.) The foreign policy establishments in both Britain and the United States thought that some kind of peaceful settlement, caked in diplomatic fudge, would almost certainly be the outcome. And on two occasions Haig and his confederates came very close to success.

The first was when Pym, now foreign secretary, returned from a visit to Washington bearing Haig's latest mediation proposals. Pym wanted to accept them; Thatcher regarded them as "conditional surrender"—with some reason. They would have disbanded the task force, withdrawn sanctions on Argentina, allowed almost unlimited Argentine immigration to the islands, and eroded the Falklanders' right of self-determination. Despite her opposition the foreign secretary exercised his right to take them to the war cabinet that evening.

Before the meeting on April 24, Thatcher privately explained her objections to her loyal deputy prime minister, Willie Whitelaw, to explain in detail why the proposals were unacceptable to her: they abandoned almost all of the points the British had declared essential and rewarded Argentine aggression. Whitelaw took her side, as he usually did, and the war cabinet went along. Rather than reject the Haig-Pym proposals out of hand, however, they adopted Nott's suggestion that Haig should put his plan to Buenos Aires first. He did so with a reasonable expectation that they would be accepted. That would have put the British in an awkward position, and Pym could have prevailed. But Galtieri, fulfilling Thatcher's prediction that a military junta would never withdraw voluntarily from the Falklands, turned Haig down.

"And so a great crisis passed," wrote Thatcher in her memoirs. "I could not have stayed on as prime minister had the war cabinet accepted Francis Pym's proposals. I would have resigned."[32]

Meddlesome Intermediaries

That rejection also marked the formal end of U.S. mediation. Washington now officially jumped to Britain's side of the fence. Reagan sent the prime minister a message promising that his official statement would "leave no doubt that Her Majesty's Government worked with us in good faith and was left with no choice but to proceed with military action based on the right of self-defense."[33] That was highly satisfactory for Thatcher. In practice, however, matters were less clear-cut.

As Geoffrey Smith has pointed out, what really happened was that the public and private U.S. policies had switched sides. America was now openly supporting Britain. That meant Weinberger was publicly able to give even more help. But Haig continued his mediation privately, even covertly, through third parties, and Reagan began regularly calling Thatcher to urge restraint and compromise almost until the surrender of Port Stanley to British forces.[34]

This pressure reflected the strategic concern, expressed most strongly within the administration by United Nations ambassador Jeane Kirkpatrick, that a British humiliation of Argentina would damage U.S. relations with all of Latin America, not merely with Buenos Aires. It was a reasonable concern. But it was trumped by all the considerations urging support for Britain, including Reagan's personal desire to help Thatcher. And in the end Argentina's defeat, as well as leading to democracy there, provoked little resentment from other Latin American countries. (The Argentines had never been popular with their neighbors.) Still, the fear of a Latin American backlash was important in Washington's calculations— not enough for the United States to side with Argentina but enough to press its British ally to accept something short of outright victory.

In early May, however, this was distinctly premature as Argentina's defeat was not guaranteed. Far from it. Haig's remote-control mediation took place against a background of the first serious fighting. The SAS and Marines had retaken South Georgia on the day after Thatcher almost resigned. On the day after the United States abandoned its formal neutrality, the SAS and Special Boat Squadron (SBS) made a first landing on the Falklands and RAF Vulcans from Ascension launched a raid on Port Stanley. Then, on May 2, a British submarine sank an Argentine battleship, the *General Belgrano*, with the loss of more than three hundred lives. Two days later, an Argentine Exocet missile sank the HMS *Sheffield* with the loss of twenty-one lives. The war had begun in earnest.

It had generally been assumed that once the fighting began, the mediation and negotiations would cease. But the scale of casualties on the *Belgrano* produced a revulsion against Britain internationally and the loss of the *Sheffield* caused heart-searching in Britain itself. This was neither fair nor rational. Ships were always going to be lost in an essentially naval war; the *Belgrano* was undoubtedly a threat to the task force and hence a legitimate military target, and its casualties were high because its accompanying destroyers had sailed away without picking up survivors. All the same, the British came under renewed pressure to consider new offers of mediation and even to make the concessions to Buenos Aires they had refused only days before. Such an offer now came from President Fernando Belaunde of Peru, at the behest of Haig behind the scenes. This Peruvian plan was in fact a lightly disguised version of earlier proposals—"Haig in a poncho"—and it reprised most of the earlier flaws. Still, it was the second occasion on which mediation came close to success.

Thatcher liked Haig in a poncho even less than Haig in seersucker. But her ability to resist had been weakened by world reaction to the *Belgrano* sinking, and this time Pym was able to sell the proposals to an anxious war cabinet. They then went to the full cabinet, which, taking a rare vote, decided with only two dissents to accept them in principle if only to "keep talking." Thatcher put on a bold front. She made clear her skepticism in the Commons. She stressed her main sticking-point left—that Britain could not accept a cease-fire if the Argentines remained on the islands. But she was forced to accept that Britain would negotiate with no preconditions on terms or outcomes. If the junta had agreed, she and her negotiating posture would have been further weakened. Britain's decision to accept the Peruvian terms was either the result of panic in the cabinet and war cabinet or a preternaturally cool calculation by Thatcher that the Peruvian plan would satisfy world opinion but not the Argentine junta.[35]

If it was cool calculation, Thatcher was vindicated. Yet again Galtieri rejected proposals that would have given Argentina at least the possibility of keeping the Malvinas without a fight. Argentina's sinking of the *Sheffield* had convinced the junta that they had a war-winning weapon in the Exocet, and they were not about to give up now.[36] But Galtieri's rejection strengthened Thatcher more than anyone. It undermined her dovish opponents in the Labour Party, in her own cabinet, in the Foreign Office, and in the U.S. State Department. It also ended any serious likelihood of mediation leading to a compromise peace. More negotiations would continue at the UN when the secretary-general unveiled his own peace proposals. Reagan would continue to press Thatcher in telephone calls and telegrams to bridge what he believed to be a modest gap between the two sides. But no mediation could bridge the gap between Argentina's demand for sovereignty and Britain's insistence on the islanders' right of self-determination.

Thatcher now reasserted this principle in the British government's final terms for a settlement. These were somewhat tougher than the Peruvian terms she had accepted under pressure two weeks before. They were drawn up on May 16, ostensibly for transmission to Argentina by the UN secretary-general in his mediating role. But Argentina was required to accept them within forty-eight hours and no negotiation was permitted. In truth Argentina was expected to reject them and did so. Their real purpose was to persuade the world that Britain had pursued a just cause in a reasonable and accommodating way. In that they succeeded. Haig privately and Labour's Michael Foot publicly both praised their reasonableness and flexibility.

As soon as Argentina had rejected the terms, Thatcher took them off the table in her speech to the Commons on May 20. The decks were now cleared for war. The next day British soldiers and Marines landed at San Carlos in the Falklands and began their land campaign to recover the islands.

Thatcher had now made by far the greater part of her contribution to winning the Falklands War. She had waged a shrewd diplomatic campaign to ensure that Britain maintained its legitimate rights in the Falklands without seeming intransigent in negotiation. She had held together the cabinet, her party, and four-fifths of the country behind a bold and risky military venture. She had organized a surprisingly wide coalition of international support for Britain against the odds. She had exploited her close political alliance with Reagan (and now Weinberger) to get vital military supplies and intelligence help for the task force at only moderate cost (if slightly higher risk) in negotiating flexibility. And within the limits of a straitened defense budget, she had given as much moral and material backing to the troops as she could.

Victory and Vindication

It was on these soldiers, sailors, and airmen—"our boys," as Thatcher took to calling them in the campaign—that the final stage of recovering the Falklands depended. Now that the diplomacy was largely over, she could do very little to assist them, and, unlike other political war leaders, she was well aware of her own incapacity in military affairs. She asked her usual probing questions when the military proposed something, but she did not get in their way with her own strategic ideas. "From the military man's point of view," said Admiral Sir Terence Lewin, the chief of the defense staff, in an interview after the war, "she was an ideal prime minis- ter....One wanted a decision and she gave it."[37] But her relationship with the forces went deeper than decisiveness. "To the men in the South Atlantic," wrote her biographer, "'Maggie' was not just a civilian prime minister playing politics with their lives. She was a leader they were proud to fight for" because they recognized in her a fighter like themselves.[38]

These feelings were returned. Thatcher had developed real admiration for the bravery and professionalism of the British military even before the war. The SAS response to the Iranian embassy siege had reinforced it. Sometimes the British armed forces seemed to be the only traditional insti- tutions that worked well. But the war had given her a sense of personal responsibility for the lives she was risking. Her aides report her sinking into silent depressions when military operations were in doubt or went wrong. She sent handwritten letters of condolence to the families of those who fell in the war. She insisted on limiting the length of negotiations because she refused to risk men and ships in dangerous seas for any longer than was militarily necessary. She did not want to let them down.

They certainly did not let her down. Twenty-four days after landing at the San Carlos beachhead, the British forces entered Port Stanley and accepted the Argentine surrender. Deprived of helicopters, lost in the sinking of the container ship *Atlantic Conveyor*, the soldiers had "yomped" across the island of West Falkland in three weeks and won major battles along the way at Goose Green, Mount Longdon, Two Sisters, Wireless Ridge, Mount Tumbledown, and Port Stanley itself. Nor were these conflicts a walkover. The British lost 255 men killed and 777 wounded, some permanently maimed. Six ships were sunk and ten more badly damaged. Nine planes were lost to ground fire and accidents.[39] But these losses, though immensely sad, were overshadowed in the public mind by the extraordinary achievements, logistical and military, of sending a vast amphibious armada eight thousand miles from home and then winning a naval, air, and land war against an enemy who was well equipped, more numerous, dug in behind strong defenses, and close to its home base.

Right up to the fall of Port Stanley, strong pressures for a diplomatic end to hostilities rather than an outright British victory came from the U.S., the UN, and even the Foreign Office. In early June Tony Parsons had to veto a UN resolution calling for a cease-fire not linked to an Argentine withdrawal. Reagan telephoned Thatcher on May 31 to urge that the British be "magnanimous" in victory and reach a compromise allowing the Argentines to save face. These pressures were backed not only by concern about the lives likely to be lost in those final days but also by arguments drawn from *realpolitik*: a British victory would allegedly saddle London with a costly commitment that would need defending indefinitely, distort British defense priorities, and alienate Latin America.

Thatcher rejected all these overtures, including Reagan's, firmly and even brusquely on the grounds that she could hardly justify risking the lives of "our boys" in order to give the Argentines half of what they had grabbed. Talking of American pressure, she told Henderson, "We were prepared to negotiate before, but not now. We have lost a lot of blood, and it's the best blood. Do they not realize that it's an issue of principle?"[40] This determination hardened in the war's final days. Her closest ally in the war cabinet, Cecil Parkinson, went on television in the final week of the war to stress that since the San Carlos landing, there had been a change of mood in Britain. There could no longer be any question of shared sovereignty or an Argentine role in the administration of the islands: "We have to be prepared to hold on to what we have repossessed." And a British sergeant fighting in the Falklands was much quoted in the British press for expressing this same national mood: "If they're worth fighting for, then they must be worth keeping."[41]

Was the continuation of conflict really worth it? Even some of Thatcher's aides and admirers have been critical of her supposed intransigence in the final weeks. But she was surely right. They were contrasting the value of the Falklands, negligible in themselves, against the supposedly heavy budgetary and diplomatic costs of winning and holding them.[42] Thatcher saw that a much larger prize was at stake. To make a diplomatic retreat the climax of what had become a great national cause would have confirmed and perpetuated the dismal myth of postwar British decline. Instead of dispelling the sense of humiliation that had sped the task force on its way, it would have piled on despair. The British people would have concluded that not even their most strenuous efforts could manage to produce an outright victory. The entire Thatcher "project" of national revival would have been derailed.

By insisting that the troops and the people deserved to clinch the victory they had all but won, Thatcher gave an enormous boost to national morale. Sailing home to the ports from which it had set out three months earlier, the victorious task force was greeted by bands playing and flags waving almost as in a Victorian imperial tableau. After years of national self-denigration, old fashioned patriotism was suddenly fashionable again.

The victory produced what became known as the "Falklands effect"—a revival of British self-confidence across the board and of Britain's reputation internationally. The British armed forces had proved themselves to be bonny fighters, a legitimate source of national pride—they later served with distinction in the Balkan, Gulf, Afghan, and Iraq wars. British military advisers and British weapons—in particular, the maneuverable Harrier—were in great demand abroad. British diplomacy, which suddenly had clout behind it, went on to foster change, from introducing Gorbachev internationally to helping settle the Angola crisis. The British economy had just started to recover from a deep recession six months before, but the Falklands victory meant that the Thatcher policies of national efficiency through free market reforms would now be given time to work. Britain has since enjoyed almost a quarter century of strong economic performance, interrupted by only one recession in the early 1990s. It has overtaken the German economy in per capita terms already and is on schedule to surpass it in absolute size in less than a decade (though both may be overtaken by China before then). The basic Thatcher model of a deregulated labor market, monetary control, and encouragement of enterprise is now seen as the standard method for an economy seeking to emerge from statist stagnation.

The main beneficiary of the Falklands effect, however, was Thatcher herself. She had watched what turned out to be the final battles of the campaign from the military headquarters at Northwood on Sunday, June 13, 1982. The next day, after a nervous meeting of the war cabinet still desperate for news of the outcome, Argentine resistance collapsed. Thatcher went from Downing Street to the Commons late that night and made a brief statement on a point of order that "white flags have been seen flying over Port Stanley." She was cheered by both sides of the House, received a graceful tribute from Labour leader Michael Foot, and was then greeted by a large crowd singing "Rule Britannia" when she returned to Downing Street. Three days later, Enoch Powell rose in the House to report what the test had revealed of Mrs. Thatcher's mettle: "It shows that the substance under test consisted of ferrous matter of the highest quality, and that it is of exceptional tensile strength, is highly resistant to wear and tear and to stress, and may be used to advantage for all national purposes."[43]

Thatcher's victory at the next election was a foregone conclusion. She postponed it for a year because she felt it might be inappropriate to exploit the war in a "khaki election." But the government was scoring above 50 percent in opinion polls and unexpectedly won an opposition constituency in a special election. The general election, when it came, gave the Conservatives a majority of 144—the highest majority won by any party since Labour's historic 1945 victory. She was to win another three-figure majority in 1987. Indeed, from June 14, 1982, right up to her last week in office, Thatcher dominated British politics as no one had since Churchill. She had the power and prestige to sustain a bold foreign and defense policy even against strong opposition over the next eight years. The White House could afford to stop worrying about her survival.

Reagan also benefited from the Falklands effect. He had arranged through Weinberger to give the British the arms and intelligence they needed for a quick victory. They had won. His telephone calls urging compromise on Thatcher had grated on her, but her fierce responses—which might equally well have grated on him—produced no negative reactions. American help continued and even increased. Against Jeane Kirkpatrick's advice he had risked U.S. strategic interests in Latin America by his support for Britain, but these strategic interests were not damaged. Quite the contrary. The junta's defeat over the Malvinas provoked a democratic revolution in Argentina itself and stimulated a wave of democratization in Latin America that the Reagan administration endorsed and assisted.[44] In short, Reagan had taken risks by supporting Britain, but the support had paid off and the risks had not materialized.

As Geoffrey Smith points out, however, the fact that Reagan took risks to support Britain makes the pressure for compromise understandable and the assistance all the more significant: "Reagan knew how much the issue meant to Thatcher. He realized that her position was hanging in the balance and he delivered."[45]

His reward was an effective partner in the long Cold War battles that lay ahead.

CHAPTER SIX

KEEPING HOPE ALIVE

In late May 1982 Cardinal Basil Hume, the modest, self-deprecating and quintessentially English head of the English Catholic hierarchy, made an emergency return visit to Rome only two days after he had left the city for London. A growing crisis between the Vatican and the British government required his mollifying diplomacy. The outbreak of the Falklands War meant that the planned pilgrimage of John Paul II to Britain in June might have to be canceled.

Both sides were distressed by this prospect. This was to be the first visit by a pope to Britain, and the entire nation, not simply the English Catholic community, was excited about it. Margaret Thatcher shared in this excitement. She had met John Paul in a side visit during the Rome summit in 1980 and been greatly impressed by him. Like the entire British government, she was grateful for his strong condemnation of terrorism in Ireland. She believed that after their Rome conversation he had pressed the Irish hierarchy to call on the first group of IRA hunger-strikers to end their fast.[1] Now she wanted to consult him on what measures the West should take in response to the imposition of martial law in Poland.

Hume had made arrangements for Thatcher to have a private tête-à-tête with John Paul during an official reception at the cardinal's house in Westminster. But the pope felt that he could not visit a country actively engaged in hostilities, especially against a formally Catholic nation like Argentina. Delicate negotiations were set in train. These had some prospect of success because of the pope's earnest desire to make the historic visit. The chances improved further when Thatcher generously proposed that no government ministers, even herself, would meet the pope or attend any of his official functions if that would make it easier for him to proceed.[2] John Paul invited an English bishop and a Scottish bishop to lunch to mull over this offer—another good sign, as "the pope believes that difficult problems can often be resolved over a meal."[3] Over lunch John Paul consented to the visit, provided that the Argentine hierarchy raised no objections.

It was this good news that brought Hume to Rome for discussions with the pope and the Argentine bishops.

"On the spur of the moment," Hume recalled later, he proposed that the pope should visit both countries.[4] This compromise was quickly agreed upon. The pope added that he would go as an advocate of peace and a messenger of reconciliation. He then concelebrated a Mass for peace with both British and Argentine bishops. Cardinal Hume had saved the day.

As a religious event, the pope's pilgrimage to Britain was the expected success. His services were attended by vast, enthusiastic congregations. He presided over a joint prayer service with the archbishop of Canterbury in the latter's cathedral, and they then signed a declaration of Christian unity. He used a sermon on the English martyrs to dispel the last vestiges of traditional British anti-Catholicism by making it an enemy of the nation's self-image: "In this England of fair and generous minds, no one will begrudge the Catholic community pride in its own history."

George Weigel has described the declaration of unity as "the high-water mark in post–Vatican II Anglican-Catholic relations." That is sadly true. Because Anglicanism worldwide has since divided over such issues as women priests and gay marriage, Christianity has become more fractured rather than less. In 1982, however, the declaration was a great ecumenical advance. (And as Anglicanism has splintered, John Paul's openness to other

Christian denominations in 1982 has had the unintended consequence of directing a steady stream of distinguished converts to Rome.)

John Paul's visit was inevitably less successful as a peace mission because of its timing. It coincided almost precisely with the British land campaign on East Falkland. Cardinal Hume's compromise was agreed on the day after the San Carlos landing, the pope arrived in Britain on the day the battle of Goose Green was fought, and he landed in Argentina only three days before the surrender of Port Stanley. He transformed his Argentine visit therefore into a more general "crusade for peace," attended by the conference of Latin American bishops, to offer spiritual consolation to the defeated Argentines.[5] The pope himself might have drawn some consolation from the BBC's war correspondent, Robert Fox, who in a nighttime lull in the battle for Goose Green overheard a British officer, Chris Keeble, successfully appealing to Argentine soldiers to surrender to superior force in the following terms: "I am Catholic. You are all Catholics. We are all Christians. I do not believe in killing unnecessarily." The battle ended without further fighting when the Argentine senior officers were persuaded that to surrender to overwhelming odds was not dishonorable.[6]

Before he left Britain, the pope had faced an equally delicate task: calling for an end to hostilities without appearing to favor either side. This he accomplished very effectively, at least in the eyes of the British, by appealing to both Britain and Argentina to negotiate and by making general anti-war statements. A letter from the British foreign secretary's office, assessing the visit two months later, concluded, "By not denouncing the Government's policy of replying to Argentina's force with force, the pope avoided causing a political storm. . . . [His] judgment [on the inadmissibility of war] seemed less a direct comment on the Falklands war, or even an abandonment of the principles of the 'just war,' than a Christian warning of the near impossibility of avoiding escalation to total war." The dispatch ended optimistically by forecasting that the pilgrimage would have "a positive impact on relations between Her Majesty's Government and the Holy See in a year which had earlier seen those relations upgraded" in part because the government had handled a potential embarrassment sensitively.[7]

Relations between the Vatican and the British government did become warmer during the Thatcher years. But the pope's visit was still a great opportunity missed. Thatcher had a high opinion of the pope, and he respected her as a woman of moral seriousness and had reason to be grateful to her. They agreed on the necessity of resisting Communism generally and the Polish crackdown in particular. Thatcher's instincts on this question were extremely sound—she grasped how Communism blighted the lives and hopes of ordinary people—but as yet she lacked John Paul's experience and his grasp of how to undermine and outwit Communist power by strategies of cultural resistance. A meeting between them at that moment could have given the British prime minister valuable early lessons in how to weaken the Soviet hold on the captive nations of Eastern Europe, and would have shaped her immediate response to the Polish crisis. But because of the Falklands War, that meeting never happened.

Cross-Atlantic Tension

Western governments in 1982 were in a state of some confusion about how to handle the imposition of martial law against Polish Solidarity. Thatcher had spent time and effort in 1981 coordinating the plans of NATO allies for sanctions in the event of a Polish crackdown. But those plans had presupposed that the crackdown would entail a Soviet invasion. They had to be rethought when Jaruzelski carried out the repression with Polish army and security forces. To complicate matters, not all Western leaders wanted a strong reaction in these new circumstances. West Germany's social-liberal coalition government, wedded to détente and *Ostpolitik*, initially took an understanding view of the crackdown. Chancellor Helmut Schmidt said that it was "necessary" to maintain stability, and Egon Bahr, the chief strategist of *Ostpolitik*, argued that world peace was more important than Poland. France, under Mitterrand's new left-wing coalition, at first took a similar view.

Even the European governments that did support a stronger response thought it should nonetheless be directed against Poland rather than the Soviet Union itself. And the smaller group willing to back anti-Soviet sanctions was still not prepared to impose the severe measures advocated by the Reagan administration. Oddly enough, this last group included the Thatcher government, then seen as both firmly anti-Soviet and loyal to Washington.

Thatcher began in the U.S. camp—or at least in mid-Atlantic. She had spoken to Reagan soon after Jaruzelski's announcement of martial law. She understood his anger and agreed with his desire to take swift reprisals. Both the British government and, at her instigation, the European Community subsequently imposed some modest sanctions of their own. To spur even this tentative action by the EC, however, Thatcher had to fight hard against the French, who wanted to continue selling Europe's vast food surpluses to the Soviets at subsidized prices. On the other hand, she also had to discourage some immoderate American ideas then floating around—such as deliberately bankrupting the Polish economy, which would threaten the European banking system more than the Soviet empire. This delicate balancing act was upset a few days after her phone conversation with Reagan, when the U.S. announced tough sanctions—the cancellation of Aeroflot landing rights, a halt to negotiations on a new grain agreement, and a ban on exporting construction materials for a gas pipeline from Siberia to Western Europe—with brief advance warning but no further consultation.

What also struck her—and positively angered other European leaders— was that the U.S. sanctions were suspiciously tailored to American politics. The gas pipeline sanctions harmed European companies, but a grain embargo—detrimental to American farmers—was not included.[8] That, she thought, was no way to run an alliance.[9]

The gas pipeline sanctions transformed the Polish crisis from one that might have damaged the Soviet Union into one that divided the Atlantic alliance for the better part of a year. American suspicion of the Siberian gas pipeline project predated the crisis itself. The Pentagon had opposed it throughout 1981 on the grounds that it would make Western Europe too dependent on Soviet energy supplies. Thatcher sympathized with this strategic argument, and with Reagan's annoyance with Europe for its seeming indifference to the Soviet-directed repression of the Polish people. But she also believed that German and French support for the pipeline made resistance to the project futile, and that the Americans' heavy-handed efforts to stop it would fail and would also disrupt Atlantic relations. That is exactly what happened when the Pentagon tacked the ban on pipeline construction equipment onto Reagan's list of Polish sanctions in December 1981.[10] The row rumbled on well into 1982.

There was an attempt to reach a compromise at the G-7 summit at Versailles in June: the Americans would lift the pipeline sanctions if the Europeans would restrict subsidized trade credits for the Soviet Union. Both sides felt they had an understanding that stopped just short of firm agreement, which would be finalized when the diplomatic caravan moved on to a NATO summit in Bonn a week later. But the Bonn summit, staged mainly to demonstrate NATO's united support for installing the cruise and Pershing missiles, passed over contentious topics such as the pipeline in the interest of unity.[11] No one seems to have realized the consequence of this in time. The deal that everyone thought was in the works—withdrawing pipeline sanctions in return for withdrawing subsidized credits—was never nailed down, so the U.S. felt free to proceed with its own policy. And on June 18, 1982, rather than withdrawing the sanctions on U.S. companies, Reagan extended them to apply to European companies as well.[12]

Up to this point, Thatcher had been sympathetic to the substance of the U.S. position, especially its opposition to subsidized trade credits for the Soviets, while regarding Washington's clumsy handling of the issue as damaging to alliance cohesion. Her diplomatic efforts had thus been directed toward getting a compromise. But the extension of U.S. sanctions to foreign companies both offended her deeply and created political difficulties. She had three grounds of complaint about American claims that U.S. law took precedence over the law of other countries: it was "extra-territorial," it was retrospective, and the resulting sanctions particularly harmed the British firm of John Brown Engineering, which had existing contracts worth $100 million to help build the pipeline. The company would probably go bankrupt if these were cancelled, which would create serious political difficulties for her in the form of higher unemployment in Scotland.[13] She began a passionate battle to get the sanctions decision rescinded.

To Western Europe, he was a trigger-happy cowboy, but to the American electorate and to Eastern Europe he represented "Reagan Country."

No pope had ever enjoyed more charisma with the modern media than Pope John Paul II—or a better understanding of the power of culture.

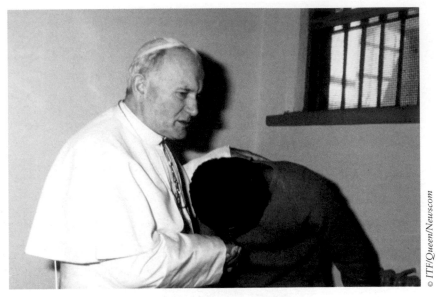

John Paul II forgiving his would-be assassin, Mehmet Ali Agca

Meeting with his fellow survivor Ronald Reagan: the two men most responsible for bringing down the Soviet Union shared a similar moral vision and a contagious optimism.

Courtesy Ronald Reagan Library

THE POPE AS COLD WARRIOR

Meeting with Lech Walesa...

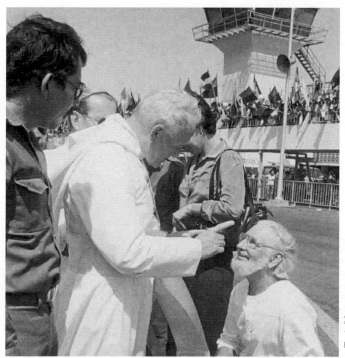

...and admonishing the Sandinista priest Ernesto Cardenal

"He's a good man but Communism is unreformable."

"You say 'trust but verify' every time we meet."
Courtesy Ronald Reagan Library

Though not a Catholic, Ronald Reagan was in many ways a cultural Catholic and found vast common ground with Pope John Paul II.

Reagan benefited from Thatcher's willingness to speak frankly, and she benefited from his admiration for her courage, political principles, and moral convictions.

The special relationship between Great Britain and America was arguably never so special—certainly not since Franklin Roosevelt and Winston Churchill—as it was under Ronald Reagan and Margaret Thatcher.

Courtesy Ronald Reagan Library

This was one of the rare occasions when Thatcher made her opposition to U.S. policy public.[14] "The question is whether one very powerful country can prevent existing contracts being fulfilled," she said in the Commons. "I think it is wrong to do so." Her government passed a new law—the Protection of Trading Interests Act—compelling British companies to ignore the U.S. sanctions and fulfill their original contracts.[15] She became, somewhat incongruously, the main public champion of European interests in the dispute.

Her opposition in private was even stronger. She arrived in Washington only four days after the sanctions decision to try to get it changed. It was a much more contentious occasion than her 1981 state visit, but it still took place in an atmosphere of overall goodwill. Geoffrey Smith describes how, in a White House meeting, she directed harsh criticisms of the policy to everyone except Reagan, who was sitting opposite her.

"Instead, she would employ the device of turning to the secretary of state or the national security adviser," he wrote, "and saying 'Al,' or 'Bill,' or 'Bud—I just don't understand your logic on this matter.'" Reagan could see what she was doing: avoiding a direct quarrel with him and giving him the chance to reconsider without undue pressure. He was amused by it.[16] Almost the central truth of their relationship is that Reagan didn't mind Thatcher's occasional brusque hectoring because he genuinely liked her and found her Boadicea act impressive at some times and entertaining at others.[17] That did not guarantee agreement, however, and on this occasion U.S. policy stayed the same and the row continued.

Reagan telephoned Thatcher again in early July to try to convince her to accept the pipeline sanction on the reasonable grounds that they both wanted pressure on the Soviet and Polish Communists to renew talks with Solidarity. She stuck to her position that existing commercial contracts should be honored. But a new note crept into this conversation on both sides. Thatcher said she hoped that the dispute would not become "a serious irritant in our relations," and Reagan thanked her for the "constructive framework" in which she had placed their differences.[18]

All sides were becoming aware that the row was out of all proportion to any possible gain. Thatcher had earlier proposed a secret meeting of major NATO allies on tougher anti-Soviet measures by Europe in return for the lifting of Washington's pipeline sanctions. Some in Washington, notably Haig's State Department, which had always been skeptical about the sanctions, wanted to mitigate what had become a major row between Europe and America, particularly since a conservative icon, the Iron Lady herself, was leading the other side. But Haig, unpopular with Reagan's close aides and shortly to be replaced, lost the internal battle in the administration. Fortunately for Thatcher, his successor was of the same mind. George Shultz resuscitated the abandoned compromise of Versailles and Thatcher's proposed secret meeting of NATO allies. On November 13, 1982, Reagan duly announced that he was lifting the sanctions in return for a NATO agreement on more restrictive controls on technology transfers and trade credits for the Soviet Union.

A major irritant in transatlantic relations had been removed. A pattern had also been established—Thatcher had joined with sympathetic forces within the Reagan administration to prevail in a struggle that was both diplomatic and inter-departmental. This would recur frequently throughout the Reagan years, and as Geoffrey Smith points out, it greatly increased Thatcher's clout, as it signified the policymakers wanted her on their side. Reagan was also reluctant to oppose her directly.

But there was little immediate cause for celebration by Thatcher or anyone else. The pipeline sanctions had been a secondary issue. The underlying problem was the reluctance of Western European governments, especially those of France and Germany, to risk détente by imposing serious sanctions on the Soviets. In the previous decade Western European governments had convinced themselves that the Communist regimes of Eastern Europe were both legitimate and popular. They were therefore reluctant to regard Solidarity either as a disproof of that legitimacy or as a harbinger of things to come.[19] Nor did they see much point in worsening profitable relations with the permanent government of the great power next door. Reagan and Thatcher disagreed with this analysis and with the policies flowing from it. Reagan's pipeline sanctions proved to be counterproductive—though they dragged the Western Europeans more than a few millimeters in his direction. Thatcher had seen that the French-

German approach was doomed to fail because it asked the Europeans to surrender too much. But if the sole response to the imposition of martial law had been a tightening of trade credits, Moscow would have been reasonably content with the outcome of its Polish gamble. There had to be something more—an alternative means of exercising pressure on the Soviets that did not require the approval of all the European governments.

Such a policy had already been determined and was even then being implemented. It was a Reagan policy supported by Thatcher and the British. But it needed the backing of an organization in Poland.

Ronald Reagan spoke to the pope in June 1982, one week after the meeting John Paul never had with Margaret Thatcher. Among the topics they discussed was an alternative approach to the Polish crisis.

Crusade for a Captive Nation

When President Reagan met Pope John Paul II on June 7, 1982, he was almost the last senior policymaker on Poland in his administration to do so. His CIA chief, William Casey; his special envoy, Ambassador Vernon Walters; and Zbigniew Brzezinski, whom Reagan had held over from Carter as an adviser on Polish policy, all met the pope before he did. Their meetings were rooted in the happy coincidence that both Reagan and John Paul believed that Poland was the key to the unraveling of the Soviet empire.[20]

On arriving in office, Reagan had impressed upon his aides that he wanted to be kept well informed on Polish developments. Richard Allen and Casey had therefore redesigned the president's daily intelligence briefing to include a special Polish update. Reagan acted quickly; Poland and Communism, after all, were topics about which he had already thought long and hard. Less than two weeks after his inauguration, Reagan met with his senior foreign policy advisers to discuss how to undermine Communist power in Poland and discourage Soviet intervention.

As often with Reagan, his methods in this were more cautious than either his rhetoric or his aims, and he did not expect immediate results. He later explained, "We did not envision ourselves as moving into a country and overthrowing that government on behalf of the people. No, this thing

had to be internal people themselves.... We could try to be useful. Solidarity, of course, was the very weapon for bringing this about."[21] Reagan's
other weapons were money, copy machines, help for the underground
press, propaganda advice, broadcasting equipment, and many of the tools
that the National Endowment for Democracy later refined into "democratization." He made it clear to his aides and, equally important, to the
foreign policy and intelligence bureaucracy that Solidarity was to get whatever help it needed to survive a crackdown. Admittedly, he was building
on the initial work of the Carter administration, which had begun to assist
Solidarity prior to the expected Soviet intervention of 1980. But Brzezinski, who had driven this earlier help through a dubious bureaucracy, points
out that Reagan's people did more than simply continue it. Of Casey he
later said, "He continued everything we did and expanded it...and led
it.... And this is why Solidarity wasn't crushed.... This is the first time that
Communist police suppression didn't succeed."[22]

Reagan was keeping hope alive, instead of relying on the ineffectual
governments of Western Europe to punish the Soviets for their imposition
of martial law on Poland. When it was fully developed, Reagan's policy
meant enabling and encouraging the "captive nations" of the Soviet bloc
to maintain moral and political independence outside the formal structures
of official Communist power. Rather than overthrowing the government,
Solidarity would push the limits of free speech and unofficial social cooperation to provide a moral counter-pole of authority. The rudiments of
such a resistance existed in Poland, even if they were temporarily scattered.
If resistance revived, its effect might begin to destabilize the regimes in
Hungary, East Germany, Czechoslovakia, and the rest of the Soviet bloc,
(as, indeed, their governments constantly complained to Moscow). In the
most optimistic scenario, the revival of the Solidarity movement might
even persuade the Western Europeans to reconsider their seemingly iron
commitment to the status quo in Eastern Europe.

Keeping hope alive was a complex business. The administration worked
both through its own intelligence networks and through a number of private and non-governmental bodies. Because Solidarity began as a labor
union, Reagan directed much American help through the AFL-CIO's links

with European labor unions. The AFL-CIO had been helping Solidarity since its birth. Irving Brown, who had helped to establish and support non-Communist labor unions in Europe in the early days of the Cold War, was now director of its international relations department. He and his boss, AFL-CIO president Lane Kirkland, became key advisers to the Reagan administration. Other sources of support were the Polish American community and the much-scorned "captive nations" network in U.S. politics with their ethnic links to home. Jan Nowak of the Polish American Congress was recruited by Richard Pipes, the Polish-born Harvard expert on Soviet Communism then on the National Security Council, to advise the administration on Polish policy. In addition to giving advice, Nowak reinforced Reagan's determination.[23]

Reagan also had a stroke of luck. In the years after martial law was imposed, an international network of Solidarity sympathizers sprang up spontaneously throughout Western Europe to raise funds and send help for Solidarity. They organized almost as a rebuke to the inaction and indifference of their governments.[24] The cause, drawing on the international reputation Walesa and Solidarity had established in 1980 and 1981, was a popular one. The network had additional political significance because it signified that Poland was at least one issue on which Reagan's policy had some European support, ranging from leftist French philosophers through the fledgling network of non-governmental organizations (George Soros's Open Society Institute among them) to conservative English aristocrats.

Robbie Lyle, now director of the Commonwealth Disaster Management Agency in London, was then a young financial executive (and an Anglican). He recalls how one such private aid effort developed:

> In 1982 my sister in Italy, Frances Sanvico, was involved in the charity Parcels to Poland, which had the help of Bishop (now Archbishop) Wesoly, head of the Polish delegation to the Vatican, and of the pope. The Vatican persuaded the Italian government to allow all post to Poland to be free of any postal charge for three months. This meant that an enormous number of goods—children's clothes, shoes, medicines, toys, and certain

foods—could be sent to thousands of addresses supplied by Sol-idarity. My sister persuaded the Red Cross in Italy to open up their warehouses, principally in Perugia, and for three months volunteers wrapped up parcels on a conveyor-belt basis and emptied almost all the Red Cross warehouses.

She next wanted to see the same kind of thing in the UK. There were already private charitable efforts to aid Poland—some of them very remarkable. Lady (Molly) Salisbury, aka the Marchioness of Salisbury, and Lady (Ginny) Beaumont, the wife of the long-serving clerk of the course at Ascot, had trained themselves to drive juggernaughts and obtained HGV licenses to do so. Through a loose tie-up with the great charity worker Baroness (Sue) Ryder, they loaded up the trucks with goods similar to those in Parcels for Poland and drove them to Warsaw, Gdansk, and other Polish cities. There must have been scenes worthy of an Ealing comedy or an Evelyn Waugh novel as these two English ladies at the wheels of huge trucks talked their way past customs officers and security guards with aris-tocratic aplomb. In any event they delivered the goods.

Well, at my sister's urging, a group of us got together in the church hall of Holy Trinity, Brompton, in London. The group was both distinguished and ecumenical: Lady Salisbury; her son Lord (Robert) Cranborne (later a cabinet minister in the Major government, now Lord Salisbury); Lady Beaumont; Lady Ryder; Norman St. John-Stevas, MP (a prominent Catholic and former leader of the House of Commons); the Anglican bishop of London, Graham Leonard; the papal nuncio Bruno Heim; Bishop Wesoly; Woodrow Wyatt (my uncle, a fiery newspaper columnist, a friend of Margaret Thatcher, and later Lord Wyatt of Weeford); the Comtesse de Borgrave, a friend of my sister's from school days; my parents; myself; and a team of parish-ioners from Holy Trinity headed by the vicar John Collins.

A number of initiatives emerged from this meeting. My uncle Woodrow wrote a series of articles about the plight of Poland in the slightly scandalous *News of the World*—which must have astonished its readers. Margaret Thatcher too was intrigued by Woodrow's sudden interest in Poland. "Whenever I meet you at the moment you bring up Poland," she said. But the main event was that the Salisburys held a ball at Hatfield to raise money for our program of aid. Drue Heinz, the great Anglo-American hostess, was a dynamo of activity behind this event. Each ticket cost £1,000—a lot in those days—the prince and princess of Wales came as principal guests, and the great Albert Roux organized the catering. Many people had to be turned away, but in the event the ball in June 1983 raised £250,000. One strong point was that the money went to immediate use for the Poles, a number of very grand people became trustees of the funds, and there was great enthusiasm for the Polish cause.

The pope was very aware of our efforts and gave his blessing to all the hard work. Less than a year later, in February 1984, at the suggestion of Bishop Wesoly, the pope granted a private audience to Molly and Robert Salisbury, Nicky and Ginny Beaumont, my sister, and myself. Each man was given a Holy Year medal by the pope, and the ladies were given rosaries. We were much photographed. The pope then insisted that we return the next morning to receive the Host in his private chapel under the Vatican. He is now buried there. Only my sister was a Catholic in our group, but the secretary general of the Vatican showed us how to receive the Host from the pope on our tongues.

Thus the pope gave five Anglicans communion in his own chapel in the Vatican as an expression of his appreciation of what we and many others had done in bringing aid to Poland. So the Ealing comedy, like the Polish crisis itself, had a happy but devout ending.[25]

It seemed that almost all roads to Poland led either to Rome or through it. There was an obvious overlap between Reagan's policy of keeping hope alive and John Paul's concept of nonviolent cultural resistance. The "captive nations" network was closely allied with the American Catholic church. Labor and intelligence networks worked in Poland with church officials and organizations because Solidarity and church networks often consisted of the same people. The intelligence presented to Reagan daily was drawn from sources including Catholic leaders with special links to Poland and the Polish pope, such as Philadelphia's Cardinal Krol. And Reagan himself had been convinced since watching the pope's 1979 arrival in Poland that John Paul was the catalyst who would accelerate the Soviet collapse. "I have had a feeling," he wrote to a friend, "particularly in the pope's visit to Poland, that religion may turn out to be the Soviets' Achilles' heel."[26]

Reagan himself had been raised Protestant. But he was culturally a Catholic. His father had been a Catholic, and Reagan felt comfortable with the kind of tough patriotic clerics like Krol, often from humble backgrounds like himself, who were still leading the Church in the early 1980s. He was comfortable enough to have an unusually large number of Catholic advisers in foreign policy positions, including Casey, Allen, Haig, Brzezinski, Walters, and Judge William Clark, who succeeded Allen as national security adviser midway through the approach to the Vatican. Jeane Kirkpatrick has rightly pointed out that their Catholicism hardly explains the Reagan administration's decision to work closely with the pope, as the same policy was supported by non-Catholics in high positions such as herself, Cap Weinberger, George Shultz, and of course Reagan. But it is probably fair to say that the policy was easier to implement because Catholics like Walters, Casey, Allen, and Clark, both sophisticated and devout, had cultivated their contacts with Krol and Pio Laghi, the pope's representative in Washington, and so enjoyed the confidence of the Vatican almost from the start.

They wanted to arrange a meeting between the pope and their boss. But it had to be a serious discussion of how to cooperate in fighting political evil rather than a merely ceremonial occasion. That meant it had to be set up in advance by emissaries with enough authority to speak for the presi-

dent on highly sensitive issues. Over the next eighteen months, CIA director William Casey and special envoy Ambassador Vernon Walters visited
the Vatican to see the pope on a number of occasions. (Walters estimated
that he saw the pope about twice a year for seven years.) They were definitely the odd couple—Walters fluent in seven languages, Casey mumbling
inaudibly in one—but they were ideally suited for their task. They were
patriotic Americans, serious Catholics, Reagan loyalists, shrewd naviga-
tors of the diplomatic and intelligence bureaucracies, and highly discreet
in very different ways, Casey hiding secrets behind his mumbles, Walters
behind a curtain of entertaining anecdotes. Casey and Walters prepared the
ground for Reagan with both skill and sincerity. They fully believed in
what they told the pope. There was no hint of diplomatic dissimulation in
their presentations; both would have shrunk from lying to the temporal
head of their own Church. And they had no sense of difficulty in serving
two masters because they were serving the one cause of religious and political liberty.[27]

Casey visited the Vatican and was granted an audience with the pope
on April 23, 1981. It was a largely exploratory visit. Casey knew that the
Soviets were also seeing the pope and wanted to know what they were saying.[28] He also had an intelligence secret to pass on to John Paul: one of
Lech Walesa's hosts on his recent Italian trip was a Bulgarian secret agent.
Casey asked the pope to warn Walesa about the Bulgarians. But the CIA
director also had larger purposes in mind. He and Reagan wanted the pope
to know that U.S. grand strategy around the world was now in harmony
with Catholic interests and Vatican policy. Reagan was committed to supporting Solidarity in Poland and to resisting Soviet subversion in Central
America, where it wore the camouflage fatigues of liberation theology.
Above all, the president did not rule out the eventual liberation of Poland
and the Soviet bloc by peaceful means. Casey received a papal blessing and
an invitation to call again whenever he wished.[29]

Walters arrived in the Vatican at a more crucial moment: November 30,
1981, just two weeks before martial law was imposed in Poland. The Soviets were already staging their usual preliminary maneuvers. Both pope and

diplomat were acutely aware of the looming threat. Walters, in addition to underlining the larger strategic arguments previously made by Casey, showed the pope photographs taken by U.S. intelligence satellites. They showed the transport and deployment of Warsaw Pact troops on the Polish borders as well as Polish troops maneuvering inside the country. The pope asked a series of practical questions about them and what they meant. Walters, shrewdly but also accurately, was not alarmist. He predicted that, despite these maneuvers, the Soviets would not invade: they were already overstretched, the Poles would fight, and an invasion would produce a bloodbath. But since a domestic crackdown was possible, as both men acknowledged, Walters gave the pope a general overview of how the United States intended to help Solidarity keep going, even if only as an underground organization. The pope said that even if the Communists cracked down, the Polish Church would not capitulate. He would not be forced back to asking permission from the Communist authorities to carry out the Church's pastoral and evangelical missions.

That exchange was the crux of the meeting. On future occasions Walters would show the pope more satellite photos and give him more intelligence briefings. On this one, he proceeded to give the pope a grand tour of Cold War flashpoints around the world—with special emphasis on Nicaragua and El Salvador—with a guide to U.S. policy in each case. The net effect was to show the Roman pontiff that the U.S. was seeking to fend off worldwide Soviet adventurism, not to pursue selfish American interests. There were some important points on which the pope remained skeptical and even opposed to U.S. foreign policy. For the moment, he was inclined to suspect that Reagan was a conventional supporter of the nuclear "balance of terror" while he was moving toward a position that might be described as "nuclear pacifism."[30] Between them, however, Casey and Walters persuaded the pope that Reagan was undoubtedly a man of goodwill and of deep Christian faith.

Not only did the pope bless Walters, but he also blessed some rosaries for Walters to bring home to Catholic friends. The U.S. diplomat ended his side of the conversation with, "Our Church has a sure and steady guide, Holy Father."[31]

Meeting of the Minds

When Reagan himself finally reached the Vatican in June 1982 for his historic meeting with the pope, he promptly fell asleep from jet lag in front of the television cameras. This enabled the media to recycle some old Reagan jokes, but it didn't really matter. Reagan had by now turned his alleged doziness and slack work habits into self-deprecatory speech material—"They say hard work never killed anyone, but I figure: why take a chance?"—so that such episodes had lost their power to harm him. In fact, the president was a diligent reader of his briefing books.[32] On this occasion, Al Haig had prepared a brief sketch of the pope's overall view of the East-West conflict and a comprehensive list of topics on which the Vatican and the U.S. might cooperate, including Poland, Central America, arms control, and the Middle East.

Brief though it was, the sketch of the pope's essential attitudes was very accurate. It showed him as an admirer of the fundamental generosity of the American people, distrustful of Soviet intentions, supportive of firmness in dealing with them, but also somewhat critical of America's wastefulness and materialism. Sections of the document dealing with Poland and Central America, classified then as "Secret," are still heavily redacted today, presumably to conceal the details of U.S. help to Solidarity and the Contras. But the declassified portions establish that there was very close agreement between the pope and Reagan on Poland; indeed, the only disagreement concerned economic sanctions, about which, for humanitarian reasons and under pressure from Cardinal Glemp, the Vatican was "dubious." The Vatican and the United States were also moving toward each other on Central America, where the U.S., reacting to attacks on bishops and missionaries from right-wing death squads in El Salvador, now proposed to work with the Church to "strengthen [the] center, encourage democracy, social justice, end violence."[33]

The document is most fascinating concerning nuclear weapons. It notes that the pope had twice written to Reagan and Brezhnev urging progress in the Geneva arms talks toward the eventual goal of eliminating all nuclear weapons. As we know from later events, notably the Reykjavik summit, this was a goal very dear to Reagan's heart. It was not U.S. policy, however, and given the U.S. military buildup then under way, it seemed to be very far from it. Reflecting the official view, Haig suggested stressing the U.S. proposals to reduce ballistic missile warheads by one-third—and also to reduce the number of missiles themselves—in the START/INF talks. Those proposals were a serious step forward, but they understated the radicalism of Reagan's private views and their closeness to John Paul's opinion.

How much of this did Reagan tell the pope when, after the public session in front of the cameras, the two men had a private fifty-minute meeting, without even interpreters present? It is almost certain that both men were entirely candid. Each saw the other as a natural ally, and this could have been their only opportunity to compare notes in person. We also know that the pope later told cardinals Casaroli and Silvestrini that Reagan had given him private assurances that he was a disarmer who wanted nuclear weapons abolished rather than simply reduced.[34] John Paul might not agree with the president that demonstrating to the Soviets that they were certain to lose any nuclear, military, or even economic competition was a stop on the road to disarmament. But that was a practical judgment that, according to Catholic teaching, is the responsibility of the proper secular authorities. What was important—and it turned out to be very important—was that Reagan had convinced the pope that he was sincerely committed to peace and disarmament and that these commitments would shape his policy.

That removed any general obstacle to the pope sympathizing with and even cooperating with other U.S. policies when they seemed consonant with Catholic values and Vatican interests. In practice that meant two things: First, the pope could condemn liberation theology in Nicaragua and El Salvador without worrying that in doing so he would be aiding the U.S. in sustaining an unjust social order there. Second, he would raise no objection to the United States (in particular through the CIA) and its allies using Church networks to help Solidarity stay alive. Both he and Reagan agreed that Poland was the key to unraveling the unjust division of Europe. Reagan recalled later, "We both felt a great mistake had been made at Yalta and something should be done. Solidarity was the very weapon for bringing this about."[35]

In contributing practically to this end, the United States was obviously more helpful to the Vatican than vice versa. The pope had directed money to Solidarity from his own papal funds to finance underground publications and broadcasts, but he could hardly match the estimated $50 million the CIA spent on helping Solidarity from 1981 to 1988. Solidarity was kept alive for seven long years in this way until, against extraordinarily high odds, it won the first free elections in Poland's postwar history and became its first free postwar government amid the general collapse of the Soviet bloc.

But had this remarkable historical reversal been achieved by a corrupt "conspiracy" between pope and president? Had there been a vulgar "deal" in which the pope had promised his silence on the installation of U.S. missiles in Europe or U.S. policy in Central America in return for Reagan's support in liberating Poland? Had John Paul traded his spiritual authority for a mess of political pottage? Or were such claims—in words that Weigel aims at Carl Bernstein and Marco Politi, who advanced these arguments in their papal biography, *His Holiness*—a "journalistic fantasy"?[36]

Reagan and John Paul certainly cooperated to help free Poland and Eastern Europe from Communism. But there is an explanation for this cooperation that is far more plausible than a "conspiracy" or "deal": both Reagan and John Paul were firmly anti-Communist, and they saw the Polish and European situations in much the same way. There was a coincidence not merely of interests between the Vatican and the United States, but also of visions between the pope and the president. Weigel spells this out in clear terms:

> The pope and the president held certain common convictions. They both believed that Communism was a moral evil, not simply wrong-headed economics. They were both confident of the capacity of free people to meet the Communist challenge. Both were convinced that, in the contest with Communism, victory, not mere accommodation, was possible. Both had a sense of the drama of late twentieth-century history, and both were confident that the spoken word of truth could cut through the

static of Communism's lies and rouse people from their acquiescence to servitude.

The pope's support for Reagan's policies on Poland, Central America, and arms control were fully congruent with Vatican policy.[37] The pope did not compromise himself at all; in fact he publicly differed with Reagan on economic questions such as foreign aid. Moreover, the financial aid that Reagan directed to Solidarity provided no economic benefit to the pope, who was contributing his own widow's mite to the same cause. Finally, as Weigel points out, the pope's greatest contribution to ending Communism was his first visit to Poland, which occurred almost two years before Reagan entered the White House. His subsequent policies toward Poland and the Soviet Union were a straight-line development of this approach (until 1988, when he softened considerably in response to Gorbachev's *perestroika* and *glasnost*.) So the allegations of a corrupt deal between prelate and politician must be discarded.

Perhaps the fairest judgment came from John Paul himself. In 1992, when *Time* magazine published an article by Carl Bernstein that contained the seeds of the "holy alliance" thesis, a reporter raised it with the pope. It was, he replied, an "*a posteriori* deduction." He went on, "One cannot construct a case from the consequences. Everybody knows the position of President Reagan as a great policy leader in world politics. My position was that of a pastor, the bishop of Rome, of one with responsibility for the Gospel, which certainly contains principles of the moral and social order and those regarding human rights.... The Holy See's position, even in regard to my homeland, was guided by moral principle."[38]

He must have been tempted to add that Poland was one of the few recorded cases in human history in which faith really did move mountains.

A New Front in the Cold War

Reagan went directly from Rome to address the British parliament at Westminster. It was a splendid event, rich in ceremony and set against the ornate background of the Royal Gallery, but also a controversial one. Some Labour members of Parliament had refused to attend in protest of

Reagan's foreign policy. But all who were present, including those who disliked what the president said, were deeply impressed by the fact that he delivered a long and eloquent speech without referring to a single note.

"I congratulate you on your actor's memory," said Thatcher immediately afterward.

Reagan laughed and replied, "I read the whole speech from those two Perspex screens." He gestured toward two apparently transparent lecterns that his audience had assumed to be some new security device. "Don't you know it?" he asked, enjoying himself. "It's a British invention."[39]

Reagan's Westminster speech is now remembered for much more than the Autocue, but it made only a modest impact at the time. Because it was delivered as British troops were closing in on Port Stanley, his audience was listening mainly for an endorsement of the British stand. He delivered a very generous one, saying of the troops, "Those young men aren't fighting for mere real estate. They fight for a cause, for the belief that armed aggression must not be allowed to succeed and that people must participate in the decisions of government under the rule of law." The assembled parliamentarians applauded loudly. But the rest of the speech left them either cold or puzzled.[40]

The Westminster address was a confident prediction that the march of freedom throughout the world would "leave Marxism-Leninism on the ash-heap of history as it has left other tyrannies which stifle the freedom and muzzle the self-expression of the people." It forecast that because Communism brought economic misery as well as denying human freedom, it would shortly run into the kind of systemic crisis that Marx had forecast for capitalism. Reagan built on these observations a series of proposals for public and private foundations that would help people in other countries move toward liberal, democratic systems of their own. These ideas eventually produced the National Endowment for Democracy and the partisan Republican and Democratic institutes that assist it. They have since helped to midwife democratic revolutions around the world, most famously the Orange and Rose revolutions in Ukraine and Georgia. It was therefore both a prophetic speech and an important statement of policy.

At the time, however, the British parliamentarians were not the only ones left puzzled, skeptical, or alarmed. Most American commentators were critical of the speech. It struck them as naïve and pointlessly hostile toward the Soviets. After all, the Soviets were a permanent part of the international landscape. "The Russians are not likely to participate in their own suicide," said Tom Brokaw. So why rile them up by denying their system any claim to political legitimacy?[41]

Nine months later, much harsher criticism greeted a Reagan speech containing anti-Soviet passages omitted from the Westminster address. Addressing the National Association of Evangelicals in Orlando, Florida, the president called the Soviets both an "evil empire" and "the focus of evil in the modern world." He got a standing ovation and a round of "Onward Christian Soldiers" in the hall, but commentators were again less kind. "Primitive," sniffed Anthony Lewis in the *New York Times*. Tom Wicker of the same address attributed a "holy war mentality" to the president. And Henry Steele Commager, a distinguished presidential scholar, described it simply as "the worst presidential speech in American history."[42]

Most of these criticisms were based on the assumption that Reagan was merely shooting off his mouth again. Such philippics had no relevance to U.S. policy, Reagan's detractors thought, because they *could* have no relevance to U.S. policy. Unless the U.S. was about to declare war on the USSR—and was in reality negotiating over arms control in Geneva— attacks on the legitimacy and mere existence of the Soviet Union were wild rhetorical excesses. And if the Soviets were foolish enough to take them seriously, they might be dangerous as well.

The Soviets did take them seriously, as we shall see. So did anti-Soviet dissidents in the Gulag, who were immensely encouraged by the sound of reality breaking into Western diplomacy.[43] Both were right to do so, as Reagan's rhetoric had a serious purpose. William Clark and an NSC staffer, John Lenczowski, had sent the president a one-page memo that stated, in part, "As the Soviets see it, to tell the truth about the USSR is to risk igniting their internal security threat—the threat of mass popular resistance to the ideology, as in Poland." This was not an entirely new insight. Scholars such as Richard Pipes and Robert Conquest and exiled dissidents such as Alexander Solzhenitsyn and Vladimir Bukovsky had been advancing similar arguments for many years. Influenced by their work, Reagan had said as much in his early radio broadcasts. But it was a minority view among Sovietologists and had not significantly influenced official U.S. policy since the 1950s. As president, Reagan adopted the Clark-Lenczowski thesis. He began to use his public speeches to tell the truth about the Soviets, putting them on the defensive ideologically.

One critic of Reagan's Westminster speech had seen what he was attempting to do. Peter Jay—British ambassador to the United States in Carter's day, the former son-in-law of Jim Callaghan, and an influential economic commentator—said of Reagan, "He seemed almost to be declaring non-military war on the Soviet Union."[44] If that was an exaggeration, it was a slight and pardonable one. Reagan saw ideas, principles, and ideology as equal fronts in the Cold War alongside the tangible economic, military, and territorial fronts. Until now, the Soviets had mounted regular attacks aimed at Western morality—assailing the West for racism, militarism, exploitation, neo-colonialism, etc., etc.—but the West had not retaliated. From now on, Reagan would call a spade a spade and the USSR an evil empire.

This ideological robustness fitted into the larger strategic pattern in Reagan's mind. Just before he left for Rome, the president had signed National Security Decision Directive (NSDD) 32, which, among much else, called for aid to Solidarity, counter-propaganda in Poland, tightening of sanctions on the Soviet Union, and a range of covert activities to achieve these objectives. Reagan sent out 328 such "Top Secret" directives to the diplomatic, military, and intelligence agencies during his presidency.[45] As Richard Reeves points out, they turned his speeches into very practical and detailed instructions on strategy and tactics. They were Reaganism in foreign policy. Three directives in particular, issued between May 1982 and January 1983, give a broad overview of what he hoped to achieve.[46]

NSDD 32 was a comprehensive blueprint for winning the Cold War, covering everything from deterrence policy to encouraging liberalization in Eastern Europe. NSDD 66 laid down U.S. responsibilities under an agreement among the major NATO allies concerning the use of financial levers, trade credits, and controls on technology transfer to weaken the Soviet Union. Ironically enough, these goals would be accomplished after the pipeline sanctions controversy. NSDD 75, drawn up by Richard Pipes, offered a set of policies for changing the Soviet Union itself, primarily to halt its external expansion, but also to encourage domestic changes toward a "more pluralistic" political and economic system.

All three documents, though their main thrust was to obstruct and penalize aggressive Soviet behavior, also offered incentives and rewards for more peaceful and/or democratic actions by them. NSDD 32 included a provision for pursuing equitable and verifiable arms control agreements, and NSDD 75 advocated cultural exchanges and (under the right conditions) a superpower summit. Though the NSDDs were statements of U.S. policy, they incorporated the results of intensive alliance diplomacy and were to that extent multilateral. Since clarity of expression is usually a sign of clarity of thought, it is also worth noting that they were well written, readable, and contained only the absolute minimum of jargon.

And, above all, they seemed to be producing results.

As 1983 began Reagan had reason to believe that progress was being made on all fronts in the Cold War. His "megaphone diplomacy" of ideological speeches, though it alarmed the Western Europeans, was badly rattling the Soviet leaders.[47] Cap Weinberger's military buildup was galloping ahead, posing enormous problems for Soviet military and budgetary planners. Fueled by Reagan's 1981 tax cuts and stabilized by Fed chairman Paul Volcker's victory over inflation, the U.S. economy—on which almost all else depended—was recovering at astonishing speed from the 1981–82 recession.[48] Poland, though superficially quiescent, was developing an underground movement of resistance to Soviet rule, and awareness of this was percolating through Eastern Europe. Outside Europe, particularly in Central America and Afghanistan, the U.S. was embarking with some success on what became known as the Reagan Doctrine: the policy of supporting local guerrillas against Soviet-assisted or Soviet-imposed dictatorial regimes and making the Soviets pay a higher price for the adventurism of the Brezhnev years.[49]

But policy toward Poland differed from the Reagan Doctrine in vital respects. Reagan had a firm concept of what to do about Poland even before he entered office: he was building on Carter's policy, and his approach was supported by almost the entire U.S. establishment. Once he had laid down the main lines of his policy and the means to implement them, especially after he had established a common outlook with the pope, he let the pressures he had instituted take their toll on the Communist regime. Thatcher helped by keeping constant political pressure on the Polish government to lift martial law, release Walesa, and negotiate with Solidarity. The pope completed the process both by restoring the spirit of Poles temporarily crushed by martial law and by uniting overly prudent Church leaders with Solidarity radicals in a common front on terms closer to Solidarity's approach.

John Paul's pilgrimage to Poland in June 1983, which the regime permitted to demonstrate that normalization was working, had exactly the opposite effect. On his arrival the pope's grim demeanor and condemnation of the "humiliation" and "suffering" of martial law showed Poles that he shared their agonies. "He is sad. You see, he understands," a Polish woman told a reporter.[50] In the days that followed, however, he began to change the national atmosphere. His sermons argued that telling the truth was the first step to liberation. This was a moral rather than a political point, but it undermined the regime's official myths that Communist power was permanent and that there would be no return to pre–martial law days. The pope insisted, over official objections, on meeting Lech Walesa. He told Jaruzelski that any "renewal" (the regime's word) of Polish society had to begin with his acceptance of the Gdansk accords on human rights. He repeatedly used what Weigel calls the "unsayable" word—solidarity— in sermons. He engaged in public dialogues with large crowds, in which he urged them with fruitful ambiguity to "persevere in hope."

Not all churchmen liked this dissidence in clerical garb. Cardinal Casaroli, the practitioner of *realpolitik*, exclaimed, "Does he want bloodshed? Does he want war? Does he want to overthrow the government? Every day I have to explain to the authorities that there is nothing to this!"[51] But there *was* something to it. By the time the pilgrimage was over, the pope had cracked the regime's façade of unshakable power. He had aligned the Church with Solidarity, dispelling the regime's hope of a separate peace with religion. He had restored the people's hope and trust in each other that his election had originally stimulated. In short, he had created the social conditions for underground Solidarity to survive and challenge the regime. Reagan's practical assistance now had deep popular roots in Polish society.

Stumbling toward Freedom in Central America

Reagan's help for anti-Communist guerrillas in the Third World enjoyed none of the advantages of his policy toward Poland. With the important exception of Afghanistan, the Reagan Doctrine was not based on an existing Carter policy; indeed, it more or less reversed Carter's policy.[52] It was highly controversial within the U.S. establishment; Democrats periodically tried to thwart it throughout the 1980s. And Reagan himself had not developed either a clear set of policies or a real commitment to them before taking office. Though some Reagan biographers see aid to the Contras as his personal obsession, for instance, this policy really began as a messy bureaucratic compromise invented on the hoof to deal with a Central American crisis that developed late in the day. It became a full-fledged doctrine only when it produced unexpectedly favorable results.

In 1981 the new administration had to deal with two Central American problems in one: the Communists in El Salvador were waging a fierce insurgency, and the Sandinista government in Nicaragua was supplying them with weapons. Earlier assurances from the Sandinistas of democracy and neutrality had proved false. Half of the problem was handled by sending a package of military aid to the friendly government of El Salvador. But Nicaragua was proving to be a second Cuba, refusing to end its assistance to the guerrillas next door. Having just been elected to halt Soviet adventurism, the Reagan administration could hardly allow this second Cuba to establish a third Cuba in El Salvador.

Haig thought that the correct response would be to "go to the source" and blockade the first Cuba. There was some justification for this bold move. As Soviet documents have since confirmed, Cuba was the first and main Caribbean staging point for Soviet arms and supplies from Vietnam that traveled via Nicaragua to El Salvador.[53] But Reagan and the rest of his administration wanted neither the major military commitment in the Caribbean that such a policy would entail nor the political storm it would provoke. Something had to be done—but not too much. As Peter Rodman observes, "The United States seems to have turned to covert action because other options were unavailable or too extreme."[54]

In November 1981, therefore, William Casey negotiated a plan with the Argentine military to train two small forces—1,500 men in all—that would harass Cuban and Sandinista military targets in Nicaragua and cut the flow of weapons to the El Salvador rebels. It was presented to a high-level meeting of the National Security Planning Group on November 16, 1981. At that stage no one regarded these forces, called Contras, as a means of overthrowing the Sandinistas; they were seen rather as a means of pressuring them toward better behavior. Reagan was especially dubious about the plan. He doubted the Contras would succeed even in exerting pressure on the Sandinistas, and he was, according to one participant, "profoundly averse to violence."[55] He refused to approve the plan.

After modifications—to minimize civilian casualties, among other things—the plan was presented again to Reagan a week later. With some reluctance he approved it as NSDD 17. Before agreeing to put it into effect, however, the president sent Haig on a secret mission to meet Castro's vice president, Carlos Rafael Rodriguez, in Mexico City. He hoped to reach some kind of deal that would make the Contra plan unnecessary. This is reminiscent of Reagan's private letter to Brezhnev in which he appealed for a peaceful Russo-American accommodation before launching his policies of military and economic competition with the Soviets. He always wanted to give the other fella one last shot. But Haig's mission to Mexico failed. His explanation, which is probably correct, was that the Cubans and Nicaraguans regarded the U.S. posture as one of weakness. They were winning the battle and doubted the Reagan administration could take the political heat of a military response. So why cut a deal? Reagan responded as he had to Brezhnev's rebuff. He had done his best to be reasonable.

Now he would have to try a harder approach. He set the Contra plan in motion with covert aid of $19 million for 1982 and 1983 in congressionally authorized funds and a further $10 million for 1983 in discretionary CIA funds. The U.S.-sponsored Contra war had begun.

Its progress over the next few years was an extraordinary exercise in survival politics. For once it was the Republicans, not the Democrats, who had reason to be grateful that a government program, once started, is all but impossible to kill. Democrats in Congress regularly sought to halt the Contra program's funding. When they failed, they restricted the purposes for which the money could be spent—for instance, it could not be used to overthrow the Sandinistas (though that is what the Contras thought they were doing). A left-wing populist movement reminiscent of the Vietnam era sprang up around America. Holding teach-ins and rallies, the protesters railed against both the Contra war and aid to El Salvador. Reagan himself, who had bigger fish to fry with his economic programs and arms control talks, made no major public pronouncements on the Contras until two years into the program, thereby allowing skeptical Democrats and leftists to set public opinion on the issue. But whenever Americans looked like they were swinging around to support Reagan's policy, the administration would commit some pointless gaffe—such as mining Nicaragua's harbors in apparent contradiction of international law—that would reverse the tide of public opinion.[56]

Despite all these drawbacks, U.S. support for the Contras and military aid to El Salvador both survived. One reason is that the two aid packages were seen (rightly, as it happens) as two sides of the same coin. Funding for the Contras thus benefited from the administration's moderation in its El Salvador policy—its push for action against the rightist "death squads," its support for centrist parties (eventually successful in 1984 with the election of a Christian Democrat president), and its backing of land reform. More important was that the Sandinistas were quite as adept as the administration at earning bad headlines. Whenever the Contra aid program seemed likely to be defeated in Congress, the Sandinistas would flaunt their Marxist credentials or Soviet links in some dramatic way.[57] On one occasion Daniel Ortega, the Sandinista leader, visited Moscow; innumerable times he and his colleagues made fiery speeches proclaiming their "revolutionary internationalism." Such provocations would push reluctant Democrats back into Reagan's camp, and Contra funding would leap over another congressional hurdle. Finally, the Sandinistas repeatedly rebuffed attempts to reach some kind of accommodation by the Americas desk at the State Department, strongly supported by George Shultz when he succeeded Haig. This revealed the intransigent nature of the Sandinistas' "revolutionary internationalism" and strengthened the administration's case for a military response.

Reagan had familiar friends and unfamiliar enemies in this struggle. As in the Polish crisis, the American labor movement under the anti-Communist leadership of AFL-CIO leader Kirkland gave his El Salvador policy strong support. Its pressure for land reform in particular was very influential. But the U.S. Catholic church, which was acting as a virtual conduit for aid to Poland, opposed Reagan on Central America. Rightist death squads had murdered four Maryknoll missionaries and the archbishop of San Salvador in 1981. These crimes took place just as Central America was bursting into America's political consciousness. Within El Salvador and Nicaragua, the Catholic Church was aware that such atrocities were committed by both sides. It supported centrist parties and moderate policies against both right-wing and Sandinista repression. But the U.S. church allowed itself to be influenced more by the Maryknolls—themselves heavily influenced by liberation theology and a romantic view of Marxist guerrillas—than by the more balanced local Catholic bishops. Hence American Catholic bishops and priests became fixtures at the Left's Central American rallies. The sins of the Salvadoran military were excoriated; those of the Sandinistas glossed over as responses to U.S. policy.

The opposition of the Catholic bishops on Central America was a potentially serious problem for Reagan. He had won in 1980 with the support of the "Reagan Democrats" who were mostly socially conservative Catholics. They were more likely than liberal Catholics to listen seriously to their bishops on political issues. Catholic clergymen and intellectuals, moreover, were drifting leftward on issues ranging from nuclear weapons to economic policy. If the bishops persuaded their congregations to oppose the administration on aid to the Contras, it could set a precedent for both stronger and wider Catholic opposition to Reagan's policies in general. That was undoubtedly what some bishops hoped. And the image of four Maryknoll missionaries being gunned down by rightist Latin thugs in El Salvador was a powerful stimulus to opposing aid to those who could be plausibly described as rightist Latin thugs in Nicaragua.

Nothing less than a direct attack by the Sandinistas on the pope, it seemed, could push American Catholics into supporting Contra aid. And on March 4, 1983, the Sandinistas directly attacked the pope.

John Paul had earlier had severe doubts about his planned visit to Managua. The Nicaraguan bishops, the papal nuncio in Managua, and his Vatican advisers all feared that the Sandinistas would try to disrupt the visit. Several priests serving as Sandinista ministers had ignored the Vatican's plea that they remove themselves from politics. The regime had established a "People's Church" under its own control and was using it to harass and, if possible, replace the "institutional church." Miguel Obando, the archbishop of Managua and originally a supporter of the Sandinistas in their struggle to oust Somoza, had turned against the regime as it established its monopoly of power. The regime wanted, in effect, to exclude Obando from any public meetings with the pope. But intensive negotiations between the nuncio and the regime seemed to have arrived at a modus vivendi by the time John Paul descended the steps of the airplane at Managua airport.

Among the dignitaries lined up to greet him was a challenge. Ernesto Cardenal, the Sandinistas' culture minister, was a priest who had defied church instructions to leave political office. The nuncio said he was sure the regime had planned for the pope's refusing to meet him.

"No, I want to greet him," John Paul said. "I have something to tell him."

When he reached Cardenal, the pope wagged his finger at the priest-minister and said (in what Weigel describes as "a warm and friendly voice"), "Regularize your position with the Church. Regularize your position with the Church." The Sandinistas put around an even friendlier version of the exchange afterward. But the press photograph that went around the world seemed to show the pope firmly rebuking the Sandinista.[58]

Worse was to follow. At the papal Mass in a Managua park, the regime packed its own supporters into seats reserved for Catholic organizations whose members were then pushed to the rear under police supervision. Sandinista leaders, including Ortega, occupied prominent positions on a platform near the papal altar, from where, throughout the Mass, they shouted "People's Power" and gave the clenched-fist salute. The public address system broke down when John Paul was criticizing the People's Church, and a supplementary "emergency" system broadcasting the slogans of the Sandinistas took over. The pope shouted "Silencio!" at one point and when the supplementary address system began broadcasting the Sandinista anthem, he strode to the front of the stage and waved his crozier back and forth above his head.

These astonishing and (to most Latin Americans) shocking scenes were broadcast on television throughout Central America and recycled in news broadcasts in the United States. Their crude manipulation of the pope's visit was a vast miscalculation by the Sandinistas. It was an act of self-demystification, revealing them as oppressive thugs rather than heroic rebels. Among its effects was the collapse of any actual support for the Sandinistas among most American Catholics—and a corresponding fall in opposition to Contra aid. The U.S. bishops conference and the Catholic Left remained hostile to that and other Reagan policies. But the Reagan Democrats stayed faithful.

One year later two codicils were attached to these events. The Vatican told the three Sandinista priests that they had exhausted all appeals against their superiors' order to leave the government and must now do so. They refused.

Then the first of two major statements on liberation theology was issued by Cardinal Ratzinger's office—the Congregation for the Doctrine of the Faith (CDF)—with John Paul's personal approval. It reiterated the essential messages of the pope's sermon at Puebla in 1979: that sin was mainly located not in political and economic structures but in the human heart, that good and evil were not political categories, that the "poor in spirit" were not the Marxist proletariat, and that Christ's death on the Cross "could not be given an exclusively political interpretation." (All of these rejected doctrines were, of course, the founding doctrines of the Sandinistas' People's Church.)

Almost two years later Ratzinger's CDF followed this up with a positive statement on a theology of Christian liberation. This was principally concerned, like the first, with establishing the primacy of religious over political doctrines. It defined liberation as freedom from sin, alienation as rejection of God's love, and a preferential love for the poor as excluding no one. But it also pointed to the political implications of an authentic Christian liberation: notably that all Christians had a duty of "solidarity" to work for the freedom of others in nonviolent ways, and that development in poor countries required open, liberal, and democratic structures.[59]

When the pope left Managua for seven other Central American countries in early March 1983, it was already clear that Sandinista rule did not conform to Catholic principles, as Cardinal Ratzinger's later two statements made explicit. U.S. policy toward El Salvador, on the other hand, was arguably an attempt to realize those principles, if in modified form. The goal was certainly to achieve an open, liberal, democratic Latin America, and the 7,000-strong Contra army encamped on Nicaragua's border was working for the freedom of others under Sandinista rule—though hardly by nonviolent means. Reagan himself had been queasy about this very point. But would nonviolent means have achieved anything?

In the future the Contras would cause Reagan almost as much political trouble as they were causing the Sandinistas. In 1983, however, they fit into an encouraging world picture. As seen from the White House, the Sandinistas were now challenged in Nicaragua, the Soviets were bogged down by an increasingly effective insurgency in Afghanistan, and the Poles were quietly resisting the martial law imposed on Soviet instructions. Almost the only part of the world that was not responding favorably to the Reagan policies of military and economic competition with the Soviets was Western Europe (cheered on by what were not yet known as the "blue states" in the United States.)

Sitting in the Kremlin, Yuri Andropov, who had succeeded Brezhnev as Soviet leader in 1982, was reaching exactly the same conclusion.

Western Europe, in 1983 as in 1947, was the new front line in the Cold War.

CHAPTER SEVEN

IMPERIAL OVERSTRETCH

~⚥~

S ix months after becoming general secretary of the CPSU, Yuri
Andropov received a highly confidential letter from his successor
as KGB chief, Viktor Chebrikov. It was classified "Top Secret—Of
Special Importance," and reported an approach to the Soviets made
through the good offices of former senator John Tunney of California. The
senior American politician making the approach was Senator Edward
Kennedy. He was requesting a personal interview with Andropov because
"in the interest of world peace it would be useful and timely to take a few
extra steps to counteract the militaristic policies of Ronald Reagan." (Chebrikov is summarizing Kennedy here rather than quoting him directly.)

According to Chebrikov, Kennedy thought that a meeting with
Andropov "would equip him with the Soviet positions on arms control
and add conviction to his own appearances on the subject in the U.S." The
senator also proposed to organize U.S. television interviews for Andropov
and other high Soviet officials who "would have the chance to address
directly the American people with their own explanation of peaceful Soviet

initiatives."[1] He claimed that his aim in all this was world peace, but the Soviets believed he had less creditable motives: namely, the hope that a meeting with Andropov would help his efforts to become president of the United States in 1988.

For whatever reason, Andropov turned Kennedy's application down flat. A signed note to Gromyko and Dmitri Ustinov, the defense minister, argued woundingly, "If the time comes to talk to the Democrats, then it would be better to meet one of the presidential candidates, the more so since Kennedy has recently reduced his political profile."

Wisely, Kennedy seems to have remained silent on this little social history. "Friends of Kennedy" told the London *Sunday Times* that he was then pressing for human rights and would have met dissidents if he had gone to Moscow. His go-between, former senator Tunney, went further, dismissing Chebrikov's letter as "someone trying to sound bigger than they were. It was in their self-interest to be seen with me and with Kennedy."

Former senators are important people, of course, but Tunney's explanation is nonsense on stilts. Chebrikov was the chairman of the KGB and, as such, the second most powerful man in the Soviet Union. He had no reason to inflate his importance in dealing with Andropov, who was one of his closest associates, and every reason to express himself as candidly as Andropov had done in writing to Gromyko and Ustinov. Furthermore, Kennedy made several subsequent attempts to advise the Soviets on the best way to outwit Reagan.

The only mystery is why Andropov turned down Kennedy's offer. The answer seems to be that, when it came to left-wing Western politicians hoping to assist the Kremlin's foreign policy, the Soviets were suffering from an embarrassment of riches.

An Empire Crumbles

And to be fair, they needed all the help they could get. By 1983, the illusions of the Brezhnev era—and their all too real costs—were coming home to plague the Soviet leadership.[2] Indeed, Brezhnev's death in 1982 looks in retrospect like an extremely shrewd political decision. His policies of avoiding serious reform at home while expanding the empire abroad had been possible only because the oil shocks of the 1970s had given the energy-producing USSR a vast windfall profit. Once energy prices fell in the 1980s (in part because Reagan and Thatcher decontrolled oil and gas prices), the underlying weaknesses of the Soviet economy were revealed, along with its incapacity to maintain an extended imperial role. Gorbachev later claimed that the USSR's growth rate had been stagnant for more than twenty years once official figures were corrected both for the oil price increase and "Brezhnev's artificial stimulation of the alcohol industry."[3]

At the same time, the bills for running an empire were rising sharply. Charles Wolf Jr. gave the global picture in an op-ed drawn from his RAND Corporation study:

> In constant 1981 dollars, using official exchange rates, costs of the Soviet empire rose about $18 billion in 1971 to $24 billion in 1976 and about $41 billion in 1980.... As a proportion of published CIA estimates of Soviet GNP, the costs of empire rose from about 1.1 percent in 1971 to about 2.7 percent at the end of the decade.... As a ratio to Soviet military spending, they rose from 9 to 19 percent during the decade.[4]

Wolf adds the important qualification that these costs are even higher when expressed in rubles because of the lesser purchasing power of Soviet currency. Even then, however, these estimates are undoubtedly lower than the real costs. Since the end of the Cold War we have discovered that the CIA consistently overstated the size of the Soviet economy and understated the size of the Soviet military. So the real costs of helping governments such as the genocidal Mengistu regime in Ethiopia, subsidizing insurrections in Mozambique and Angola for decades, and financing a world terrorist network may have amounted to as much as 5 to 6 percent of Soviet GDP. And if that GDP was stagnant and the costs were rising, other calls on the Soviet budget would inevitably go unmet.

There is an almost poignant hint of this in Anatoly Chernyaev's diary entry for September 19, 1981. Chernyaev, from his perch in the Communist Party's International Department, commented on the Polish situation:

Judging from my information, nobody here [in Moscow] even thinks about "repeating Czechoslovakia." On the contrary, we gave Poland a huge loan, which is quite painful for ourselves. We did not publicize this, although the Poles, and the whole world, did. But we cannot tell our people about their own selfless internationalism. As far as food is concerned, things are very bad here.[5]

And what was the Soviet Union getting in return for such painful costs? Almost all the Soviet advances of the 1970s, which had caused such alarm in the gardens of the West, had either faded or soured. Some of the Third World regimes it upheld were rogue states that reflected little credit on their Soviet ally; others barely clung to power against persistent domestic insurgencies. Still others had drifted away from the Soviet bloc altogether as the capitalist world economy boomed following the revival of the U.S. economy in the early 1980s. There was more than a touch of necrophilia in the Soviet Union's fraternal relations with such incompetent and genocidal kleptocracies as Ethiopia.

As oil prices fell and Western economies became more attractive markets, raw material cartels lost what small appeal they ever had. The concept of "limits to growth" evaporated with them as rises in known reserves of raw materials overtook their depletion rate in the 1980s boom. The Third World's campaign for a new world economic order of "stable" raw material prices and international wealth redistribution under UN auspices had been halted in its tracks by Reagan and Thatcher at the 1981 North–South summit in Mexico. Now the Soviets turned against it as well when some of their client states employed its arguments to try to claim economic concessions from Moscow.[6] The Third World itself began to lose shape and meaning as the 1980s wore on. Economically, the rise of newly industrializing countries such as Singapore, South Korea, and Hong Kong meant that it was no longer either a club of the poor or an anti-capitalist pressure group. Politically, the Afghan war drove the generally anti-Western Islamic world into opposition against the Soviets, further dividing the West. And, historically, the ending of the post-colonial period meant that its artifacts, of which the Third World was one, gradually disappeared as well. By the end of the Cold War the Third World existed only as an idea in the mind of Western Marxist intellectuals.

As Peter Rodman points out, the Soviets began to abandon Third-Worldism while it was still in vogue in the West. A collection of scholarly essays by leading figures in the official Soviet intelligentsia, including future prime minister Yevgeny Primakov, concluded in 1982 that countries of "socialist orientation" (i.e., those allied with but not part of the Soviet bloc), far from becoming more independent of the capitalist world, were increasingly becoming integrated into it. They were no longer reliable allies in the fight against imperialism. And their progress—or regress—compelled a reassessment of the entire Marxist structure of historical inevitability.[7]

Such academic exercises were rarely merely academic in Moscow. Andropov picked up these themes when addressing the Central Committee on June 15, 1983. He cast doubt on the socialist credentials of various Soviet allies: "It is one thing to proclaim socialism as one's goal and quite another thing to build it." He complained about the expense of supporting them, hinting that in the future they would have to look after themselves. He also warned that good relations with the West and avoiding nuclear war must take preference over Soviet obligations to Third World allies.[8] It would be some time before these warnings were translated into hard policy decisions. Both Andropov and his successor Gorbachev continued to fund their client states. But the ideological justifications for retreat—and their accompanying psychology—were already in place. And the financial pressures would only get worse.

Nor had the Soviets solved their Polish problem. As early as March 1982, the Soviets realized that martial law had, in Macbeth's words, "scotched the snake, not killed it." Brezhnev told Jaruzelski at that time, "We agree with you that counter-revolution is not completely destroyed. It has not surrendered and, furthermore, it wants revenge. We can hardly hope that all these KOSs [Committees for Social Resistance] and KORs [Workers Defense Committees] will leave the political arena voluntarily. On the contrary everything shows that they may raise their heads again, as soon as martial law is weakened. The enemies of socialism also connect their hopes with the church, and not without reasons."[9]

Moscow believed that Jaruzelski and the Polish Party were insufficiently ruthless with the Church. More than that, Jaruzelski apparently believed that the Church was an indispensable ally in normalizing the country—or at least that Poland could not be normalized against its determined resistance. Gromyko told a Politburo meeting in April 1984 that he and Ustinov had told their Polish comrades of their deep concern about this: "Basically the Church has already turned into a party which takes anti-state stands. . . . The PORP [Polish Communist Party] does not conduct active ideological work and, in particular, fights the Church too weakly. The matter has gone as far as many thousands of people crawling on their knees in front of the pope. [This seems to be a reference to the pope's 1983 pilgrimage.] We told Jaruzelski that we in the Soviet Union were very worried about this."[10]

Jaruzelski was being not weak but realistic. His regime had sufficient force to maintain public order, but he could no longer command even the Poles' hypocritical acquiescence to Communist ideology. The general had his episcopal allies in both Rome and Warsaw, who—partly from a responsible desire to avoid bloodshed, partly from a lazy and unimaginative assumption of Soviet permanence—sought to avoid provoking the regime by open opposition. But the mass of Poles had absorbed the pope's subtle techniques of cultural resistance. They demonstrated their hostility to Communism not by riots but by openly showing their allegiance to God, Our Lady, the Church, and John Paul. They would live their lives with as little reference to government as possible. They were now linked by an underground Solidarity organization that, in addition to its growing moral authority, was drawing on material assistance from Washington, London, and millions of conscientious Europeans. And the murder of a charismatic priest, Father Jerzy Popieluszko, by three state security agents had given the Polish people an inspiring new martyr.[11]

Father Popieluszko had been, after John Paul himself, the boldest practitioner of cultural resistance in Poland. His eloquent sermons in his Warsaw parish church had attracted thousands of worshippers from widely varied backgrounds and ideologies. He had taught that resistance was a moral obligation in the face of unaccountable power and that nonviolence was the Christian form of resistance. The Warsaw correspondent of the *New York Times* wrote of him wonderingly, "Nowhere [from East Berlin to Vladivostock]...was anyone else openly telling a crowd that defiance of authority was an obligation of the heart, of religion, manhood, and nationhood."[12] Father Popieluszko had expressed what Poles at their best felt, and he had been silenced.

For ten days after his disappearance, his Warsaw church was packed with worshippers attending hourly Masses. One was in progress when the news arrived that his trussed body had been retrieved from the River Vistula. A fellow priest and friend, Father Antoni Lewek, fearing that the congregation would be roused to angry demonstrations, asked them to remember Christ weeping over the death of Lazarus. He recalled the congregation's response: "Something very moving happened.... Three times they repeated after the priests, 'And forgive us our trespasses as we forgive those who trespass against us. And forgive us our trespasses ...'"[13] In saying these words and dispersing quietly afterward, Father Popieluszko's mourners were expressing courage as well as Christian love. They would have found it harder to forgive if they had been more frightened. But they knew the priest's murder signified the weakness of the regime. When Father Popieluszko's grave became a religious and political shrine, this weakness was laid bare.

The regime recognized its failure. Jaruzelski saw that the most he could hope to achieve would be maintaining remote bureaucratic rule over a sullen nation. The ideological offensive that Moscow wanted would mean resistance, bloodshed, and perhaps even collapse. The Soviet Politburo, in turn, saw that Jaruzelski's strategy would result in the regime's gradual isolation from real political life. One day it would simply crumble before more vigorous social forces, including the Church. Both views were correct. Martial law had proved to be a historical cul-de-sac.

The Soviet view was more prudent than Jaruzelski's in one respect: it took into account the impact of Polish events on the rest of Eastern Europe. The fact that Jaruzelski followed his own strategy rather than the

Politburo's meant that the Polish infection, so long quarantined within the nation's borders, began at last to spread to its neighbors.

John Paul was yet again the Typhoid Mary of this epidemic. In June 1985 he published his fourth encyclical, *Slavorum Apostoli*, celebrating the missionaries Saint Cyril and Saint Methodius, who had brought Christianity to the western Slavs. This gave further stimulus to a Czech Catholicism that was already beginning to flex its evangelical and pastoral muscles. In 1982 Cardinal Frantisek Tomasek had banned priests from taking part in partisan politics, thus extracting them from the Czech government's Catholic front, Pacem in Terris, and effectively neutralizing it. The cardinal had also spoken out in defense of the human rights movement Charter 77, led by imprisoned playwright (and later national president) Vaclav Havel. And in April Tomasek read a letter of pastoral instruction from the pope to one-third of Czechoslovakia's priests, who were gathered in Velehrad for what Weigel describes as "the largest display of Catholic and priestly solidarity in Czechoslovakia since 1948."[14] It was also a strong message that priests had a duty to defend the faith against the persistent soft subversions of the regime as much as against outright persecution.

John Paul applied for a visa to attend the celebrations, also in Velehrad, for the 1,100th anniversary of the death of Saint Methodius in July. The regime, tougher and more devious than Jaruzelski, not only denied the pope's application, but also tried to turn the Velehrad pilgrimage into a Communist peace festival. But the growing spirit of resistance in Czech Catholicism ensured that these tactics backfired—badly. Two hundred thousand pilgrims arrived in Velehrad. When the peace festival partisans tried to welcome them with the usual ideological patter about world peace, the pilgrims responded with: "This is a pilgrimage! We want the pope! We want Mass!"[15]

If cries like these—cries that denied and defied the ideological monopoly of the Communist Party—were spreading throughout the Soviet bloc, the West was being handed a major strategic advantage, even if it showed no signs of realizing it. Andropov could not avoid recognizing it; it continually confronted him and his colleagues. They had to find some equal and opposite reality on their side of the ledger. Where was the pope *un*popular? Where was Reagan regarded as more of an oppressor than Andropov? Where were the ideological currents of opinion still trending leftward? Above all, where was there a pro-Communist equivalent to Solidarity?

As always, once the right questions were put, the answers were easy—the place: Western Europe; the time: 1968 to the present; the principal players: the European social democratic left and the "peace movement."

Missile Diplomacy

On a July afternoon in 1982, Paul Nitze, the U.S. negotiator on intermediate range nuclear (INF) weapons in the Geneva arms control talks, went for a walk through the Swiss countryside outside Geneva with his Soviet counterpart, Yuli Kvitsinsky. They hoped that as they strolled through the woods, they would be able to break the deadlock in the talks that had developed in the previous year. When they returned some hours later, they thought they had succeeded.

The problem they were addressing had arisen in the 1970s when the Soviet Union planted SS-20 missiles in Eastern Europe aimed at Western European cities. West German chancellor Helmut Schmidt had then persuaded NATO to install cruise and Pershing missiles in Western Europe both to counter the SS-20s and to ensure that Europe could not be strategically "decoupled" from the United States. If there were American missiles in Europe, a Soviet attack would automatically bring the U.S. into the war.

No one wants nuclear missiles in their backyard. Strong opposition to NATO's proposed missile installation developed, especially among leftists, throughout Western European countries. To mollify these protests, in 1979 NATO's governments had agreed on a "dual track" strategy—i.e., they would negotiate at Geneva to reduce missiles on both sides as they simultaneously prepared to install the new missiles. When Reagan became president, the Pentagon reopened the debate on this strategy. As we have already seen, however, Thatcher joined the State Department in successfully defending it, to the general relief of European governments.

Still, the agitation of the "peace movement" continued. It gained particular influence in Germany, where most of the missiles would be stationed. So the German foreign minister, Hans-Dietrich Genscher, proposed a more ambitious version of NATO's policy that became known as the "zero-zero option"—no INF missiles at all on either side. This was a very appealing proposal from a public relations standpoint, as it offered what the peace movement claimed it wanted. But it had a number of hidden drawbacks, and the process of negotiating it within NATO produced some unusual diplomatic alliances.

Thatcher joined with the U.S. State Department in resisting Genscher's "zero-zero" proposal, which she suspected was a PR stunt. She also felt that if it were ever accepted—which it was six years later by Gorbachev—it would undermine Schmidt's main reason for originally asking for U.S. missiles in Europe.[16] Withdrawing the missiles would indeed risk a strategic "decoupling" of Europe from the United States. At the same time, the West could hardly keep some INF missiles in Europe if the Soviets removed all theirs. And suppose Moscow "withdrew" them to just across the Soviet border, enabling them to hit almost as many Western European cities as from their original positions? Altogether, "zero-zero" was too risky a proposition.

Ranged against the Thatcher–State Department alliance was the hybrid Genscher-Pentagon axis. This unusual combination united the dovish Genscher with the hawkish Weinberger and Perle, and did feature strong arguments of its own. It was undeniable that "zero-zero" would be a brilliant diplomatic stroke, both undermining the Soviets and mollifying the peace movement. That met Genscher's political needs. The Pentagon supported the proposal from the more hard-headed calculation that the Europeans would never summon the necessary political will to deploy the cruise and Pershing missiles anyway. For Weinberger and Perle, "zero-zero" was a way of getting the Soviets to withdraw their SS-20s in return for the Western Europeans not doing what they never would have done anyway.[17]

This was the trump card used by Weinberger to persuade Reagan to adopt "zero-zero" at an NSC meeting. As Haig recounted it, Weinberger said, "Western Europe is unreliable and will not deploy the Pershings.

Therefore, Mr. President, you must come forward with a public relations ploy to deflect what is happening."[18] Although disproved by later events, this was a realistic argument at the time and doubtless played its part in swaying Reagan.

It is almost certainly true, however, as Geoffrey Smith and others argue, that Reagan was finally convinced by the fact that "zero-zero" would mean abolishing an entire category of nuclear weapons. No one outside a small coterie of senior advisers and close political friends like Thatcher then realized that Reagan was a nuclear disarmer. But his anti-nuclear stance worried his colleagues in both the Pentagon and the State Department, alarmed Thatcher (who became their principal ally on matters nuclear), and complicated internal NATO debates in ways that would have astonished outside experts if they had known. They were sufficiently astonished as it was when Reagan announced in November 1981 that the United States and NATO would propose to eliminate all INF missiles at the Geneva arms talks.

As most of the participants in the "zero-zero" debate had expected, the Soviets did not accept the offer. It would have required them to withdraw weapons already in place—a diplomatic retreat—whereas NATO would merely have not gone ahead with installing new missiles. They defended their apparent intransigence by arguing that the SS-20s were replacing older missiles and so should not be considered a new threat. This initially gave NATO the predicted PR advantage, but it was short-lived. The anti-nuclear and peace movements in Western Europe were never exactly what they seemed. They were not truly advocating disarmament, though they included such advocates, but were in reality anti-American movements. They invariably vented greater hostility at the U.S. missiles defending them than at the Soviets missiles targeting them. And before long they were criticizing "zero-zero" as unrealistic, when they would have hailed it as a breakthrough to world peace if the Soviets had proposed it.

"Zero-zero" was announced in November 1981; deployment of cruise and Pershing missiles was scheduled for November 1983. Within those two years East and West engaged in a titanic struggle for the political soul of Europe. Stripped of its technicalities, the question at issue was the deployment of the U.S. missiles. If that could be stopped, the Soviet Union would enjoy superiority in both INF missiles and conventional forces, and would be regarded as the main European superpower. In Raymond Aron's ironic reworking of Marx: "A specter is threatening Europe; the specter of the Red Army." If deployment went ahead, on the other hand, it would be a Soviet defeat in the central theater of the Cold War at a time when the USSR was meeting reverses almost everywhere else. The stakes were very high.

The West waged this battle by trying to separate the genuine disarmers from the calcified anti-Americans. "Zero-zero" was the first attempt to do this. When it produced deadlock at Geneva, Nitze and Kvitsinsky went for their famous "walk in the woods." This was their own initiative, but it reflected the support of Thatcher, the State Department, and the Europeans for something short of "zero-zero" if it would break the deadlock. When they emerged from the forest, the two negotiators had agreed on a deal: 300 American cruise missiles and 225 Soviet SS-20s would remain on their respective sides of the Iron Curtain.

Neither government accepted the deal. Massive demonstrations throughout Western Europe against missile deployment were making the Soviets overconfident. Reagan, for his part, opposed the proposals on both idealistic and practical grounds. As a disarmer he preferred the "zero-zero option" to a deal that would add more missiles to those already in Europe; as an old union negotiator, he thought it was simply a bad deal. He had built up American military strength in order to force a significant Soviet retreat that would include a sharp reduction in nuclear arms. What Nitze had obtained just didn't cut the mustard. Also, it was too soon—the Soviets needed to realize that they were losing the Cold War before they would offer serious concessions. Their rejection of the Nitze deal suggested as much.

Nitze wondered what he would tell the Soviets.

"Just tell them you work for one tough son of a bitch," said the president.

That was both true and false, a useful reputation in some circumstances, a hindrance in others. In reality Reagan was idealistic in adopting his aims, tough in defending them, and flexible in achieving them. He had turned down Nitze. But in March 1983 he bowed to pressure from Thatcher (again backed by the State Department) for a new NATO offer that would keep "zero-zero" as an eventual objective but accept lesser missile cuts in the interim. In return for this flexibility, he asked Thatcher to stop the Europeans from publicly demanding American flexibility, as this weakened him at the bargaining table.[19] When the Soviets shot down a civilian South Korean airliner in October 1983, he lambasted them vigorously and imposed modest sanctions, but he did not withdraw from the Geneva talks, as some of his supporters desired. He stayed at the negotiating table for two years until the Soviets walked out, but he refused to make self-destructive concessions while there.

Reagan's policies were reasonably well calculated to reduce the peace movement to its left-wing anti-American core. But they were outweighed by his public image as a trigger-happy cowboy, which served as a recruiting poster for the movement. Moscow was further aided by deep-seated trends in European politics. After Vietnam and the revolutions of 1968, Labourites and social democrats—honest left-wingers as well as corrupt agents of influence—were more than willing to make common cause with the Communist left and its various front organizations. A new popular front was born, christened the Broad Left.

If they were losing in Geneva, might not the Soviets recoup their losses in the streets and in the voting booths?

The Peace Front

In May 1980 Boris Ponomarev, the head of the CPSU's International Department, received a letter from his East German counterpart, Herman Aksen. It argued that the traditional Soviet method of conducting peace campaigns through organizations that were securely (and obviously) under its own control, such as the World Peace Council, meant that Moscow was missing a great opportunity. Aksen noted that there now existed in Western Europe and the United States a large number of independent left-wing "peace" bodies, with significant public support, that were being repelled by front organizations known to be taking orders from Moscow. The

Netherlands' No to the Neutron Bomb, Belgium's Action Committee for Peace and Cooperation, America's Mobilization for Survival, and Britain's Campaign for Nuclear Disarmament were all more influential than Moscow's cloned protesters. So why not employ more flexible tactics to work with them?

"Realization of our common goals requires...support from a popular mass movement," wrote Aksen. "However, the popularity and effectiveness of this movement depends to a great extent on whether we manage to activate the broad peace-loving forces, far beyond the limits of the World Peace Council–led movement."[20] A month later, from June 14 to 16, the "problems of coordination of mass peace movements" were discussed in Budapest by the Central Committee secretaries of the Soviet bloc.

Aksen's strategy was not entirely novel. The Soviets had supported popular front cooperation against fascism in the 1930s, when the rise of Hitler convinced Stalin to collaborate with non-Communist left-wing parties he had heretofore denounced as "social fascists." Suspended during Stalin's short-lived alliance with Hitler, the anti-fascist popular front of Communists and bourgeois democrats was revived during World War II and, because of the heroic Soviet resistance to Hitler, even became a central orthodoxy of Western politics. Stalin again ensured that this was short-lived. Between 1947 and 1968, fear of the Soviet Union was the main factor in European politics. The West united under American leadership. And anti-fascism was replaced by anti-totalitarianism as the prevailing mindset.[21] But the Vietnam War and the anti-Vietnam movement it had spawned shifted progressive opinion back to the idea of Broad Left unity against an "Amerika" and a "Free World" that masked a new kind of corporate fascism. As the "sixty-eighters" conducted their long march through the institutions, they pushed them steadily leftward and, among other "reforms," removed the previous constraints against cooperating with left-wing totalitarian parties. Gradually the conditions favorable to a new popular front were created.

This was a revolutionary social movement across the entire West. Its first effects were protests in France that almost brought down Charles de Gaulle, the anti-Pentagon sit-ins, the 1968 siege of the Chicago Democra-

tic convention, and the riots and demonstrations that disrupted universities almost everywhere. But as it matured and settled down—and as it
failed to achieve an early revolution—the movement began to effect less
dramatic but more significant changes: the McGovernization of the Democratic Party in the United States, *Ostpolitik* in Germany, Euro-Communism
in Spain and Italy, the Socialist-Communist alliance in France, and the rad-
icalization of the social democratic and liberal left almost everywhere.
None of this had been planned or orchestrated by the Soviets. At first they
had been mystified and even embarrassed by it—for instance, when it took
the form of "socialism with a human face" in Czechoslovakia they
stomped on it. But as the 1970s wore on they began to see its usefulness
and strove to exploit it.

In some cases the social democrats arrived on the Soviets' doorstep begging to be exploited. Soviet records now available show that in the 1970s
and 1980s senior figures in the British Labour Party were almost embarrassing in their desire to cooperate with Soviet foreign policy goals. Such
apparatchiks, notably the late Ron Hayward, who was general secretary
of the Labour Party from 1972 to 1982, were either ignored or circum-
vented when Labour was in power. But they exercised considerable influence over Labour policy when the party was in opposition—which it was
during Hayward's time from 1972 to 1974 and again from 1979 to 1982.
Also during his period of office, the "proscribed list" of Communist front
organizations was abolished and "party-to-party" links with Communist
parties were permitted. (This allowed the "party-to-party" visit to London
by Soviet notables in 1976 that led in turn to the parliamentary row
between Thatcher and Callaghan over the propriety of a democratic party
having fraternal relations with a Leninist one.)

In June 1973 Hayward led a Labour delegation including the party's
deputy leader, Edward Short (now Lord Glenamara), and two back-bench
MPs to Moscow.[22] They asked for Soviet help to get Labour into power at
the next election. They particularly wanted high-level meetings on this trip
to demonstrate its success to the media in England. Gromyko was consulted and, according to Chernyaev's diary, responded with shrewd
alacrity:

Gromyko immediately caught the most important thing. The largest social democratic party of one of the major countries comes to Moscow and almost entreats us to help them to get into power. After slighting the "Bolsheviks" for so many decades, they are finally addressing us with such a humble request. This is our chance. We cannot lose anything and we can gain a lot.

The delegation met Gromyko, Ponomarev, and the chief ideologist, Mikhail Suslov. They had moderately fruitful conversations for a first visit. The Soviets complained about past Labour governments. Hayward assured them that although Labour's past policy had been anti-Soviet in certain respects, some "positive shifts in the party" had now occurred. Alas, Brezhnev declined to see the delegation. So to mitigate their disappointment, Suslov showed them his office.[23]

Hayward and other Labour left-wingers had a series of semi-clandestine meetings with Chernyaev and his International Department colleagues over the next nine years. To judge from Chernyaev's accounts, these occasions were sinister, sad, and comic by turns, with the Labourites sounding like groupies keen to impress the Comrades with the seriousness of their "socialism" and the Soviets wondering how to evaluate the nervous and occasionally drunken boasting of their contacts that they had salted Labour with sympathizers. The Soviets also had to soothe local British Communists who complained, like Rodney Dangerfield, that they got no respect from Labour and were now being two-timed with them by Moscow. It must have been quite a tough posting.

The Soviets had to wait some time before this assiduous courting paid off. When Labour did control the government between 1974 and 1979, prime ministers Harold Wilson and James Callaghan, both firmly pro-American, conducted foreign and defense policy with almost no reference to the Labour Party outside Parliament. Nor, however, did they replace left-wingers in the party machine with their own loyalists. As a result, when Thatcher won the 1979 election, the Labour organization was still firmly under the control of the left and packed with Hayward's appointees.

More "positive shifts in the party" now occurred. Over the next three years the Labour Party moved sharply leftward, embraced an economic program of socialist autarchy, adopted a defense policy of unilateral nuclear disarmament, effectively drove four former Labour ministers to found a new center-left party, the Social Democrats, and replaced Callaghan as leader with Michael Foot, who, though a decent democrat, was also a committed unilateralist and left-winger. All this played into Thatcher's hands, as we shall see, but for the next eight years the main opposition party in America's closest ally was unilateralist, anti-NATO, anti-American, and solidly in support of the international "peace movement."

What happened to Labour was an extreme case. Many other politicians on the European left (and some neither on the left nor European) went to Moscow to discuss cooperating with the Soviets for "peace" and against Reagan.[24] Few identified themselves so completely with Soviet goals and the victory of "socialism" as Hayward and some of his colleagues. Other social democratic parties in Europe moved leftward in the late 1970s and early 1980s to oppose the missile installations and endorse the peace movement. Few did so as flamboyantly or as self-destructively as Labour. Still, the underlying reality in European politics was that it was now respectable on the left to cooperate with local Communists and the Soviets against Reagan and for "peace."

Thatcher set out to oppose this tendency from her first days in office—and to rally her European colleagues to do likewise. In September 1979, Helmut Schmidt, anxious about the drift of public opinion and his own SPD party against deployment, asked her to accept 16 of the cruise missiles allotted to West Germany in addition to the 144 she had already accepted for stationing in the UK. She agreed. That same month she urged the Dutch and Belgian prime ministers not to renege on their commitment to deploy the missiles. In October she conferred with Francesco Cossiga, the Italian premier and a staunch NATO loyalist who was determined to deploy. They agreed to pile more pressure on the Dutch and Belgians, partly because a refusal to deploy the missiles by the Low Countries would undermine Schmidt in Bonn. This attempt to rally European governments succeeded. At the December NATO meeting Holland and Belgium (with modest conditions) and West Germany all reaffirmed their NATO commitments.[25]

But this was merely a respite. Social democratic parties continued to move leftward and to push their leaderships to oppose missile deployment. In 1982 this finally brought about the collapse of Schmidt's social-liberal coalition in West Germany and its replacement by a coalition of the liberal Free Democrats and Christian Democrats under new chancellor Helmut Kohl. Kohl joined Thatcher and Cossiga in strongly backing deployment, but he would have to contest an election fairly soon in which it would be a central issue. Elections also loomed in Britain, Holland, Belgium, and Italy before the November 1983 date of deployment, in which "peace" would be the slogan of the main left-wing party. There was a real possibility that deployment could be stopped electorally.

To help bring this about, a vast "peace" campaign of sophisticated propaganda, mass petitions, street demonstrations, and political organization was launched. It is hard in retrospect to convey the sheer size of the enterprise. Millions of people signed "peace" petitions; hundreds of thousands marched through European city centers; groups of people never before associated with Soviet propaganda or street protests, such as bishops and generals, emerged as members of a broad-based "peace" coalition. This coalition's spirits were high, and not without reason: an earlier such campaign against the neutron bomb had been smaller and less diverse, and it had succeeded. Carter had announced that he would not deploy the enhanced radiation weapon even after persuading Schmidt and Callaghan to go out on a political limb by supporting it. The anti-INF campaign was even better organized and it employed powerful new themes designed to appeal to the paranoia of the European Left. An endless blitz of plays, films, pamphlets, magazines, and documentaries not only opposed deployment but also peddled the fantasy that NATO countries were ruled undemocratically by a "secret government" of intelligence agencies, far-right political circles, and the United States.[26]

This was a combination of chutzpah and Freudian projection. Though it was a breach of political etiquette to suggest that the Soviets might be financing or organizing the peace campaign, Soviet diplomats and "journalists" were expelled from Denmark, Portugal, Belgium, Holland, and Norway for doing precisely that. One of them incautiously admitted that he could summon thousands of Dutch protesters onto the street overnight through his networks—significantly, not through his networks of local Communists, but through "conscientious objectors."[27]

Overwhelmingly, the peace movement was a voluntaristic Broad Left enterprise—helped and even manipulated by the Soviets but not controlled by them. Many tendencies fed it: religion, ecology, the student movement, trade unions, Trotskyism, syndicalism, anarchism, and above all antinuclear factions such as CND in Britain. Half the sermons in Holland, the Dutch prime minister had told Thatcher, advocated nuclear disarmament by the West. The leaders of the German "peace" movement were Petra Kelly, a Green, and Gert Bastian, a general.[28] Britain's "peace" leadership was divided between E. P. Thompson, a distinguished historian of the Labour movement, and the "Greenham Women," a group of radical ladies who camped out on the edge of Greenham Common with the intention of obstructing the deployment of missiles there.

Aksen's "peace" strategy had proved to be a brilliant one. It cloaked an important Soviet strategic interest in a multicolored garment woven from environmentalism, religion, pacifism, anarchism, and old-fashioned radical eccentricity. At its height it could bring millions into the streets overnight. It reshaped the political culture of the left and thus of countries where the left was culturally dominant. It was so successful that it was imitated wholesale by the American left in the "nuclear freeze" movement.

It could do anything, in fact, except win elections.

Thatcher made the unilateral disarmament policy of the Labour Party her main target in the 1983 election. She was almost certain to win the election, no matter what topic she chose to emphasize, because she was the recent victor of the Falklands War. So her choice of target was significant: it revealed that she intended to use her election victory as a mandate for deployment. Thatcher had always liked Michael Foot, the Labour leader, personally. Their relations were courteous, even friendly, and in her memoirs she writes, "If I did not think it would offend him, I would say he was a gentleman."[29] But she fought a merciless campaign against him and the Labour Party on the grounds that its leftist defense and other policies would leave Britain open to external attack and prey to internal left-wing subversion. She received help from others on this score. An anonymous Labour front-bencher described the party's manifesto as "the longest suicide note in history."[30] Alexander Solzhenitsyn, visiting Britain, spent an evening with the prime minister; he later told the press that supporters of unilateral disarmament were "naïve." And Reagan ensured that Thatcher basked in the media limelight at the Williamsburg G-7 summit in the midst of her campaign. The result was a landslide victory, a parliamentary majority of 144, and a secure second term of office.

Kohl had already secured a firm majority for his conservative-liberal coalition in elections earlier in 1983. The Dutch and Belgian elections similarly returned governments that supported deployment. But the 1983 Italian elections were the most severe disappointment for the peace campaign. Though the Christian Democrats lost ground, they did so mainly to a group of smaller centrist parties rather than to the left. In the parliamentary haggling that followed, the Italian socialists who had been allies of the Communists for most of the postwar years switched sides and formed a coalition with the center and the right under their own leader, Bettino Craxi. This coalition, which strongly supported deployment, proved to be the most stable and enduring Italian government since 1945.

Still reeling from these election results, the "peace" movement suffered yet another blow in September 1983, when the Soviets shot a civilian South Korean airliner out of the sky because it had strayed over a strategically sensitive area near the Sakhalin islands. Though the peace campaigners could dismiss this as irrelevant to their campaign or even argue that it demonstrated the need for disarmament all around, it cast a harsh light on their anti-American bias. They had concentrated all their opposition on U.S. missiles, yet the Soviet Union had revealed itself as the more reckless superpower. European opinion shifted a little away from Andropov and toward Reagan.

With November only two months away, Thatcher could feel that her strong public support of deployment and her strong private pressure for American flexibility in negotiations had paid off. If the Soviets showed flexibility in return, there might still be an INF deal and the withdrawal of at least some SS-20s. If not, U.S. missile deployment would now go ahead unhindered. She was facing the unusually pleasant prospect of a "win-win" situation. For once, it was hard to see what could go wrong.

One month later, on October 25, Reagan invaded the queen's own island of Grenada.

Socialism Marches through the Caribbean

A small island in the southeastern Caribbean, Grenada had some banana plantations, a modest tourist trade, and a U.S.-owned private medical school with mainly American students. It was an independent state, but like many former British colonies it was also a constitutional monarchy whose head of state was Queen Elizabeth. Her exiguous official duties, except on the rare occasions when she visited the island, were in the hands of her governor-general, Sir Paul Scoon. In general the island was so obscure that when Reagan invaded, Moscow's television news illustrated the story with a map of Granada, Spain.[31]

Yet Grenada had been an unnoticed cockpit in the Cold War for the previous four years. In 1979 Maurice Bishop and his New Jewel Movement had seized power in a Marxist coup and established the People's Revolutionary Government. The PRG promptly revoked the 1974 independence constitution and ruled thereafter by decree. But the constitutional position was more ambiguous than the government's title suggested. Bishop made his peace with the Commonwealth and London, which continued, somewhat fitfully, to give Grenada development aid. Scoon remained in place as the queen's representative, and the PRG treated him as possessing a modicum of legitimacy. Bishop established close links with Cuba and the USSR, arrested and tortured opponents, imposed press restrictions, armed a militia of his supporters, and postponed elections indefinitely. He also began building a large modern airport, with Cuban help. This last was defended as a step toward increasing tourism, but it could also help the Cubans supply arms to Latin American guerrillas or ferry troops to southern Africa.

These developments unnerved Grenada's neighbors. Some of them had Marxist rebels of their own, and they feared that Bishop might encourage or even directly assist them. Bishop and his colleagues certainly saw themselves, however absurdly, as historical figures creating a Caribbean-wide revolution, as records of their debates showed.[32] The Soviets indulged and may even have shared these fantasies, as borne out by their own records. Among Caribbean Marxists in Britain and the United States there was real excitement over this new Anglophone Cuba.

The United States gradually became anxious about Grenada as a potential source of Caribbean instability. On October 4, 1983, the Reagan administration issued NSDD 105, demanding a more active security policy for the region. Europeans, including the British Foreign and Commonwealth Office (FCO), were more relaxed, recalling Claud Cockburn's idea of a dull headline: "Small Earthquake in Chile. Not Many Dead." Countering both points of view, English diplomatic historian David Carlton argued at the time that Grenada was in fact a minor irritant but a major strategic asset for Washington. The island was small, defenseless, and sitting in America's backyard. If the time ever arrived when Washington needed to demonstrate its power and determination without any risk, Grenada was available.[33] Something almost like that is what happened.

The weekend of October 22–24 brought two crises to the United States. In Lebanon, 242 American Marines and 58 French paratroopers were murdered by suicide bombers early on Sunday morning. In Grenada, a coup against Bishop by an even more extreme group of Marxists was threatening the lives of the American students and doctors at the medical school.[34] The massacre of the Marines came as a complete surprise, even though hostility to them in Beirut had been worsening for some time. The Grenada crisis had been developing more gradually.

The coup had begun on October 13, when an internal dispute in the PRG led to the ousting and house arrest of Bishop and his replacement by would-be Leninists Bernard Coard; his wife, Phyllis; and "General" Hudson Austin. Rumors of a hard-line coup now spread around the island, reaching London and Washington through the UK High Commission and the U.S. embassy on Barbados. Bishop escaped from house arrest on the following Wednesday and led his supporters to Fort Rupert, an old colonial prison looming over the capital. There he was confronted by three armored cars that fired on the crowd, killing between thirty and forty people. Bishop and several of his ministers were then shot by firing squad. Grenada's new rulers declared a curfew, and an uneasy calm settled over the island. But the regime was narrow, unpopular, and feared. The situation on the island was unstable, the American medical students risked death or imprisonment, and Washington and London both began their exercises in crisis management.

On Friday, October 21, Grenada's neighbors, the Organization of East Caribbean States, now thoroughly alarmed, voted to form a multilateral force that would "depose the outlaw regime in Grenada by any means." Supported by Jamaica and Barbados, the organization informally contacted Britain and the United States about mounting such an intervention. Richard Reeves, in his biography of Ronald Reagan, implies that this request was a pretext engineered by the United States.[35] But that underrates the importance of two local leaders, Tom Adams and Eugenia Charles, prime ministers of Barbados and Dominica respectively. Both were formidable anti-Marxists who wanted to protect their own countries from genuine local threats and were determined to draw the United States and Great Britain into the struggle if at all possible. They were far keener on intervention than either Britain or America.

But they failed to get Britain on their side. The FCO had already poured cold water on any suggestion of joint intervention when the U.S. raised the matter on the day Bishop was murdered. Its mindset was one of "retreat from empire" that deprecated anything that smacked of gunboat diplomacy. It downplayed any Cuban role in the crisis that would tend to justify intervention and never understood Reagan's concern about a potential hostage crisis. Indeed, the FCO now appeared to see its main diplomatic role as diverting Washington from action. In his study of the Grenada crisis, Gary Williams says that that the FCO never even put the case for intervention to Downing Street.[36] Certainly, Thatcher said that she never received the OECS appeal, which meant that the FCO was becoming an obstacle to understanding between London and Washington, as well as between London and the OECS.[37]

Washington, meanwhile, was moving into crisis-management mode. In response to the informal OECS appeal, Reagan ordered a flotilla of ships loaded with Marines bound for Beirut to divert to the east Caribbean. This was a precautionary move, but a serious one. Handling of the crisis was given to the Special Situations Group, chaired by Vice President George H. W. Bush. The group reached a "75 percent" decision to intervene. Bush's aides knew that Reagan was preoccupied with avoiding another Tehran-style hostage crisis. Top administration officials expected that the intervention would go ahead.

Thatcher had also ordered a ship, HMS *Antrim*, to sail toward Grenada but with the instruction that it was to remain "beyond the horizon." That signified merely that a rescue of British subjects might become necessary, and an SAS contingent was on board for that purpose. But Thatcher and her new foreign secretary, Geoffrey Howe, were relatively unconcerned about Grenada; one set of Caribbean Marxists had replaced another. Surely that was no big deal. A British official had paid a day's visit to Grenada and reported to the Foreign Office that the regime was willing to arrange for British subjects to leave the island if they wished. His report had also described the situation ambiguously as "calm, tense, and volatile." But FCO briefings and even ministerial replies gave a milder impression: "Small Earthquake in Grenada. Not Many Dead. No Britons Are Believed to Be Missing." The FCO mindset of "retreat from empire" was shaping a policy that reflected neither British interests nor Anglo-American comity—and least of all concern for the Grenadian people.

This "retreat from empire" was also provoking a hostile response in Washington. The State Department, noting a marked lack of sympathy for

U.S. policy, had started to stonewall and even mislead the British embassy. British diplomats were told that nothing much was happening but that the Americans would call if things looked likely to change. The reality was very different; detailed plans for intervention were going ahead. At the SSG, the question was raised of when to tell Thatcher. "Decision: notify her at the last minute."[38] Reagan explained this in his memoirs (and to Thatcher later) as something necessary for security at the Washington end. But it was dangerous to deceive a close ally, even if British behavior had provoked such caution—and it was probably mistaken on other grounds as well.

Moreover, the last minute was fast approaching. Early on Saturday morning Reagan was awakened in Augusta, Georgia, and told that the OECS had now formally requested U.S. intervention. Security was also beginning to break down. Intervention was being discussed as a possibility at a meeting of CARICOM, the Commonwealth Caribbean trade group. Reagan asked his new national security adviser, Bud McFarlane, how quickly an invasion of Grenada could be mounted.

"Forty-eight hours," was the answer.

Stressing that his priority was the safety of the six hundred American students, Reagan ordered the intervention for early Tuesday morning. He still had two days to change his mind.

One night later he was again disturbed in the early hours with the terrible news that the 242 Marines had died in Beirut. He was shaken and angered by the news—the more so because there was little he could do about it. France's Mitterrand, among others, told him that no effective retaliation was possible against the terrorists or their Syrian masters. Cap Weinberger at the Pentagon, who had always opposed the Lebanon commitment, wanted to withdraw the troops as soon as possible. (As they were being withdrawn, he ignored a presidential order for an air strike on the terrorist camps, lest it draw the U.S. back into the conflict.) And American public opinion had no appetite for maintaining a Lebanon commitment that even its diplomatic advocates had difficulty in explaining.

Almost every consideration now endorsed the invasion of Grenada. If Reagan could do nothing in the Middle East, he could still demonstrate the continuing might of the U.S. in the eastern Caribbean. And if he did nothing there and some of the 600 American medical students were added to the 242 casualties in Beirut, his presidency would be over. Carlton's cold-blooded calculation now had blood to back it up. Reagan could no longer halt the invasion of Grenada.[39] He and the medical students both depended on its success.

One small problem remained. No one had yet informed the Grenadian head of state in London: namely, Her Majesty the Queen, the president's old riding partner. Nor was the British prime minister, the president's old friend, aware of the plan. Not until a few hours before the invasion began, early evening London time, did the president send a message to Downing Street that he was contemplating invasion. A British cabinet meeting earlier that day had already decided in principle to oppose intervention, and Howe, misled by State Department stonewalling, had assured MPs that the U.S. had no intention of doing anything so rash.[40] Thatcher had no choice but to order the preparation of a draft reply counseling strongly against such a course. Before this could be sent, however, a second message arrived from Washington saying that the president was proceeding with the invasion. After consulting with Howe and Defense Secretary Michael Heseltine, she sent a message expressing opposition to the intervention in unusually strong language:

> This will be seen as an intervention by a Western country in the internal affairs of a small independent nation. I ask you to consider this in the wider context of our wider East-West relations and of the fact that we will be having in the next few days to present to our parliament and people the siting of cruise missiles in this country. . . . [I] hope that even at this late stage you will take it into account before events are irrevocable.

But it was too late. The Marines were already landing in Grenada. The operation was far from flawless—nineteen U.S. soldiers were killed—but the result was never in doubt. Six hundred and fifty Cuban "construction workers" fought bravely but they were overwhelmed and returned to their homes, along with a rag-tag and bobtail of advisers from other Communist countries. The American students were rescued and, on returning to the United States, ran down the airline steps and kissed the ground. In Grenada itself the intervention was enormously popular. Order was established, elections held, and the first of a series of democratic governments elected. When Reagan visited the capital of St. George's months later, he received a rapturous welcome, which subsequently appeared in his 1984 election commercials. He had already been given a similar welcome on returning to the White House on the day after the "liberation." Signs proclaiming "Your Finest Hour" possibly overstated his success. Conservative columnist George Will remarked drily that Grenada proved the United States was at best a regional superpower. But the signs reflected the political fact that Grenada had been a success both in its own right and in Carlton's terms. It had obliterated the impression of defeat and impotence that had been left in Beirut.

Thatcher and Howe uttered barbed criticisms of the "liberation" without condemning it outright, in the face of a delighted and vengeful Labour opposition over the next few days. Howe especially suffered because he had been so forthright in dismissing talk of intervention only hours before it happened. But the quick American victory, its undeniable popularity with Grenadians, Churchill's principle of always staying close to the United States, and the axiom that there was no use crying over spilt milk (or blood) all combined to convince Thatcher to put the episode behind her and to re-establish the Reagan-Thatcher partnership on its previously warm footing. Reagan himself made it easier with a personal telephone call that began with a characteristic piece of light self-deprecation:

President Reagan: If I were there, Margaret, I'd throw my hat in the door before I came in.

Prime Minister Thatcher: There's no need to do that.

President Reagan: We regret very much the embarrassment caused you, and I would like to tell you what the story is from

our end. I was awakened at three o'clock in the morning, supposedly on a golfing vacation down in Georgia. The secretary
of state was there. We met in pajamas out in the living room of
our suite because of this urgent appeal from the Organization
of East Caribbean States pleading with us to support them in
Grenada. We immediately got a group going back here in
Washington, which we shortly joined, on planning and so
forth. It was literally a matter of hours. We were greatly concerned, because of a problem here—and not at your end at
all—but here. We have had a nagging problem of a loose
source, a leak here.

Thatcher responded to this friendly apology in like vein:

Prime Minister Thatcher: . . . I'm very much aware of sensi-
tivities. The action is under way now and we just hope it will
be successful.

After Reagan had given her a full briefing on the military and political
progress of the intervention, they ended on the old "Ron" and "Margaret"
terms, with Margaret asking Ron to pass on her best wishes to Nancy and
Ron encouraging Margaret to "eat 'em alive" down at the House of Commons. It is a fascinating conversation. Both are eager to heal the breach
between them, and they succeed. Both were also slightly hurt and disappointed. Reagan almost certainly shared the view of some of his aides that
Thatcher would probably support the intervention—maybe with the kind
of private misgivings she sometimes expressed over nuclear policy—but
clearly and publicly.[41] He would also have been more than human if he had
not hoped for some payback for his help over the Falklands; McFarlane certainly believed the U.S. had been let down on that score. Thatcher felt hurt
because she had been deceived and excluded from the decision-making—
and she felt the hurt doubly because the exclusion was so public.

Thatcher also had other reasons for opposing America's unilateral intervention in Grenada: she was afraid it would undermine support for

installing the INF missiles in Europe. That did not happen, but it was sensible to guard against such European fears. She was sensitive to the insult to the queen as well (although the queen herself instructed Scoon to give vigorous help to the Americans in restoring democracy on Grenada, which he did). Finally, Thatcher was nervous that the Grenada intervention would be used by the Soviets to justify invading other countries. That was a prudent consideration, but it hardly outweighed the value of rescuing more than one hundred thousand people from murderous anarchy and stabilizing the eastern Caribbean. Besides, the specific conditions of Grenada—a constitutional limbo, the collapse of the PRG into civil war, the massacre of ministers, the threatening presence of armed Cubans, the appeal of neighbors nervous about regional instability, and finally the request for intervention by Governor-General Scoon once he was free—were too uncommon to be a useful precedent for Soviet aggression. And if by some extraordinary chance they were to be repeated elsewhere, a precedent for intervening to restore order and save lives would be good rather than bad.

Public debate in Britain following the immediate crisis hashed over these and other points. This proved slightly embarrassing for the prime minister, however, because almost all her usual supporters on foreign policy issues took Reagan's side. In the House of Lords debate on Grenada, for instance, liberals such as Max Beloff, Noel Annan, and Hugh Thomas as well as more conventional Tories were both baffled and alarmed by Britain's apparent willingness to allow the Grenadians to fall into the Cuban-Soviet orbit. The *Daily Telegraph* and the *Times* were hostile to Thatcher's refusal to endorse American action. And one of her strongest intellectual supporters, Paul Johnson, confessed that he was astounded at her inability to see that Grenada was an issue as morally clear and compelling as slavery. Thatcher's support came only from Tory "wets" and mocking Labourites.

This post-crisis debate had several positive effects. It accelerated and deepened Thatcher's reconciliation with Reagan. If her own people supported him, she had to recognize that he had a far stronger case than she had first realized—and the mission's success gave her additional reason to respect his judgment. It meant also that when Reagan requested the right to use British bases for the 1986 bombing raid on Libya, she was disposed to consider it sympathetically. As always, she asked hard questions about targeting, legality, the evidence of Libyan involvement in the terrorist nightclub bombing for which this was the response, and so on. But she agreed to the use of bases for the raid when no other European country would do so. That effectively wiped away any lingering resentment over Grenada. It reinforced her heroine status with Americans at large. And finally, the debate persuaded Thatcher to take a slightly more skeptical attitude toward international law. In response to Grenada, she convened one of her seminars on the topic and, as she writes in her memoirs, was surprised to find that "the lawyers were inclined to argue on grounds of *realpolitik* and the politicians were more concerned with the issue of legitimacy."[42] Even if she were slightly more skeptical, however, she still liked to have the lawyers telling her that the letter of the law was on her side. She was, after all, a lawyer herself.

Was then Grenada just a "small earthquake in the Caribbean"? Not really. For the United States it set Reagan surely on the road to victory in the 1984 election. For the British it was a little like an episode of the sitcom *Yes, Prime Minister*, in which the FCO tells the politicians what they should know—and not an iota more. For the Grenadians it was blessed relief from evil under the sun.

And in faraway Moscow it was a cloud no bigger than a man's hand.

"Reagan's 'Firmness' Has Paid Off"

As the prime minister was being driven to the airport on her way to Yuri Andropov's funeral, Robin Butler, the senior civil servant in attendance, noticed that she was wearing high-heeled court shoes. Would she be attending the funeral, he asked, in those shoes? Yes? In that case he insisted on diverting the car to a shoe shop where she could buy a pair of fleecy fur-lined boots—the only footwear suitable for a Politburo funeral that would involve standing for hours in below-freezing Red Square. After buying the boots, Thatcher complained about their exorbitant price all the way to Moscow.

The next day was as Butler had predicted: Thatcher had to stand for hours in the cold. After the burial, she paid a brief courtesy call to shake hands with Andropov's successor, Konstantin Chernenko, at the Kremlin wake, drank a glass of champagne, and then returned to her limousine for the drive back to the Moscow airport. No sooner had she settled back onto the limo's cushions than she apologized generously to Butler.

"Robin, I should never have made such a fuss about the price of those boots," she said. "When I saw Chernenko in the reception line, I realized at once that they were a prudent long-term investment." Make that medium-term, Prime Minister. Chernenko died a year later.

Vice President Bush had the same thought as Thatcher. Saying farewell to the U.S. embassy staff after the funeral, he had quipped, "Next year, same time, same place." And Reagan, when asked why he was the first postwar president not to have had talks with a Soviet leader, replied, "They keep dying on me."

It was no accident, comrade. Andropov's death was also the death of a strategy. He had come to power late in the day, but he had been the first apostle of "new thinking" following Brezhnev's long era of stagnation. Along with the Finnish-born Otto Kuusinen, he had recruited a cadre of clever young apparatchiks, open-minded, technically able, ambitious, and eager to rescue the Soviet Union from its looming decline. To the rest of the world, Andropov might appear to be a cold-eyed KGB brutalitarian who had suppressed the Hungarian uprising by the cruelest methods. To his young protégés, however, he was a thoughtful, civil, imaginative, and even kindly boss. One of them, Georgi Arbatov of the Institute for the U.S. and Canadian Studies, said, "I know of no instance when he intentionally committed any base act for its own sake." As Peter Rodman points out, this praise is both hilariously ambiguous and appropriately Soviet.[43] But it may not be completely false.

When Andropov became the general secretary of the CPSU, reports in the Western press painted him in exaggerated colors as a proto-liberal, fond of jazz, scotch whiskey, John Wayne movies, and Western novels. All the admiring descriptions—steel-trap mind, brilliant linguist, fine chess player—were trotted out in Western media portraits until Vladimir

Bukovsky confessed he was afraid to turn on his vacuum cleaner for fear it would start babbling on about the virtues of the new Soviet leader. Nothing in Andropov's short tenure at the top suggested there was any truth in this glowing portrait; he is chiefly remembered for having launched a massive intelligence operation in 1983 to check his suspicion that NATO's Operation Able Archer was the disguise for a preemptive nuclear strike. No one with even a slender knowledge of the open societies of the West would have believed that the United States could launch a secret preemptive nuclear strike. It was either pure Soviet paranoia or disinformation calculated to frighten the West into halting its arms buildup.

Andropov's strategy to deal with Brezhnev's imperial overstretch was not especially imaginative. Like any sane accountant, he proposed to cut down the empire's expenses on its marginal client states. He placed an ever higher priority on cutting defense costs through negotiating arms reductions with the West. Neither retrenchment really occurred. The war in Afghanistan went on unabated; the repression in Eastern Europe was not relaxed; the peace campaigns in Western Europe, though more effectively deceptive than under Brezhnev, failed to halt missile deployment; and he did not even stick to his accountant's fiscal caution when a client state got into trouble. Thus, Chernyaev wrote in his diary for November 12, 1983:

> Yesterday, I read through more than a hundred coded messages from all over the world. One of them had an alarming note from Andropov on it. He orders: "Do everything possible to prevent Reagan's invasion of Nicaragua (similar to one of Grenada). It would be a terrible blow on Cuba, on all Castro's policies, and hence on us—both as a superpower and as a stronghold of the socialism and liberation movements."

As for the second half of the strategy, because Andropov was both highly suspicious of Western governments and hopeful that the peace movement could prevent the installation of the INF missiles, he failed to pick up the hints dropped by both Reagan and Thatcher in 1983 that they were now in the market for serious talks. But it really didn't matter, because both the Soviet Union and Yuri Andropov were suffering from terminal illnesses.

Two unmistakable symptoms of the USSR's condition became visible in fall 1983. The most important was when cruise and Pershing missiles were installed in November, as NATO had agreed two years before. Millions of people continued to march and sign petitions, but their governments simply ignored them. Voters trumped marchers. The Soviet Union, despite its preponderance of missiles and conventional forces, had failed to bully Western Europe.

At this point Reagan had won the Cold War in Europe, although it would be another five years before the formal end of hostilities. The Soviets would still try to reverse their defeat by maneuvering at the bargaining table, but their superpower image lagged way behind the reality of their decline. Reagan had fulfilled his promise to Dick Allen: "We win, they lose."

Ailing and frustrated, Andropov pulled the Soviet negotiators from the Geneva talks. His colleagues in Moscow were not deceived. Writing in his diary for December 7, 1983, Chernyaev notes sadly that the Soviet Union is now negotiating from weakness:

> The main problem is negotiations. Obviously, we are closing all of them, including Vienna....But the whole world demands negotiations. Our antiwar friends and social democrats are warning us that the USSR may "lose face" if it is "too stubborn." The more so because for many years Ponomarev himself has everywhere (including the Party congresses) asserted the principle of negotiations as the only alternative to nuclear holocaust. The more so, because we already have "experience" of this. In 1979, after the NATO decision, we also declared through Gromyko and all our propaganda that there would be no negotiations unless they were to cancel their "military buildup" decision. But he had to go to Geneva later anyway!
>
> Obviously: tactically we need to be tough (for prestige). But what do we do after that?[44]

The other symptom of Soviet decline was Reagan's takeover of Grenada. Here both Soviets and dissidents realized something to which most Westerners were blind: Grenada was important out of all proportion to its size. Unlike El Salvador or Afghanistan or Angola, Grenada was a socialist country rather than merely a country of "socialist orientation." It was theoretically possible for the latter to slip back into the capitalist camp, but according to Soviet ideology, once a socialist country, always a socialist country. If Grenada could revert to capitalism, then history could run backward and water uphill. It was therefore impossible.

As Bertrand Russell remarked, however, the existence of something is absolute proof of its possibility. The invasion of Grenada, its easy success, and above all the welcome it received from the masses—these events thrilled the subjects of the Soviets because they exposed the lie of irreversibility. By an equal measure, they alarmed Soviet leaders, especially those with responsibility for the Caribbean, because they opened up an abyss of freedom into which anyone or any country might now fall. Chernyaev's diary for the last few months of 1983 shows that he and his colleagues were becoming increasingly desperate and devoid of ideas. It also shows the absurdities of the revolutionary Leninist mindset.

October 27, 1983:

The U.S. invasion of Grenada. It is "my" country. Our contacts with Grenada started from me: I met Coard at a congress in Jamaica, and he made an impression of an educated Marxist and a "firm Leninist." Then there was his visit to us, after that diplomatic relations were established, and so on.

And now Coard looks like the murderer of Bishop, like the man who has provoked the intervention. On the other hand, this is quite a normal, historically sanctified development for any revolution. It is not for us to throw stones at those who tried to accelerate it or at least to strengthen it. All the more so since we've given no economic help at all to this tiny state (it probably has a smaller population than my Kropotkinskaya

Street in Moscow), to prevent them reaching 40 percent unemployment in two or three years.

Now, the most important thing is that Reagan has proven, once again, that he is going to commit any outrages he wants in his "crusade." He is going to put us into an ever more stupid position—that of a "superpower" which is unable to stop him.

The same day:

Now they've invaded Grenada, and they'll probably do the same in Nicaragua soon. And what are we doing? Yesterday evening Andropov announced cardinal proposals on mid-range nuclear missiles for the Geneva negotiations.

So the Cubans honor and mourn their men, who had heroically fought the U.S. Marines to the bitter end on Grenada. The whole world is shocked, even Thatcher "condemned" Reagan, while we look like distracting the world's attention from it. Of course, disarmament is really vital for the humankind. But we are losing in moral sense; we look like egoists.

In addition, they will start humiliating us now: Reagan's "firmness" has paid off. The USSR obviously made big concessions as a result of it.

November 5, 1983:

I quarreled with [Ponomarev] over his usual pseudo-theory about "imperialism's failures" (what with the Grenada revolution being crashed, Romania's position, socialism disappearing in Poland, Angola's one foot in the grave...what with the American missiles being deployed in Europe, our helpless inability to defend Lebanon or Nicaragua, the hardest attack yet on Castro's whole revolutionary strategy in Latin America, etc.). [Ponomarev] either fails to realize what is happening with the revolutionary process or deliberately employs optimistic

demagogy. This means we have either completely subdued theoretical analysis to routine propaganda, or that we are indeed
unable to face the truth.

November 15, 1983:

A reception for Guyana delegation (the special representative
of the president, the commander in chief, two members of the
ruling party's leadership). They brought a message to
Andropov. They told me that Guyana is going to be next after
Grenada and Nicaragua. Therefore, they plead for help: economic aid, military aid. I kept fooling them with promises, and
finally packed them off to the [relevant] offices for "specific"
discussions on their requests. Before that, I received Ponomarev's instruction: we would not give them military aid. If we
did, we would put them at risk of an American attack "while
we cannot do anything about it."[45]

Andropov never left the hospital to deal with these accumulating problems. In February 1984 he died, like Brezhnev, at the end of his tether. The
remedies of his "new thinking" had proved inadequate against the massive
sickness of the empire. And his successor, Chernenko, was a perfect symbol of the vacuum at the center of Soviet power. When his elevation was
announced, Peter Rodman, who would soon be appointed director of the
State Department policy planning staff, unable to recall him to mind, had
gone to his scrapbook and looked through more than a decade of photographs of superpower diplomacy. Chernenko was in some of them. But
Rodman, even thus prompted, was unable to remember anything that he
had said or done. No one had even bothered to introduce him to the Americans present on those occasions.[46]

In his brief period of power, until his death in March 1985, Chernenko
prosecuted the war in Afghanistan more harshly, strengthened Soviet ties
with such client states as Ethiopia, and avoided any meaningful economic

reforms. His tenure put East-West relations into cold storage. And the problems of the empire had quietly got worse.

When it came to Chernenko's successor, the smart money was on Mikhail Gorbachev, an Andropov protégé admired by the old guard and regarded as one of their own by the younger apparatchiks. Gromyko, proposing him, had said he had a nice smile but "iron teeth." Compliments like that from the stone-bottomed Gromyko would not normally be accompanied by praise from the West. But Gorbachev had been talent-spotted in advance by Canada's Pierre Trudeau and Peter Walker, one of Thatcher's senior colleagues. Prompted by them, she had invited him to Chequers in December 1984 for a "getting-to-know-you" session.

At Chequers Thatcher and Gorbachev had engaged in a spirited six-hour debate on, among other things, the relative merits of capitalism and communism. He advanced orthodox Communist arguments but also presented himself as a reformer. He did so in a fresh and lively way, quite unlike any other Soviet apparatchik the British had previously encountered. Maybe the KGB had told him that the way to Thatcher's heart was to disagree vigorously with her. In any event she was impressed and sent Reagan a long and favorable account of the meeting and of Gorbachev. He struck her as the kind of flexible Soviet leader that she and Reagan had been waiting for since mid-1983.

She summed it all up in her public statement after Chequers: "I like Mr. Gorbachev. We can do business together."

Now Gorbachev was in charge. Within a relatively short time, he and Reagan agreed to hold a summit meeting in Geneva in November 1985. In the eight months between coming to power and meeting Reagan, the new Soviet leader had impressed the Western press with his energy and charisma. He received even more favorable reviews than had the early Andropov. As the summit approached, there was almost kindly media speculation on whether the old actor in the White House would be capable of meeting this dynamo on equal terms.

He had facts at his fingertips! He had brilliant negotiating skills! He dominated any room he was in! He was the most formidable Soviet leader since . . . well, perhaps best not to specify. He had drive! He had energy! He had charm! He had charisma! He was the man to beat!

Alas, poor Gorby. He was beaten before he began. The weapon Reagan used to beat him was something that all the smart reporters, experts, and advisers had dismissed as a boomerang—the Strategic Defense Initiative.

CHAPTER EIGHT

TRIUMPH AND DISASTER

On the morning of March 24, 1983, Cap Weinberger found himself in a deeply embarrassing position. The previous evening he had briefed his fellow defense ministers at a meeting of NATO's nuclear planning group on the president's speech introducing the concept of the Strategic Defense Initiative (SDI) that would be delivered later that night. Weinberger, however, had not mentioned missile defense in his briefing. Originally skeptical, he had decided to support the idea after all but thought announcing it would be premature. Now it was the leading news item across at least two continents.[1]

Weinberger was not the only one feeling surprise and doubt. The reactions of most reporters, national security analysts, think tank strategists, allied defense and foreign ministers, and even a majority of Reagan's own advisers ranged from dubious to mocking. The Soviet response was bitterly hostile—which meant that they took the idea seriously. So did many ordinary Americans—because it seemed common sense to defend the country against a nuclear attack rather than to avenge its destruction from the grave. But relatively few informed people took it both seriously and favorably.

Those who did were generally scientists and military researchers working on missiles, lasers, computers, and related technologies. In her memoirs, Margaret Thatcher claimed to be one of them because she had been reading about Soviet progress in lasers in the technical scientific journals.

Thatcher was one of the few Western leaders to express initial support for SDI—and even then she had to fight disagreement within her own cabinet and the Foreign and Commonwealth Office. But her backing was carefully defined. She saw missile defense as one element in an overall strategy of deterrence. If an attacking power could not know which missiles might be shot down, then it could not safely launch a preemptive strike. She shared the skepticism of Reagan's critics about achieving full defense through an anti-nuclear "astrodome" that would destroy all incoming missiles. It seemed to her utopian. As Reagan's vision of strategic missile defense became clearer, she often tried to restrain him from (in her opinion) his riskier flights of fancy. And because her more constrained idea of missile defense was supported by almost every pro–missile defense expert and adviser in both London and Washington, she was perhaps slow to grasp the revolutionary possibilities of Reagan's more visionary plan.

Even today the extent and character of Reagan's missile defense concept are not fully understood. That applies as much to his admirers and supporters as to his critics. Rather than considering missile defense one facet of the nuclear deterrent, as Thatcher did, Reagan saw it as the central element in a global system of nuclear arms reduction. From this standpoint, a system of defense against incoming missiles would make it safer for a government to reduce its stockpile of offensive missiles. In the hypothetical case of an impenetrable shield, then a nation need have no offensive missiles at all, as the shield itself would make an attack pointless. Even if the shield were imperfect, however, a country with missile defense would still need far fewer deterrent missiles than one without it. Missile defense both improved the deterrent and made it safer to reduce offensive nuclear stockpiles. It was the ultimate confidence-building measure.

But in order to reduce stockpiles on both sides, missile defense would have to be available to all nuclear powers. Reagan realized this and repeatedly stated his willingness to share U.S. technology with the Soviets for that purpose. People found it hard to credit this. Whether that was due to Reagan's reputation as a Cold Warrior cowboy or because they believed great powers never used an advantage for altruistic purposes we cannot know. But the president constantly had to reiterate this point—and its underlying logic—to incredulous interviewers. Here is one such exchange with a BBC correspondent:

> **BBC:** Are you saying then, Mr. President, that the United States, if it were well down the road towards a proper SDI program, would be prepared to share its technology with Soviet Russia, provided, of course, that there were arms reductions and so on on both sides?
>
> **Reagan:** That's right. There would have to be the reductions of offensive weapons. In other words, we would switch to defense instead of offense.[2]

Skeptics sometimes argued that Reagan's vision foundered on the reality that nuclear weapons cannot be un-invented. Not only did Reagan take this reality into account, but he also used it to bolster his argument for missile defense. In the BBC interview quoted above, Reagan also pointed out that a system of agreed global defense would protect everyone against what he called "some madman...secretly set[ting] out to produce some [nuclear weapons] with the idea of blackmailing the world." This argument foresaw contingencies like those we face today: an Iranian bomb, a nuclear device in the hands of al Qaeda, even the risk of an accidental launch by a nuclear state. It was, as Mark W. Davis points out, a look ahead into our own world of nuclear proliferation.[3]

Reagan's link between missile defense and nuclear stockpile reduction is the key to understanding the mysteries surrounding SDI. It explains, for instance, why a firm Cold Warrior like Reagan contemplated reductions in nuclear missiles far more sweeping than those accepted by Nixon and Carter in the heyday of détente. It also explains his wholesale withdrawal of those concessions when Gorbachev would not agree to serious research on SDI—unless missile defense were part of the package, nuclear disarmament would be unsafe. It would be vulnerable to deceit, to nuclear development by third parties, and to an accidental launch from the remaining stockpiles. Reagan believed not in a flawlessly invulnerable shield but a "mix" of missile defense and nuclear disarmament.

Reagan was impelled toward missile defense because of his strong moral objections to the theory of deterrence known as Mutual Assured Destruction (MAD). Like the nuclear pacifists, he believed that it would be abhorrent to kill millions of innocent Russians in retaliation for a Soviet nuclear attack on the United States. And like the Western governmental strategists, he believed that to threaten such retaliation was legitimate if it were the sole means of deterring the Soviets from a first strike. Where he departed from strategists of both East and West, however, was in believing that a strategy based solely on retaliation—namely, MAD—would cease to be legitimate if there were a means of defense against nuclear missiles. Such a defense was not available in 1980. But might one be invented?

Reagan had come to think so in 1979, on a trip to the North American Aerospace Defense Command (NORAD). Accompanied by adviser Martin Anderson and a Hollywood scriptwriter friend, Douglas Morrow, the presidential candidate visited the command center where young military technicians hunched over computer screens looking for signs that a ballistic nuclear missile had been launched from somewhere against the United States. Officials explained to Reagan that NORAD could track incoming missiles almost from the moment of their launch until they hit their U.S. targets. It was an impressive display of U.S. technology. But as General James Hill pointed out, they were powerless to stop or divert the missiles; this technology could only ensure that a U.S. retaliatory response was launched before the Soviet missiles arrived. Reagan was distressed; he felt that "there had to be a better way."[4]

Some skeptics, such as Frances Fitzgerald, profess surprise that Reagan learned as late as 1979 that it was impossible to defend America from ballistic missiles that could not be halted in flight.[5] This criticism is disingenuous. Reagan's many columns on arms control in the 1970s show that he had a solid grasp of matters nuclear. What surprised and upset Reagan at

NORAD was the disparity between the excellence of the technology and the modesty of its purpose. If we could track missiles from their launch, he asked reasonably, could we not develop a means of halting them? He told Anderson to study the issue and encouraged the delegates at the 1980 GOP convention to put missile defense into the party platform. Once ensconced in the White House, he asked Ed Meese to chair a small secret committee to take the idea further. Reagan then instructed the Joint Chiefs in December 1982 to consider the prospects for strategic missile defense. They presented him with a favorable report on February 11, 1983; Admiral Jim Watkins, the chief of naval operations, was particularly supportive. Two days after unveiling the idea in a March 23 speech, Reagan issued an executive order instructing William Clark to superintend a research and development program on the idea.[6]

Thus was SDI launched into public debate. Like the ballistic missiles Reagan had viewed on the NORAD computer screens, once launched, SDI could not be recalled. It flew unerringly to its target: the technological backwardness of the Soviet Union. Unlike a ballistic missile, however, it did so by a roundabout route.

The Prelates Oppose

Three months later Reagan found that he was the rope in a tug of war on SDI, pulled in one direction by John Paul and in the other by Margaret Thatcher. When they met in June 1983, Reagan told the pope not only of his general approach to East-West relations but in particular of his personal commitment to disarmament. As we have seen, the pope told cardinals Casaroli and Silvestrini after their meeting that Reagan had emphasized his desire to abolish nuclear weapons rather than simply reduce them. Since Reagan had already announced his intention to proceed with missile defense, it is hard to believe that he did not discuss with the pope both that policy and its underlying moral-cum-strategic arguments. If that had happened, pope and president would have found themselves in close agreement on a number of issues. Both were close to being nuclear pacifists; they reluctantly tolerated nuclear weapons as a temporary deterrent only until a defense against them could be found. Both were anti-Soviet; they accepted that high levels of defense spending and preparedness, including nuclear deterrence, were justified by the Soviets' inherently aggressive nature. Both were also tough-minded idealists; they believed that a strong moral and cultural resistance to the Soviet bloc might weaken and transform it without a violent conflict. Given this similarity of outlook, John Paul would have understood and almost certainly approved of the twin aspirations of missile defense and nuclear arms reduction that underpinned Reagan's strategic thinking. And because he would have understood that these were Reagan's aims, he would probably have accepted the short- to medium-term policy of building up America's military power, including its nuclear stockpiles, since the buildup was intended not for use but to underline the futility of competing economically and militarily with the United States.

This potential for understanding was not true, however, of the U.S. Conference of Catholic Bishops (USCCB). It is certain that the bishops collectively disapproved of Reagan's nuclear policy and highly likely that they did not understand it. The USCCB had been discussing a joint pastoral letter on war and peace for two years when Reagan delivered his speech. A revised draft submitted to the Vatican was found wanting. In January 1983 the bishops and experts who had worked on the first two drafts were summoned to Rome to discuss these questions with Vatican officials, other bishops, and experts from European countries with a direct interest in U.S. nuclear policy. Father Jan Schotte of the Pontifical Justice and Peace Commission was handed the delicate task of writing a "synthesis" of the discussions to guide the American prelates in their third attempt. It was sent to the USCCB for transmission to the bishops. Archbishop John Roach, the USCCB chairman, and then cardinal-elect Joseph Bernardin, the chairman of the joint pastoral drafting committee, duly forwarded it with the assurance that the Vatican had not raised serious questions and that no major changes would be needed in the final draft.[7]

Those assurances were not strictly true. Following the Vatican's intervention (and presumably as a result of it), the USCCB letter—"The Challenge of Peace"—was significantly rewritten. The second draft had originally treated the "pacifist" and "just war" traditions as almost equal in Catholic thought; the third made clear that the just war tradition was the sole authentically Catholic one. While acknowledging that individual Catholics could take a pacifist stance for themselves, the final draft now pointed out that no nation could adopt a pacifist position, on the grounds that governments have a responsibility to protect their citizens. It expanded the justifications for deterrence from one ("preventing the use of nuclear weapons") to several, including the discouragement of aggression. Deterrence was now granted a "strictly conditioned moral acceptance." And in response to the Vatican's criticisms that levels of authority had been muddled earlier, the final draft reluctantly conceded: "The applications of principles in this pastoral letter do not carry the same moral authority as our statements of universal moral principles and formal church teaching."[8] That was an elegant understatement. Most of the bishops' proposals in the final version were prudential judgments that were not binding on Catholics, that were arguably an intrusion into the legitimate sphere of the laity, and on which the bishops spoke with no particular authority.[9]

Even with these improvements, the document was unsatisfactory, and because of them it was internally inconsistent. As George Weigel argued in his 1987 study of American Catholic thought on international relations, though the letter drew upon traditional Catholic theology, including "just war" arguments, it was actually driven by very different ideas and emotions. Echoing the arguments of anti-nuclear "survivalists" such as the *New Yorker*'s Jonathan Schell and Australia's Dr. Helen Caldicott, it suggested that nuclear weapons were a unique threat to human survival. Accordingly, such countervailing considerations as resisting totalitarianism could be granted much less weight in policy. It showed no interest in the growing cultural resistance to Communism in Eastern Europe despite its evident significance for peace and war in the nuclear age. And it was influenced by the intellectual snobberies of anti-anti-Communism and hostility to Reagan.[10] These impulses jostled uncomfortably alongside the genuinely Catholic "just war" insertions upon which the Vatican had insisted. In the end "The Challenge of Peace" was recognizable more as a production of the "nuclear freeze" movement than of the Catholic faith.

In one respect that did not matter. Reagan gave his SDI speech three weeks before "The Challenge of Peace" was published. So it is understandable that the document did not deal with strategic missile defense. But if the USCCB had been persuaded by its own arguments, it would have subsequently welcomed SDI—and in particular it would have responded warmly to Reagan's advocacy of missile defense as a means to reduce and eventually eliminate nuclear stockpiles. Nothing of the kind actually happened. Most individual episcopal comments were hostile to Reagan's innovation. And when the USCCB got around to collectively making a statement on it in 1988, it concluded that "proposals to press deployment of SDI do not measure up to the moral criteria outlined in this report." Further down the page, these criteria were found to include "that the framework of arms control agreements and negotiations not be eroded or made more difficult" and that "the stability of deterrence not be weakened."[11] Since the INF treaty eliminating an entire category of nuclear missiles had been signed the previous December, almost five years after Reagan's SDI speech and partly because of it, the bishops seemed to be either unobservant or illogical. The mordant comment of one distinguished Catholic layman, William F. Buckley Jr., serves as a final judgment: "That a congregation of men dominated by moral hierarchical reasoning should reject the search for a shield to use in place of a sword defies penetration."[12]

In retrospect it is clear that many of the bishops and most of their bureaucrats had allowed their political sympathies to overwhelm both their prudential and moral judgment on nuclear war and peace in the Reagan years. Above all, the USCCB, unlike other national hierarchies such as the West German government, gave insufficient weight to the challenge (and evil) of totalitarianism. John Paul sought to restrain the USCCB from these rash and one-sided positions well before his meeting with Reagan.[13] Following that meeting he made no criticism of SDI and offered no support to the USCCB's later criticisms of it. There were rumors that a critical report on SDI would be issued by the Pontifical Commission on Peace and Justice in early 1985, but this never materialized. And in February 1985 John Paul refused a direct request from Soviet foreign minister Andrei Gromyko to speak out against SDI. This record leads to two conclusions: first, that the pope had never shared the absolutist rejection of nuclear weapons after which the USCCB plainly hankered; and second, that after meeting with Reagan, John Paul believed the American president to be sincerely committed to nuclear disarmament and devoted to SDI as a means of achieving that end. As Catholic doctrine teaches that decisions on matters such as war and peace are principally to be decided by the responsible political authorities, the pope was prepared to trust Reagan's judgment on SDI once he had established that the president would be guided by the proper moral considerations.

On the American side, both Reagan and Weinberger, now a zealous convert to SDI, missed no opportunity to stress that SDI was inspired by a moral objection to MAD and was intended to promote disarmament. There is no reason to doubt their sincerity; it was in fact a great irritant to some of their allies, as we shall see. But Reagan would almost certainly have been aware that if he deviated in a major way from his commitment to SDI as a tool of disarmament, he would have been guilty of deceiving the pope. All we know of Reagan, including his high respect for John Paul, tells us that he would have shrunk from such a course. To be sure, Reagan saw SDI as useful in promoting other goals, notably in goading the Soviets to the bargaining table. But he was remarkably consistent—some would say stubborn—in not forgetting SDI's primary purpose. This required considerable flexibility on his part in dealing with the British prime minister.

Unacceptable Destruction

Thatcher had told Gorbachev at their famous first meeting in Chequers not to bother trying to separate her from Reagan over SDI. She had said simply, "Don't waste any time on trying to persuade me to say to Ron Reagan: 'Do not go ahead with SDI.' That will get nowhere." She was as good as her word. But her word did not quite convey her full opinion of missile defense.[14]

As a scientist with a healthy respect for U.S. technology, she never shared the outright scorn for SDI expressed by most European governments and military experts. A nation that had sent a man to the moon in the 1960s might well develop the capability to shoot down missiles in the 1990s. Thatcher also calculated that if Britain went along with Reagan's program (particularly if others did not), she would then be able to secure lucrative contracts for the many British companies specializing in advanced military technologies. And though she had some misgivings about SDI, her method of dealing with disagreements between herself and Reagan was to give him strong support in public while fighting for what she wanted in private. All that disposed her to support SDI.[15]

Her misgivings, however, were not trivial. The lesser question was technical: would it work? Experts at the time decisively dismissed SDI. It would not work and, even if it did, it could easily be overwhelmed if the other side built more missiles. But even these detractors realized that these obstacles might be overcome. After all, the Soviets, while denouncing Reagan's proposals as both impractical and barbaric, were also conducting research on their own missile defense system. That suggested the idea might work. If it did, many analysts believed, the Americans might be encouraged to retreat behind their missile shield and neglect the strategic interests of their European allies. European governments had developed that anxiety within days of Reagan's March 23 speech. Even launching the idea of missile defense had upset them. In addition, Thatcher had a parochial concern: would such an anti-missile shield, if developed by both the United States and the Soviets, neutralize the smaller independent British deterrent—the Trident on which she had spent so much money? But her main concern was whether SDI would strengthen or weaken deterrence—the balance of terror that had kept the peace in Europe for almost forty years. She adhered to "a slightly qualified version of the doctrine known as MAD," or what she called "unacceptable destruction." This revised theory held that the destruction following a nuclear exchange would be so severe that it would deter both nuclear war and conventional war. If SDI was likely to undermine such deterrence, she had to oppose it, as the Soviet Union enjoyed a large preponderance of conventional forces. A total missile defense, in addition to risking a suicidal outbreak of conflict, would therefore necessitate a large and immediate increase in spending on conventional defense. Her government was already increasing defense spending by 3 percent annually. Still more would be crippling.[16] Thatcher's argument here revealed the dirty little secret underlying MAD: nuclear weapons were a relatively cheap form of defense. SDI threatened to replace them with something more expensive.

Thatcher soon saw a silver lining in the mushroom cloud: an impenetrable defense was simply impractical. Neither life nor science was like that. But SDI could make deterrence both safer and more stable. If an SDI system could shoot down even a few incoming missiles, then a potential aggressor could never be certain that he would destroy all or enough of the means of retaliation. So the Soviets could not risk a first strike. Her task therefore was to persuade the president to develop SDI within limits that would enhance deterrence in this way rather than replace it with defense—especially since the latter approach would leave Western Europe vulnerable to a conventional assault. Napoleon had once said that you could do anything with bayonets except sit on them. Similarly, you could do anything with missile defense except halt the advance of tanks and infantry with it. The prime minister set off to Washington by way of China to make that point.

Immediately following her talks with Gorbachev at Chequers in December 1984, Thatcher went to Beijing to sign the Hong Kong agreement, transferring, with certain protections, sovreignty over Hong Kong from Britain to China, and then journeyed on to Camp David to meet with Reagan and his advisers. It was a grueling schedule but it ended with a great diplomatic coup. Because there was no clear agenda for the Camp David talks—and in particular because the Americans had no expectation that SDI would be the main topic of debate—Cap Weinberger and his Pentagon experts were not present. But George Shultz and the State Department, who were largely sympathetic to Thatcher's anxieties and saw her as representing Europe on the issue, were there. And when the British delegation focused discussion almost entirely on SDI, it prevailed. The British knew what they wanted, had prepared their case carefully, and argued for it forcefully. Reagan, national security adviser Bud McFarlane, and Shultz, in the absence of Weinberger, were taken by surprise, divided and conquered—though they were more or less willing prisoners.[17]

Thatcher elicited agreement on a four-point program that placed the development of SDI in a NATO and Geneva context. The four points were:

1. The U.S.—and Western—aim was not to achieve superiority, but to maintain balance, taking account of Soviet developments.
2. SDI deployment would, in view of treaty obligations, be a matter for negotiation.
3. The overall aim was to enhance, not undercut deterrence.
4. East-West negotiations would aim to achieve security with reduced levels of offensive systems on both sides.

One-sided diplomatic coups rarely survive, and there was something for both sides in this statement. Thatcher got item three, Reagan item four, and they shared the honors on items one and two. But the overall effect of the agreement was to subject America's development of SDI to NATO debate and to a restrictive interpretation of its potential.[18]

Thatcher fought strongly to maintain these limitations in the run-up to the November 1985 Geneva summit. In July of that year she attended a White House seminar on arms control along with almost all the senior political-military figures in the U.S. government. According to other participants, she talked almost nonstop about how the administration's constant talk about SDI was delegitimizing nuclear weapons. After the meeting Shultz said to Reagan, "Boy, she's not a very good listener, is she?" Reagan replied tolerantly, "But she's a marvelous talker."[19]

Reagan's patience, however, did not extend to his acquiescence when Thatcher directly challenged his cherished concept of SDI as a means of nuclear disarmament. That exchange, occurring over lunch in the White House, revealed the stark difference between the two leaders' views of SDI—and also disproved the casual assumption of many people, even those around Reagan, that the old boy didn't really grasp the implications of his "astrodome." The kerfuffle began after Thatcher had outlined her familiar argument that SDI would never enable the United States and the West to have complete nuclear armament.

"If you follow that logic to its implied conclusion," she said, "and do get rid of nuclear weapons, you expose a dramatic conventional imbalance, do you not? And would we not have to restore that balance at considerable expense?"

"Yes," replied Reagan, "that's exactly what I imagined." As he said this, the president looked the prime minister squarely in the eye. There was a brief silence. Both their staffs felt that this exchange should never become public knowledge.[20]

Yet the row did them both credit. They had boiled down their disagreements over SDI to the essential dispute and staked out their respective positions with great clarity. For the moment it seemed that they could agree on developing an SDI research program and leave their ultimate argument to be settled later.

Reagan had the comfort of knowing he had the pope on his side. Meanwhile, Thatcher did not realize she had the moral support of the U.S. Catholic bishops for her contrary policy. It would probably have alarmed her if she had known. Yet she would need support from somewhere sooner than either of them expected. They might have thought that their dispute could be settled by the future—but that future was only two years away.

The Geneva Prelude

On the fortieth anniversary of D-Day, Reagan delivered a justly famous tribute to "the boys of Pointe du Hoc" who had stormed the cliffs overlooking Omaha Beach. He did so standing on the same cliffs in front of the survivors of that bloody day and, through the injustice of genetic inheritance, looking younger than the "boys," now fatter and bespectacled, who were his juniors.

"These are the boys of Pointe du Hoc. These are the men who took the cliffs. These are the champions who helped free a continent. These are the heroes who helped end a war," said the president.

It was an affecting moment. There was the moving contrast between the boys of the past and the elderly men of the present. There were the simple but powerfully evocative words of speechwriter Peggy Noonan. And there was Reagan himself, who spoke them eloquently because he believed them deeply. He had volunteered for the U.S. Army six years before the outbreak of war because he sensed the coming conflict, but due to poor eyesight and deafness in one ear, he had been assigned on the outbreak of hostilities to help make films for the armed forces not far from Hollywood. He always felt a special respect and obligation to those who risked harm for the common good. On one occasion, when he was participating in a military school graduation, Reagan threw out the official program that called for him to leave after awarding ten certificates. "I may have to ask these young people to risk their lives," he told Dick Walters. "I think I can stand for an hour or two and greet them all personally."[21]

The ceremony on Pointe du Hoc made an especially deep impression on the French. Franco-American relations were at a high point in 1984, a sign that Europeans generally were warming up to the cowboy president. Reagan and Mitterrand got on well personally despite a seemingly wide gulf of ideology; polls even showed that Reagan was France's favorite in the forthcoming presidential election that fall.[22] And the anniversary of D-Day, when many GIs returned with their families to meet those they had liberated, had awoken warm memories of the wartime alliance. Reagan captured all those feelings in his address. Later that day, Evan Galbraith, the U.S. ambassador to Paris, brought the president some heartwarming news. The French government had decided to award him a decoration. Galbraith had not been told exactly what decoration; he thought it might be the Croix de Guerre.

"The Croix de Guerre," said Reagan, looking distinctly upset. "I couldn't possibly accept that. That's for bravery. All I did in the war was to fly a desk." He asked Galbraith to find out if it were true and to solve the problem. Some time later the ambassador returned with the good news that the decoration was the Legion d'Honneur. But Reagan was still not quite satisfied. What was the citation? What were they giving him the honor for?

"For statesmanship," replied Galbraith.

"Oh, statesmanship!" said Reagan and relaxed. "I can play that."[23]

He played that eighteen months later in Geneva. In advance of the first Reagan-Gorbachev summit, the Western media had been touchingly solicitous about the American president's age and infirmities compared to the youth and vigor of the new Soviet leader. This concern was famously rendered absurd when on the summit's first day—a cold Swiss November morning—Reagan, coatless and hatless, bounded down the steps of their meeting place at the Villa Fleur d'Eau to greet a Gorbachev who looked all too Soviet as he emerged in coat, trilby, and muffler from his official ZIL.

Years later Reagan's official biographer asked Gorbachev what he had sensed as he looked into Reagan's eyes. Gorbachev replied, "Sunshine and clear sky. We shook hands like friends. He said something, I don't know what. But at once I felt him to be a very authentic human being." He used the Russian word *lichnost*, which his interpreter translated to Edmund Morris as "someone of great strength of character who rings true all the way to his body and soul."[24] By then, however, Gorbachev's historical reputation was bound up with that of the American president. If they had been friends from the first, Gorbachev would look like a far-sighted peacemaker rather than an outmaneuvered opponent. The reality was that both men were jostling for advantage and also for a deal reciprocal enough to satisfy the other.

Gorbachev faced the more serious dilemma in his negotiating strategy. On one hand, he badly needed a deal reducing armaments so he could divert military resources to the starved Soviet consumer; on the other hand, he had to get SDI abolished. The Soviet Union could not match the American SDI program either economically or technologically. Even if Gorbachev believed his own side's propaganda about the impossibility of an effective missile shield, he could not afford to risk being wrong. And if he accepted a deal that retained SDI, the Soviets would have to spend more money vainly striving to compete than they would save on offensive missiles. Gorbachev could have accepted Reagan's offer to share SDI technology, but routine Soviet paranoia blocked that exit for the moment. Whatever kind of *lichnost* Reagan might be, Gorbachev was not going to bet the collective farm on his authenticity on the first day of the summit season.

Reagan was under no such pressure. He had just been re-elected to his final term. The U.S. economy was booming. And though he was being pressed by Nancy and others to construct a peacemaker's legacy, he knew that Geneva was merely the first of a series of summit meetings. This was the "getting-to-know-you" scene; the denouement was some way off. The most Geneva could offer him was a rise in his opinion poll ratings as he gradually shook off his Cold Warrior image. As for his peacemaker's legacy, he was a Cold Warrior of some thirty years' standing. He could live with being one for a while longer.

Gorbachev could hardly win on such an uneven playing field if Reagan stood firm. The Russian's best hope was that the president would be pressured by his advisers into making concessions against his better judgment. Reagan was in fact bombarded by such advice, sometimes irritated by it, and occasionally willing to be persuaded by it.[25] In preparation for the summit he had agreed to advance a 50 percent cut in strategic offensive systems on both sides. (This was an odd sort of concession, though one typical of arms control deals, since the official U.S. position on INF missiles had long been the "zero-zero option." By keeping some U.S. missiles in Europe, the United States would save Moscow from the diplomatic humiliation of having to remove all its SS-20s.) But the U.S. president had not denounced the evil empire for thirty years and then narrowly survived an assassination attempt simply in order to pursue a more cautious version of Nixon's détente. He had his sticking points. Unfortunately for Gorbachev, the main one was SDI.

Given these limitations, the Geneva summit was a modest success—more modest for Gorbachev and more of a success for Reagan—but a success all the same. It was orchestrated not to fail, of course. Even the "surprises," such as Reagan inviting the Soviet leader to join him in a tête-à-tête by the lake, were cleared with the other side in advance so that no one would actually be surprised. The joint communiqué and news conference were likewise planned in advance. But Geneva's success went a little deeper than the public relations patina. The negotiations were blunt and even tough without becoming bitterly hostile. Reagan's opening remark in the plenary session—"Let me tell you why we mistrust you and are suspicious of you"—illustrated this. It was harsh but it also initiated a plea for greater trust. In this frank atmosphere, each side got a clearer view of the other. The Americans ended up more pleased than the Russians. Gorbachev spoke forcefully—extremely so on SDI—but he struck Reagan's advisers at times as almost pleading for an agreement so that the Soviets could enjoy the prosperity of the Germans and Japanese, who "spend so little on weapons."[26] Reagan dispelled the Soviet view that he was an inattentive and lazy pawn of his advisers. Though he was sometimes vague on the details of nuclear weaponry, he was seen by Gorbachev's team as sharp and commanding on the big issues—and determined.

Other questions were discussed—regional disputes, arms reductions, what classes of weapons to include in the proposed 50 percent cut—but SDI was the central issue. Just before the first plenary session broke up, Reagan offered to share SDI technology with the Soviets: "I have made an argument—to share with you our anti-missile shield.... You've been researching such a system also.... If either one of us comes up with a solution, let's share it, make it available to everyone, remove all fear of a nuclear strike." After lunch Gorbachev responded with a firm rejection: "The SDI is a terrible arms race—a race in space. We would have to take steps to smash your shield like a porcelain plate." Whether "spears" or "shields," he added, the space-based weapons were undeniably military.

Reagan gave him the same steady gaze as he had given Thatcher the year before: "No, I don't agree."

"We seem to have reached a dead end," said Gorbachev.

They continued debating SDI for another day. Those further debates finally climaxed in much the same way. Gorbachev threw down his pencil and said, "I regret you can't see it our way." But failure to agree on SDI—which would dominate Soviet–American relations for another two years—had not scuttled the summit. Reagan and Gorbachev had at least begun to like each other. Gorbachev was charmed by Reagan's jokes and, like everyone else, curious about his Hollywood celebrity. He asked the veteran actor what it was like to see his younger self on the screen.

"You've set me up for a great one-liner," replied Reagan. "Like meeting a son you never knew you had."

Reagan in turn picked up on a reference to God in Gorbachev's opening remarks: "We are not at war with each other and let's pray to God we never shall be." This remark deeply impressed Reagan, who later told the West German president that he was convinced Gorbachev believed in God. He wanted to get him alone for a religious discussion. Reagan was almost certainly mistaken here—Gorbachev's remark was either a throwaway colloquial expression or, more likely, a calculated attempt to appeal to what the Soviets well knew was a strong religious strand in Reagan's psychology.[27] Whatever it was, it worked. Reagan told Pat Buchanan, his communications director, that he had taken three anti-Soviet passages out of the draft of his closing remarks at Geneva: "Pat, this has been a good meeting. I think I can work with this guy. I can't just keep poking him in the eye."[28]

And despite the careful choreography of Geneva, Reagan pulled off a genuine surprise. After their conversation in the lakeside house, as both leaders were walking toward Gorbachev's limousine, Reagan extended an unscripted invitation to the Gorbachevs to visit him in Washington for a second summit. Gorbachev was taken aback—some accounts say he paled—and then issued a return invitation to Moscow which Reagan in turn accepted. Both men then shook hands with unusual warmth. Reagan complained later that his hand had almost been crushed.

They were right to be pleased. The promise of further summits was the final guarantee of Geneva's success. It meant that the relatively modest formal agreements—cultural exchanges, civil air safety regulations, and a 50 percent cut in nuclear arsenals "appropriately applied"—were seen not as disappointing half-measures but as first steps in a hopeful process. Returning home, Reagan went directly from the plane to a joint session of Congress, where he was vociferously cheered. He told his diary: "I haven't gotten such a reception since I was shot." The next day his approval ratings reached the low eighties.

And SDI had not been even slightly compromised.

Keeping the Faith in a Dying Empire

Not everyone was pleased, however. Senator Edward Kennedy visited Moscow in February 1986 and met Gorbachev for the first time. His reception was much friendlier than the dusty dismissal he had received from Andropov four years earlier. The transcript of their meeting has been reclassified by the Putin administration. But Vadim Zagladin, the deputy head of the International Department, reported quite fully to Gorbachev and the Politburo on his own extensive talks with the U.S. senator. It is plain from his accounts that Kennedy and the Soviets saw eye-to-eye on several important matters. So Zagladin was alarmed to report that Kennedy was not entirely happy with the outcome of the Geneva summit:

> E. Kennedy emphasized the following ideas. 1. The recent meeting has changed the climate of the world in many respects.... The change is for the better, the birth of hopes for a better future. However, this process also has a negative side. President Reagan actively uses the new climate. And the problem is not only that his popularity is growing after Geneva. In fact Geneva allowed Reagan to slow down the process of movement to any positive results in negotiations with the USSR. He says that the situation has already changed, that he has instituted dialogue with the Russians, while in fact he does nothing or manages things in the old direction, i.e., that of increasing military preparations. From the Democrats' point of view, all of this is very bad. This does not mean they are against Geneva or the spirit of Geneva—they are for it. But they think it important not to allow Reagan to abuse a good thing for bad purposes.... In his [Kennedy's] opinion, it is important to keep increasing pressure on the administration from different sides, both abroad and at home. He would like, during his conversation with Comrade Gorbachev, to suggest some specific ideas on this issue.[29]

After the senator's meeting with Gorbachev, he again had dinner with Zagladin, who reported that the encounter had been a great success:

> 1. The senator [came away with] a strong impression from his talk with Comrade M.S. Gorbachev. "I liked him very much," Kennedy said. "He is a firm, though flexible, leader who knows what he wants." 2. At the same time, in E. Kennedy's opinion, "my Soviet friends have not yet thoroughly understood the psychology of the Americans and the essence of Reagan's tactics."... The average American sees the situation as follows:

"Reagan has managed to establish contacts with the Russians, gaining much from them, but giving nothing. He is a great leader!"...The senator's speculations seemed to suggest that Geneva was a great success for Reagan and a doubtful one for us. So I asked him a direct question: "Well, do you think it was a mistake to go to Geneva?" The senator replied without hesitation: "No, it was not, but you should keep pressing, be firmer."

According to Zagladin, Kennedy finished with some practical guidance on how to outmaneuver Reagan in future negotiations:

"We should choose two or three points which could be achieved and constantly put pressure on Reagan in order to restrict his freedom of maneuver. These points might be the following: confirmation of the ABM treaty; restriction of the nuclear test limits and a cut in their number; missiles in Europe" (though Reagan, Kennedy said, will demand the elimination of missiles from Asia).

Summarizing, Kennedy said, "The present complacency of the Americans, their almost Christmas mood, must be broken. You should put more pressure, and firmer pressure, on Reagan....And, of course, I shall think over what can be done on my side, on the Senate's side. At the Congress session, I shall report on my meeting with Gorbachev. I will speak in the country as many times as necessary. Gorbachev is right, we should not miss this opportunity."[30]

One of the many ironies of this conversation is how little Kennedy understood the situation and standing of the Soviet Union in early 1986. He speaks to Zagladin—and presumably to Gorbachev—as if the USSR were a superpower equal to his own country in economic and military strength. He advises them to stand firm and put pressure on Reagan. He assumes a strategic reach and a freedom of maneuver that for the Soviets must have had the powerfully tacky aroma of 1970s nostalgia. To leaders

with the narrowing horizons of Gorbachev and the Politburo, his promise
of congressional help may have sounded like the trumpet call of the U.S.
Fifth Cavalry. But could they really believe it?

They were far more likely to reason like the Soviet apparatchiks negotiating with a canny Parisian jeweler in the movie *Ninotchka*: "Let's
uphold the prestige of the Soviet Union for another ten minutes"—and
then give in. Or, in Gorbachev's case, for one more summit meeting.

But Western leftists, both in America and Europe, were trapped in a
time warp by the mid-1980s. Their own ideological predilections—and the
predictions based upon them—deterred them from noticing two major
developments. The first was that the Soviet Union was a declining power
both economically and militarily. John Kenneth Galbraith, the distinguished Harvard economist who enjoyed almost saintly status among
American liberals, declared in 1984, "That the Soviet system has made
great material progress in recent years is evident both from the statistics
and from the general urban scene.... One sees it in the appearance of well-
being of the people on the streets . . . and the general aspect of restaurants,
theaters, and shops.... Partly, the Russian system succeeds because, in contrast with the Western industrial economies, it makes full use of its man-
power." At the time the Soviet economy was near catatonic. As late as
1989, well-known economic columnist Lester Thurow opined, "Can economic command significantly...accelerate the growth process? The
remarkable performance of the Soviet Union suggests that it can.... Today
it is a country whose economic achievements bear comparison with those
of the United States."[31] By far the most embarrassing case of intellectual
myopia, however, was that of Paul Samuelson, winner of the 1970 Nobel
Prize in economics and author of the best-selling economics textbook since
World War II. As non-economist Tom Bethell pointed out in a 1988 article in *National Review*, successive editions of Samuelson's *Economics*
showed a graph of relative growth rates for the U.S. and Soviet economies
with the Soviet growth rate rising more steeply than the American one.
Though starting from a lower base, the Soviets were projected to overtake
the U.S. in about twenty-five years. Bethell's denouement deserves to be
quoted in full:

With each new edition of the book, the date of intersection with the U.S economy was shifted out into the future. Samuelson's seventh edition (1967), for example, put the Soviet economy at 50 percent of the U.S. economy in 1960, with growth paths showing a probable intersection point in about 1990. In a cautionary note, however, Samuelson warned that "from 1960 to 1967 it would appear that the United States has moved at the very top of its range," while the USSR, "because of bad weather and crops and shortening of the work week, may have moved at the bottom of her projected range."

By the tenth edition (1976), nonetheless, the Soviet GNP had moved ahead to 57 percent of the U.S. economy. The Soviets had narrowed the gap—despite bad weather and long weekends, the seventh-edition graph was reproduced exactly, although updated along the time axis, this time showing a probable intersection point around the year 2000. The graph has been dropped from Samuelson's latest (twelfth) edition, co-authored with William Nordhaus.[32]

If liberal economists were wrong, the performance of Sovietologists, historians, strategists, and foreign policy experts was no better. In a 1982 article in *Foreign Affairs*, the house journal of the foreign policy establishment, Columbia University Sovietologist Seweryn Bialer had written, "The Soviet Union is not now, nor will it be during the next decade, in the throes of a true systemic crisis, for it boasts enormous unused reserves of political and social stability." That same year historian Arthur Schlesinger Jr. declared confidently that "those in the United States who think the Soviet Union is on the verge of economic and social collapse [are] wishful thinkers" and only "kidding themselves." "Each superpower has economic troubles," he maintained; "neither is on the ropes."[33] And in 1981 Strobe Talbott, then of *Time* magazine, later of the Clinton administration, had written, "Though some second-echelon hardliners in the Reagan administration... espouse the early 1950s goal of rolling back Soviet domination of Eastern Europe, the U.S. simply does not have the military or political power to do that."[34] Such judgments were even refined down to the level of strategic nuclear warheads, with liberal strategists arguing that the Weinberger defense buildup was militarily futile since the Soviet Union would always be able to match any U.S. increase.

Kennedy was living in a mental universe shaped and bounded by these intellectuals. To their influence was added the simple impressiveness of any structure that has been around a long time. In 1988 it required a daring act of imagination to envisage a world without the Soviet Union as a major player. Three years later it had disappeared altogether. Finally, what Seymour Martin Lipset and Gyorgy Bence once remarked of most Sovietologists applied more broadly to Kennedy and the Left: their politics "undermined their capacity to accept the view that economic statism, planning, [and] socialist incentives would not work." So they dismissed as futile Reagan's shrewd policy of competing the USSR into the ground.

Gorbachev knew in the most painful way how false and complacent were these assessments. At a White House dinner in December 1987, when he could afford to be forthcoming, he found himself at a table with Richard Perle, late of the Pentagon. Perle asked him if he knew how much the Soviet Union spent on defense. Gorbachev replied he did know but that it was a state secret.

"Let me give you my estimate," said Perle. "Twenty-five percent of your gross national product."

Gorbachev smiled and passed on to another topic. His smile may have been one of relief that the Americans had not been better informed. Perle's guess was higher than any official U.S. estimate—the CIA's was 16 percent. But it was still almost certainly an underestimate.[35]

The Counter-Revolution Rolls On

If Western leftists were wearing blinkers when they gazed upon the Soviet Union, that was an intellectual disability. When they failed to notice the transformation of their own (and Asian) economies by Reaganism and Thatcherism, that was a self-inflicted and potentially fatal wound.

Almost all the intellectual energy of both American and British leftists was spent in attempting to demonstrate the failure of these policies by criteria that were short-term, parochial, and irrelevant to the dramatic character of the economic changes they were instigating.[36] American liberals, for instance, denounced vast deficits extending indefinitely into the future when they were in fact replaced by surpluses in less than a decade. Labour critics of Thatcherism in Britain could hardly complain about deficits since the public sector had a run of surpluses in the mid-1980s. They denounced instead the high levels of unemployment under Thatcher. But higher unemployment was inevitable as a temporary byproduct of reducing inflation; it came down once inflation was wrung out of the economy. The Western European countries such as France, Spain, and Germany that followed Labour's interventionist "social model" have had unemployment levels of between 10 and 20 percent for almost two decades now, while in contrast, the British unemployment rate has been consistently in single digits, and in August 2006 was at 3 percent. (If unemployment is a temporary effect of fighting inflation, it is a permanent result of tolerating it—and also an effect of pricing workers out of jobs by inflating their wages with social benefits.)

Reaganism and Thatcherism were in essence the same basic free market approach applied in different circumstances. Thus, an important component of Thatcherism was labor market deregulation whereas the U.S. labor market was already deregulated. Reaganism, on the other hand, pruned the excessive Depression-era financial regulations that in Britain were handled by a more flexible and informal system of self-regulation.[37] Both sought to provide a framework of monetary stability within which individuals and companies could pursue their own projects with as little hindrance as possible and as much finance as the market would grant. Given the acceleration of scientific and technical knowledge, these projects were likely to include processes, jobs, and industries that had not previously existed. Attempts to explain this during the period of rising unemployment were resented and mocked by those in existing industries suffering from recession. Critics of both Reagan and Thatcher were judging their policies as if they were designed to revive the immediate postwar economy of heavy industrial manufacturing. In fact, though neither Reagan nor Thatcher could have made this precise prediction themselves, they were replacing that economy with a new "post-industrial" one based on rapid communications. Because the critics were looking at the wrong gauges, they never noticed the information revolution igniting under their noses.

This revolution took place in two stages. In the first stage the two leaders set about establishing a stable monetary framework by defeating inflation—a policy with heavy political costs. This was the period when Reagan, against the advice of his own aides, gave strong public support to an embattled Thatcher with the promise in 1981 that both would be "home safe and soon enough." Reagan himself endured unpopularity to back Paul Volcker, Carter's appointee as chairman of the Federal Reserve, who was squeezing double-digit inflation out of the U.S. economy by means of monetary restraint. Unemployment rose to 10 percent in 1982. The Republicans lost twenty-six seats in the House of Representatives and barely held the Senate in that year's mid-term elections. But Reagan was a confirmed monetarist and stayed the course. Economically, it was morning in America less than a year later. Inflation was defeated, and under Volcker's successors Alan Greenspan and Ben Bernanke, it has remained under firm control up to the present. Christopher DeMuth summed up this success:

> Since the inflation-breaking year of 1982, the Federal Reserve Board has pursued a consistent low-inflation policy, and inflation has averaged less than 2.6 percent—as compared with 7.6 percent for the decade before 1982. Over the same periods, unemployment fell from an average of 7 percent to less than 6 percent, and continues to fall. No one is arguing today that inflation is something we should tolerate in order to achieve low unemployment or other economic goals.[38]

Thatcher accomplished the same triumph over inflation against heavier odds, since inflation was more entrenched in the UK economy. In her case, however, the monetary squeeze also fell foul of the law of unintended consequences. Because the targeted monetary measures proved to be unreliable, Thatcher and her principal economic ministers, Geoffrey Howe and Nigel Lawson, imposed a far tougher squeeze on the economy than they either intended or initially realized. They thought they were imposing a Friedmanite policy of monetary gradualism when they were in fact applying a short, sharp monetary "shock" as advocated by F. A. Hayek.[39] This had numerous ill effects, notably job losses and factory closures, but it had one extremely valuable effect that mattered more: coming after the "winter of discontent," it dramatically altered the attitudes of workers and labor unions. In order to keep their jobs in a growing recession, they abandoned restrictive practices, shed over-manning, worked new capital machinery efficiently, ignored their more extreme labor union leaders, and in general allowed management to manage. It was a strange paradox: a macroeconomic monetary squeeze of unintended severity forged the psychological attitudes needed for a successful microeconomic supply-side revolution.

No less important was the success of the monetary policy—the so-called Medium-Term Financial Strategy (MTFS). In spring 1980, during the preparations for the British budget, Nigel Lawson, the architect of the MTFS, was asked by a senior treasury official what level of inflation (then 20 percent) he forecast for 1983–84. To general skepticism he guesstimated 5 percent. In the event the figure turned out to be slightly lower. And as Lawson underlines with justifiable pride in his memoirs, even though the method of controlling the money supply changed later, the abiding legacy of the MTFS was a general consensus that macroeconomic policy should provide a stable non-inflationary monetary environment favorable to the launch and success of supply-side initiatives.[40]

The second stage in creating a new information economy was the introduction of incentives for—and the removal of barriers to—economic innovation. In both countries these were the reduction of marginal income tax rates and financial and economic deregulation. Reagan added antitrust policy in the U.S., and Thatcher brought in labor market deregulation and privatization in Britain. Almost all these policies were strongly resisted by political opponents. They eventually passed into law (or practice) only as a result of determined political leadership by president and prime minister. Reagan's first landmark tax reform program got through because a wounded president in dressing gown and pajamas made call after call to doubtful congressmen shortly after his release from the hospital in 1981.

But the final entrenchment of "Reaganomics" as the new governing orthodoxy can be precisely dated: it was October 22, 1986, when the president signed a second landmark tax reform. The bipartisan bill eliminated exemptions in return for lowering tax rates and fixing a top income tax rate of 28 percent. At a time when Reagan was said to be losing his clout, he had first persuaded the House Republicans to swallow a liberal bill crafted largely by the Democratic majority and then overawed the House Democrats into accepting the more conservative version from the Republican Senate. It was a tour de force of democratic leadership—and it established the basic ground rules for Washington budgetary politics since then.[41]

Thatcher had even harder opposition to overcome. Her labor market deregulation not only had to run the gauntlet of Labour MPs and nervous Tory "wets," but even after passing into law it had to survive a major non-parliamentary challenge in the 1984–85 miners' strike. This was no conventional industrial dispute. It was a violent attempt by a minority of the miners' union, led by the Marxist revolutionary Arthur Scargill, to force the majority of union members to strike in order to compel London to subsidize loss-making mines indefinitely. Such a defeat would also have meant, as Scargill and others repeatedly argued, not only the abandonment of Thatcher's entire economic strategy, but also a new political situation in which the labor unions would exercise an effective veto over government policy across the board. In pursuit of this blend of economic irrationalism and Leninist democracy, Scargill led physical attacks on miners who stayed at work and on the police who protected them. Pitched battles with serious casualties, including at least one death, occurred throughout mining areas. It dominated national politics for more than a year. As Thatcher noted in her memoirs, it was an "insurrection" rather than a strike.

If Scargill could not count on his union's members—they defeated him in a national strike ballot—he was able to recruit support elsewhere. On February 4, 1985, a top-secret note from the CPSU International Department proposed that one million rubles be transferred to Scargill through the All-Union Central Council of the Trade Unions in Moscow and an American bank in Dublin. According to Scargill, this routing "would make

it absolutely impossible to discover the source of the money."[42] Supporting documents show that Scargill sought this help from the Soviet embassy
in London on the grounds that "M. Thatcher wants to break the unions
by any means... [or] she will have to resign herself." The request was
approved and signed by, among others, Gorbachev. Two months after the
Chequers meeting, the Soviet leader had shown that he was a man who
could do business with a variety of partners.[43]

Scargill gained little except time from this transaction. Expecting him to
launch a political strike, Thatcher and her energy ministers (first Lawson,
later Peter Walker) had spent the previous few years building up supplies
of coal at the power stations. No other unions gave the striking miners
serious support. The country was neither brought to a halt nor suffered
serious economic damage. Eventually the miners returned to work, march-
ing behind banners and accompanied by brass bands, but utterly and completely routed. This was a victory for Thatcher as important as the
Falklands War. It removed the last lingering, nervous fear of both the voters and the markets that labor unions could render Britain ungovernable
and the elected government impotent. It weakened the extreme left everywhere, including in the Labour Party, by demonstrating that its trump
cards amounted to a busted flush. And though Labour took some years to
realize the fact, Thatcher's victory entrenched her economic and labor
reforms as the new consensus of British politics.

Financially stable and economically deregulated, the American and
British economies now began their respective long booms combining economic growth with price stability. Since 1982 the U.S. has enjoyed twenty-
four years of high economic growth interrupted by only two very short and
shallow recessions. The UK has enjoyed the same period of growth, interrupted by a single but more serious recession in the early 1990s,[44] and now
boasts the fourth-largest economy in the world. (These overall figures naturally conceal some policy failures, such as America's persistent inability
to restrain spending and the recent growth of re-regulation in the UK under
pressure from the European Union.)

But these statistics also conceal the massive restructuring of the two
economies that Reaganism and Thatcherism achieved—and the social-

psychological changes accompanying them. Loss-making industries were either closed down or reduced in size. Manufacturing industries shed labor, often while increasing output, as they restructured to meet foreign competition. New industries in the financial services, information, and high-tech sectors were established—often by new companies or entrepreneurs from academic and non-industrial backgrounds. Privatization transformed inefficient state-owned industries into dynamic private sector ones. New financial instruments allowed entrepreneurs to take over sluggish low-earning companies and put their assets to more profitable uses. In general the Anglo-American economies were characterized by change, profitability, growth, and the better allocation of resources, including labor.

Pure business efficiency was not the most important result of the Reagan-Thatcher revolution, however. There was a social side to economic liberalization. Start-ups, small businesses, and self-employment played an important role in the restructuring of both economies. Nigel Lawson points out a number of them in the British case:

> For many years there was an average increase of five hundred new firms per week—after deducting closures. There was a rise from little more than one million to over three million in the number of self-employed. The UK venture capitalist industry, which scarcely existed when we first took office, had by 1985 become twice as large as its counterparts in the rest of the European Community taken together.[45]

This spirit of enterprise had flourished in the U.S. for so long that such expressions of it were neither novel nor especially impressive. The 1980s merely saw more of them as deregulation and antitrust policy opened up greater opportunities for business outsiders. In Britain the same developments signified something more fundamental—the spread of an enterprise outlook from the small-business middle class to much wider swathes of society.[46]

Allied with the spread of enterprise was the spread of capital ownership. Thatcher had drawn the battle lines with Labour in a 1987 election speech:

"Labour believes in turning workers against owners; we believe in turning workers into owners." The early first step in this policy was to sell state-owned low-income houses to their tenants at discounts that took account of rent paid over the years. It was a great success socially, politically, and even financially: nearly two million tenants bought their homes, many of them voted Conservative for the first time, and local authorities were no longer saddled with the costs of maintaining the houses sold. Selling shares in newly privatized industries to the general public was the second step. This was even more popular. Two-thirds of Britain's state-owned industries were sold to the private sector, resulting in more efficient industries and wider capital ownership. Between 1979 and 1989 the proportion of the British public owning shares rose from 7 percent to fully one-quarter.

Taken together, the spread of both the enterprise outlook and wider ownership were part of a revival of what Shirley Robin Letwin, the distinguished Anglo-American political theorist, called the "vigorous virtues" in her philosophically groundbreaking study of Thatcherism.[47] These are such qualities as self-reliance, diligence, trustworthiness, and initiative that enable someone who exhibits them to live and work independently in society. Though they are not the only virtues—compassion and cooperation might be called the "softer virtues"—they are essential to the success of a free economy and a civil society as both of these rely on dispersed initiative and self-reliant citizens. The revival of the vigorous virtues (in addition to being the heart of Thatcherism) was an indispensable part of the successful transformation of the U.S. and British economies in the 1980s. It was a psychological restructuring that helped sustain the physical restructuring.

That transformation did not stop at the Atlantic's edge. Reagan and Thatcher were also changing the world economy by virtue of the demonstrative effects of Reaganism and Thatcherism (then rapidly becoming known under the portmanteau term of "neo-liberalism.") They had provided the world with successful models of free and deregulated economies. Their own leftists might disparage the new employment opportunities as "McJobs," but other countries began replicating the same policies. Tax cuts were America's principal intellectual export, as privatization was Britain's. Of the two, privatization was probably the more important on a global basis since both Third World and post-Communist economies were lumbered with a vast number of inefficient state industries. Privatization expertise became one of the City of London's most profitable services over the next two decades.

Even the Soviets and Western European Communists were forced to change course by the widespread adoption of privatization internationally—and also the equally widespread acceptance of the market logic behind it. Thus in a 1986 conversation between Gorbachev and Alexander Natta, the general secretary of the Italian Communist Party, there occurs this fascinating little exchange:

> **Natta:** At the same time we, the Communists, having either overestimated or underestimated the functions of the "welfare state," kept defending situations which, as it became clear only now, we should not have defended. As a result, a bureaucratic apparatus, which serves itself, has swelled. It is interesting that a certain similarity with your situation, which you call stagnation, can be seen here.
>
> **Gorbachev:** "Parkinson's law"[48] works everywhere...
>
> **Natta:** Any bureaucratization encourages the apparatus to protect its own interests and to forget about the citizens' interests. I suppose, that is exactly why the right's demands of re-privatization are falling on a fertile ground in Western public opinion.[49]

In general the recovery of the British economy on free market lines was curiously more impressive than America's revival because it started from a lower economic point—Britain in 1979 was frequently compared unfavorably to East Germany—and occurred in a country that had pioneered social democracy. Still, the essential principles of both experiments were the same. Once the command economies of the Soviet bloc collapsed in 1989, revealing the extraordinary bankruptcy of state planning, it was the Reagan-Thatcher model that the new democracies sought to emulate.

Even in the mid-1980s, however, when Gorbachev looked out from Moscow to the developing world, he saw Asian countries such as Singapore, Hong Kong, South Korea, and Taiwan defying history. Twenty years previously he, Brezhnev, and even the West had expected such vulnerable nations to either fall victim to Marxist guerrillas in black pajamas or join the winning socialist side in a new world economic order of administered trade. Now that the "Asian Tigers" were booming free economies, other Asian countries, even China itself, began converting to capitalism. The Third World's finance ministers were increasingly disciples of Friedman, Hayek, and Adam Smith. Neo-liberalism had replaced Marxism as the ideology of the future.

Selling *perestroika* to his nervous Politburo, Gorbachev pointed out that tiny Singapore was exporting more annually than the vast Soviet Union. He could not hope to compete with the ex–Third World, let alone catch up to the new information economies of the Anglosphere, unless he drastically reduced military spending. But reform came with a built-in dilemma. Competing with the U.S. on missile defense would mean diverting more resources to the military, but abandoning that competition would mean losing the Cold War.

He decided to gamble everything on a single throw of the dice. He would convince Reagan to abandon SDI by exploiting the president's one gaping vulnerability: his idealism.

A Near-Miss in Reykjavik

Gorbachev arrived in Reykjavik on October 10, 1986, for what the American side expected to be merely a one-day preparatory meeting for the Washington summit. Reagan had not even brought Nancy along—and, like Gorbachev, who had brought Raisa, he valued his wife's moral support. By contrast, the Soviets had spent weeks preparing for this event. Gorbachev was eager to present as radical a package of arms control reductions as possible. His aide Anatoly Chernyaev sent him a note during these discussions that said: "The main goal of Reykjavik, if I understood you correctly...is to sweep Reagan off his feet with our bold, even risky approach to the central problem of world politics."[50] In order to succeed in this, he had to swoop down on Reagan and catch him by surprise, rather as Thatcher had done at Camp David.

Gorbachev in particular, but also the Soviets in general, had reassessed their original opinion of Reagan. Anatoly Dobrynin later admitted that in 1981 Brezhnev had made a serious error in responding to Reagan's personal appeal with such stilted agitprop. Reagan had been sincere and they had missed an opportunity. They had come to realize that he was a firm opponent of the Soviets who would resist any number of threats or pressures—who would indeed become tougher in response. But he had also demonstrated at Geneva and in his earlier diplomatic contacts with them two qualities to which they might appeal.[51] He believed in the "human factor" in politics—namely, that if he could engage Gorbachev in a one-on-one discussion or show him the friendliness of the ordinary American, he would have a good chance of persuading Gorbachev to reach a genuine peace accord. Reagan also was a sincere disarmer who wanted to rid the world of as many nuclear missiles as was safely possible.

Reagan also had a third quality, the Soviets came to believe, which magnified the importance of the first two. Though the Western media kept treating Reagan as the pawn of his staff, he had shown his opponents at Geneva that he was firmly confident in his own judgment. He would listen to his aides and experts but make up his own mind. Nixon confirmed this impression in a conversation with the Soviet leader. But Gorbachev still needed some persuasion on this point. He had to be argued by Mitterrand, whom they also consulted, out of the belief that Reagan was merely a tool of the military-industrial complex whose personal qualities and beliefs were secondary matters. Mitterrand managed to convince him that Reagan was both eager to catch the tide of peacemaking and capable of rising above ideologically stereotyped thinking. (He also warned them presciently that Reagan would never give up SDI.)[52] So they devised and honed a negotiating strategy, rooted in Reagan's personality, to catch the U.S. off its guard at Reykjavik.

If Gorbachev, trading on the personal trust with Reagan he had established in Geneva, were to propose progressively but rapidly dismantling the nuclear missile stockpiles on both sides, might he not persuade the president to sacrifice SDI for such an extraordinary gain? After all, he could argue that SDI would be unnecessary in a world without nuclear weapons. Almost all those around Reagan—Shultz, Weinberger, Perle, Nitze, arms control director Ken Adelman—would be likely to scan the fine print and urge caution. So would Thatcher from across the pond. But if the disarmament offers were sufficiently dazzling, and the pace of the negotiations suitably swift, Reagan might be tempted to override any objections from his aides and allies and reach an agreement then and there with his new best friend. It was a well-crafted strategy, and it almost worked. It failed because Reagan kept a cooler head than his advisers.

Gorbachev and Reagan met on Saturday morning, October 11, in Hofdi House—the Icelandic government's hospitality house rumored to be haunted—overlooking Reykjavik's harbor. The Soviet leader began by announcing that he would be "bold," and he was. He ignored the small change of future summit arrangements, declared that both sides wanted the total elimination of nuclear weapons, and presented a plan for reaching at least the halfway mark. Its main points were a 50 percent cut in the strategic offensive weapons of both sides, the "zero-zero option" for INF missiles in Europe (plus talks on INF missiles in Asia), and a prohibition on space-based missile defenses under the ABM Treaty, which itself would be observed by both sides for at least ten years.

Both sides then broke for a lunch at which they had a lot to digest. Reagan's advisers, including usually skeptical hawks like Perle, were impressed by the ambition of the Soviet proposals. Only Reagan—whom Gorbachev had thought distracted during the session—was wary. Inside the secure communications "bubble" at the U.S. embassy he told his team, "I'm afraid he's going after SDI."[53]

After lunch Reagan spoke for an hour, attempting to persuade the other side that SDI was something to embrace rather than fear. By now this was familiar to Gorbachev, who sat "stone-faced" through it. But Reagan went beyond his usual assurances and proposed to put his offer of sharing missile defense technology in treaty form. It must have been a powerful performance, especially impressive after the apparently distracted Reagan of the morning session. One Russian aide described the president's negotiating technique, an odd mixture of lethargy and star power, in very admiring terms: "He is like lion! When lion see antelope on the horizon, he is not interested, he go to sleep. Ten feet away, too much, leave it. Eight feet, the lion suddenly comes to life!"[54] The lion concluded his remarks by offering a treaty that would combine sharing SDI with the complete elimination of ballistic missiles.

Gorbachev and Reagan then began an auction on missile systems. Would Reagan agree to a 50 percent reduction in strategic missiles? Yes. So the Russian pressed on: let us then agree to cut all strategic systems by 50 percent—land-based, sea-launched, and those carried in bombers. Reagan became cautious and tried to kick this back to the "experts." Following the well-crafted Soviet negotiating strategy, Gorbachev tried to avoid this: if it were left to the experts, he said, it would be "kasha [porridge] forever."[55] But Reagan resisted a detailed debate. He preferred to persuade Gorbachev of the virtue of sharing SDI, which the Soviet leader repeatedly dismissed as implausible—and an unreliable promise too, since who could know what Reagan's successor might decide.

Both leaders parted that Saturday night in a slightly tense mood. There had been much talk of bold and historic disarmament decisions, but no actual proposals had been agreed upon and the SDI issue still divided both sides. Overnight, however, the experts hammered out a series of agreements. Paul Nitze told Reagan at Sunday breakfast that they had made more progress in arms control in ten hours than in the previous ten years. Reagan replied, "Literally a miracle is happening." A fever of optimism— quite unsuspected in the outside world, which thought this was a planning session for the next summit—began to overtake the negotiators. As bold agreements over strategic systems and INF missiles were settled, they told themselves that an agreement over SDI must surely now be possible.

A final meeting was scheduled for late that Sunday afternoon. Edward Shevardnadze, Gromyko's more outgoing successor as Soviet foreign minister, told the U.S. negotiators that they were creative and experienced enough to come up with some compromise formula that would include SDI. They did. Perle and his NSC colleague Air Force Colonel Richard Linhard produced a crisp draft designed to satisfy everyone:

Both sides would agree to confine themselves to research, development, and testing, which is permitted by the ABM Treaty, for a period of five years, through 1991, during which time a 50 percent reduction of strategic nuclear arsenals would be achieved. This being done, both sides will continue the pace of reductions with respect to all remaining ballistic missiles with the goal of the elimination of all ballistic missiles by the end of a second five-year period.... At the end of the ten-year period, with all offensive ballistic missiles eliminated, either side would be free to introduce defenses.

Reagan liked the draft but, discussing it with Perle and White House chief of staff Donald Regan, he worried about any further limitations on SDI that Gorbachev might wish to add. If they were as serious as Perle feared likely, the president indicated that he would not acquiesce "simply so we can leave here with an agreement."[56] When Gorbachev's amendments arrived, they were exactly what Perle had anticipated.

Gorbachev proposed two changes. The first replaced "offensive ballistic missiles" (a smaller category) with "strategic offensive arms" (a larger category). This was a tactical maneuver. Each side tried to smuggle through wording that would leave it with an advantage in strategic weaponry as the stockpiles were drawn down. It was a real difference but probably soluble. But the second proposed change was a killer: "The testing in space of all space components of anti–ballistic missile defense is prohibited, except research and testing in strategic laboratories." That meant a ban on serious testing and deployment of SDI. The trap had been sprung: Reagan had to choose between a historic deal eliminating nuclear weapons in ten years and keeping SDI. Reports of the meeting tell of an excited Gorbachev unable to sit still as the debate went back and forth.

At times it was sharp, even bitter. Reagan asked why the Soviets didn't get rid of their Krasnoyarsk radar complex—believed by the U.S. to be part of a defensive missile tracking system—if they were such strong believers in the ABM Treaty. (He later observed of Gorbachev's silence in the face of this accusation: "When you tag them with something that's really true, they don't deny it. They just don't react, as if you hadn't said it.")[57] At other times the conversation became almost sentimental. Reagan said to his counterpart, "Ten years from now I'll be a very old man. You and I will come to Iceland and bring the last missile from each country. We'll give a tremendous party for the whole world.... I'd say, 'Hello, Mikhail.' You'd say, 'Ron, is it you?'" Gorbachev, who tried to keep smiling throughout this testing late-afternoon debate, replied, "I don't know if I'll live ten years, especially after negotiating with you, you're sapping all my energy."

But they always came back painfully to SDI and one word: "laboratory." If it were included, Gorbachev would sign the deal; if it were omitted, Reagan would do so. They sent out the aides one last time to develop a compromise. When they were reviewing their efforts at 5:30 that Sunday afternoon, there was a final burst of near-manic optimism. It was almost as if they were trying to forget their dispute over SDI. Reagan asked why they were merely reducing nuclear weapons—why not eliminate them altogether?

Gorbachev said, "We can do that. We can eliminate them." He was echoed by the usually cautious George Shultz, who had now forged almost a friendship with Shevardnadze, with the euphoric words, "Let's do it!"

But neither would budge on strategic missile defense—and Gorbachev insisted that all other arrangements depended on that issue. Reagan, as Mitterrand had predicted, was determined not to surrender SDI. They finished their meeting in an atmosphere of intense disappointment. Both leaders walked into the hallway and put on their raincoats.

"You planned from the start to come here and put me in this situation," said Reagan. Gorbachev replied that there was still time to reach an agreement. They could go back to the bargaining table.

"I think not," replied the U.S. president, and strode out of Hofdi House toward his car. Gorbachev trailed along beside him, still pleading that a deal was possible. He told Reagan that he was missing the opportunity to go down in history as a great president who had achieved nuclear disarmament. Reagan said that applied to both of them.

"I don't know what else I could have done," said the Soviet leader in their final exchange.

"You could have said yes," replied Reagan, who got into his car and was driven to the airport.

These last few minutes might have been scripted in the Crimean sessions that Gorbachev held in preparation for the Reykjavik summit—except for the curtain line. Reagan was supposed to choose his historical legacy over his commitment to SDI. Most of his advisers, Perle excepted, would have accepted the word "laboratory" in return for sweeping arms reductions if their boss had agreed. And Reagan was undoubtedly tempted.

He was able to resist that temptation mainly because of the force of his convictions. But his refusal was also made easier because he was in a strong position not only vis-à-vis Gorbachev (who was playing a weak hand brilliantly) but also in U.S. politics. Reagan was going back to Washington to sign a landmark bipartisan tax reform law one week later. If Reykjavik was regarded as a failure, he could absorb the blow; he did not need a foreign policy success to mask political weakness. There is at least the possibility that he might have swallowed "laboratory" if he had been politically on the ropes.

Reagan returned to Washington on October 12. On November 4 the Republicans lost control of the U.S. Senate and the *New York Times* ran a story headlined: "Iran Says McFarlane and 4 Others Went to Tehran on a Secret Trip." It has been a damned close-run thing.

The Reagan Doctrine

In January 1985 Mark Palmer pondered something that ran boldly counter to Washington's conventional wisdom. Guerrilla fighters in the Third World were no longer invariably Marxist. Many were indeed anti-Marxist—and not only the Contras in Nicaragua. There were anti-Communist guerrillas in Angola, Mozambique, Afghanistan, Cambodia, the Horn of Africa, and several other countries. Admittedly, there had been anti-Communist guerrilla movements in the past. Lithuanian partisans had kept a low-level anti-Soviet war going in the countryside until well into the 1950s. Yemeni royalists (led by a maverick British Tory MP) had fought Nasser's invading army in the 1960s. Some of the African civil wars in the 1960s and 1970s had been waged by mercenaries whose ideologies probably went beyond anti-Communism. But these were spasmodic and unrelated reactions with no chance of success.

Suddenly, however, there seemed to be a more general movement of resistance in response to the Brezhnevite expansionism of the 1970s. Some of these anti-Marxist rebels were even respectable democrats. (The U.S. State Department in 1988 estimated, for instance, that only 200 out of 16,000 Contras had previously served in Somoza's National Guard.)[58] And those with different ideologies, such as some mujahadeen groups in Afghanistan, were fighting to free their countries from foreign occupation.

Mark Palmer was later a strong champion of the Hungarian democratic revolution as U.S. ambassador to Budapest in the late 1980s. In 1985 he was deputy assistant secretary of state on the European desk. He had helped to draft Reagan's Westminster speech, and he was seen as an up-and-coming man. So Peter Rodman, then head of policy planning at the State Department, paid attention when a memorandum from Palmer arrived on his desk suggesting that these anti-Communist guerrillas represented a new opportunity for American foreign policy. U.S. assistance to such movements would be in a long tradition of American support for patriots resisting foreign rule stretching back to Bolivar and the Polish nationalists of the nineteenth century.

Rodman had already been alerted to this opening from another angle. The previous year a young Harvard Sovietologist serving on the National Security Council, Steve Sestanovich, had written a *Washington Post* op-ed pointing out that the USSR's Third World client states were an increasing financial and sometimes military burden to Moscow. As we saw earlier, the Politburo's own academic experts were arguing the same thing. Sestanovich observed that this imperial overstretch was potentially a major strategic vulnerability. Washington could increase the costs to Moscow substantially if it decided to exploit it.[59]

Rodman had another consideration in mind. The U.S. had assumed obligations of its own to various resistance movements over time. Some were popular on Capitol Hill, such as the Afghan mujahadeen, who enjoyed wide bipartisan support. Others, such as the Contras, were highly controversial and their funding was perpetually at risk. But each case was treated separately. There was no overall rationale for supporting such movements. They were not seen as representing an important cause or an imperative of history. They were simply U.S. clients, vulnerable therefore to congressional attack or to media criticism. Why exactly were we funneling money and weapons to guerrilla groups in Central America or Afghanistan? Wasn't that the kind of thing we criticized the Soviets for? How could we justify it?

Rodman saw that if a persuasive overarching answer could be given to such questions, the U.S. could cause great difficulty for the exhausted Soviets at very modest cost to itself. As it happened, such an argument could be found in the promotion of liberty that Reagan had proclaimed in his Westminster speech. U.S. foreign policy was already being reshaped by this. Indeed, under Elliott Abrams at the Human Rights and then the Americas desk of the State Department, the liberty test was being applied impartially against both enemies and authoritarian allies. In the next few years Augusto Pinochet in Chile and Ferdinand Marcos in the Philippines would both be forcefully encouraged to leave office by the United States. If Washington was prepared to push out dictatorial friends, why should it not assist friendly patriots to reclaim their country from Moscow-backed ideological cliques that held power by force of foreign arms?

Rodman asked for more thoughts from Palmer, added some of his own, and sent the first draft of a speech advocating support for "freedom fighters" to George Shultz. Impressed, Shultz arranged a meeting for Rodman with Casey and McFarlane to discuss it. The idea began to spread at the top of the administration that open support for freedom fighters against dictatorial Communist regimes could be an important part of U.S. foreign policy. Rodman brought in skilled wordsmiths such as Robert Kagan and Luigi Einaudi to work on the final draft, and Shultz delivered the speech to the Commonwealth Club of San Francisco on February 22, 1985.[60]

Shultz's speech combined a number of important themes. Its main argument was that if Communists continued to aid Marxist rebellions against democratic regimes, then the U.S. would no longer be inhibited from supporting democrats fighting against Communist oppression. A secondary, but not trivial, consideration was that such help would also tilt the "correlation of forces" worldwide toward liberty since the Soviets were increasingly overstretched. The third theme was a qualified olive branch: the U.S. was seeking not to overthrow regimes but to modify their behavior. If the Sandinistas, for instance, would liberalize their political system and allow the Contras and other opposition groups to participate fully in politics, the U.S. would welcome such a change and tailor its own policy accordingly.

This conclusion alarmed some conservatives on the NSC, such as the redoubtable Constantine C. Menges. They feared, not wholly unreasonably, that the Contras and the mujahadeen would be sold out by a State Department whose highest priority was diplomatic compromise. But some willingness to compromise was unavoidable. In attempting to solve some of these "regional problems," the U.S. was engaged in diplomatic talks with allies like Pakistan and adversaries like the Soviets. It had to make clear it would settle for less than an outright military victory—which is what finally happened anyway. But the U.S. also had a duty to ensure that the interests of its guerrilla allies would be accommodated in any settlement. In the two most important cases—Afghanistan and Central America—it did so.

The flipside of these anxieties was that Shultz's support for freedom fighters helped to unite the administration behind the policy and to recommend it to moderate Democrats. Reagan himself, having overcome his early doubts, was on board even before Shultz. A reference in his 1985 State of the Union address—"we must not break faith with those who are risking their lives . . . to defy Soviet-supported aggression and secure rights which have been ours from birth"—was picked up and elaborated upon by columnist Charles Krauthammer. Krauthammer argued in a *Time* magazine essay that this "overt and unashamed American support for anti-Communist revolution" was a major innovation in recent U.S. foreign policy, and named it the "Reagan Doctrine." What had begun in 1981 as a series of hesitant, uncoordinated, and defensive responses to the Soviet advance had graduated by degrees to the status of a foreign policy "doctrine" alongside those of Monroe, Truman, and Nixon.

Getting the plan implemented was another matter. Support for the Afghan rebels was strong and bipartisan in Congress; covert U.S. military assistance more than doubled from $280 million in 1985 to $630 million in 1987. (Total Western and Saudi aid was much larger.) The problem was with the CIA and military bureaucracies, which were reluctant to supply the mujahadeen with the kind of advanced military supplies they wanted— in particular, with badly needed Stinger ground-to-air missiles.

Shortly after taking office, Gorbachev had given the Soviet armed forces two years to win the war in Afghanistan.[61] In turn the Red Army had launched a much tougher and effective counter-insurgency campaign using helicopter gunships and fighter-bombers. Against these tactics the muja-hadeen used Blowpipe ground-to-air missiles provided by the British and Soviet SA-7 shoulder-fired missiles purchased secretly in Europe by the CIA.[62] These were effective at first, but the Soviet forces eventually devel-oped tactics to outwit them. Pakistan's president Muhammad Zia-ul-Haq told a delegation of U.S. congressmen in late 1985 that the rebels desper-ately needed better missiles, in particular the Stinger. It took almost a full year to overcome the resistance of the military and intelligence bureaucra-cies in order to get them to the Afghans. Reagan signed an order to do so in April 1986; the first delivery of Stingers was made in September of that year.

A U.S. Army study later concluded that the Afghan resistance fired 340 Stingers, downing 269 aircraft.[63] The balance of war on the ground swung back strongly in favor of the Afghans at the very moment when Gor-bachev's deadline for success was approaching. In effect, their supply was the decisive military event of the war.

It was also the decisive political event of the war. Radek Sikorski, now Poland's defense minister, then a young journalist covering the conflict from the mujahadeen side, reached both conclusions. He acknowledged the military effect of the Stingers, but he thought that the supply of British Blowpipes was also important because, though less effective than Stingers, they were an open political commitment that helped overcome the resis-tance of U.S. bureaucrats to supplying the Stingers. If the British could ignore "plausible deniability," so could the U.S.[64] And the mere fact that the U.S. was now prepared to openly assist anti-Communist forces—which was the essence of the Reagan Doctrine—was itself a crucial strategic inno-vation. It added to the long list of reasons for the Soviets to reconsider their various Third World commitments.

Diplomacy, in particular the UN negotiations at Geneva, now took on some importance; these negotiations provided the diplomatic fig-leaf for a Soviet withdrawal. The Geneva accords were signed in April 1988, and Soviet troop withdrawals began in August. On February 15, 1989, General Boris Gromov crossed the bridge to the Soviet Union—the last Soviet soldier to leave Afghanistan—one decade after the Soviets had confidently invaded.

The Afghan war did not end there. The Soviets continued to send military supplies to their Afghan allies, who clung to power for another three years. Since the fall of Kabul in 1991, Afghanistan has suffered from endless sectarian conflict, a civil war, an invasion, and a revived civil war. It remains in crisis at the time of this writing. In 1989, however, the country had delivered a historic strategic defeat to the Soviets. Their friends and their enemies knew it. The subjects of their European empire were now encouraged to seek their own liberation. And Soviet influence elsewhere began to retreat.

As Rodman notes, almost all Brezhnev's military commitments to the Third World were abandoned between 1988 and 1992.[65] Cuban troops were withdrawn from Angola following an agreement signed in December 1988 in New York. The Vietnamese withdrew from Cambodia in 1989. The Sandinistas were defeated in a democratic election in Nicaragua in 1990. And there was a political settlement that essentially reconciled the losing Communist guerrillas to a democratic status quo in El Salvador in 1992. These events, marking the end of the Soviet Union as a superpower, represented an astounding success for a foreign policy doctrine of four years' standing. But the Reagan Doctrine's victory in Central America had not come simply, painlessly, or without casualties. It wounded, in particular, the president of the United States—and almost fatally.

Central America—in particular aid to the Contras—was a recurring controversy in U.S. domestic politics from 1981 until the 1990 Nicaraguan elections. The broad American Left outside Congress bitterly opposed Reagan's policy. Congress, narrowly divided, regularly came close to cutting off aid and instead compromised by imposing restrictions on it (the various "Boland Amendments"), and the administration sought ways around the restrictions. For five years, however, Reagan got most of what he wanted, in part because of the administration's willingness to compromise and in part because of the Sandinistas' intransigence and brutality. The Reagan administration showed its reasonableness in El Salvador, where it supported centrist Christian Democrat politicians, land reform, and restraints on the military. The Sandinistas showed their unreasonableness by sending out violent mobs to attack opponents in a 1984 election that had been designed to establish their legitimacy. They did so again, as Reagan biographer Richard Reeves dryly points out, by visiting Moscow whenever a close congressional vote on Contra aid was scheduled. Both these sets of actions enabled Reagan to win support for his Central American policy from a coalition of moderate Democrats led by Congressman Dave McCurdy.

But when the Iran-Contra scandal[66] broke, this narrow but effective coalition was weakened. The germ of the scandal was the administration's attempts to get around the effective prohibition of congressional restrictions on aiding the Contras. Most of these attempts—encouraging private citizens and friendly governments to aid the Contras—were legal. But a White House cabal, led by deputy NSC director Admiral John Poindexter and the gung-ho Colonel Oliver North, who undoubtedly believed that they were carrying out Reagan's wishes, conceived an ingenious plan to direct funds to the Contras from profits on arms shipments to Iran that were themselves designed to secure the release of American hostages held by terrorists linked to the Iranian mullahs. Whatever the legality of this arrangement—the Iran-Contra planners believed they were operating through legal loopholes and, because of the unutterable legal confusion that eventually descended on Iran-Contra, their contention was never decisively disproved—it was the worst possible politics.

Ayatollah Khomeini was so despised in America that the idea of supplying him with rockets struck ordinary citizens as outrageous and allies as a betrayal of Reagan's principled stand against terrorism. There were arguably legitimate arguments for the supply of arms to Iran: developing a strategic rapprochement with a major regional power in the Middle East and saving the lives of U.S. hostages. In retrospect, however, these look unrealistic: the outreach to Tehran had failed in any event, the American negotiators had been taken to the cleaners, only a few of the hostages were released, the dealings in Tehran smacked of amateur conspiracy addicts, and an atmosphere of illegality and deception hung over the entire enterprise. The momentum of scandal familiar since Watergate now took over. Reagan's approval ratings dropped precipitously and for the first time since the attempt on his life he looked politically mortal. A quasi-legal process of investigation and accusation was launched. The Democrats, now back in control of both houses of Congress, moved to destroy the Reagan presidency. And for almost an entire year the business of the U.S. government was delayed and distorted by the scandal mania.

Reagan was forced into humiliating gestures of apology and amnesia in the course of this hunt. But he survived owing to two errors on the part of his partisan critics. What really agitated the voters was that Reagan had struck a deal with the mullahs only six years after the Tehran hostage crisis. His liberal critics were far more concerned with the diversion of funds to the Contras. They never managed to instill their indignation into the voters, who after a time accepted the president's apology for arms dealing. Second, the media and the Democrats had spent six years trying to convince America that Reagan was a doddering old dimwit asleep at the wheel. That now suited Reagan's defense perfectly. The Democrats' new image of him—a Machiavellian mastermind orchestrating a vast conspiracy—was actually closer to the truth, but it seemed so uncharacteristic that *Saturday Night Live* produced a hilarious sketch showing Reagan barking commands to juggle currencies and transfer arms in fluent French and Farsi and eventually exclaiming in exasperation, "Do I have to do everything myself?"

In the end Iran-Contra dribbled into the sands of legal appeals and newspaper recapitulations. Reagan revived his presidency; some reforms of the NSC, including its own legal counsel, were introduced; stronger congressional oversight of the CIA was brought in; and George H. W. Bush won the 1988 election after campaigning as Reagan's heir. Even the Contras survived. Iran-Contra had forced Reagan to accept a seriously flawed diplomatic process that, in effect, ended aid to the Contras in return for promises of better behavior by the Sandinistas, including an election in 1990. When this diplomatic process began in 1987, such a bargain looked like surrender in disguise—exactly what conservatives like Constantine C. Menges had feared from the start—because it was easy to assume that the Sandinistas would never seriously abide by it.

By 1990, however, a new sort of international pressure for honest democracy had evolved. Not at all ironically, it flowed in part from Reagan's Westminster speech and the institutions it had created, such as the National Endowment for Democracy. What Rodman calls "the full panoply of election monitoring," including visits from Jimmy Carter, was accordingly unleashed on Nicaragua. The presence of serious election observers both hindered Sandinista election rigging and encouraged the ordinary Nicaraguans to vote their true preference. (The Sandinistas were probably overconfident as well.) To the surprise of almost all observers— from the Bush administration to left-wing "Sandalista" sympathizers abroad—the pro-American democratic opposition, including some Contras, won the election handsomely. The Soviet attempt to install Communist surrogates in America's backyard—an attempt going back to the early 1970s—had collapsed completely.

Such an outcome would have seemed utopian four years earlier, when the Iran-Contra scandal had broken. Reagan had then been shattered by the sudden contumely. He was told his presidency was over every time he turned on the television. He remarked in a *Time* magazine interview, "I have to say there is bitter bile in my throat these days."[67] Almost as he was saying this, Margaret Thatcher was writing him a highly personal letter. She had been briefly angered by the fact that Reagan had broken his own rule that governments should never deal with terrorists. But her letter bore not a trace of disapproval. In her own hand, she wrote on December 4, 1986:

Dear Ron,

I was glad that we were able to talk on the telephone the other day so that I could tell you directly how very much you and Nancy are in our thoughts at this difficult time. The press and media are always so ready to criticize and get people down. I know what it's like.

But your achievements in restoring America's pride and confidence and in giving the West the leadership it needs are far too substantial to suffer any lasting damage. The message I give to everyone is that anything which weakens you weakens America; and anything that weakens America weakens the whole free world. Whatever happened over Iran is in the past and nothing can change it. I firmly believe that the message *now should be* that there is important work to be done and that you are going to do it." (Emphasis in original.)[68]

It was a warm-hearted letter of encouragement from a dear friend. But it was also an accurate political assessment. There *was* important work to be done. Indeed, there was a world to win.

CHAPTER NINE

CHECKMATE

❧ ❧

"Failure," *wrote Jack Matlock*, resident Sovietologist on the National Security Council, on his pad as he traveled back to Washington with the president on Air Force One. It foreshadowed the headlines that would shortly decorate all the stories American reporters were then writing about Reykjavik for the next day's papers. It also captured the mood on the plane. With all the euphoria of the afternoon in Hofdi House—sober Shultz shouting, "Let's do it!" and Shevardnadze urging U.S. negotiators Paul Nitze and Max Kampelman to "come up with something"—they had in the end built up to an awful letdown. The bitter parting of the two principals had occurred in front of the world's media, and it shaped the world's initial reaction.[1]

Shultz's briefing at the press center had reflected this disappointment. Sam Donaldson of ABC reported, "Shultz looks like his dog has just been run over by a truck."[2] When the secretary of state was asked later why he looked so tired and depressed, he said the reason was simple: he was tired and depressed. His actual words were less downbeat, but the reporters wrote them down filtered through the dull green glow of his expression. The gloom seemed omnipresent.

Only two people contradicted this mood. At Keflavik airport, Gorbachev reassured the disappointed Icelandic prime minister that his country had not hosted a complete failure.

"There will be more coming out of this meeting than anyone realizes," he said. "For the first time in forty years, both great powers tried to eliminate all nuclear weapons. This is the beginning of the end of the Cold War." Whether or not Gorbachev then realized exactly how the Cold War would end, it was a remarkably prescient forecast that showed an ability to rise above immediate feelings and perceive the underlying truth of the moment.[3]

The other seer was Charles Z. Wick on Air Force One. Wick was one of Reagan's old Hollywood friends, a former dance band leader who had become a successful businessman in media and other industries. He had been an effective director of the United States Information Service, establishing Radio Marti to broadcast to Cuba. He seemed invariably optimistic and upbeat. But his almost professional cheerfulness masked a shrewd political mind. He now spoke up.

"Ronnie, you just won the Cold War. They admitted they can't compete. They don't have the money to fight the dollar."

Reagan, still dispirited, replied, "I just hope you're right."

Victory in Defeat

But Don Regan was prompted to rally the crowd: "We can't go home this way, like a team that lost the World Series." His short pep talk rejuvenated Reagan's inner circle. Press spokesman Larry Speakes outlined a media crusade against the foolish notion that Reykjavik had been a disappointment. He scheduled almost the entire top tier of the administration on television shows to refute this absurdity. John Poindexter, Bud McFarlane's successor as NSC director, explained to the reporters on the plane that Reykjavik had not ended in bitterness—indeed, it had not really ended at all.[4]

"We are going to find some way to preserve SDI and still have reductions in nuclear weapons," he said. "Both sides need to reflect on what happened."

Poindexter's analysis was not very different from Gorbachev's words to Iceland's prime minister. After he had shaken off his fatigue and depression, Shultz too came to believe that the Reykjavik summit had been an unrecognized success. The Soviets had shown what they were prepared to concede, the Americans now knew their bottom line, and most of the Soviet negotiators had told the Americans how much they regretted narrowly failing to achieve an agreement. Moreover, the Soviet military had been more accommodating than the Soviet diplomats in the Reykjavik negotiations—which suggested internal pressures in Moscow for a deal. Without realizing it the negotiators had agreed not to permanently break off negotiations.[5]

Reagan effectively confirmed this on television the following night. Blaming Gorbachev for the failed agreement, he reiterated that SDI was needed as a safety guarantee if the Soviets reneged on their arms control promises. But his bottom line was that the American offer was still on the table.

"We are closer than ever to agreements that could lead to a safer world without nuclear weapons," said the old Cold Warrior. He also noted that another offer was still on the table: his invitation to Gorbachev to attend a summit in Washington. That would have to wait some time, however. Not only did the president become embroiled in the Iran-Contra affair a few weeks later, but Gorbachev had also fiercely attacked him as a "primitive" and a "caveman" at a secret Politburo meeting.[6] It is possible that Gorbachev had been genuinely irritated by that final sharp exchange, but more likely that he was justifying the failure of his Reykjavik strategy.

Both leaders also wanted to gauge how public opinion would react to the events in Iceland. Shultz was convinced that Gorbachev believed Reagan's intransigence over SDI would alarm Western opinion and force him into a retreat. Instead, argued Shultz, the public actually reasoned that if Gorbachev was so keen to abolish SDI, it must really be worthwhile.[7]

And indeed, given that the coverage of Reykjavik had stressed failure and disappointment, the initial reviews were surprisingly positive for Reagan. *Time* magazine reported on its own poll:

By almost every measure, Ronald Reagan emerged from Reykjavik a winner. Among Americans who kept abreast of the summit, two out of three support Reagan's decision to reject the
Soviet offer. Most blame Mikhail Gorbachev for the failure to
reach agreement, and an overwhelming majority believes the
president is more committed to arms control than is the Soviet
leader. Most agree with Reagan that SDI should be developed.
Apparently, most do not see SDI as a stumbling block to future
negotiations; a majority is optimistic that Reagan and Gorbachev will eventually sign a pact. Significantly, confidence in
Reagan's ability to negotiate an arms-control agreement has
nearly doubled since a year ago.[8]

If the public relations war was going well, there were rumblings of discontent elsewhere. As inside accounts of the Reykjavik negotiations dribbled out—notably, that Reagan had been prepared to abandon all nuclear
missiles—the foreign policy establishment became increasingly critical.
They feared that Reagan's utopian vision of SDI was threatening the
nuclear deterrence that had actually kept the peace for forty years. Inside
the administration, Admiral Bill Crowe, speaking for the Joint Chiefs, told
Reagan that they were alarmed at the idea of giving up ballistic missiles,
which, in addition to their peacekeeping virtues, were a very cheap form
of defense. Outside the administration, James Schlesinger, a former defense
secretary, reiterated the point Thatcher had made earlier to Reagan at
Camp David: nuclear deterrence had defended the West not only against a
nuclear first strike, but also against the Soviet Union's enormous stockpile
of conventional forces. He concluded bluntly, "The American position at
Reykjavik seems to have reflected no understanding of these simple fundamentals."[9]

Thatcher herself was horrified when she first heard the reports. As she
told Geoffrey Smith, she felt as if there had been an earthquake: "There
was no place where you could put your political feet. No place where you
were certain you could stand."[10] Her nervousness was shared by her senior
colleagues and by most of America's other European allies. They had

fought the peace movement in Europe throughout the 1980s to defend nuclear deterrence in general and the INF missiles in particular. Now this chair was being pulled out from under them by the White House.

Thatcher had two other reasons for concern. The sweeping abolition of ballistic missiles proposed at Reykjavik would mean that the independent British deterrent would vanish as well. Gorbachev had actually conceded that any U.S.-Soviet disarmament deal need not include the French and British deterrents. When his military chiefs objected, he told them not to be silly: "England and France are not going to attack the Soviet Union." But the Reykjavik deal would render that concession worthless. Washington could hardly supply Trident to the Brits if it were not building the missile for U.S. forces. That would be a major blow to the Thatcher government—and to Thatcher personally. Though Reagan could calmly contemplate nuclear disarmament because he believed SDI would protect the countries that disarmed, Thatcher had the discomfort of no such conviction.

Her second anxiety was electoral. The Labour Party had adopted a policy of nuclear unilateralism. That would be a main focus of the Tory Party's negative campaigning in an election expected in spring 1987. If Reagan's disarming intentions were fully grasped, they would rescue Labour and make the Tories look positively bellicose. In the event, that never happened. The initial focus of British media reporting of Reykjavik was on Reagan's supposed intransigence over SDI. And though his willingness to abolish all nuclear weapons on both sides subsequently became known—and some Labour strategists grasped the opportunity this gave them—contempt for the cowboy president was so strong in the Labour Party and in the left-leaning media that they were never able to capitalize effectively on this. Praising Reagan to damn Thatcher was simply too counterintuitive for them and their supporters. Accordingly, when the election was held, the Tories won another landslide victory on a campaign that stressed the booming economy and the risks of electing a semi-pacifist Labour government.[11]

Thatcher flew over for an Anglo-American summit on November 15. This time she could not pull off the kind of friendly ambush she had staged at Camp David. Both sides were aware that serious differences existed between them. Her principal adviser on foreign policy, Charles Powell, had told the White House in advance what she wanted from the visit: "Reassurance that strategic arms will not overlook conventional imbalances in Europe; reassurance that political delicacies in Britain will be taken into account; reassurance that negotiating positions do not undermine Britain's Trident program; reassurance that we know where we are heading."[12]

What she got was a joint communiqué that met her political needs, blurred the divergence in British and U.S. policy, and endorsed all but one of Reagan's goals at Reykjavik. The British Trident program was to be protected; a 50 percent cut in strategic weapons over five years was endorsed, along with deep cuts in INF missiles; SDI research was to go ahead. Only the idea of scrapping all strategic missiles over ten years was left unmentioned. It had not been dropped, however; it was merely pushed discreetly into the background. The truth was that the Reykjavik disarmament proposals were still firmly on the table and, more important, still on the president's personal agenda, even if he could not pursue them directly at the moment.[13]

Thatcher had obtained a serviceable agreement that she could argue fulfilled most of her objectives. Deterrence with a "mix of systems" remained the basis of NATO strategy. The commitment to deep cuts in INF missiles was hardly a concession on her part, as the "zero-zero option" had been agreed NATO policy since 1981. SDI research was to take place within the limits of the ABM Treaty even if interpretations of the treaty differed. Scrapping all ballistic missiles had not been disavowed, but it had not been endorsed either—and Thatcher could reasonably argue that it was a utopian aim unlikely to be attained. The U.S. side was happy to see the joint statement interpreted in the British prime minister's favor; indeed, they were eager to do so, as Reagan wanted her to win the forthcoming election (which she did the day before Reagan called on the Soviet leader to "tear down this wall"). And if she did not score an unqualified diplomatic victory on the central issue of nuclear weapons, as before, she gained an unexpected one on the vexed topic of arms for Argentina.

Four years after the Falklands War, the Reagan administration wanted to resume arms sales to Argentina in order to strengthen the new democratic government there. American strategists had recommended weapons that in their view could not be used against the Falklands. The president had been fully briefed on the arguments—and on the likelihood that Thatcher would oppose the plan. Over lunch, following the agreed statement on nuclear arms, Reagan and Thatcher discussed a variety of topics in high good humor. Reagan made no mention of arms to Argentina. No one did until the very end of lunch, when Thatcher, almost as an afterthought, looked down a list of topics from her handbag and said, "Oh, arms for Argentina. You won't, will you?"

"No," said Reagan. "We won't." And that was that.[14]

It was a small but satisfying ambush, which Reagan probably granted because he could not meet all her larger requests. Paradoxically, Reagan and Thatcher's difference over deterrence brought them closer together. When she left Washington, Thatcher had good reason to be even more supportive of SDI than before. It was now the main obstacle blocking another Reykjavik. As long as Gorbachev insisted that SDI research be confined to the laboratory as a condition of disarmament, there could be no wholesale scrapping of the strategic missiles and the nuclear deterrent that kept the peace cheaply.

Or so it seemed. But the surrounding strategic environment was poised to change so dramatically that such questions would shortly become irrelevant.

As Wick had realized amid the encircling gloom on Air Force One, Reagan had already won the Cold War. The Soviets could no longer meet U.S. economic and strategic competition. They therefore had to meet Reagan's terms. Gorbachev announced his acceptance of the "zero-zero option" on INF missiles on July 22, 1987. Shultz and Shevardnadze met in Washington in September to work out the details of a new treaty. There was a brief hiccup in early October, when Gorbachev was distracted by then unknown Boris Yeltsin, who attacked him in internal party councils as an international gadabout with failing domestic policies. But Yeltsin was forced to apologize in the pre-*glasnost* style of Soviet self-humiliation. He was instantly forgotten, and the diplomatic process resumed. In October Reagan announced that Gorbachev would be visiting Washington in early December to sign the treaty eliminating INF missiles worldwide. He also revealed that he had in turn accepted Gorbachev's invitation to a Moscow summit in 1988, when they hoped to sign an agreement to cut long-range strategic missiles by 50 percent. There was no mention of SDI.

Reagan was not in good form for the December Washington meeting with Gorbachev. He was so querulous—especially about SDI—and distracted that after the first session Shultz took him aside and told him so. Reagan agreed to do his "homework" better. But despite his personal performance, Reagan's policies prevailed. When he raised SDI again the following day, Gorbachev replied, "Mr. President, do what you think you have to do. And if in the end you think you have a system you want to deploy, go ahead and deploy." And after all the drama of Reykjavik, that was that.

It was terrific PR for the Soviets, but it was also the silver plate on a coffin. Gorbachev was mobbed by enthusiastic crowds of Washingtonians on Connecticut Avenue. His star rose in the opinion polls. "Gorbymania" swept Europe and America. He was popular because he had ended the Cold War with a civilized handshake and his signature on an arms reduction treaty.

Not everyone noticed that he had also lost the Cold War. It was a negotiated surrender that left the Soviet empire intact (if shrinking) against a background of clinking champagne glasses. Some skeptical conservatives warned that Gorbachev might manage to snatch victory from the jaws of defeat, as eliminating INF missiles and reducing strategic missiles would have left NATO relatively weak against the Warsaw Pact's preponderance of conventional weapons. Thatcher may have been right to be wary of Reagan's idealistic drive for this at the expense of the erosion of deterrence—most Western experts then thought so. Her concern was a rational one, especially in the light of history. It may also have been a needless fear.

We will never know for sure, however, because two years later the Warsaw Pact collapsed.

A Ray of Light through the Iron Curtain

Thatcher's Eastern European diplomacy began in 1984 with her visit to Hungary. It was written up at the time as evidence of her "softening." She had visited a street market in Budapest and received a "warm, indeed passionate" welcome from crowds of shoppers. The British press reported that she had discovered Communists were human beings like herself. In fact Thatcher had always known that. What she discovered—or rather, confirmed for herself—was that the shoppers were not Communists. Wherever she went in Eastern Europe before the fall of Communism, she received a warm, indeed passionate welcome because she was regarded by ordinary Eastern Europeans as a symbol of opposition to Communism.

Thatcher's visit to Budapest had been conceived as a roundabout method of reopening contacts with the Soviet Union. Janos Kadar, who had ruled Communist Hungary since the Soviet suppression of the 1956 Hungarian Revolution, was close to the Soviets and especially to Andropov, who as Soviet ambassador to Budapest in 1956 had masterminded that bloody action. Kadar was a cynical but faithful old Communist who made plain the rules of Hungary's Cold War game: the Soviets would allow him considerable freedom to experiment with a quasi-capitalist economy provided that he kept the country in the Warsaw Pact. That did not surprise Thatcher, who was hoping to send Kadar as a messenger boy to the Kremlin.

Thatcher and Reagan had been sending out feelers for better East-West relations for a year. But these had either been ignored or not understood as such by a paranoid Andropov. Thatcher reiterated these messages to Kadar, telling him that Reagan had been disappointed at the summary dismissal of his personal appeal to Brezhnev. Andropov should know that Reagan was still interested in better relations. In turn Kadar told Thatcher that Andropov was a hard, calculating man, but one who listened and could do business. Wasn't he ill? Yes, but he was improving.

All this information about Andropov proved useless as well as misleading when he died six days later. Thatcher reported back to Reagan that improving relations would be a "long and slow process." But Gorbachev had already been identified by the British as a better prospect—and five months later, during the short rule of the sickly Chernenko, she met Gorbachev at Chequers and the process of bettering relations began in earnest.

There was, however, a subtext to Thatcher's Hungarian visit that would prove highly significant. One motive for the Hungarians in inviting her was to demonstrate the relative success of the "liberalized" Hungarian economy. Communists all over the Eastern bloc were increasingly aware that the legitimacy of their regimes was quietly collapsing. They were looking for a substitute legitimacy as Marxism became more and more of a laughingstock. Some opted for extreme nationalism—notably, Slobodan Milosevic in Yugoslavia. Others saw that democracy was the only real modern legitimacy. They were calculating that they should reinvent themselves as social democrats, lose the first multi-party elections, and return to power when the chaos they had left behind doomed the first democratic government. (Hungarian, Czech, Slovak, and Polish Communists all managed this trick in the next decade.) Still others believed that legitimacy lay in successful economic "reform" of a capitalist kind. In the waning days of Communism there sprouted all kinds of Marxists—Thatcherite Marxists, Singapore Marxists, and even "Pinochet Marxists"—offering a free market economy with degrees of political liberty ranging from full liberalism to none at all.

Thatcher was already known abroad as a tough and effective economic reformer. The Hungarian Communists would have liked her imprimatur on their reforms, and she was quite open to persuasion on their value. But she was extremely disappointed. She visited a housing estate—chosen because it had been an Anglo-Hungarian joint project with a British company—where the tenants were allowed to buy their own homes. But she discovered that if they moved on, they had to sell the homes back to the Hungarian state. In other words, they did not really own them at all. Noting acidly that this was the same policy the Labour Party had proposed for British council housing, she saw that it revealed the narrow limits that even a liberalized Communism placed on economic freedom.[15]

Still, the Communists' desire for capitalist approval, in particular for Thatcher's approval, gave rise to a distinctive British diplomacy over the next few years. It had three stages: first, to establish better trade and commercial relations with Eastern Europe in order to lessen its reliance on the COMECON bloc; second, to condition the improvement of these economic ties on improvements in human rights; and third, to insist on internal political reforms in return for greater investment. This economic diplomacy was supplemented with gestures of political support for democratic and religious dissidents; for instance, the British foreign minister was the first Western diplomat to place a wreath on the grave of Father Jerzy Popieluszko, the anti-Communist priest killed by the Polish security services. In other words, as the Communist political structures of Eastern Europe began to crack under such pressures as John Paul's campaign for religious liberty and the growing resistance of dissident movements, Thatcher stepped forward to offer economic inducements for Communist governments to increase liberty. And as time went on, her conditions for help became tougher.

Her next visit was to the Soviet Union in 1987. This was one trip from which she had something personal to gain—an election was approaching and she would benefit from the sheer glamour of the Iron Lady conquering Moscow, if only by agreement. From that standpoint the visit was an unqualified success: she enjoyed enormous and almost entirely favorable publicity. The international press reported that her debate with Gorbachev over the relative merits of communism and capitalism had gone well over schedule because both sides enjoyed it. She also debated three Soviet political commentators on Moscow television and, as even Gorbachev privately admitted to the Politburo, made mincemeat of them with her experience in parliamentary repartee.[16] As in Hungary, she was mobbed by friendly crowds at a Moscow housing estate and on a trip to Georgia. All of this— against exotic Russian and Georgian backgrounds—greatly boosted her election prospects at home.

Thatcher's visit was less interesting from a diplomatic standpoint. Gorbachev was negotiating directly with Reagan now. This was six months after Reykjavik. Thatcher was no longer an intermediary on his behalf; she was, if anything, an obstacle. Overall, in their ideological debates, which have now been published in full, Thatcher gave somewhat better than she got.[17] Gorbachev seems to have confused Thatcher with his wife, Raisa.

His arguments have the musty smell of Marxist apologetics even when they were making practical points.

Who gained most from the visit? Thatcher's image as an international stateswoman helped her win the 1987 election in a landslide. She also improved her international image, which was already high but colored somewhat by her perceived bellicosity. The Moscow visit gave her a more rounded and even sympathetic image. Gorbachev later told the Czech Communists, "We should do justice to her; she is a bourgeois politician who is able to defend her principles."

Discussing the impact of her visit with the Politburo, Gorbachev summarized, "Apparently there are hardly any benefits from her visit. But there are no losses either."[18] That is almost certainly a favorable gloss. Thatcher's televised debate with the Soviet journalists alone—with the unrestrained forcefulness of her replies and the previously hidden information she revealed about such matters as Soviet nuclear policy—had quickly become the talk of Moscow. Not hugely significant perhaps, but it was still another nail in the coffin of Soviet thought control. By the time Thatcher left Moscow, she had concluded that the ground was cracking under the Soviet system—even if, as she noted, the regime still had enough residual power to stage a delegation of "impeccably distinguished Soviet stooges" to hymn the achievements of socialism in advance of her meeting with the great dissident Andrei Sakharov and his wife, Yelena Bonner.[19] But *perestroika* and *glasnost* were generating more hopes than they could fulfill. And as Thatcher observed, quoting Tocqueville, the moment a despotism begins to reform is the moment of its greatest danger.[20]

If Thatcher's visit to Poland in November 1988 was more consequential, that was because Poland's Communist system had advanced further toward disintegration. The "artificial peace of totalitarianism" imposed by the declaration of martial law seven years earlier had failed to "normalize" the country. The pope's third pilgrimage to Poland the previous June had cracked the ice and revived Solidarity. And the shoots of free politics were now beginning to grow again.

This second coming of democracy had begun in January 1987, when General Jaruzelski, still Poland's Communist head of state, visited the Vatican for an audience with John Paul. His visit demonstrated his recognition that Poland could not be governed over the opposition of the Catholic Church. Though that had always been true, it had become much more significant under martial law and in particular after the murder of Father Popieluszko. The martyred priest's church had become a center of the kind of cultural resistance that Archbishop Wojtyla had pioneered twenty years before in Cracow. The Kolbe church in Nowa Huta, run by the chaplain of the Lenin Steelworks, was another such center. But this was cultural resistance on a much larger scale than in the 1970s. The Kolbe church housed a private university, a theater, a jazz club, art exhibitions, and classical concerts. Four hundred workers graduated from classes taught by distinguished academics from such institutions as Jagiellonian University. And sometimes more than a thousand people would attend events advertised solely by word of mouth.[21]

Such institutions and practices—preserving civilization as much as mounting resistance—were also beginning to appear under other Eastern bloc regimes. Plays by banned authors (sometimes starring banned actors) were performed in private homes in Czechoslovakia, where the recognized leader of the Charter 77 dissident movement was playwright Vaclav Havel. Roger Scruton, the conservative English philosopher, helped to organize an underground university in Prague and recruited intellectuals to lecture and smuggle books into the country.[22] There were innumerable such small attempts to reestablish the links between the two halves of Europe sundered by totalitarianism. Communist regimes in the rest of the bloc still had the power to harass such outcrops of civilized resistance into the ground—or into prison—but in Poland the Church had the power to protect them.

Jaruzelski wanted better relations with a Catholic Church that commanded more social power than the government. He needed economic recovery, which depended on the willingness of Poles to accept economic reforms. He hoped that the Church would urge ordinary Poles to make sacrifices for a depressed Poland in such mundane ways as working harder and more honestly. In a society where the most quoted joke was "They pretend to pay us and we pretend to work," this was an important demand. The general was prepared to pay a price for the Church's help in meeting it: maybe a formal diplomatic link between Poland and the Vatican eventually, but a papal visit immediately. John Paul insisted on a price in return: he would visit the birthplace of Solidarity, the city of Gdansk on the Baltic Sea, which he had been forbidden to visit on his second Polish pilgrimage in 1983. This was reluctantly granted.[23]

But John Paul could not grant Jaruzelski's larger request. Workers could not reasonably be asked to help a society that was denying them any say either in political decision-making or in the sharing of social goods. Also, he was more prepared to say this explicitly now than in the more unstable and threatening conditions of 1983. The day before he arrived in Gdansk, John Paul signaled his intentions at a Mass for sailors in the nearby town of Gdynia. He delivered a profound sermon on the Christian meaning of solidarity. Not only did he repeat the word "solidarity" throughout the sermon, but he also explicitly argued that man had a right to struggle for his rights and his own genuine progress. In Gdansk itself, before a congregation of at least one million, he drew out the lesson further. The rights of workers, he said, were not confined to their work; they had a right to "make decisions concerning the problems of the whole of society."

This was a direct challenge both to the Communist monopoly of political power and a reply to Jaruzelski that said, in effect, that only a state that recognizes the rights of its people has the right to ask sacrifices of them. A disappointed Jaruzelski remarked with bitter sarcasm as the pope left, "May the word 'solidarity' flow from our Polish soil to those people who still suffer from racism and neo-colonialism, exploitation and unemployment, persecutions and intolerance." His bitterness was understandable. Support from the Church had been the last hope of his regime for economic recovery and political stability. If the Church would not provide it, then the days of Polish Communism were numbered.

In April 1988 strikers downed tools in Bydgoszcz. Strikes quickly spread
to Nowa Huta and the Gdansk shipyards. The strikers' demands included
the legal re-recognition of Solidarity. Demonstrations with the same
demands spread to Warsaw, Cracow, and Lublin. In August new strikes
broke out in the Silesian mines. Again, sympathy strikes spread throughout Poland. Unable to control the situation, the Polish Communists
appealed for help to Lech Walesa, who convinced the strikers to return to
work. And in November 1988 Thatcher arrived in Warsaw as the guest of
Jaruzelski.

Thatcher had consulted the pope before setting out. They both understood that Eastern European Communism, especially in Poland, was at the
point of collapse. The regimes were so discredited that they had to rely on
the moral authority of their opponents for their continued power—first the
pope, then Walesa, now Thatcher. Jaruzelski's main motive for inviting the
British prime minister was to enlist her support for his economic reforms.
On the eve of her visit, the regime announced that it was closing the Lenin
shipyard on the "Thatcherite" grounds that it was sustaining heavy losses.
A trap was being sprung for her: she was supposed to endorse treating
Walesa as if he were Arthur Scargill.

If that was what the regime expected, what it got was a lecture in the
true nature of free market economics. Thatcher pointed out that profits
and losses were concepts that made sense only if there was a market. Since
the Lenin shipyard was selling to only one customer, namely the Soviet
authorities, its viability depended almost entirely on changes in the ruble-
zloty exchange rate. And even so the Lenin shipyard was making smaller
"losses" than its "competitors." It was being proposed for closure because
the regime resented it politically. Throughout the official portions of her
visit—including her state dinner with Jaruzelski—she made these and similar points about Poland's economic troubles. She also repeated the pope's
moral arguments for Solidarity: if the Communist government wanted the
Polish people to show economic responsibility, it should grant them the
freedoms that went with it. And she gave these contentions a sharp personal edge: when it came to applying tough economic reforms to deep-
seated problems, she told Poland's Communist leaders, the difference

between them was that she had been elected three times to carry the reforms out.

More important than her official engagements, however, was Thatcher's demonstration of sympathy with the opposition. She laid a wreath on Father Popieluszko's grave and visited his parents and his church. The next day she flew to Gdansk where, accompanied by Walesa, she laid another wreath on the shipyard memorial to the workers who had been shot down in 1970. She had a meeting over lunch (cooked by Walesa's confessor, Father Jankowski) with the Solidarity committee in Gdansk. She then visited the Solidarity church, where a packed congregation of families rose at her entrance and sang "God Give Us Back Our Free Poland." Everywhere in the city she was cheered by huge crowds—from the moment she arrived, when hundreds of workers threw their caps into the air in unison, to the moment of her departure in a small boat, when the huge shipyard cranes were dipped seawards in her honor.

It was, she writes in her memoirs, one of the most moving days of her life. She was unable to hold back her tears. But she also drew a very practical lesson from it. Before leaving Warsaw, she saw Jaruzelski a final time and told him, as one hardheaded politician to another, that Solidarity looked to her like an unstoppable political force. He made no comment.[24]

Two months later, on January 19, 1989, Solidarity was recognized as an independent labor union. Three weeks after that the round-table negotiations on new political structures began. An agreement on new elections was signed in April, and the elections themselves were scheduled for June. The method of voting was an unusual one: the voters crossed out the names of candidates they wanted to reject. Voters joyfully crossed out the names of the Communists who had oppressed them for forty years. Solidarity won every contested seat but one. In July the new parliament dominated by Solidarity kept a promise given in the round-table negotiations and elected Jaruzelski president—by one vote. One month after that, Jaruzelski, whose own candidate for prime minister had failed to form a government, asked Tadeusz Mazowiecki (whom he had jailed eight years before) to be the next prime minister.

Mazowiecki took office at the head of Poland's first postwar democratic government on September 12, 1989—exactly ten years and three months after John Paul II had landed in Poland and appealed to God, "Let Your Spirit come down and renew the face of the land—this land."

Two months later the Berlin Wall was opened. By spring 1990 the Soviet empire had shrunk down almost to the territory of the USSR itself. But even then, the retreat was not quite over.

A Victory Lap through a Freer World

Almost as if he were a matinee idol, Ronald Reagan left office amid popular acclaim and critical hostility on January 11, 1989. He also marked the end of a great political partnership by signing a warm letter of thanks and appreciation to Margaret Thatcher.

It was Reagan's relaxed self-confidence as much as Thatcher's stern abilities that had enabled this extraordinary partnership to work so well for so long—the full length of Reagan's two terms. Their personalities and gifts were very different. Sir Percy Cradock, Thatcher's foreign policy adviser, contrasted them as "the bossy intrusive Englishwoman, lecturing and hectoring, hyperactive, obsessively concerned with detail," and "the lazy, sunny Irish ex-actor, his mind operating mainly in the instinctive mode, happy to delegate and over-delegate, hazy about most of his briefs, but with certain stubbornly held principles, a natural warmth, and an extraordinary ability to communicate with his constituents."[25] But they complemented each other. Each brought to the partnership qualities the other lacked that made it work better. Each gained from the other's contribution. And since they wanted the partnership to work and were prepared to overlook faults in each other, it worked better than well. It worked splendidly.

Still, given that Washington lore during his presidency held Reagan to be not very bright—the "amiable dunce," in Clark Clifford's famous phrase—it was inevitable that a common belief arose that Thatcher held Reagan in low esteem intellectually. Many of Thatcher's advisers disparaged Reagan's intellect, and their estimation may well have influenced her; she made one or two private remarks early in their relationship that seem to reflect it, saying on one occasion that "there's not much grey matter, is there?"[26]

But there are compelling reasons to doubt that this was (or is) her considered view, beginning with the fact that she denies it. The more we know about Ronald Reagan, the more false and superficial the "amiable dunce" thesis seems. Recent Reagan scholarship—both biographies and his own republished writings—has demolished the once conventional wisdom that Reagan was lazy (he was extremely diligent), that he was manipulated by his aides (he was happy to give them credit for actions he had ordered), and that he was ignorant of the major political issues (he had analyzed them in detail in his columns and radio broadcasts). If Reagan did not see any point in engaging in prolonged analytical argument or detailed policy examination, it was because he had long ago thought through these matters and reached firm conclusions. He saw his task as giving general directions to his administration to pursue aims he had determined before reaching office. Richard Reeves, his most recent biographer and a political liberal unsympathetic to his philosophy, underlines the result in a series of rhetorical questions: "Could the shrewd secretary of defense, Caspar Weinberger, have more than doubled the Pentagon budget? Could the experienced secretary of state, George Shultz, have believed Russia would be applying for membership of NATO in 1993? Could Donald Regan... have raised the morale of a nation?"[27]

It is implausible to the point of absurdity to think that these things were achieved by an amiable dunce. A shrewd observer herself, Thatcher was bound to notice in them clear proof of a high, if unorthodox, intelligence. And as someone whose male colleagues sometimes found her own thought processes infuriatingly hard to follow, she would not have dismissed Reagan's broad-brush directions as merely instinctive. She would have recognized that while one world historical success might be luck, a succession of them looked more like carefulness on Reagan's part.

Indeed she did recognize this. Her considered judgment on Reagan is in her memoirs. On the occasion of his 1980 victory, she writes pointedly, "It was easy for lesser men to underrate Ronald Reagan." She further notes that his "apparently detached and broad-brush" style of work and decision-making enabled him to revive the American economy, American power, and American morale. She concludes by giving him the principal credit for winning the Cold War since his "policies of military and economic competition with the Soviet Union forced the Soviet leaders, in particular Mr. Gorbachev, to abandon their ambitions of hegemony and to embark on the process of reform which in the end brought the entire Communist system crashing down."[28] In other words, without Reagan, no *perestroika* or *glasnost* either.

We can account for her few dismissive remarks about the president quite easily. Thatcher was given to letting off steam at the end of a busy day over a drink with her close aides. At the end of a particularly frustrating day, she would avenge the concessions forced from her by sharply criticizing the people to whom she had made them. Those around her recognized these remarks as an expression of her frustration—the equivalent of punching a cushion—rather than of her true opinions.[29] And they were forgotten the following morning when policy had to be made again. Since there were moments when the U.S. president took positions she had strongly opposed, as at Reykjavik, there were times when he became the unknowing victim of this private dismissal. Reagan gave her few occasions for such criticisms. They became less frequent over time as her respect for him grew to match her affection.

Reagan's signature on a letter to Thatcher was his last official act as president. On Inauguration Day 1989, however, it was hard to recall exactly what Reagan's last *political* act had been. He seemed to have been coasting to retirement, doing a series of victory laps around the international arena, for the best part of a year. The Moscow summit in May 1988, his farewell to the Republican convention, the tripartite meeting on Governor's Island with Gorbachev and Vice President George H. W. Bush only the previous month, all attended by cheering crowds—no one could recall a president going out in such style and with such popularity since Calvin Coolidge.

The critics—including most editorial writers, columnists, and historians—thought the comparison only too valid. Reagan's favorite president was Calvin Coolidge, whose picture had been restored to prominence in the White House in 1981. More to the point, Coolidge's departure from office had been swiftly followed by the 1929 crash and the Great Depression. Reagan's media scolds predicted firmly that something similar would now happen to dent or even destroy Reagan's reputation. But after eighteen years of high growth with stable prices, scarcely interrupted by two mild and shallow recessions, they have given up hope. Any future major economic reverse will have to be blamed on some other Republican. In the meantime the critics have largely retreated to the position that the 1980s were a shameful "decade of greed." This accusation is a Halloween child: something pretty in grim disguise. If the figures for charitable giving are any guide—and they are—the 1980s were a decade of generosity. And the one economic item for which Reagan can be legitimately criticized, namely the deficit, was declining when he left office. Besides, it bought victory in the Cold War, peace with Russia, and Clinton's "peace dividend."

If Reagan's presidency had been a movie from his Hollywood days, it would have ended not in January 1989 but on one of three other dates. The first would be May 31, 1988, when he addressed the students of Moscow University during the Moscow summit. Though the summit itself was regarded as having produced meager results—the Strategic Arms Limitation Talks made only slow progress—it was a triumph for the human factor in politics. Reagan was mobbed by ordinary Russians on a walkabout in the Arbat shopping district (and distressed by the heavy-handed tactics of the Soviet police in clearing the crowd). The old actor wowed the Moscow intellectuals with a speech in which he quoted Russian filmmaker Sergei Eisenstein on vision as the basis of leadership. He was given a guided tour of Red Square by Gorbachev.

It was his address to Moscow University, however, that was the moral highlight of the visit. Most of the students present had come to maturity when the Soviet media was denouncing the American president as a dangerous warmonger. They were too young to remember his Hollywood days. But he was cheered enthusiastically because he spoke to them as an ambassador from the future. Reagan described to the students the new information economy rooted in human creativity that his own policies had helped to bring forth: "Like a chrysalis, we're emerging from the Industrial

Revolution—an economy confined to and limited by the earth's resources—into, as one economist titled his book, *The Economy of the Mind*, in which there are no bounds on human imagination and the freedom to create.... Think of that little computer chip. Its value isn't in the sand from which it was made."

Around them were the ruins that Communism had made of the industrial economy. But Reagan was pointing to an information economy that would be open to them now that ideology no longer blocked their way. They applauded the old spell-binder and he left them sharing his vision, as he had left so many American audiences.[30]

The second date would be December 6, 1988, when Reagan hosted Gorbachev and President-elect (and still vice president) George Bush for a lunch on Governor's Island off the end of Manhattan. Gorbachev had just announced at the United Nations that the USSR would unilaterally reduce its conventional armed forces by 500,000 men, its tank divisions by a quarter, and its combat aircraft by 500. The cuts sharply reduced, if they did not entirely eliminate, the Warsaw Pact's predominance in conventional arms that had worried Thatcher and made her reluctant to weaken nuclear deterrence. Over lunch Gorbachev asked the retiring president his opinion of the UN speech.

"I heartily approve," said Reagan, repeating the phrase later that afternoon to the press. It was indeed the kind of massive arms reduction that he had always said he wanted—and that the experts had told him was utopian.[31]

The third date would occur after he left office—November 9, 1989, when the Berlin Wall was finally torn down, not deliberately by Gorbachev as Reagan had requested, but as the result of a bureaucratic mistake. As the rebellions against Communism spread across Eastern Europe in the fall of 1989, the beleaguered East German authorities, anxious to create a safety valve for the popular discontent fueling nightly riots, ordered a more liberal approach to allowing their citizens to visit West Berlin. Misunderstanding their instructions, the guards let people through the gates. A trickle came through, this news was broadcast, the trickle became a flood, and the flood, now intoxicated with liberty, began to chip away at the hated structure. Berlin became a single united city in a few hours, and East Germany ceased in a matter of days to be an effective Communist dictatorship. Over the next few months, the Soviet empire in Eastern Europe gradually collapsed, to be replaced by independent market democracies.

The breach of the Berlin Wall was the real climax of the Reagan presidency. His everyday departure in January had been handled well. His last presidential address to the American people was a friendly farewell that treated the presidency as a sort of joint enterprise with the people to guard America, his "shining city upon a hill": "My friends, we did it. We weren't just marking time. We made a difference. We made the city stronger. We made the city freer. And we left her in good hands. All in all, not bad. Not bad at all. And so, goodbye."

On his last morning in office, his national security adviser, Colin Powell, had given him the daily national security briefing. It was short and sweet: "Mr. President, the world is quiet." Reagan handed over power to Bush and returned to California.

But the world was not quiet. It was fermenting with the idea of freedom that Reagan had both preached and personified. Ten months later the Berliners followed Reagan's advice. They tore down that wall.

Down Go the Dominoes

East Berlin and East Germany had fallen because of a bureaucratic mistake. It was a metaphor for the end of Communism more generally. On the night of Bush's inauguration, the Soviet ambassador surprised the class enemy at a *National Review* celebratory dinner when he said that the Soviet Union would not intervene if Eastern European states decided to abandon socialism and follow the capitalist road. William Safire took out his reporter's pencil and started making notes, and Jeane Kirkpatrick set about cross-questioning the ambassador. He stuck to the idea of Soviet neutrality. They were hearing what later became known as the "Sinatra doctrine"—the idea that the Eastern Europeans could do it their way without asking permission from Moscow. Already at the printer that week, *National Review*'s cover story was a prescient article titled "The Coming

Crack-Up of Communism" by young Polish journalist Radek Sikorski. Even so, the editors and their guests found it hard to credit that Soviet imperial Communism would go quietly into voluntary liquidation anytime soon.

Their suspicion was not wholly unjustified. It was Soviet policy to reform the empire, not dismantle it. Gorbachev and the Politburo had concluded by the start of the Bush presidency that the USSR's allies were a costly embarrassment. But neither in the Third World—where the Soviet Union was sending arms to Communist rebels in El Salvador until 1991—nor in Eastern Europe did the Soviets intend to introduce genuine multi-party democracy. What was needed in Hungary, East Germany, Poland, Czechoslovakia, and the other satellites, they calculated, was *perestroika* and *glasnost* carried out by reform Communists like Gorbachev himself. Such governments would draw their ministers from non-Communist parties, but the leading role of the Communist Party would be retained, and they would pursue enlightened economic policies along "market socialism" lines. Existing Communist governments headed by hard-liners such as Erich Honecker obstructed this outcome, and would have to be maneuvered or forced out. This could be done, if necessary, by reform Communists cooperating with dissidents to broaden the regime. When that happened, socialism with a human face would be established throughout the bloc—and the Warsaw Pact would rest on more stable and popular foundations.

This strategy was first applied in Hungary and Poland through the device of round-table talks with the opposition. The round-table strategy was designed to exploit the Communist Party's real but fading power to negotiate a new constitution in which the Communists would "share" power but on terms (reserved parliamentary seats, for instance) that gave them, unless things went badly wrong, a dominant political position. In Poland, Gorbachev authorized such talks because Solidarity was simply too strong to suppress and the government represented not socialism with a human face but, in Adam Michnik's phrase, "Communism with a few teeth knocked out."[32] But Gorbachev and his local allies had miscalculated. Communism was by now so discredited and unpopular that opposition parties won majorities massive enough to overwhelm any number of special protections for Communist power. In Hungary the reform Communists believed that their leader, Imre Poszgay, would emerge as president from the round table and control any further process of democratization. But the opposition (led by the first post-Communist prime minister, Josef Antall) insisted on the president being elected by the new parliament. As a result the first competitive elections, held in 1990, returned an anti-Communist majority, thus depriving the Communists of control of all the levers of power and splitting the party in two.[33]

It seemed that everywhere, once the progress of liberalization started—with such reforms as competitive elections—the reform Communists soon lost control. Long-suppressed social forces emerged from nowhere to capture the process and push it in fully democratic directions. Finally, any event, large or small, political or religious, bold decision or bureaucratic mistake, could start the reform avalanche moving once people began to believe that major political change was possible.

Thus the crisis in East Germany began in September 1989 when Hungary opened its borders to East Germans eager to flee to the West. Thirty thousand did so, creating a crisis for the Berlin regime, worsening relations between two Communist states, and sparking the ferment that led eventually to the overthrow of the Wall.

In Czechoslovakia hundreds were injured when riot police brutally crushed a protest march by students in mid-November. This produced massive public revulsion against the regime. Vaclav Havel brought dissidents together under the umbrella organization Civic Forum to mount a more serious resistance. The Church threw its influence behind the resistance. Cardinal Tomasek told Catholics, "In this hour of destiny for our country, not a single one of you may stand apart.... Religious liberty cannot be separated from other human rights. Freedom is indivisible." Over the next six weeks, as the nation mobilized to seek its freedom, the Communists attempted to transform the revolution into an internal maneuver that would replace the hard-liners with their own reformists. But the public rejected the new government. Mass demonstrations and nationwide strikes continued for weeks, until the regime collapsed and a coalition dominated by dissidents took power to organize genuine multi-party elections.

One incident captures this process in miniature. A reform Communist from the days of "socialism with a human face," Zdenek Mlynar, returned to Prague from exile abroad. He had been the chief ideologist of Alexander Dubcek's "Prague spring," and as such he had sincerely tried to reconcile a Communist economy with a liberal democratic political system, essentially by giving independent pressure groups some influence in the political process. He had high if slightly inconvenient credentials—he had been Gorbachev's roommate at college—and he was exactly the kind of figure Gorbachev hoped would replace the old guard. Because of Mlynar's past decencies, Havel invited him to address a massive crowd in Wenceslas Square. But he spoke in the stale jargon of reform Communism. Whatever his private convictions, he represented 1968's halfway house to liberty. The crowd whistled him off the platform. Five weeks later Havel was installed as president of a democratic Czechoslovakia and Gorbachev's roommate had returned to academic theorizing.[34]

One by one the Eastern European Communist states tumbled uncontrollably toward democracy and independence. Gorbachev is praised for not sending in the tanks as in Hungary in 1956 or as in Czechoslovakia in 1968. Such praise is deserved even if, as Peter Rodman observes, only a Soviet leader is praised for not actually shooting his own people. But Gorbachev's restraint was as much a recognition of reality as it was a moral choice. The year before, Gorbachev had explained to Reagan and Bush at Governor's Island the reasons he was cutting the number of Soviet troops and tanks in Eastern Europe: "I'm doing this because I need to. I'm doing this because there's a revolution taking place in my country. I started it. And they all applauded me when I started in 1986, and now they don't like it very much, but it's going to be a revolution, nonetheless."[35] He was also doing it because the Afghanistan debacle had created a crisis of morale both within and outside the Red Army. Soldiers had returned from doing their "international duty" to report of atrocities against whole villages fighting for their independence. There was no appetite for another exercise in fraternal repression.

So Gorbachev had no real ability to crush the revolution that was now devouring his reformist friends. Worse, it would soon be lapping at the very door of Moscow.

In Search of a New Credo

Though Gorbachev was losing Eastern Europe politically in 1989, he still had a slim chance of keeping it strategically—and he hoped to recruit two unusual allies in achieving this: John Paul and Margaret Thatcher. From 1989 to 1991 all the great powers were wondering how to cope with the freedom revolutions redrawing the map of Europe. In particular Gorbachev wanted to prevent a reunited Germany remaining in NATO, as that would increase the strategic threat to the USSR. One of his maneuvers was to advocate a "Common European Home" that would include Russia and exclude the United States. He knew that Thatcher was hostile to German reunification and that the pope might be brought to sympathize with the Common European Home idea. In December 1989, therefore, Gorbachev made his historic visit to the Vatican.

Whatever else it was, Gorbachev's visit was an important admission that official atheism had been defeated by religious belief. He made this quite explicit when he introduced his wife to the pope, saying, "Raisa Maximova, I have the honor to introduce the highest moral authority on earth." Then he added, "And he's Slavic, like us."[36] That was no mere pleasantry. Ever since Gierek had told the Soviets of the pope's Slavic sympathies in 1981, they had wondered how to exploit them usefully. The post-1989 crisis seemed to be just the occasion.

Almost the first recorded words of the meeting take up a Slavic theme. Gorbachev said, "I highly value your words that, among all other things, we are two Slavs. I don't want to sound like a pan-Slavist, but I do believe in the mission of the Slav nations to assert universally the understanding of the value of human life, peace, and the good." John Paul responded favorably to this, as well he might; he had often argued that Europe must breathe with the two lungs of the Roman and Byzantine Christian traditions. As the conversation progressed, the Soviet leader argued several times that the West should not impose its models on the whole of Europe. The pope agreed. Gorbachev stressed the role of Europe in the world—that its traditions gave it "a historical peacemaking mission" in the world. Also, the new "European credo" was an invitation to think collectively about the world's problems—very different from the ambition of *some* Western countries to insist that the renewal of Europe must be based on Western values.[37]

It is sometimes hard to grasp exactly what Gorbachev was driving at in this conversation. He seemed to want to say something like: "Look here, we Slavs are half of Europe and we want our national and cultural traditions to be given more weight in continental bodies. We could sort all this out very amicably if the Americans weren't around. They keep insisting that everyone has to handle things their way. Let Europe be Europe." But he couldn't quite bring himself to say anything so clear, partly because he was nervous in the pope's presence, as eyewitnesses suggest, and partly because he sensed dimly that it would be highly inappropriate. So he threw out vague hints wrapped in platitudes. The pope, by contrast, was admirably clear and practical, calling for religious freedom, better treatment of Lithuanian and Ukrainian Catholics, and the passage of legislation in Russia protecting their rights. He responded favorably to Gorbachev's invitation to visit the Soviet Union (though for diplomatic reasons he could not accept it until the Russian Orthodox Church extended its own invitation and in fact it never happened).

John Paul clearly liked Gorbachev, whom he was known to have called "a providential man."[38] But they were talking at cross purposes. For the pope, the idea that Europe should breathe with two lungs was essentially a religious and cultural one about the Slavic contribution to Christianity. It was not an argument about defense, foreign policy, or international institutions, whether economic or strategic. If Gorbachev imagined that the pope would intervene in European politics to help reshape the Continent in line with Soviet foreign policy, he had seriously misread the nature of John Paul II. Since the Soviets had seen their Polish satrapy move toward independence under his spiritual leadership, they may have seen him as a political "player" with whom they could deal. In reality he was a spiritual leader who would outline the moral principles to be heeded in building a new Europe but would not design it himself. Gorbachev may also have realized that the Poles would have resisted any attempt to evict the United States from Europe even if—fanciful notion—it had been proposed by the Vatican.

Insofar as Gorbachev's criticism of the imposition of Western values was intended to refer to economic models, Gorbachev should have saved his breath to cool his *kasha*. John Paul had been thinking deeply about economics, but he was moving in exactly the opposite direction from the Soviet leader.

During his papacy theretofore, John Paul II had written two powerful encyclicals on social and economic justice. All such encyclicals have certain things in common: for instance, they rightly warn against greed and materialism as dangerous sins. John Paul's first, *Laborem Exercens* (On Human Work), was published in 1981. It continued the general tradition of social encyclicals which, while rejecting socialism, tend to stress the rights of labor, including the right to strike, its priority over capital, the fallacy of "economism" (i.e., treating workers merely as "hands"), the desirability of a "family wage" or one income sufficient to support a family, and so on. Where *Laborem Exercens* strikes out in an original direction is in treating work not as a punishment for the Fall but as a positive good in which the worker both realizes himself and approaches closer to God. To make work in our world conform more closely to that ideal, the pope proposed new patterns of work and ownership that would give the worker a greater share of both and thus a more creative role. He would cease, in Marxist terms, to be alienated from the product of his labor.

John Paul's second encyclical, *Sollicitudo Rei Socialis* (On Social Concern), was published in 1988 and was generally interpreted by the media as denouncing communism and capitalism about equally. That was not an accurate description of John Paul's opinion. In praising Gorbachev as a good man, the pope had added the aside, "But Communism is unreformable." And while the encyclical is full of proposals for reform—for instance, the idea of a right to economic initiative—these are largely concerned with making capitalism fairer rather than abolishing it. But it undoubtedly bore the influence of priests and laymen associated with the Catholic left. And some of its language—the "two blocs"—smacked of moral equivalence.

Both encyclicals, despite the originality and power of *Laborem Exercens*, are distorted by an important flaw: they address themselves to the capitalism of the past, the "Fordist" industrial capitalism of manufacturing industry and production lines, rather than to the information capitalism of computers and silicon chips that Reagan and Thatcher had midwifed.

John Paul remedied this in his third great social encyclical, *Centesimus Annus*, published in 1991. This identifies the source of modern wealth neither as raw materials nor possession of the "means of production," but as knowledge, know-how, and creativity, or, in economist's language, "human capital." Since all people have abilities of some kind, they have a responsibility to develop them as fully as possible. Society in turn is responsible for smoothing people's path to knowledge and for combating exclusion. An economy is to be judged as just or unjust by how effectively it opens access to knowledge and skills. A free economy is likely to do that best—but only if it is shaped by an independent culture of virtue and trust and operates within a framework of humane but liberal law. A capitalism that meets these criteria is clearly justifiable from a Catholic standpoint, and a socialism that intrudes excessively into private economic decisions and pauperizes the poor is equally clearly not.

Anglo-American capitalism under Reagan and Thatcher developed more fully and rapidly in the direction of the "know-how economy" than did any other economic system. Insofar as "Western values" were a shorthand term for this form of economic development, John Paul had favored them in *Centesimus Annus* and could oppose them only at some cost in consistency. In addition the pope argued that society now consisted not of two polarities, the state and the economy, but of three independent spheres—the state, the economy, and the cultural milieu. He favored a society in which capitalism was shaped and restrained by culture and cultural institutions as much as by the state, and probably more so. That was a movement away from what the Soviets and even the democratic socialists of Western Europe wanted.

Within a very short time Gorbachev would have realized that he had emerged from the Vatican empty-handed. The pope had significantly revised Catholic social teaching in the light of the Reagan-Thatcher transformation of capitalism.[39]

Birth Pangs of a New Europe

If Gorbachev could expect little help from the pope to maintain the Soviet strategic position in Europe—drowning men clutch at straws—he had better grounds for thinking that Thatcher might do so. She had two plausible motives for this implausible sympathy. First, at this stage she believed that he was the key to continuing *perestroika* in the USSR and even perhaps to the establishment of democracy there. Any developments that weakened him, she feared, were likely to threaten these things. It was even possible that if he were to fall, then the Soviets might rescind the Sinatra doctrine and seek to recoup their strategic position, thus threatening the peace and stability of Europe.

These calculations were not unreasonable, but they exaggerated Soviet power and misunderstood the purpose of *perestroika,* which was not democracy but a more liberal and sustainable Communism. Also, they were distorted by the human factor. Like Reagan, Thatcher liked Gorbachev. He had cooperated with them both in ending the Cold War. They interpreted his *perestroika* as the first stage of the abandonment of Communism. And, in addition, Thatcher had gained some credit as the one who had identified Gorbachev as someone with whom they could deal. She continued to see him as a reformer who was essential to a process of stable reform—though doubts were beginning to arise.

Thatcher had a second motive for possibly supporting the Soviet strategic position in Europe—namely, her passionate hostility to the reunification of Germany and a desire to delay it as long as possible. She feared that a too-powerful Germany would dominate Europe either from within or without the European Community. When reunification crept quietly onto the European political agenda in summer 1989 with the fall of Erich Honecker amid the growing troubles of Eastern European Communists, she looked for allies to obstruct it—and found very few. Mitterrand was one, Gorbachev another—both temporarily.

These two considerations distorted her foreign policy for the following six months, as she has freely conceded in her memoirs, describing her policy on German reunification as having met with "unambiguous" defeat. Her failure was one sign, among others, that her political position was getting weaker at home and abroad. Until the Gulf War broke out in August 1990, President George H. W. Bush was signaling that he wanted to make relations with Germany a higher priority than those with Britain. Within Britain a row between Thatcher and her chancellor, Nigel Lawson, over the responsibility for rising inflation had divided the Thatcherites, gravely weakened the government, and undermined her own dominance. And though she would be reluctant to admit it, she missed Reagan, who had provided (except on SDI) a stable anchor of policy. She had known where she stood with him, but she did not feel quite as confident about Bush. She felt therefore that she had to be more aggressive in advancing her own positions. As a result Thatcher sought to make common cause with Mitterrand and Gorbachev against German reunification over the summer and fall of 1989 as the Communist dominoes fell.

Her campaign included one conversation that requires an extended digression: In September 1989 Thatcher stopped off at Moscow for a meeting with Gorbachev devoted to the transformation of Eastern Europe and the possibility of a reunited Germany. At one point she asked him to turn off the tape recorder. He did so and, after the meeting, set down his recollection of her comments.

According to Gorbachev, Thatcher told him that neither Britain nor Western Europe was interested in reunification. It would mean altering postwar borders, which nobody wanted, and would undermine international stability and threaten security. She went on: "Neither are we interested in the destabilization of Eastern Europe and the collapse of the Warsaw Pact. Of course, the internal changes in all Eastern European countries are natural. Somewhere they go further, somewhere—not yet. But we want these processes to be exclusively internal. We will not intervene there and encourage de-Communization of Eastern Europe."[40]

So did Thatcher go wobbly?

In fact she said almost nothing on that occasion that she had not said, or did not later say, to Bush, or to others, or that she has not written in her memoirs. On the day after the Berlin Wall fell she wrote a letter to Gorbachev, which she copied to Helmut Kohl. Horst Telchuk, Kohl's adviser, noted in his diary of these events for November 10:

> Helpful by comparison is the letter from Margaret Thatcher to Mikhail Gorbachev, of which we have received a copy.... The English prime minister agrees with the Soviet president that a risky instability is not excluded, and therefore ordered steps for the maintenance of stability and prudence are necessary. Like the federal chancellor, she too stresses unmistakably that long-term thoroughgoing reforms in the GDR are "the most solid foundation" for stability. And she lists these reforms by name: free elections, multi-party system, complete freedom of movement, real democracy and an economic system that supports it. The agreement with the federal chancellor on this point is impressive. Addressing Gorbachev, she expressly refers to the telephone conversation with Kohl. She and the federal chancellor are both of the opinion that a destabilization must be avoided. Nobody in the West has the intention of interfering in the internal affairs of the GDR or endangering the security interests of the GDR or the Soviet Union. I am sure that this letter to Gorbachev will have a very calming effect.[41]

When Thatcher saw Bush in Camp David after the Wall had fallen, she said, according to Bush's memoirs: " 'The overriding objective is to get democracy throughout Eastern Europe,' she told me. 'We have won the battle of ideas after tough times as we kept NATO strong.'... She added that such change could only take place in an atmosphere of stability. 'That means NATO and Warsaw Pact should stay, NATO anyway. . . . Focus on democracy now.' "[42]

Another preoccupation of Thatcher's surfaced in a telephone conversation she had with Bush on November 17, one week after the Wall fell. She feared that German reunification would threaten Gorbachev's political survival. "Destabilize him and we lose the possibility of democracy in the Soviet Union," she warned.[43]

Her confidants report her as arguing that securing democracy in the individual Eastern European countries should take priority over destroying an already crumbling Warsaw Pact. Bush and Secretary of State James Baker had advocated a similar position before the Wall came down, when the president was swept away by the general enthusiasm and by the firm determination of Kohl to push for German unity. The Thatcher position was still supported by National Security Adviser Brent Scowcroft, who after the Camp David meeting between Bush and Thatcher wrote:

> I was not as optimistic as the president about the outcome and I had some lingering sympathy for Thatcher's position. She had her eyes on some very important priorities. The changes which had already taken place in Europe were breathtaking in their scope, and managing their consequences would take the best efforts of all to prevent dangerous possibilities from developing. To add to this already unsettling brew the potentially most destabilizing issue of all—German unification—could be asking for trouble.[44]

When Thatcher spoke to Bush in November, democracy had already won in Poland, Hungary, and East Germany, and it was advancing in Czechoslovakia. She had given strong public support to its victory in all these countries. In her own memoirs she reports frankly that she had told Gorbachev of her opposition to reunification, immediately adding, "Of course, I did not want East Germans—any more than I would have wanted anyone else—to have to live under Communism. But it seemed to me that a truly democratic East Germany would soon emerge and that the question of reunification was a separate one, on which the wishes and interests of Germany's neighbors and other powers must be fully taken into account."[45]

What then explains Gorbachev's memory that she had opposed the "de-Communization" of Eastern Europe? This is clearly either a misstatement or a misunderstanding of her position. All her diplomacy, private and public, for 1989 and 1990 was devoted to ensuring the successful establishment of democracy throughout Eastern Europe. She wanted stability precisely so that this development should not go into reverse. And she feared that a Western policy encouraging the dissolution of the Warsaw Pact would produce such a backlash. Gorbachev apparently compressed this train of argument into simple opposition to "de-Communization" and thus distorted it out of recognition.

If going wobbly meant abandoning or weakening her support for Eastern European democracy, Thatcher did not wobble even slightly. She argued that it should be prudently supported so that the process might continue, as it did, into the Soviet Union itself. But if going wobbly meant fighting a losing battle against an almost irresistible force, namely the German people's desire in 1989 to live in one democratic state, then she wobbled like a spinning top running down. Thatcher's opposition to reunification could only have been sustained by preventing the Germans from voting for it—and since her commitment to democracy never wavered, her opposition to reunification was doomed.

That period between the collapse of the Wall and the creation of a united Germany was almost exactly one year. Kohl argued consistently and effectively for reunification in public and in the "four-plus-two" talks that had been created to resolve the question. He carried the Americans with him. Gorbachev and Mitterrand both opposed it privately—the latter passionately—but were more circumspect in public. In the end, both abandoned their opposition before Thatcher did.

What still remained to be settled was Germany's position in NATO. Accepting her defeat on reunification and knowing that the stability she sought required anchoring a united Germany in Western institutions, Thatcher went to see Gorbachev in June 1990. It was her last great service to him. She helped persuade him to accept NATO membership for Germany in return for Western credits to alleviate his fast-deteriorating economy.[46] In effect she reconciled him to the collapse of his hopes of maintaining Soviet strategic power over a democratic Eastern Europe.

Thatcher's initial fears about the destabilizing effects of the rapid emergence of a new Eastern European political structure fortunately proved groundless. If anything, the fast pace of change paved the way for the democratization of the Soviet Union rather than retarding it. The Warsaw Pact was peacefully dissolved. A United Germany joined NATO and the European Community. By the middle of 1990 all of Eastern Europe was free; by the start of 1991 a new structure of a democratic Europe had been put in place.

Reagan and Thatcher both made triumphal tours of the region, where they were greeted as champions of liberty in the victorious fight against Communism. And Thatcher could not resist intervening in their elections to urge voting against left-wing parties and half-hearted reforms.

By then, however, another battle was shaping up—this time one in which Gorbachev and Thatcher were on opposite sides.

A Failed Experiment

At a lunch in Paris for the heads of government of the Conference on Security and Cooperation (CSCE) in Europe in November 1990, Thatcher was talking to the new president of the semi-democratic Romania, the former Communist apparatchik Ion Iliescu, about the importance of having a clear stopping point in negotiations—the point beyond which you would not go. Gorbachev, who had been listening across the table, suddenly leaned forward to express agreement.

His stopping point, he said, was the external borders of the Soviet Union. He had conceded much, but he would not concede changes in that.[47]

In November 1990, however, Gorbachev was already losing this battle. Three separate crises roiled the Soviet Union and undermined Gorbachev in 1990: the Soviet economy was collapsing; the Communist Party was being destroyed by revelations of its past crimes; and the Soviet nationalities were seeking to leave the Soviet Union through various means. *Perestroika* had not solved the first of these crises; in conjunction with *glasnost*, it had instead helped to create the other two. And all three together had forged a crisis of legitimacy for the entire Soviet regime and for Gorbachev personally. The eerie symbolism of three dates was pointed out by David Pryce-Jones in his obituary for the USSR: on May 1, 1989, Gorbachev reviewed the traditional May Day parade from the Red Square reviewing stand with other members of the Politburo; one year later he was booed and had to decamp from the scene; and on May 1, 1991, the May Day parade was cancelled.

Ostensibly, the economic crisis was the worst. By the 1980s the Soviets contributed only 2 percent of world trade. Their per capita consumption was less than half of Western European levels. Sugar, meat, animal fats, and even that famous Soviet "sausage" were rationed. Three hundred large towns and cities lacked central sewage systems. Life outside Moscow, Leningrad, and a few other major cities was primitive. Only a fifth of the roads were all-weather, and more than 100 million people were crammed into what amounted to less than nine square meters of living space (generally in communal apartments). Pollution was so bad that the health minister could seriously offer the advice: "To live longer you must breathe less."[48]

But Soviet citizens had been living in such squalid conditions for seventy years. They had long ago ceased to believe any of the regime's promises of economic improvement. If other circumstances had not changed, they would probably have continued to adapt for another seventy years. But *glasnost* meant that these failures could be openly discussed and blamed on the Communist Party. In addition, the Party itself began to reveal the extraordinary series of crimes against humanity—mass murder, genocide, the Gulag, institutionalized corruption—that had been its modus operandi since Lenin. Very few families were not touched by these atrocities; both Gorbachevs had relatives who had been purged. And as the official reports established, the number of victims of Stalin's terror even exceeded the estimates of the most distinguished Western scholar of Soviet totalitarianism, Robert Conquest, whose accounts had been criticized by some Western Sovietologists as exaggerated and alarmist.

Gorbachev had allowed these revelations, paradoxically, in order to conduct a more civilized purge—he wanted the old guard out and reform Communists in. But their effect was far more comprehensive: after all, if the Communist Party had committed these terrible crimes, how could it possibly claim to be the vanguard of humanity entitled to the "leading role" in government and society? Moreover, because Gorbachev had also allowed some competition in elections, the Soviet voter could purge for himself—and the likelihood was that he would purge officeholders in proportion to their importance in the Party. The Party itself was thus under siege. Ambitious politicians had a choice: they could either side with the hard-liners and oppose reforms or they could leave the Party. But where was an alternative party?

This was now provided by the third crisis: the nationalities problem. In the Baltic states, in Georgia, and in the Muslim republics, newly formed nationalist organizations demanded secession from the USSR. Gorbachev strongly opposed independence, as he told Thatcher and Iliescu in Paris. So he ordered Communist apparatchiks to cooperate and even infiltrate such bodies to transform them into loyal opposition parties within a reformed Soviet Union. Some did as he asked, but overall this effort proved as futile as it had in Eastern Europe. The Communist parties in the constituent republics were moribund, the new nationalist bodies had energy and commitment, and the apparatchiks either went over to the nationalists' side altogether or were defeated in elections and recalled to Moscow.

Between 1989 and 1991, therefore, the history of the Soviet Union was one of gradual dissolution. In March 1989, the Baltic nationalist parties won elections by huge majorities; in May Latvia, Estonia, and Lithuania declared "sovereignty" (i.e., that their laws superseded those of the Soviet Union); in August two million people formed a human chain linking Riga, Vilnius, and Tallin (the three Baltic capitals) in protest at the Soviet occupation; and in November Georgia declared independence. This process accelerated sharply in March and May 1990, with the three Baltic republics declaring full independence from the USSR. Gorbachev announced that these declarations were illegal and instituted an economic blockade of Lithuania. But he called it off in June when it became clear that the Lithuanians preferred their liberty to the subsidies they had enjoyed as members of the USSR. Following this successful defiance, Ukraine, Belorussia, and the various "Stans" all rushed to declare their own independence in the summer and fall of 1990. When Gorbachev had declared to Thatcher the sanctity of the USSR's borders, he was not making an academic point; he was informing her obliquely that he was on the verge of attempting to crush a series of rebellions that were breaking up the Soviet Union.

In December 1990 Gorbachev reshuffled his cabinet, bringing in hard-liners and accepting the resignation of moderates like Shevardnadze (who warned of an impending dictatorship). Between January 2 and January 13, 1991, Soviet interior ministry troops (the so-called "Black Berets") surrounded public buildings in Vilnius, Lithuania. They closed the airport and railway station, seized the television station, and shot fifteen people. Gorbachev claimed the following day that they were responding to a request for intervention from a "national salvation committee." The next day Gorbachev denied he had ordered the raid, blaming it on the national salvation committee. So it was a very unfortunate coincidence that the following week another national salvation committee was formed in Riga, Latvia. Alas, forgetting their previous error, on January 19 the Black Berets intervened in Latvia, seizing various public building and killing four people. This time Gorbachev blamed the intervention on the Baltic parliaments.

But it was too little too late against populations led by intelligent and brave politicians that were determined not to be pushed back into the Soviet prison of nationalities. This time, moreover, the Baltics had the sympathy of Russian reformers: 300,000 demonstrators marched in support of Baltic independence in Moscow on January 20. In the following month the Baltic states voted overwhelmingly for independence. Again, the other constituent republics followed them in rapid succession, and the breakup of the Soviet Union accelerated until the hard-line counter-coup of August that year.

As these events were unfolding, they had one effect, initially unnoticed, that gradually transformed the entire picture. The more the constituent republics peeled off the Soviet Union, the more important the leader of the Russian Republic naturally became. That leader was Gorbachev's old rival, Boris Yeltsin, whose humiliation at Gorbachev's hands had briefly delayed the Washington summit. A series of political changes brought him to the top of the Russian political structure, both Party and state, in 1990. And whereas Gorbachev was threatened by all three crises, in particular by the legitimacy crisis of the USSR, Yeltsin was strengthened and given new opportunities by them. He now set out to oust and replace Gorbachev—and one of his first steps was to ask to meet Thatcher in April 1990.

Yeltsin posed a problem for Thatcher, but though she did not yet realize it, he also provided her with a solution to a bigger problem. Although she agreed to meet him, she made it politely clear that she would remain loyal to Gorbachev, whom she liked and admired. Yeltsin accepted this quite happily as the basis of the conversation, almost certainly because he guessed that the facts of the Soviet situation would eventually push Thatcher into his arms. Once that stipulation was agreed, she was curious to see him. Her briefing stated that "some pundits even suggest that if [Yeltsin] is elected as president of the Russian Federation, he may end up with a more important job than Gorbachev's presidency of a crumbling Union. This is an exaggeration." Yeltsin soon did, in fact, eclipse Gorbachev, and even then it was clearly a possibility. So Thatcher listened carefully, and she liked what she heard.

Essentially, Yeltsin's message was that Gorbachev's *perestroika* didn't go nearly far enough because he was still a Communist wedded to state control and intervention. What was needed in the USSR was democracy, free markets, and decentralization, which he supported. It is doubtful whether Yeltsin truly believed this or, if he did, that he realized its full implications. His interest in such ideas was purely utilitarian: he would use them as instruments to replace Gorbachev (in reality if not formally). But Thatcher knew from both reading and experience that this diagnosis was correct. She concluded that Yeltsin was someone who had shed the Communist mindset still hobbling Gorbachev. From this point on, she was in two minds: publicly and formally she supported Gorbachev, while privately she hoped that Yeltsin's remedies would prevail, ideally through a coalition of the two men. Outside events would shortly enable her to change horses in mid-coup. In the meantime she would imbibe the lessons of Yeltsin's visit.[49]

The most important such lesson was that the Soviet Union no longer represented a force for stability. In the long run—and perhaps even in the short—it was a cause of conflict. That conclusion now put her at odds not only with Gorbachev but also with Bush, Baker, and Scowcroft, who, after their flirtation with risk-taking over German reunification, had now decided to shore up the crumbling USSR in the interests of stability. They shared that opinion with most Western European leaders. So in 1990 the U.S. government was allied with Gorbachev against the nationalist forces in the Baltics, which were quietly backed by Yeltsin and radical democrats in Russia, with Thatcher now leaning to support the latter.

Thatcher did not know it yet, but she had only a short time left to fight such battles. In that short period she won two more battles for liberty. And she was on the battlefield when the totalitarian beast finally died.

The first battle was her intervention at the Rome summit of the European Community in October 1990. The United States was already applying pressure on the Baltic states against independence. Secretary of State James Baker had told the Lithuanians in May 1990 that they should "freeze" their declaration of independence—and the United States continued to exert such public and private pressure throughout that summer. At Rome, European Commission chairman Jacques Delors further proposed that the EC issue a declaration in favor of preserving the existing external borders of the USSR. That would have meant formal European approval for imprisoning the Baltics indefinitely, and would have damaged their morale, which was already depressed by the lack of Western support. Thatcher alone objected. She pointed out that the West had consistently refused to recognize the incorporation of the Baltic republics into the USSR since 1940. The Soviets themselves had just admitted that it was based on the "secret protocols" of the Nazi-Soviet pact. Why would we change now? Delors replied that he had Gorbachev's private assurance that the Baltics would eventually be free to leave. Thatcher objected that such

Soviet guarantees had not always been worth a great deal. Embarrassed by the debate, Mitterrand and Kohl withdrew their support for Delors. The proposal was dropped.

Three months later the Black Berets attacked Vilnius and Riga, on the orders of their "national salvation committees." One year later the Baltic republics were once again independent states. But only one month after the Rome conference—in November 1990—Thatcher had already fallen from power.

She did so in the most dramatic circumstances. While at the CSCE conference in Paris, attended by Bush, Kohl, Mitterrand, and Gorbachev, held to discuss a new security structure for a free Europe, Thatcher was told by her aides that she had not gained a sufficient majority in the election to remain leader of the Conservative Party and thus prime minister. Declining to contest the second round, she left office on November 28, 1990. As Churchill was dismissed by the voters on the morrow of his great achievement in leading the British people to victory against Hitler, so she was dismissed by an ungrateful party at the very moment of her great international triumph.

But she had one final service to render in the battle for liberty. When Soviet hard-liners briefly imprisoned Gorbachev in his Crimean villa during the August 1991 coup, Yeltsin, by now the elected president of the Russian Federation, telephoned Thatcher to seek her support for the democratic resistance he was leading in Moscow. Western governments were dithering: Mitterrand referred on television to Yanaev, the principal putschist, as "the new leader" of the Soviet Union; Kohl said merely that he trusted the Soviets would abide by the treaties Gorbachev had signed; but Thatcher went onto the doorstep of her new private London office and via television condemned the coup and urged Russians to take to the streets in support of their liberty. Within four days the coup collapsed and Gorbachev returned to Moscow.

But he returned to a changed city. The coup had been carried out by Gorbachev's own appointees. It was the last whimper of the Soviet system. Gorbachev was one of the losers of the coup debacle. Power had been transferred from him to Yeltsin, who promptly outlawed the Communist

Party, dissolved the Soviet Union, and humiliated its last leader, his old rival, in a joint conference before the world's press. Thatcher had also, by her intervention, effectively transferred her political trust from Gorbachev to Yeltsin. She hailed his dissolution of the Communist Party as a triumph for liberty.

With the corpse of Soviet Communism on the floor and its last leader sitting glumly beside him, Yeltsin took questions from the press. What was his opinion of Communism, he was asked.

"It is an experiment," he replied, "that should have been tried in a much smaller country."

Reputations

Days after President Reagan's funeral in June 2004, CNN assembled a group of journalists to discuss the significance of what had been an extraordinary few days. Perhaps because Reagan's death had been long expected and was seen by almost everyone as the release of his soul from the imprisonment of an enfeebled body, the mood of the nation had not really been one of mourning. To be sure, the formalities of mourning had been impeccably observed. Long lines of ordinary Americans had moved quietly past the flag-draped coffin in the Capitol; the eulogies in the National Cathedral before the world's mighty had been powerful and affecting; and with the final interment of the body in California against the setting sun, it almost seemed as if nature herself was obeying the protocol laid down for presidential departures.

But though America wept, the mood underlying all these events was one of celebration. Across the country and throughout the world people celebrated the life and achievements of Ronald Reagan, a pleasant man who had turned out to be a great president. There was under the solemnity almost a festive atmosphere. Wherever people gathered—sports fans in bars where for once the television was showing news programs, foreign dignitaries in Washington's smart hotels, political junkies on Capitol Hill, mourners lining up to show their respects—they were telling Reagan's old jokes, remembering lines from his great speeches, recalling his nobility on the day his life almost ended in 1981, and discussing how he had changed the world for the better. It was a remarkable week and, even for a strong Reagan admirer like me, an unexpected one.

In the CNN discussion, Bernard Shaw, recently retired from CNN as a news anchor, said to the chairman of the group, reporter Wolf Blitzer, that he would like to raise "a sensitive issue." Blitzer agreed and Shaw continued:

Shaw: The news media, and how we failed to thoroughly cover and communicate the very essences we're talking about, possessed by Ronald Reagan. What I've been reading and what I've been hearing, I did not get during his two terms in office. Or did I miss something?

Blitzer: I think you're on to something, Bernie.

Shaw: I think we failed our viewers, listeners, and readers to an appreciable extent. I can't quantify it, but I'll, I'll put it there. Because I certainly missed a lot.

Blitzer: I think you're absolutely right, Bernie. We've learned a lot more about this presidency in the years that have followed Ronald Reagan's two terms in office. And I suspect as more of his diaries, more of his papers, more of his speeches, more information is released by the presidential library in Simi Valley, we'll learn even a great deal more.

Shaw had hit a very sensitive point indeed. Reagan's reputation when he left office had been high with ordinary Americans but low with political, media, and academic elites. And it is elites, unfortunately, who determine reputations. For the first few years of his retirement, therefore, the former president had been constantly assailed by stories about how he had been placed among the least successful presidents by some coven of history professors or was seen as a less successful ex-president than Jimmy Carter. He was even treated to polite condescension by the Bush administration, not by the gentlemanly George Bush himself, but by various political appointees who lost few opportunities to suggest that now the adults were in charge and we would see a more rational foreign policy. After a few years Reagan won exemption from personal criticism by the graceful and courageous way he told America of his onset of Alzheimer's, after which he disappeared from the lives, but not the thoughts, of Americans at large and was cared for quietly by his devoted wife.

Between his announcement of the onset of Alzheimer's and his death, however, Reagan's reputation recovered remarkably. By the time of his funeral the Reagan presidency was regarded as a historic success on a number of grounds: he had won the Cold War (without firing a shot); he had revived the U.S. economy, which was enjoying its twenty-second year of consecutive economic growth; he had restored the spirit of America; he had established a new conservative dominance in American politics based on small government and low taxes. All of these claims are subject to qualification, but they are all essentially true.

How had this transformation occurred? In his controversial biography of Reagan, *Dutch*, Edmund Morris reports that he attended an academic conference at which many of those present, including some distinguished Russians, had argued persuasively that the former president had won the Cold War at Reykjavik with SDI. He wrote a letter to Reagan describing the debates and throwing in some of the good jokes, notably Whittle Johnson's "Eisenhower had the military-industrial complex to contend with; Reagan had the academic-media complex."

Reviewing the book after Reagan's Alzheimer's had become public knowledge, I commented that the further revival of his reputation would now depend on others. It was probably the safest prediction I ever made; it turned out to be completely wrong. The publication of books of Reagan's own earlier writings—his columns, his radio broadcasts, his love letters to Nancy, his letters to the general public—demonstrated beyond any doubt that Reagan was a well-informed man of high ability who took great pains to familiarize himself with important political issues and who understood them well enough to be able to explain them simply, clearly, and sometimes wittily to other people.[50] So it became impossible to sneer at the former president—something that had served too many intellectuals as a substitute for intelligent appraisal.

Once people *had* to examine Reagan's achievements, his ultimate success was assured. After all, such achievements as winning the Cold War and restoring the U.S. economy from stagflation to two decades of growth are hard to disparage. As the theologians put it, they compel assent. These accomplishments have been seconded by America's former adversaries. One of the themes cited by Morris in his letter to Reagan was the astonishment of Russians at the refusal of American intellectuals to give any credit to Reagan for his undeniable achievements. It has been an amusing feature of international conferences since 1991 that American liberals (in particular Sovietologists and Latin America specialists) cower under the blows of praise for Reagan from Russians and, even more so, from Eastern Europeans. Such praise contradicts the first rule of the academy formulated by a rare French neo-conservative, the late Jean-Francois Revel: "The Left may sometimes be wrong, but the Right can never be right." But until the conformity of academia obliterates memory entirely, Reagan will continue to enjoy the regard of those whose had to live under the evil empire. And in today's world of instant communications, that means he will always have well-informed supporters celebrating his reputation.

Of course, Reagan never lacked faithful friends, from Margaret Thatcher downward. Books by former colleagues, journalists, and admirers have rolled off the presses in large numbers. Almost all of them paint Reagan in colors that are favorable but in some sense unexpected—he is shown to be cleverer, shrewder, and more hardworking than we knew. He is now a major publishing industry in his own right—and, more ominously, an academic industry. But he is protected against that last threat by an important social fact. He is the president we all feel we know well because we see his old movies on television. And if he was persuasive in every role except his one casting as a villain (in *The Killers*), he is unlikely to be successfully transformed into a villain by an assistant history professor at Midstate U.

Recent years have seen an opening of many public records, both in America and in other countries, that would once have been closed for up to fifty years. We are likely to see, as Wolf Blitzer noted, additional information about—and further exploration of—Reagan, his life, and his achievements in the future. If the first tranche of material is anything to go by (some of it displayed on earlier pages), new information is likely to raise rather than lower the president's standing. And at the moment Reagan's reputation rivals that of FDR as a twentieth-century president who made his party dominant at home and his country dominant in the world.

When Reagan died, Pope John Paul sent Nancy Reagan the following telegram:

> Having learned with sadness of the death of President Reagan, I offer you and your family my heartfelt condolences and the assurance of my prayers for his eternal rest. I recall with deep gratitude the late president's unwavering commitment to the service of the nation and to the cause of freedom as well as his abiding faith in the human and spiritual values which ensure a future of solidarity, justice, and peace in our world. Together with your family and the American people I commend his noble soul to the merciful love of God our Heavenly Father and cordially invoke upon all who mourn his passing the divine blessings of consolation, strength, and peace.

Even allowing that it was couched in the language of consolation, this message is a strong moral endorsement of the president's policies. In the space of a few lines he is identified with service, freedom, solidarity, justice, peace, and nobility. It seems reasonable to conclude from this that in the pope's eyes Reagan's policies not only had beneficial results, but were actuated by good intentions. If so, it indicates that their first meeting in 1982 at the Vatican, when they discussed Reagan's foreign and defense policies, was a hinge of history. After that, the pope felt no difficulty in approving and—where it was practicable and appropriate—in assisting America's attempt to liberate the subjects of Soviet rule in Poland and everywhere else.

Less than a year afterward, on April 2, 2005, John Paul II died. Six days later he was buried at a funeral attended by the largest gathering of heads of state in history. Leaders of the Eastern Orthodox churches, Protestant churches, Judaism, Anglicanism, and (for the first time) the Ethiopian Orthodox Church attended. An estimated one billion people watched the funeral on television. Almost more impressive than either the dignitaries or the numbers, however, were the crowds who for those six days and for several days earlier, when the ailing pope was approaching death, had watched, prayed, and sung in the great square of St. Peter's.

Like the crowds who walked past Reagan's catafalque, they were not grieving in the normal sense of the word. Before the fact they were praying that his death would be an easeful one and saying goodbye; afterward they were giving thanks for his life and calling for his speedy canonization—"Santo Subito!" If the crowds had been all Poles or all Catholics, such reactions would have been readily understandable, but they came from all over the world and from several faiths. Interviews revealed that one was a Jew from Chicago, who upon hearing of the pope's likely death had boarded a plane for Rome to thank him for reconciling his Church with the Jewish people with love rather than legalisms. Cardinal Ratzinger, who was about to assume the burden of the papacy and who was perhaps the pope's closest confidante, almost proclaimed "Santo Subito" himself:

> None of us can ever forget how in that last Easter Sunday of his life, the Holy Father, marked by suffering, came once more to the window of the Apostolic Palace and one last time gave his blessing *Urbi et Orbi*. We can be sure that our beloved pope is standing today at the window of the Father's house that he sees us and blesses us. Yes, bless us, Holy Father. We entrust your dear soul to the Mother of God, your Mother, who guided you each day and who will guide you now to the eternal glory of her Son, our Lord Jesus Christ.

Yet this outpouring of ecumenical love and affection for the late pope requires explanation, for John Paul II died fourteen years after the collapse of Communism. Helping to bring down the evil empire was universally agreed to be his great historical achievement. But what had he done in the fourteen years since then? If the Western media were to be taken at face value, the answer would be that he became a truly great tourist. He went to exotic places and put on amusing headgear. The typical "serious" account of a papal pilgrimage—and there were many such pilgrimages in those fourteen years—went something like this: "The pope arrived to cheering crowds in Manila/Delhi/Capetown/Rio yesterday. But many thoughtful Catholics believe that the Holy Father is obstructing necessary reforms such as married priests. And statistics show that though the faithful cheer him, they don't obey him when it comes to using artificial methods of contraception."

Not all of this wearisome critique was false. Many otherwise faithful Catholics in Europe and America *did* blithely disregard the church's teaching on sex. But what Christian pastor was ever surprised by disobedience? After all, it's on page one of the story.[51] The pope himself could have added greatly to the media's list of his failures and disappointments. He was distressed that Eastern Europe and, above all, his beloved Poland, had adopted the materialist consumer culture of Western Europe when Communism collapsed. He had hoped at least to begin the reunion of Christendom but had been frustrated by the reluctance of some Orthodox leaders. He grieved that the European Union, which the Vatican had vigorously promoted for five decades, would not put either God or the Christian heritage of Europe into the preamble of its constitution. And though he made every effort to effect a rapprochement with Islam, kissing the Koran for instance, he was disappointed by the failure of Muslim clerics to make corresponding gestures of charity and tolerance. (They were, he believed, deterred from doing so by threats from extreme jihadists.)

But these failures hardly explain the singing and praying crowds outside his window in the week he died. Many were present for the simple but adequate reason that they thought him a truly good and holy man. They wanted to tell him so and to express gratitude to God for his life. Others, like the Jewish man from Chicago, were responding to particular *successes* in the pope's life—in that case, his development of Catholic regard for the

Jews as the "elder brothers" of Christianity. But the size and diversity of the crowd in St. Peter's square testify to something else—namely, the great success of the pope's visits abroad and in particular to the developing world. Those papal pilgrimages were missions—and they converted vast numbers of people both directly and indirectly.

According to Philip Jenkins, Africa had 16 million Catholics in 1950; it has 120 million today, with the number expected to rise to 228 million by 2025—a fourfold increase in seventy-five years. The *World Christian Encyclopaedia* estimates that 75 percent of Catholics will be living in Africa, Asia, and Latin America by the same year.[52] What the Western media somehow failed to notice in their parochial reporting of the papal pilgrimages was that John Paul II was making the Catholic Church considerably more Catholic—and not just demographically. These new Christians tend to be more orthodox than their northern brethren. Under John Paul II the number of bishops and cardinals from these countries greatly increased—a trend that is certain to continue under his successor. So the late pope bequeathed to Pope Benedict XVI a Catholic Church that was large, growing fast, becoming more orthodox, and possessing an advantage over the other rapidly growing Christian churches in the southern parts of the world—namely, that papal authority ensures these new Christians will be an undiluted source of strength rather than, as in Anglicanism and liberal Protestant churches, a source of both strength and division. That may one day come to look like a greater achievement than his role in the defeat of Communism—and not only in the eyes of God.

As for Margaret Thatcher, her reputation is higher in the rest of the world than in Britain. But in her own country she still regularly scores high in polls on the "most admired Briton" or some such title. Her eightieth birthday party was attended by both the Queen and the Labour prime minister—both marks of high regard. And she has the devotion by about half the population.

Even so, her reputation is handicapped by a number of disadvantages. To begin with, she is not dead—and death reduces, if it does not eliminate, the partisan element in political judgments. Secondly, she left office not through an established constitutional formula as Reagan had done, nor through death like John Paul, but as a result of a political coup in her own party and government that left behind a residue of bitterness. Even now, David Cameron, the current Tory leader, apparently thinks that the best way to establish his own distinctive political identity is to distance himself from her and her policies. Thirdly, she remained in politics for many years after her tenure as prime minister, taking controversial positions and fighting for them. And, finally, she was the driver of a social and political revolution in Britain that reduced the influence of such groups as the cultural intelligentsia, which accordingly have not forgiven her. Dame Mary Warnock's observation that her looks were "not vulgar, just low" and the attack by theater director Jonathan Miller on her "odious suburban gentility" and "sentimental saccharine patriotism" were among the more snobbish barbs directed at Thatcher.

All in all, Thatcher as a politician is more like FDR than Ronald Reagan: she was engaged in political battles of such bitterness that most of her old opponents will never forgive her. Even though her policies are now almost universally regarded as correct, she still bears the burden of the hatred they aroused. The irreconcilable enemies she made then on the academic and cultural left exercise a disproportionate influence on how she is now seen.

All of these disadvantages, like life alas, are likely to disappear in time. No doubt her social critics regret their snobbery already, if only because it revealed too much about them. The Conservative Party cannot afford *not* to venerate its greatest twentieth-century peacetime prime minister. Once it recovers from its continuing nervous breakdown, it will surely set her next to Churchill in its pantheon. Rank-and-file Tories never ceased to hero-worship her. Her academic and media enemies will retire eventually as well (and with them their disproportionate influence on Thatcher studies). The two main political issues on which she campaigned vigorously were issues on which it is now clear that she was bravely right: leaving the ERM (a European fixed exchange rates system) marked the end of the recession and beginning of Britain's thirteen years of uninterrupted growth, and America's eventual intervention in Bosnia brought the Serbs to the bargaining table and led to the Dayton Accords that have kept the peace and saved lives.

And finally there is the issue of Britain's relationship with Europe—which is the main reason that some critics remain angry with her. They argue that her Euro-skepticism has prevented Britain playing a more constructive role both in Europe and the wider world. But since both John Major and Tony Blair entered Downing Street intending to place Britain "at the heart of Europe" and both discovered that other European states simply did not want the economic and political structures that suited Britain, that criticism looks increasingly unrealistic. Thatcher's willingness to negotiate a new, looser relationship with Europe may not yet be within the realm of the politically possible in Britain, but her *analysis* of the unsuitability of the European idea to Britain's national interest is quietly but widely accepted. So now that she has retired from public life, maybe her critics can forgive her infuriating habit of always being right against the odds.

There are already signs of an uptick in Thatcher stocks. Her memoirs will play a part in pushing them further upward since they will significantly shape what future generations know of her. Her recent biographer, John Campbell, wrote of *The Downing Street Years* that "the book has its *longueurs*, but it is still by far the most comprehensive and readable of modern prime ministerial memoirs." Campbell's own biography turned out to be far more favorable to her than he probably expected. He finishes by examining two contrary views of her—brave and great national leader versus narrow ideologue of selfishness—throwing up his hands and concluding that they are both true! It is a revealing ambivalence. For how would it have been possible to reverse the ravages of unionized socialism without incurring the charge of selfishness? If tax cuts are a stimulus to economic revival, they nonetheless benefit high earners disproportionately. If over-manning is destroying industry, then restoring profitability will nonetheless require higher unemployment for a period. To demand painless political achievement is a form of that very British vice: sentimentality. It is to want earnings without work, victory without struggle, the palm without the dust. Thatcher's record must be judged by more realistic standards.

By those standards, defeating inflation, restoring British industry, and helping to win the Cold War don't seem at all bad. But such achievements could not have been won without incurring heavy costs. Once that fact is digested by the British people, they are likely to join the rest of the world in recognizing Thatcher's greatness with more or less no qualifications.

Yet will such a post-religious people be able to comprehend them? In all three cases—Reagan, Thatcher, and John Paul—it is a spiritual element that best explains them and their achievements. All three, in subtly different ways, taught and embodied the virtue of hope. John Paul's sermons and speeches in Poland were injunctions to people not to despair in the face of overwhelming force, but instead to hope in God and trust their fellow man. Reagan preached confidently of a coming age of liberty that would bring about the end of Communism. Thatcher believed in "vigorous virtues" that, once liberated from the shackles of socialism, would enable the British and people everywhere to improve their own lives. In very different styles, all were enthusiasts for liberty.

In the late 1970s they encountered difficult practical problems ranging from inflation to religious oppression to Soviet military power. Worse, the problems had coalesced to form a nightmare in people's minds. A nightmare is a more intractable problem than the separate difficulties that compose it because it paralyses the will with despair. John Paul, Reagan, and Thatcher all tackled the problems before them in a commonsense way; more important, they all were confident they would win. They drove out despair with hope; they dispelled the nightmare. With daylight the problems had become manageable. Eventually they were solved.

We have very different problems today, but every reason to hope. After all, to adapt Lady Thatcher's resonant last line of her eulogy for President Reagan: We have an advantage that they never had. We have their example.[53]

ACKNOWLEDGMENTS

H ow idly and irresponsibly I have passed over the acknowledgments
    pages of other people's books! And how bitterly I now realize that I
have thereby remained ignorant of their true authors. For the work that an
author puts in is merely the famously deceptive tip of an iceberg constituted by
other people's help, advice, research, criticism (both constructive and negative),
encouragement, and above all their blind eye turned to one's absence. For all
these things and more I would like to thank all the people mentioned below and
many others whom I have temporarily forgotten but will surely remember when
I next need their help.

Thanks are first of all owed to my indulgent colleagues at the Hudson
Foundation, in particular Herb London and Ken Weinstein, who have both
helped me on numerous points of fact and opinion and tolerated my disappearance for writing and research. Rich Lowry, Jay Nordlinger, Ramesh Pon-
nuru, and my other colleagues at National Review have generously allowed
me to skip my normal writing duties there. Dorothy McCartney has kindly
switched from giving me research help on NR articles to research help on the
book. I hope they will like the results.

In writing this book I received invaluable research assistance from four people. Pavel Stroilov and Vladimir Bukovsky gave me generous access to their
cache of files from Soviet archives on the Cold War and related matters. Some
of these documents come originally from the documents of the Communist
Party of the Soviet Union, copied by Vladimir Bukovsky when he was invited
by Boris Yeltsin to be a witness in the constitutional trial of the CPSU. Mr.
Bukovsky has made most of these documents available on the Internet, and
they are quoted freely in his book, Judgment in Moscow, mentioned in the
text.

Others are documents from the files of the Gorbachev Foundation. Inventory 1-1 of the Gorbachev Foundation documents are the transcripts of Gorbachev's talks with foreign leaders, politicians, etc. The top-secret originals are
in the Presidential Archive of Russia. The GF copies were available for
researchers till 2003, although no one was allowed to copy them. In 2003 the

access was closed altogether under pressure from Putin's administration, which had finally learned that top-secret documents had been available elsewhere. So the transcripts are still classified. Inventories 2-2 and 2-3 are the stenographic notes made at Politburo meetings by Chernyaev and other of Gorbachev's aides. Inventory 3-1 are Zagladin's memos and reports about his communications with various Western figures.

Christopher Collins, who did the research for Lady Thatcher's memoirs and is now, among his other duties, the presiding genius of the Margaret Thatcher Foundation website, guided me to many fascinating aspects of Lady Thatcher's life and work of which I was unaware. He also protected me from errors and omissions. And, finally, Laura Stallworthy delved deep into the Reagan and Thatcher administrations by means of FOIA requests that turned up information that gave a new slant on the cooperation between my three heroes.

The other friends and colleagues who helped me include William F. Buckley, who has encouraged me to write this book for almost a decade; Father Richard Neuhaus, who told me that the only way to write a book is to write a book; Radek Sikorski and Piotr Naimski, who helped me through the pitfalls of Polish politics; George Weigel for advice on the Catholic doctrines of peace and war; Martin Walker and Arnaud de Borchgrave for conversations on the politics of the Cold War; Norman Lamont for the fruits of his experience in the Thatcher governments; Ken Minogue for putting things into proper perspective; and Peter Brimelow for his willingness to help me unravel some tangles of writing and logic on the way.

I have been helped beyond measure by my editors at Regnery, Harry Crocker, Paula Currall, and Jack Langer, who have given exactly the right mix of encouragement and guidance to a first-time author.

I am greatly indebted to Lady Thatcher for giving generously of her time and recollections for this book, and to Mark Worthington, Robin Harris, Cynthia Crawford, and Bob Kingston for their memories and assessments of the Thatcher years.

Finally, I want to thank my mother, May, to whom this book is dedicated, and my sister Margaret for giving me the sanctuary of peace and quiet while I was writing the British sections of the book; my stepdaughters, Katherine and Amanda, for sweetly not playing hard rock too often; and my wife, Melissa, for love, help, and encouragement always.

NOTES

Chapter One: The Indian Summer of Liberaldom

1. Interestingly, her husband disagreed. Denis Thatcher told the well-known Anglo-American political theorist Shirley Robin Letwin at a cocktail party in the early 1960s that his wife would be the first female prime minister. Mrs. Letwin recognized a uxorious husband and was skeptical.

2. George Weigel, *Witness to Hope: the Biography of John Paul II* (New York: HarperCollins, 1999).

3. Acta Synodalia, III-2, 530–32, quoted in Weigel.

4. Carl Bernstein and Marco Politi, *His Holiness: John Paul II and the History of Our Time* (New York: Penguin Books, 1996).

5. Ibid., 83.

6. Weigel, 209–10.

7. Richard John Neuhaus, "The Truce of 2005?" *First Things*, February 2006.

8. Weigel, 189–91.

9. Ibid., 221. This is itself a fascinating observation about a group of (presumably) conservative clerics. It suggests that deeply rooted and socially widespread intellectual deformation might have underpinned their reactions. Making a very similar observation about a very different social group, namely cultural critics, George Jonas, the distinguished Hungarian Canadian writer, who lived under both Communism and Nazism as a child and young man, wrote in the course of favorably reviewing the film *Sunshine*, that as always in such films the fascist thugs were simply thugs but the Communist thugs were figures of "intriguing complexity."

10. Weigel, 229.

11. Ibid., 227.

12. U.S. National Archives II (State Department files, RG 59, Central file 1970–73, box 2652). Also available on the Margaret Thatcher Foundation website, PDF 92K: http://www. margaretthatcher.org.

13. Gleysteen was an experienced diplomat who served in the U.S. diplomatic service for thirty years. His postings included Suriname, Egypt, Germany, and Britain. He retired three years after this conversation and later founded the Yale lectures that bear his name.

14. Margaret Thatcher, "What's Wrong with Politics?" Conservative Political Center Lecture, 1968.

15. Mrs. Thatcher referred to him as "the late Colm Brogan." She was corrected by the *Telegraph*'s deputy editor, Colin Welch, who said that far from being "late," Colm was in fact alive, though infirm, and a great admirer of hers. About a month later, Colin, Frank Johnson, and I took Colm out to lunch. As soon as he sat down, he triumphantly produced a handwritten letter from Mrs. Thatcher saying how much she had enjoyed his books and urging him to return to the intellectual fray. In fact, Colm had never really left it. But because he was writing mainly for Americans as the London correspondent for *National Review*, he had dropped out of sight in Fleet Street. Colm died not long afterwards, writing brilliant satires on Harold Wilson's Britain until the week of his death. Mrs. Thatcher publicly acknowledged her debt to him and others in *The Downing Street Years* (London: HarperCollins, 1993), 12–13.

16. "Wet" was originally a British private school term meaning "timid" or "feeble." It was applied pejoratively to Tories who were nervous about or opposed to the conservative economic and labor union reforms that Mrs. Thatcher implemented in her first two terms. They in turn embraced the word as a term of praise.

17. Mrs. Thatcher's phrase for the 1984–1985 miners' strike led by the Marxist union leader, Arthur Scargill.

18. Four days after the second 1974 election, Frank Johnson, my colleague at the *Daily Telegraph*, and I turned up at the Centre for Policy Studies for an appointment with Sir Keith to discuss his media relations (which, by and large, were lousy). We were ushered into a study and given cups of coffee. The door opened and in walked Mrs. Thatcher (whom neither of us knew at all well). Without any preliminaries, she said, "Gentlemen, I am Sir Keith's campaign manager for the leadership. What can I do for you—and what can you do for me?" That was the first time anyone—except perhaps Denis Thatcher and Lady Joseph—knew for certain that there would be a leadership challenge to Edward Heath.

19. I was another of the sympathetic journalists at the meeting, a dinner in the Reform Club attended also by T. E. Utley and Michael Harrington about ten days before the first round of the election. The late Alfred Sherman, an adviser to Sir Keith Joseph and Mrs. Thatcher at the Center for Policy Studies, who

had arranged the dinner, stayed for drinks and then discreetly withdrew. To the best of my knowledge, this was the only example of discretion in Sir Alfred's rumbustious career.

20. Ford Library (White House Central File, CO160, Box 56). Also available on the Margaret Thatcher Foundation website, PDF 89K: http://www.margaretthatcher.org.

21. Ford Library (NSC Country File Box 15). Also available on the Margaret Thatcher Foundation website, PDF 97K: http://www.margaretthatcher.org.

22. Quoted in *Ronald Reagan: A Political Biography*, by Lee Edwards (Belmont, MA: Nordland Publishing & Caroline House), 1981.

23. Reagan had been offered a twice weekly television commentary by Walter Cronkite for ABC News. He was to be "balanced" by two weekly commentaries from the liberal journalist Eric Sevareid. Reagan surprised his staff by turning down what seemed a dream offer on the grounds that the public would tire of him on television and "they won't tire of me on the radio." He agreed instead to the proposal of Peter Hannaford, his director of public affairs at Sacramento, that the new firm of Deaver and Hannaford Inc. would manage a nationally syndicated newspaper column, speaking engagements around the country, and a five-day-a-week radio commentary that would be produced and syndicated by the radio producer Harry O'Connor. The radio broadcasts and other pre-presidential writings by Reagan are collected both in *Reagan in His Own Hand*, collected and edited by Kiron K. Skinner, Annelise Anderson, and Martin Anderson (New York: Simon & Schuster, 2001), and in *Reagan's Path to Victory: The Shaping of Ronald Reagan's Vision*, collected and edited by Kiron K. Skinner, Annelise Anderson, Martin Anderson, and with an introduction by George Shultz.

24. Henry Kissinger's third volume of memoirs gives a gripping account of the final days of South Vietnam as seen from Washington. Neither president nor secretary of state was able to prevail against a curious mood of eager defeatism in establishment Washington, influencing senior members of both parties, some of whom had publicly committed themselves to support military aid to Saigon after America's withdrawal, but almost all of whom now wanted a North Vietnamese victory so that the United States could wash its hands of Indochina.

25. Radio broadcast, "Communism, the Disease," May 1975.

26. Skinner, et al., *Reagan's Path to Victory*, Introduction.

27. Ronald Reagan, "Wanted: A New Dream of America," *Daily Telegraph*, November 20, 1975. I had helped to arrange this article, acting as a go-between for *Telegraph* editor Bill Deedes with the Reagan campaign. Reagan's people knew that they were scooping themselves but thought it would arouse interest outside the United States. This it did: the BBC World Service news led with it. Not as a result of this favor (though it helped), the *Telegraph* was probably the British newspaper most favorably inclined to Reagan for many years. Three years after the article, the same contacts made Bill Deedes the host of an off-the-record press breakfast for Reagan and aides on his 1978 European tour. It was the only media event on the British leg of the tour, and the first (and for some the only) time that leading editors and columnists in Britain had a chance to meet and question Reagan. By and large they liked him but doubted that a man of nearly seventy could become president. This misjudgment may have been the result of Reagan's being jet-lagged, having stepped off a transatlantic plane only hours before. For a retrospective account of the breakfast, see "Breakfast with the Governor," by Ferdinand Mount in the London *Spectator*.

28. Edwards, 182.

29. Ibid.

Chapter Two: The Nightmare Years

1. These figures are drawn from David Frum's superb social history *How We Got Here: The 1970s* (New York: Basic Books, 2000).

2. Ibid., 12–13.

3. David Carlton, *The West's Road to 9/11* (New York: Palgrave Macmillan, 2005). This is a melancholy account, relieved by the dry wit of its author, a British diplomatic historian, of the West's long appeasement of international terrorists—and of the meager returns on this policy.

4. Malcom Sutton, University of Ulster, http://cain.ulst.ac.uk/sutton/ crosstabs.html.

5. Frum, footnote, 380

6. Nigeria was the worst victim of the excessive capital spending—especially on grandiose civil engineering projects—that had been induced by the OPEC myth. But even Saudi Arabia, whose government was more financially cautious, miscalculated. On a visit to the country in the late 1980s, I saw for myself roads that stopped in the middle of nowhere and half-built hotels on the Arabian Gulf, all of them projects that had been abandoned when oil prices fell and the money ran short.

7. Frum, 315.

8. Ibid., 313 and following.

9. Ronald Reagan, Annelise Anderson, Martin Anderson, *Reagan in His Own Hand: The Writings of Ronald Reagan That Reveal His Revolutionary Vision for America* (New York: The Free Press, 2001), 118.

10. Carlton, passim.

11. *The Economist*, February 1974, quoted in Frum, 319.

12. Leo Labedz, article on the Student Revolution, *Survey*, circa 1968. *Survey* was a small London-based quarterly devoted to critically examining developments within Communism and the Left. It was, however, disproportionately influential. Its Washington subscribers, for instance, included Senator Daniel Patrick Moynihan.

13. Frum, 156.

14. "The Second Coming," by William Butler Yeats, from Richard J. Finneran, ed. *The Collected Poems of W.B. Yeats* Revised Second Edition (New York: Scribner, 1996), 187.

15. I was one of two conservatives in the cinema. In addition to applauding, members of the audience gave clenched-fist salutes and shouted "Algiers Yesterday, London Tomorrow" and other improbable slogans. Gillo Pontecorvo's fine film was, however, criticized by some leftist critics as an example of "bourgeois objectivity" because it depicted the horrifying human consequences of both FLN terrorism *and* French torture.

16. Jean Raspail, *The Camp of the Saints* (Petoskey, MI: Social Contract Press, 1994).

17. Raspail was denounced by various dyslexic reviewers at the time as a fascist who had written an offensive but ridiculously paranoid diatribe. To judge the worth of this critical verdict, the reader should know that Raspail told *Social Contract* magazine in a recent interview that he could not bring himself to fire on the Third World invaders his imagination had conjured up. His paranoid forecasts have meanwhile come true at the Gibraltar Straits and the U.S.–Mexican border if not as yet on the Côte d'Azur. Non-dyslexic readers have no difficulty in seeing that the real enemy depicted in his book is "the Beast" rather than the Third World—and not only in fiction.

18. The brother of the Israeli politician Bibi Netanyahu, who later became prime minister. An institute for the study of terrorism was established in honor of Jonathan Netanyahu in the 1970s. The Jonathan Institute has since held a series of influential conferences on terrorism.

19. Frum, 342.

20. "The bomber will always get through," was a famous line of Stanley Baldwin, who was the British prime minister from 1934 to 1937, the dominant figure in inter-war British politics, and far more responsible for the policy of appeasing the dictators than the better-known Neville Chamberlain. His pessimism about the ability of defense forces to resist mass bombing proved unfounded owing to the invention of radar, the courage of the RAF pilots, and the fortitude of the British people. But it is uncannily similar to modern liberal estimates of the invincibility of terrorism.

21. The revolutionary "students" included the current president of Iran, Mahmoud Ahmadinejad.

22. Frum, 343.

23. Even this was too robust for Secretary of State Cyrus Vance, who secretly resigned in protest at the decision to launch the rescue mission. He loyally postponed his resignation until the mission was complete. The mission's failure meant that his reputation suffered no damage.

24. Private conversation with the author.

25. Steven F. Hayward, *The Age of Reagan* (New York: Prima-Forum, 2001).

26. George Weigel, *Witness to Hope: the Biography of John Paul II* (New York: HarperCollins, 1999), 252.

27. Carl Bernstein and Marco Politi, *His Holiness: John Paul II and the History of Our Time* (New York: Penguin Books, 1996), 169.

28. Weigel, 254–55.

29. Bernstein and Politi, 175.

30. Quote from Callaghan speech to 1978 Labour conference: "We used to think that you could spend your way out of a recession and increase employment by cutting taxes and boosting government spending. I tell you in all candor that that option no longer exists, and in so far as it ever did exist, it only worked on each occasion since the war by injecting a bigger dose of inflation into the economy, followed by a higher level of unemployment as the next step."

31. Geoffrey Smith, *Reagan and Thatcher* (New York: W. W. Norton, 1991).

32. Reagan, et al., 47.

33. I am grateful to Steven Hayward for drawing this quotation to my attention.

34. There is some irony in the fact, therefore, that Brzezinski argues that Carter's phrase about America's "inordinate fear of Communism" was rooted in his conviction that the Soviet Union was a declining power. He made this point very forcefully at a recent conference organized by the *American Interest* magazine.

35. Peter Schweizer, *Reagan's War: The Epic Story of His Forty-Year Struggle and Final Triumph Over Communism* (New York, Random House, 2002), 107.

Chapter Three: Did God Guide the Bullets?

1. This account of the attempt on the pope's life is drawn mainly from George Weigel's *Witness to Hope: the Biography of John Paul II* (New York: HarperCollins, 1999). Weigel bases it in part on the account in *Be Not Afraid*, by Andre Frossard and John Paul II (New York: St. Martin's Press, 1984). Frossard's account itself was based on extensive interviews both with the pope's secretary, Stanlislaw Dziwisz, and with the Gemelli chief surgeon, Francesco Crucitti, who features heavily in the events. It draws also on the account in Carl Bernstein and Marco Politi's *His Holiness: John Paul II and the History of Our Time* (New York: Penguin Books, 1996).

2. Frossard, 251.

3. Bernstein and Politi, 295.

4. My account of the Reagan shooting and its aftermath is drawn mainly from the most recent timeline, that in Richard Reeves's critical but fair-minded biography, *President Reagan: The Triumph of Imagination* (New York: Simon & Schuster, 2005.) But it also includes information from Edmund Morris's *Dutch: A Memoir of Ronald Reagan* (New York: Random House, 1999), who had unique access to Reagan as his official biographer, and finally from a worm's eye-view of the event recounted by President Reagan himself to a group of conservative editors and activists, including the author, at the White House in 1983. This small episode is itself covered later in the chapter.

5. Reeves, 35.

6. Morris, 429.

7. This account of the Brighton bomb is based in part on Lady Thatcher's own account in *The Downing Street Years* (London: HarperCollins, 1993), and in part on my own recollection. As a *Daily Telegraph* journalist covering the Tory conference, I had been in the Grand Hotel until about 2:15 p.m. and then went to the hotel next door and to bed. Less than a minute after I had turned out the lights, the bomb exploded. We were ushered out onto the boardwalk. That night almost the entire Tory cabinet, innumerable MPs, senior news correspondents, and television personalities, most in pajamas and dressing gowns, milled about carrying their few rescued possessions, exchanging stories of narrow escape, and gossiping excitedly. A vivid account of a night to remember can be found in the *London Times* of Saturday, October 13, 1984, by Frank Johnson.

8. Thatcher, 380.

9. Ibid., 381.

10. Magee was released as a result of the Good Friday Agreement, married a novelist, and has since made a television film about "reconciliation" with the daughter of his victim, Anthony Berry. But he continues to justify his murders with the argument that he had no political avenue to pursue his grievances. Since he was a citizen of an advanced democratic country, this amounts to arguing that unless his wishes were granted, he was being denied a hearing. But we should expect neither honesty nor logic from unrepentant murderers.

11. Bernstein and Politi, 296–97.

12. Thomas P. Melady, "John Paul II rejected assassination inquiry," *National Catholic Reporter*, April 29, 2005. When Melady reported these conversations to the State Department, his superiors asked him to establish whether the pope regarded Gorbachev as "trustworthy." Melady put this question to Casaroli: "While his response was not specific, I reported that he said Yes on behalf of the Holy Father."

13. Gorbachev archives. "Meeting Between Gorbachev and Andreotti," May 22, 1991.

14. John Follain, "Brezhnev Hatched Plot to Kill Pope," *Sunday Times* (London), March 12, 2006.

15. Ibid. Among the intelligence agencies that suspected a Soviet role was the KGB. Both Vasili Mitrokhin and Oleg Gordievsky, two important defectors, report that KGB officers around the water cooler were themselves divided fifty–fifty over whether their organization were responsible for the attemped assassination. Half of them thought that it was too risky for the KGB to undertake, even through the Bulgarians, the other half thought it had been carried out by Department S of Directorate S, which carried out assassinations. Vasili Mitrokhin and Christopher Andrew, *The Sword and the Shield: The Mitrokhin Archive and the Secret History of the KGB* (New York: Basic Books, 1999), 897–98; Oleg Gordievsky, *The KGB* (Knotting, UK: Sceptre Press, 1991), 639.

16. Bernstein and Politi, 300.

17. Weigel, 440.

18. Thatcher, 459–60.

19. John Campbell, *Margaret Thatcher Volume One: The Grocer's Daughter* (London: Pimlico, 2001). This is the first volume of a superb two-volume biography of Thatcher.

20. Thatcher, 10. William Pitt, the Elder, First Earl of Chatham, (1708–1778), had led Britain to victory in the Seven Years' War.

21. Campbell, 753.

22. Henri E. Cauvin, "President Offered in '83 to Meet with Hinckley," *Washington Post*, June 12, 2004. Quoted in Paul Kengor's *God and Ronald Reagan: A Spiritual Life* (New York: Regan Books, 2005).

23. Mrs. Thatcher was hardly in a position to forgive her would-be assassin. Since she had not been harmed, she would have been forgiving injuries done to others. Any forgiveness would come better from those who had been injured or bereaved. That, however, would not have been right in the circumstances. The murderers were members of a criminal terrorist group that was still pursuing a campaign of murder. Now that they have been caught, convicted, and released, they remain impenitent. Patrick Magee, for instance, seeks "reconciliation" with his victims on the argument that they were simply unlucky to be maimed by his just and necessary actions. Without repentance there can be no forgiveness. To forgive someone for a crime of which he remains proud, in addition to being absurd, is an incentive to future murders.

24. Morris, 435.

25. In her funeral eulogy for President Reagan, Lady Thatcher turned this formulation around with, "Surely the Big Fella Upstairs never forgets those who remember Him."

26. Reeves, 54.

27. Anatoly Dobrynin, *In Confidence*, quoted in Morris, 790.

28. I was one of the activists.

Chapter Four: Be Not Afraid

1. Remarks by Richard V. Allen, "Pope John Paul II, Ronald Reagan, and the Collapse of Communism: An Historic Confluence," Pope John Paul Cultural Center, Washington, D.C., November 14, 2004.

2. This is allegedly the case. See George Weigel, *Witness to Hope: the Biography of John Paul II* (New York: HarperCollins, 1999), 279.

3. Since Krol later became a close confidante of President Reagan, the conspiracy must have been even more far-ranging and convoluted than even Andropov guessed.

4. Vadim Valentinovich Zagladin was the first deputy head of International Department of the CPSU until 1987. He then became an adviser to Gorbachev. This conversation is to be found in the Gorbachev Archives.

5. See Chapter Nine for an account of Gorbachev's visit to the Vatican, December 1, 1989, when he appealed to the pope as a fellow Slav.

6. *Redemptor Hominis*, 17.8. Quoted in Weigel, 289.

7. Andrei Gromyko, *Memoirs* (London: Hutchinson, 1989), quoted in Weigel, 298–99.

8. Quotations are from Janusz Rolicki, *Edward Gierek: Przewana dekada*, (Warsaw, 1990), cited both in Carl Bernstein and Marco Politi's *His Holiness: John Paul II and the History of Our Time* (New York: Penguin Books, 1996), 191, and in Weigel, 301.

9. David Martin's *Tongues of Fire: Explosion of Protestantism in Latin America* (Oxford: Blackwell Publishing, 1990) was the first major look at this new and important religious phenomenon. It is fundamentally a work of reporting and analysis, but the author (a British sociologist specializing in religion and a practicing Anglican) made no secret of his sympathy for these new religious movements. His book was bitterly attacked by reviewers sympathetic to liberation theology such as Hugh O'Shaughnessey of the *Financial Times*. Their critiques bear some similarity to the attacks on Christian "fundamentalism" of more recent times.

10. The quotations from the pope's speeches in the following paragraphs are drawn from Weigel, 281–87.

11. Author interview with Piotr Naimski. See also Weigel, 193.

12. Ronald Reagan, Annelise Anderson, Martin Anderson, *Reagan in His Own Hand: The Writings of Ronald Reagan That Reveal His Revolutionary Vision for America* (New York: The Free Press, 2001), 149.

13. Author interview with Naimski.

14. Bernstein and Politi, 216–17.

15. Weigel, 317, 915.

16. Author interview with Naimski.

17. Weigel, 320–23.

18. Anatoly Chernyaev was deputy head of the International Department of the CPSU until 1986. This excerpt from his diary is the entry for November 6, 1976. That year he became Gorbachev's assistant on international affairs. His diary is in the Gorbachev Archives. A book based on its entries during the 1981 Soviet hard-liners' coup has been published. Chernyaev's diary for 1985 is online at the National Security Archive, http://www.gwu.edu/~nsarchiv/ NSAEBB/NSAEBB192/index.htm. Ironically in light of this excerpt, he later became a great admirer of Mrs. Thatcher.

19. Margaret Thatcher, *The Downing Street Years* (London: HarperCollins, 1993), 66.

20. Ibid., 65–71.

21. *New York Times*, June 5, 1979, quoted in Weigel, 915.

22. Carter also gave her a mixed review: "A tough lady, highly opinionated, strongly willed, cannot admit she doesn't know something." Jimmy Carter, *Keeping Faith*, 113, quoted in John Campbell's *Margaret Thatcher Volume Two: The Iron Lady* (London: Pimlico, 2003), 57.

23. *Time*, October 15, 1979, quoted in Weigel, 349.

24. Weigel, 361–62; Bernstein and Politi, 307–08.

25. Campbell, 57.

26. Sir Nicholas Henderson, *Mandarin: The Diaries of an Ambassador* (London: Weidenfeld & Nicolson Ltd, 1994), 316, quoted in Campbell, 58.

27. Campbell, 58.

28. See Antonio Martino's similar reaction to the Desert One failure quoted in Chapter Two.

29. The following account of the long, drawn-out Solidarity crisis is drawn from several sources, principally my interview with Piotr Naimski, Weigel's *Witness to Hope*, Timothy Garton Ash's *The Polish Revolution: Solidarity* (London: Jonathan Cape, 1983), and Bernstein and Politi's *His Holiness*. The reference to "sausage" is to a poem by a Solidarity sympathizer, quoted in Garton Ash, 301, which includes the lines "The times are past/when they closed our mouths/with sausage."

30. Earlier language from the Gdansk accords, acknowledging the leading role of the party, was cited in an appendix.

31. Bukovsky Collection, item 0401; Vladimir Bukovsky, *Jugement a Moscou: Un Dissident dans les Archives du Kremlin* (Paris: Editions Robert Laffont, 1995), 440.

32. Quotations from top-secret minutes of Politburo meeting in October 1980 are from Bernstein and Politi, 247 and following.

33. Bukovsky quotes extensively from this tranche of top-secret CPSU documents in his book. He has also made them available online at the Bukovsky Collection at http://www.2nt1.com/archive/ buk/html. Up to the present, however, this book has been published in Poland, France, Germany, Italy, Bulgaria, Romania and Russia, and but not in the U.S. or the UK. I am grateful to Mr. Bukovsky for giving me free access to these archives and for allowing me to quote freely from his book.

34. For instance: "Top Secret. Translated from the Spanish. To the CPSU Central Committee. Hereby I apply for your party to provide 6 (six) places for our party members to attend the courses of special (military) training on the following areas: 1. The security of the party. 2. Preparation of the identity documents. 3. Communications. 4. Armed struggle in the town (leading this struggle.) 5. Armed struggle in the country (leading this struggle.) 6. Staff service. It is desirable to organize the said courses in May–November of this year. We are expressing our fraternal gratitude to you, and pass our warmest greetings. Louis Sacos Sanco, The First secretary of the Nicaraguan socialist party Central Committee. 17 March 1976. Translated by [signature] (K. Kurin.) Bukovsky Collection, Item 0920.

35. Steven F. Hayward, *The Age of Reagan* (New York: Prima-Forum, 2001), 560–66.

36. Bukovsky, 41.

37. Ibid., see also items 0947 and 0967 at the Bukovsky Collection.

38. Ibid., 37–40; see also items 0925, 0958, and 0959 at the Bukovsky Collection.

39. Zagladin, from the transcript of his meeting with Karsten Voigt, October 16, 1980. Gorbachev Archives, 3-1.

40. Zagladin's report on his meeting with with Eugen Selbmann, Gorbachev Archives, 3-1.

41. Weigel, 404–06.

42. Author interview with Naimski.

43. Bernstein and Politi, 252.

44. Bukovsky Collection, item 0414; Bukovsky, 445–48.

45. Ibid.

46. Bernstein and Politi, 254–55.

47. Weigel, 407.

48. There is a vivid account of this meeting, seen largely from Jaruzelski's point of view, in Bernstein and Politi. It includes a fascinating scene in which Jaruzelski, remembering the fate of Dubcek in 1968 and thinking that he might not return from the meeting, places his wife and daughter under the protection of his friend General Michal Janiszewski. If this is true, it is an astonishing revelation of the actual mindset of the man whom the Soviets regarded as absolutely reliable.

49. Quotations are from the Politburo minutes for December 10, 1981, quoted in Bernstein and Politi, 331–32.

50. Bukovsky Collection, item 0424.

51. During and after the crisis, Jaruzelski continued to use the threat of Soviet intervention as a reason for his imposition of martial law long after he had been told of its impossibility.

52. Weigel, 432–33

53. Ibid., 433–34.

Chapter Five: Friends in Need

1. Sir Nicholas Henderson, *Mandarin: The Diaries of an Ambassador* (London: Weidenfeld and Nicolson Ltd, 1994).

2. Not actually the first foreign leader. As John Campbell points, out the leaders of Jamaica and South Korea had beaten her to it. *Margaret Thatcher Volume Two: The Iron Lady* (London: Pimlico, 2003), 263.

3. Geoffrey Smith, *Reagan and Thatcher* (New York: W. W. Norton, 1991), 23. Smith's book, which draws on candid interviews with most of the senior officials in London and Washington shortly after the events in which they were involved, remains by far the best account of the Reagan-Thatcher relationship.

4. Campbell, 264.

5. The Thatcher government's early economic policy included tighter control of the money supply along with a switch of the tax burden from direct to indirect taxation, sharp cuts in personal income tax, tougher control of public spending, the encouragement of enterprise, and the reduction of subsidies to state-controlled industries such as steel and automobiles. This covered much more than monetarism. In addition the government's monetary targets proved unreliable, partly as a result of financial liberalization, and were eventually abandoned in favor of targeting the exchange rate. Thus British monetarism itself was an unorthodox one. But as Milton Friedman remarked at the time, the working definition of monetarism in the UK in the early eighties was "anything Margaret Thatcher does." The single best account of economic policy during the Thatcher years is to be found in the memoirs of her second finance minister, Nigel Lawson: *The View from Number Eleven* (London: Bantam Press, 1992). The book is also a comprehensive primer in the workings of British government and, despite its length and topic, extraordinarily readable.

6. Smith, 42–46.

7. All this was on top of a hectic schedule of other diplomatic and political meetings arranged by Secretary of State Al Haig and British foreign secretary Lord (Peter) Carrington. See Smith, 41–42.

8. Mrs. Thatcher always remembered this phrase and quoted it back at the president in a speech she delivered when he was leaving office eight years later.

9. Smith, 51, based on an interview with Reagan in retirement.

10. Jacques Attali, *Verbatim* (Paris: Fayard, 1995), quoted in Campbell, 262. Mitterrand more famously remarked that Mrs. Thatcher had "the eyes of Caligula, the mouth of Monroe."

11. Smith, 46–48.

12. Perle interviewed for the documentary *The Thatcher Factor*, produced in 1988 by Brook Lapping. Quoted in Campbell, 267.

13. Memo to the president, from Richard V. Allen, Ronald Reagan Library, quoted on the Margaret Thatcher Foundation website: http://margaretthatcher.org.

14. Max Hastings and Simon Jenkins, *The Battle for the Falklands* (New York and London: W. W. Norton & Co., 1983). This book was written and published within months of the war's end. But it remains the best account. It is readable, balanced, and comprehensive with Hastings covering the military conflict and Jenkins the political and diplomatic negotiations, both brilliantly. The two chapters covering the Falklands war in Thatcher's memoirs, based on an aide-mémoire she dictated immediately following the conflict but published after the Hastings-Jenkins book, are a vivid and indispensable account of the war as seen from Downing Street. And Geoffrey Smith's picture of Anglo-American relations during the war offers a cool and accurate disentangling of a myth-laden episode.

15. Smith, 68–71, based on interviews with Perle and Robert "Bud" MacFarlane, then deputy national security adviser, who were members of the Trident negotiating team along with Ambassador Richard Burt, then assistant secretary of state for European affairs.

16. Hastings and Jenkins.

17. Ibid., 48.

18. Ibid., 59–60. As the authors point out, there is some dispute on when the final decision to invade took place. But the decisions necessary to start the process of invasion certainly began that weekend.

19. Ibid., 56–63.

20. Margaret Thatcher *The Downing Street Years* (London: HarperCollins, 1993), 179.

21. According to most accounts. In her memoirs, however, Thatcher remembers Leach as being in civilian clothes.

22. Hastings and Jenkins, 67. Leach's prediction was not far off the truth. After the sinking of its battleship, the *Belgrano*, the Argentine navy retired to its home ports, where it stayed for almost the remainder of the conflict. Thus the service most strongly in favor of Operation Goa played the least glorious role in it, and the air force, which had been lukewarm, performed bravely and well in British as well as Argentine eyes.

23. Telegram from Reagan to Thatcher, April 1, 1982.

24. Hastings and Jenkins, pages 68–73.

25. Enoch Powell to Margaret Thatcher in the House of Commons, April 3, 1982.

26. Thatcher, 183–84.

27. Thatcher, nervous about Suez at the time, was always more anxious to keep on the right side of international law than her image suggested. This caution explains some of her skepticism about Grenada and her intensive questioning before she agreed to help the Libyan raid. Though she lamented what she called the "Suez syndrome" in the introduction to *The Downing Street Years*, it left its mark on her too.

28. Smith, 82–88.

29. Ibid., 84, based on an interview with Lawrence Eagleburger, who was then undersecretary of state for political affairs.

30. Ibid., 85, based on an interview with Haig.

31. Thatcher, 200. This assurance originally contained a claim that British access to the U.S. facilities on Ascension Island had been "restricted" in accordance with customary usage. Haig showed it to Thatcher in advance, however, and she hit the roof, pointing out that Ascension Island was British territory leased to the United States. He omitted the offending sentence in the message finally sent to Buenos Aires.

32. Ibid., 207–08

33. Ibid., 210.

34. Smith, 90–91.

35. Ibid., 90–92; Campbell, 144–47. Campbell takes the view that if Galtieri had accepted the Peruvian proposals, "Britain could not have defied American and world opinion by pressing on" [with the war.] That is questionable. International outrage at the *Belgrano* was already fading as the *Sheffield* showed the task force's vulnerability. The junta was bound to put a foot wrong even before negotiations. Britain would probably have had grounds for keeping up the military pressure within days and in a warmer political climate.

36. Hastings and Jenkins, 168–69.

37. Lewin, interviewed for *The Thatcher Factor*, quoted in Campbell, 139.

38. Campbell, 138.

39. Hastings and Jenkins, 316–17.

40. Henderson, 465–68, quoted in Campbell, 152.

41. Hastings and Jenkins, 261.

42. In fact, the diplomatic costs never really materialized. The budgetary costs of maintaining "Fortress Falklands" are real enough. But the end of the Cold War changed British defense priorities, including naval strategy, so completely that the kind (though not the size) of navy Leach wanted is now the latest strategic thinking.

43. Thatcher, 184. Ian Gow, her parliamentary private secretary, had this quotation and Powell's earlier intervention printed and framed for her as a Christmas present in 1982.

44. Interestingly, this is Gorbachev's view. Documentation will follow shortly.

45. Smith, 94.

Chapter Six: Keeping Hope Alive

1. Margaret Thatcher, *The Downing Street Years* (London: HarperCollins, 1993), 390.

2. This was a sacrifice on several levels. In addition to her wish to consult the pope on Poland and Eastern Europe, Thatcher hoped that a warm official greeting for the pope would remove the lingering impression of Irish Catholics that the Tory Party was tainted by anti-Catholicism. Thatcher felt this strongly. She is an O'Sullivan on her father's side and free of any religious prejudice. She believed that this anti-Catholic reputation was an obstacle in her diplomacy on Northern Ireland. It was certainly an obstacle to winning Irish Catholic votes in Britain at the time. Like almost all religious factors in British politics, however, it has since evaporated.

3. Letter to the foreign secretary from Sir Mark Heath, British ambassador to the Holy See, dated June 28, 1982, reference number 226/6.

4. Private letter from Hume to Weigel, quoted in George Weigel, *Witness to Hope: the Biography of John Paul II* (New York: HarperCollins, 1999), 435 and 927. Sir Mark Heath's letter contains the same account with minor variations.

5. Weigel, 435–36.

6. Robert Fox, *Eyewitness Falklands* (London: Methuen, 1982), 189. Both sides were astonished to discover after the surrender that the odds were not in fact overwhelming. There were fewer British and more Argentineans than either of them had realized in the fog of war.

7. Letter from Foreign and Commonwealth Office to head of Western European Department, Her Majesty's ambassador to the Holy See, dated August 3, 1982.

8. A grain embargo had been seriously discussed within the administration. But Reagan had given a pledge during the election to remove it—which he had done in his goodwill letter to Brezhnev—and he felt bound by it. It was, however, a diplomatic problem that American grain sales to the Soviet Union rose rapidly and profitably while the United States campaigned against the Siberian pipeline.

9. Thatcher, 251–56.

10. Geoffrey Smith, *Reagan and Thatcher* (New York: W. W. Norton, 1991), 71–75.

11. Thatcher, 258–59.

12. Smith, 98–101.

13. John Brown Engineering had an especially strong case as they had cleared their contracts with the U.S. State Department before signing them.

14. Another such occasion was Grenada.

15. John Campbell, *Margaret Thatcher Volume I: The Grocer's Daughter* (London: Pimlico, 2000), 268. The British government was on slightly slippery ground here because at least some of the existing contracts had a clause requiring the signatory company to obtain the permission of the U.S. State Department before transferring technology to third-party countries. Hence John Brown's earlier approach to Foggy Bottom.

16. Smith, 97–103.

17. Boadicea was the warrior queen of the (ancient) Britons.

18. Reagan to Thatcher, July 2, 1982, quoted in Campbell, 269.

19. Hans-Dietrich Genscher, German foreign minister in the Social-Liberal Coalition, had refused to meet representatives of Solidarity on his visit to Warsaw in 1981.

20. On arriving in Fatima to give thanks for his deliverance from Agca's assassination attempt, however, the pope remarked that "in the designs of Providence there are no mere coincidences." Quoted in Weigel, 440.

21. Carl Bernstein and Marco Politi, *His Holiness: John Paul II and the History of Our Time* (New York: Penguin Books, 1996), 262 and following. The Reagan quotation comes from an interview with the authors in 1991.

22. Ibid., 260.

23. Ibid., 264 and following. Nowak later told the authors that "without the policy of Reagan, there would be no victory of Solidarity."

24. Interview with Piotr Naimski.

25. Interview with Robbie Lyle. He adds a small postscript: "I gave the pope a carriage clock from Asprey's. They had packed it up without a key. We discovered this because I gave a similar one to the Ansidei family (Raphael's patrons) in Verona as a present for looking after my niece when my sister had been caring for my mother in Britain during her last days. The second clock did not have a key either. Back in London I telephoned Asprey's, who at first were incredulous until I showed them a photograph of the pope with the Asprey parcel in his hands. Someone was dispatched that day to Rome with two keys!"

26. Quoted in Richard Reeves, *President Reagan: The Triumph of Imagination* (New York: Simon & Schuster, 2005), 108.

27. I had the benefit of several long conversations with Walters on the *National Review* cruise of the Baltic in 1989. What follows is shaped by those conversations. I also had the good fortune to meet Casey over a small lunch when he was CIA director. Conversation on that occasion was mainly devoted to two topics: the continuing controversy over whether a former head of Britain's MI5 had been a Soviet agent (Casey was inclined to believe so) and U.S. support for the Contras. Friends of Casey since then have persuaded me that he and Walters brought the same attitudes to their meetings with the pope. I have also drawn heavily on the account of these meetings in Bernstein and Politi's book.

28. They were seeking to exploit an apparent coincidence of interest in the run-up to martial law in Poland: the pope wanted to avoid bloodshed; the Soviets wanted to "stabilize" the situation. But since the pope believed that recognizing Solidarity and the rights of independent social bodies such as labor unions was an essential foundation of "stability," he was never manipulated into excusing the government's crackdown. He sometimes counseled Solidarity to be prudent, but he invariably placed the blame for disorder on the despotic regime that refused to recognize such basic rights. Other Catholic leaders in Poland were not always so clear on this point.

29. Bernstein and Politi, 286–91.

30. This reflected the generally held opinion that Reagan was a trigger-happy cowboy who could not be trusted with nuclear weapons. Reagan's real attitude to nuclear weapons was very different. This question is dealt with more extensively in the next chapter.

31. Bernstein and Politi, 321–29.

32. More recent books on Reagan have demolished the canard about his laziness. See in particular *How Ronald Reagan Changed My Life*, by Peter Robinson. Robinson, a speechwriter for both Reagan and Bush who wrote the famous Berlin Wall speech, noticed that his speech drafts for the president were invariably returned overnight corrected and improved in the president's own hand. Upon checking with his colleagues, he found this to be true of all the official papers that the president took to his private quarters at night.

33. Memorandum for the president, S/S 8214633, May 22, 1982. Declassified in part August 29, 2002.

34. Bernstein and Politi, 355–61.

35. Interview with Ronald Reagan, ibid., 358.

36. Weigel, 441.

37. The Vatican's criticism of the first draft of the U.S. bishops' pastoral letter on nuclear weapons might seem at first to support the "conspiracy/deal" thesis. This is dealt with (and refuted) in the next chapter. But in any event the pope's private dialogue with Reagan on disarmament is sufficient explanation for the Vatican's subsequent treatment of nuclear issues.

38. Quoted in Weigel, 927.

39. Namely the Autocue, which Thatcher soon mastered. Thatcher, 258.

40. There were exceptions. David Owen, one of the leaders of the new Social Democrat Party and a former foreign secretary, thought after hearing it that Reagan might go down as a much better president than most Britons then thought, and Ray Whitney, an experienced diplomat and Tory MP, described it as "very hard-hitting." Reeves, 110.

41. Reeves, 109.

42. Quoted in ibid., 141.

43. There are a number of stories that tell of Gulag political prisoners passing news of the speech to each other—and of how the behavior of their guards improved after it. Among the most powerful is that told by Richard Reeves in the introduction to his Reagan biography. In early 1985, former senator James Buckley, then serving as president of Radio Free Europe, passed on to the president two small pieces of rice paper smuggled out of the Gulag. They contained a message, written in a tiny hand that required a magnifying glass, for Reagan himself: "We women political prisoners congratulate you on your re-election to the post of president of the U.S.A. We look with hope to your country which is on the road to freedom and respect for human rights. We wish you success." "Oh, golly," said Reagan, "Golly, how could anyone write that small.... Dammit, it is an evil empire."

44. Reeves, 110.

45. They have now been declassified and are almost entirely available on the Internet.

46. Lee Edwards, *The Conservative Revolution* (New York: The Free Press, 1999).

47. The phrase "megaphone diplomacy" was coined by Lord Carrington for a speech he was giving on East-West relations. He thought better of it before giving the speech and deliberately omitted it. But the press release had already given the phrase currency. This episode aggravated fears in Washington that Carrington was a weak sister. These fears were mistaken. Though a domestic "wet," Carrington was a tough Cold Warrior. But they were an obstacle later to his becoming general secretary of NATO. Thatcher fought hard for his appointment and gained the day. Carrington proved an excellent NATO head and won the respect of both the Pentagon and the State Department.

48. Paul Volcker was Jimmy Carter's appointee as chairman of the Federal Reserve. But he has always acknowledged that he could not have "stayed the course" of monetary disinflation if he had not received strong political backing from Reagan. He has also conceded that Reagan paid a heavy political cost, including Republican losses in the 1982 election, for that steady support.

49. Peter Rodman's *More Precious than Peace* (New York: Scribners, 1994) is an indispensable guide to the history of the Reagan Doctrine. It benefits greatly from being both an insider's well-informed memoir, as Rodman was head of policy planning at the State Department during the relevant period, and a wider dispassionate history as he also brings a diplomatic historian's perspective to the topic. Peter Schweizer's *Victory* (New York: Atlantic Monthly Press, 1994) is also a very fine account.

50. Weigel, 461. My analysis of this pilgrimage follows closely upon his account in pages 459–64.

51. Quoted in ibid., 462–63.

52. The Carter administration had begun helping the Afghan resistance since 1979. Angola and Cambodia, where the Reagan Doctrine was also applied, raise issues similar to those in Central America and Afghanistan. But they are less important to Reagan and hardly involved Thatcher or the pope at all. They are therefore not treated in detail in this book.

53. See Chapter Two, where this evidence is presented and discussed.

54. Rodman, 236.

55. Thomas Enders, the assistant secretary for the Americas, quoted in Rodman, 238.

56. Ibid., 233–46.

57. From their different standpoints both Rodman and Reeves stress this point.

58. Weigel, 453–55.

59. Ibid., 456–58.

Chapter Seven: Imperial Overstretch

1. Tim Sebastien, "Teddy, the KGB, and the Top-Secret File," *Sunday Times*, February 2, 1992. Sebastien was one of the first Western journalists to obtain access to secret Soviet files after the collapse of the Soviet Union. The article on Kennedy, based on a Politburo memo taken from the files, was a sidebar to a much longer article on Soviet meetings with British Labour Party notables.

2. Peter Rodman, *More Precious than Peace* (New York: Scribners, 1994), Chapter 12, "The Gorbachev Revolution," passim.

3. Mikhail Gorbachev, *The Ideology of Renewal for Revolutionary Restructuring* (Moscow: Novosti Press Agency Publishing House, 1988), 35–36. Quoted in Rodman, 293.

4. Charles Wolf Jr., "Costs of the Soviet Empire," *Wall Street Journal*, January 30, 1984. Quoted in Rodman, 297–98.

5. Chernyaev, Gorbachev Archives.

6. Rodman, 294.

7. "Socialist Orientation in the Liberated Countries," quoted and summarized in Rodman, 293–97.

8. Rodman, 296–97.

9. Confidential message from Moscow to Erich Honecker, the East German Communist leader, found in the East German archives. Stiftung Archiv der Parteieu und Massenocganisationen der DDR im Bundesarchiv (SARMO-BArch), DY 30/J IV – 2/20 – 1/13.

10. Transcript of Politburo meeting, April 26, 1984. Vladimir Bukovsky, *Jugement A Moscou. Un Dissident dans les archives du Kremlin* (Paris: Editions Robert Laffont, 1995.)

11. George Weigel, *Witness to Hope: the Biography of John Paul II* (New York: HarperCollins, 1999), 479–80.

12. Ibid., 460–61.

13. Ibid., 479–80.

14. Ibid., 500–02.

15. Ibid., 501–02.

16. This objection had much less force in 1987 than in 1981 because the Cold War was winding down. Even then, however, it was not completely baseless, and Thatcher later fought to keep short-range nuclear (SNF) missiles from being scrapped to maintain some degree of NATO deterrence and to keep the U.S. and Europe safely "coupled."

17. Geoffrey Smith, *Reagan and Thatcher* (New York: W. W. Norton, 1991), 50–58.

18. Ibid., 57, based on an interview with Haig.

19. Margaret Thatcher, *The Downing Street Years* (London: HarperCollins, 1993), 269–70.

20. Bukovsky Collection.

21. David Gress's *From Plato to Nato* (New York: The Free Press, 1998) has a very interesting discussion of the content and significance of these ideological shifts.

22. Unpublished article by Pavel Stroilov, drawing on Chernyaev's diaries. Short, a Labour moderate, was seemingly uncomfortable at finding himself part of this circus. When he ran into Chernyaev with Hayward a year later at a Labour conference, he affected not to recognize him.

23. Stroilov, quoting Chernyaev.

24. Examples galore will be found in the Bukovsky Collection.

25. Thatcher, 236–44.

26. See, for instance, Chris Mullin's thriller *A Very British Coup*, which had the Soviet Union rescuing Britain from a U.S. intelligence agency–backed coup with a timely infusion of foreign aid. Ken Loach's film Hidden Agenda dealt with similar themes.

27. Jeffrey G. Barlow, "Moscow and the Peace Offensive," Heritage Backgrounder 184, May 1982.

28. Bastian and Kelly became both lovers and political celebrities. But their celebrity faded along with the peace movement, and their affair ended tragically with what might be either a mutual suicide or a murder and suicide. Their story has not yet found its Dostoevsky.

29. Thatcher, 265.

30. Believed to be Gerard Kaufman, a Labour moderate, who held several front-bench posts in the 1980s.

31. This account of the Grenada crisis draws on the Thatcher memoirs, several Reagan biographies, Geoffrey Smith's *Reagan and Thatcher*, other standard sources, and in particular the article " 'A Matter of Regret': Britain, the 1983 Grenada Crisis, and the Special Relationship," by Gary Williams, in *Twentieth Century British History*, Volume 12, No. 2, 2001, 208–30. This scholarly paper corrects many misunderstandings of the crisis, including some held by those who participated in it, and is currently the best available guide to finding out what happened and why. Williams is completing a book on Grenada covering both the revolution and the crisis, to be published in 2007.

32. Paul Seabury, *The Grenada Papers* (Oakland, CA: ICS Press, 1984.) See also "Grenada Documents: An Overview and Selection." Departments of State and Defense, Washington, D.C., 1984, OCLC 11273740.

33. Conversations with Dr. Carlton at the time.

34. Some historians argue that their lives were not in fact threatened. That is not the view of several doctors whom I have interviewed over the years in visits to Grenada. They tell me that they genuinely feared for their lives and those of their students and were immensely relieved to be saved by the intervention.

35. Richard Reeves, *President Reagan: The Triumph of Imagination* (New York: Simon & Schuster, 2005), 179.

36. Williams, 215, based on an interview with Sir Robin Renwick in July 1997.

37. If Thatcher meant she had never received a formal appeal from the OECS, she is correct. Eugenia Charles simply forgot to mail the formal letters in all the hurly-burly of the crisis. But the OECS informally approached the High Commission in Barbados at the same time as they approached the Americans. The FCO knew this. If the prime minister was not told, that would be a serious lapse on its part.

38. Williams, 217.

39. Dr. Conor Cruise O'Brien in *The Observer* was alone among commentators in the British press in advancing this interpretation after the event.

40. Telegrams from British diplomats in Washington and Barbados had arrived in London suggesting that an invasion was now a real possibility before Howe spoke in the Commons. Unfortunately, he had not seen them. He therefore strolled much further out on the limb of dismissing its likelihood than he should have.

41. Private information from one of the Grenadian decision-makers.

42. Thatcher, 335.

43. Rodman, 295–96.

44. Chernyaev, Gorbachev Archives.

45. Ibid.

46. Rodman, 299.

Chapter Eight: Triumph and Disaster

1. Geoffrey Smith, *Reagan and Thatcher* (New York: W. W. Norton, 1991), 112–16.

2. Quoted in Mark W. Davis, "Reagan's Real Reason for SDI," *Policy Review*, 103. I am indebted to Mr. Davis's very interesting article for this and other information in this chapter.

3. Ibid.

4. This account is based on Martin Anderson's *Revolution* (New York: Harcourt, 1968), in which he describes the visit to NORAD. It has been confirmed by General Hill.

5. Frances Fitzgerald, *Way Out There in the Blue: Reagan, Star Wars, and the End of the Cold War* (New York: Simon & Schuster).

6. George Shultz, *Turmoil and Triumph: My Years as Secretary of State* (New York: Scribner's, 1993).

7. George Weigel, *Witness to Hope: the Biography of John Paul II* (New York: HarperCollins, 1999), 464–65.

8. "The Challenge of Peace: God's Promise and Our Response," Pastoral Letter, United States Conference of Catholic Bishops, 1983, 26.

9. George Weigel, *Tranquillitas Ordinis: The Present Failure and Future Promise of American Catholic Thought on War and Peace* (Oxford and New York: Oxford University Press, 1987), 275–80.

10. Ibid., 280–85.

11. "A Report on the Challenge of Peace and Policy Developments 1983–88," United States Conference of Catholic Bishops, June 1988.

12. William F. Buckley Jr., "The Bishops and SDI," *National Review*, August 1988.

13. Weigel, *Tranquillitas*, 282.

14. Smith, 149.

15. Ibid., 149–50.

16. Margaret Thatcher, *The Downing Street Years* (London: HarperCollins, 1993), 463–66. Oddly enough, the U.S. Catholic bishops ended up agreeing with Thatcher in their 1988 statement quoted above. Their opposition to SDI presupposed that it might undermine deterrence and divert public spending from more desirable social objects.

17. Smith, 156.

18. I am indebted to Thatcher's excellent book for this summary.

19. John Campbell, *Margaret Thatcher Volume Two: The Iron Lady* (London: Pimlico, 2003), 292.

20. Smith, 167, based on an interview with Bud McFarlane.

21. Conversation with General Walters.

22. "Seemingly" because Mitterrand was almost as anti-Communist as Reagan, if in a more serpentine way.

23. Conversation with Ambassador Galbraith.

24. Edmund Morris, *Dutch: A Memoir of Ronald Reagan* (New York: Random House, 1999), 556–57.

25. According to Chernyaev's diary, Gorbachev told people on his return that Donald Regan, the White House chief of staff, had wandered over to the Soviet delegation and told them to keep up the pressure on Reagan "for his own good." We have to treat this report with some caution. Chernyaev heard it from Ponomarev, who heard it from Gorbachev in Moscow later. Nor does it specify on what topic Reagan should be pressured for his own good (even if we might suspect it was SDI). A later anecdote may throw some light on this: Regan was asked by Richard Reeves what the biggest problem was in the White House during his tenure. Regan said that everyone there thought he was smarter than the president. "Including you?" asked Reeves. "Especially me," replied Regan.

26. Morris, 561.

27. Ibid., 550–75. Morris was present at the Geneva, Reykjavik, and Washington summits. His accounts of them are among the most vivid pages in his book. And because they are free of the postmodern literary techniques he employs for the earlier parts of Reagan's life, they are also reliable accounts.

28. Richard Reeves, *President Reagan: The Triumph of Imagination* (New York: Simon & Schuster, 2005), 293.

29. Quoted in an unpublished article by Vladimir Bukovsky and Pavel Stroilov.

30. Though one should always be wary of reports of conversations, since the transcriber may have an interest in exaggerating his success and downplaying any rebuffs, there is no sign of such flaws in the thousands of transcripts made by Zagladin, who was a senior and trusted figure near the very top of the Soviet hierarchy. When the Bukovsky-Stroilov article was being prepared for publication by *National Review*, the editors contacted the senator's office and sent him the Zagladin transcripts. Senator Kennedy commented, "I had a close working relationship with both President Reagan and President Bush on these visits to Moscow to see Gorbachev. I met with them before and after each visit, and they obviously wanted to miss no opportunity for progress on nuclear arms control in the 1980s and on U.S.–Russian relations after the fall of the Berlin Wall. Gorbachev shared these interests and I was glad to have a small role in making successful compromises possible. The 1987 treaty banning intermediate-range nuclear forces was one of President Reagan's finest achievements."

31. There is no shortage of such quotations, alas. I have taken these from Dinesh D'Souza's cornucopia of anti-Reagan condescension: *Ronald Reagan: How an Ordinary Man Became an Extraordinary Leader* (New York: Free Press, 1997).

32. Tom Bethell, *National Review*, 1988. Samuelson also wrote in his 1981 edition, "It is a vulgar mistake to think that most people in Eastern Europe are miserable." Vulgar, eh? How perfectly frightful.

33. Quoted in D'Souza, chapter one, and in Peter Schweitzer, "Who Broke the Evil Empire?" *National Review*, May 1994.

34. Quoted in Schweitzer, "Who Broke the Evil Empire?"

35. Reeves, 438.

36. There is an interesting exception to this criticism. Some Marxist writers in Britain gathered around the (now defunct) journal *Marxism Today* were among the first to notice that a new sort of economy was replacing the previous "Fordist" model of industrial organization, and that this new economic structure, more decentralized and less dependent on manual labor, was giving birth to a new sort of conservative politics. *Marxism Today* may also have coined—it certainly popularized—the term "Thatcherism," which it defined as a combination of economic freedom and social authoritarianism. That is not quite right, but it captures something.

37. This was itself deregulated in Thatcher's third term by the "Big Bang," which removed restrictions on foreign banks entering the City of London's major financial and banking institutions.

38. Christopher DeMuth, "Two Wins, a Draw, and Two Losses," *National Review*, August 2006.

39. One of the debates about British monetary policy at the time centered around the question of whether tight control of the money supply could be sustained against popular pressure as unemployment rose. Two distinguished Nobel Prize laureates, both admired by the Reaganauts and Thatcherites, Milton Friedman and F. A. Hayek, were associated with a "gradualist" policy that would squeeze inflation out of the system slowly. Unemployment under such a policy would rise only moderately but it would stay high for a long period. Hayek argued that a government could survive a shorter period of high unemployment better than a longer one of moderate unemployment. Hence it should pursue a tough monetary squeeze that would change inflationary attitudes more quickly and require a shorter period of higher unemployment. That is what the Thatcher government found itself doing inadvertently. The results seem to have justified Hayek without disproving Friedman.

40. Nigel Lawson: *The View from Number Eleven* (London: Bantam Press, 1992), 66–73.

41. DeMuth argues in his *National Review* article that Reagan failed to entrench the bipartisan agreement on tax and spending that he achieved over monetary policy and deregulation. That is true. It is partly explained by the fact that expert opinion is more divided over the former two questions than over the latter two. Even so, though Reagan's success was less complete, he bequeathed to the GOP the advantage of defending a popular status quo rather than proposing a novel and perhaps risky reform.

42. Scargill had also been detected by the London *Sunday Times* soliciting support from Colonel Gadafi and the Libyans.

43. Bukovsky Collection. Available on the Internet at http://psi.ece.jhu.edu/ IRUSS/BUK/GBARC/pdfs/terr-wd/num01-84.pdf, where Gorbachev's signature is on page five.

44. Unlike the two minor U.S. recessions, the British recession of the early 1990s raises important policy questions. It is dealt with in the next chapter.

45. Lawson, 981–82.

46. I don't recall a single person in my graduating class of 1964 in Queen Mary College, London University, who intended to start his own business. A handful wanted to work in the family firm. But most were ambitious to become trainee managers at Imperial Chemical Industries or Metal Box. By the mid-1980s, every graduating class included scores of would-be entrepreneurs.

47. Shirley Robin Letwin, *The Anatomy of Thatcherism* (London: Fontana, 1992).

48. C. Northcote Parkinson, a British scholar of the economics of bureaucracy, coined several laws. The most famous is "Work expands to fill the time available." But Gorbachev may have been thinking of his law on the expansion of bureaucracy. Parkinson also wrote a critique of Marxism under the title "Left Luggage."

49. This passage is taken from the study "EU-USSR" by Bukovsky and Stroilov.

50. Reeves, 341.

51. In a two-hour conversation with Shultz and Dobrynin in March 1983, Reagan told the Soviet ambassador that he would consider the release of six Pentacostal Christians living in the basement of the U.S. embassy an important sign that better U.S.–Soviet relations were possible. He would not make political capital out of their release (even though as a broadcaster he had campaigned for it). See Reeves, 138–39.

52. Ibid., 341–42. In general the degree to which Gorbachev's thinking continued to be shaped by Marxist categories has probably been underestimated by historians and commentators. Morris argues (pages 594–95) that Gorbachev's view of Reagan was partly shaped by the failure of the U.S. administration to react favorably, or indeed at all, to his 1986 string of speeches and proposals advocating "new thinking" in Soviet foreign policy away from military solutions and toward diplomacy. These interpretations are not incompatible; the administration's reserve may have reinforced Gorbachev's lingering Marxist suspicions.

53. Ibid., 144.

54. Serge Tarasenko, quoted in Morris, 596, 828.

55. Reeves, 346–47.

56. Ibid., 348–53.

57. Morris, 596.

58. Peter Rodman, *More Precious Than Peace* (New York: Scribners, 1994), 407. My account here draws heavily on conversations with Rodman and on his book, especially chapters 11, 12, 13, and 14.

59. Ibid., 260–88.

60. Rodman, 272–75. Kagan, then on Rodman's staff, went on to become a columnist and commentator whose book *Of Paradise and Power: America and Europe in the New World Order* (New York: Knopf, 2003), became an international bestseller. Luigi Einaudi, then of the Inter-American Bureau, later served as U.S. ambassador to the Organization of American States.

61. Don Oberdorfer, *The Turn: From the Cold War to a New Era* (New York: Poseidon Press, 1991), 237–39, quoted in Rodman, 327.

62. Rodman, 339.

63. Ibid., 600.

64. Radek Sikorski, *Dust of the Saints: A Journey to Herat in Time of War* (Washington: Paragon House, 1990.) Also a conversation with Sikorski.

65. Rodman, 324.

66. The scandal was aptly described by Rodman as "the bastard child of the Reagan Doctrine" and wittily termed "Iranamok" by Michael Kinsley.

67. *Time*, December 8, 1986, quoted in Reeves, 370.

68. Margaret Thatcher Foundation website: http://margaretthatcher.org.

Chapter Nine: Checkmate

1. Richard Reeves, *President Reagan: The Triumph of Imagination* (New York: Simon & Schuster, 2005), 348–49.

2. Ibid.

3. Edmund Morris, *Dutch: A Memoir of Ronald Reagan* (New York: Random House, 1999), 599.

4. Interviews with Regan and Wick, quoted in Reeves, 353–56.

5. George Shultz, *Turmoil and Triumph: My Years as Secretary of State* (New York: Scribner's, 1993), chapter 36, passim.

6. Reeves, 355.

7. Shultz, chapter 36, passim.

8. *Time*, October 27, 1986.

9. Reeves, 356.

10. Interview with Thatcher, quoted in Geoffrey Smith, *Reagan and Thatcher* (New York: W. W. Norton, 1991), 214.

11. One Tory campaign poster showed a soldier holding up his arms in the gesture of surrender under the heading "Labour's Policy on Arms." This was given greater credibility in the course of the campaign when Neil Kinnock, the Labour leader, suggested that guerrilla fighting could be an alternative to the possession of nuclear weapons. In other words, he assumed that a Britain without nuclear weapons would be defeated. Thatcher could hardly believe her luck and delivered the most devastating riposte the following day: "Labour's non-nuclear defense policy is in fact a policy for defeat, surrender, occupation, and, finally, prolonged guerrilla fighting." Kinnock never recovered. He went on to two election defeats and the gilded obscurity of a commissionership in the European Union.

12. U.S. embassy briefing, November 5, 1986 (National Security Council, Box 90902), quoted in John Campbell, *Margaret Thatcher Volume Two: The Iron Lady* (London: Pimlico, 2003), 294.

13. Campbell, 292–96.

14. Smith, 224–25.

15. Margaret Thatcher, *The Downing Street Years* (London: HarperCollins, 1993), 454–58.

16. Report to the Politburo, April 2, 1987, as recorded by Chernyaev.

17. They are available, for instance, on http://www.margaretthatcher.org.

18. Report to the Politburo, April 2, 1987, as recorded by Chernyaev.

19. Thatcher, 474–85.

20. Ibid., 485.

21. George Weigel, *Witness to Hope: the Biography of John Paul II* (New York: HarperCollins, 1999), 528–30.

22. *Dogg's Hamlet and Cahoot's Macbeth* by Sir Tom Stoppard, the great Anglo-Czech playwright, is a funny and moving riff on this theme.

23. Weigel, 546–47.

24. Thatcher, 777–82.

25. Sir Percy Cradock, *In Pursuit of British Interests* (London: John Murray, 1997), 58, quoted in Campbell, 262.

26. Chris Ogden, *Maggie* (New York: Simon & Schuster, 1990), 236, quoted in Campbell, 262.

27. Reeves, xv–xvi.

28. Thatcher, 157, 813. As someone who helped Mrs. Thatcher in the writing of her memoirs, I recall that she devoted a great deal of thought to getting such personal judgments right.

29. With a few exceptions. George Urban, the distinguished Anglo-Hungarian historian, was one of the small circle of conservative foreign policy experts who gave occasional advice to Thatcher when she was prime minister. Supportive of her Cold War policies but disillusioned by her Euro-skepticism, he subsequently wrote a book quoting some of her fiercer diatribes against the EU as if they were her considered opinion. It was serialized in the London *Times* and caused grave scandal to the naïve.

30. Reeves, 472–75.

31. Ibid., 483–84.

32. Weigel, 529.

33. David Pryce-Jones, *The Fall of the Soviet Empire, 1985–1991* (London: Weidenfeld and Nicolson, 1994), 221 and following.

34. Conversation with Vladimir Bukovsky.

35. Reeves, 484.

36. Weigel, 602.

37. Gorbachev Archives.

38. Weigel, 604.

39. For whatever reason, Gorbachev devoted only one page of his voluminous memoirs to his historic visit to the Vatican. See ibid., 600–05.

40. Gorbachev Archives, Inv.1-1, transcript of Gorbachev-Thatcher meeting, September 23, 1989.

41. *329 Tage: Innenansichten der Einigung [329 Days: Inside Views of the Unification]*, Siedler Publishing, 1991.

42. Gorbachev Archives.

43. George Bush and Brent Scowcroft, *A World Transformed* (New York: Alfred A. Knopf, 1998), 192.

44. Ibid., 193

45. Ibid., 190.

46. Campbell, 639.

47. Thatcher, 802.

48. Pryce-Jones, 3–4.

49. Thatcher, 802–04.

50. Almost all of these books were collated, edited, and included commentary by Kiron K. Skinner, Annelise Anderson, and Martin Anderson. They are important contributions to a full understanding of Reagan and thus to the history of our times. See in particular their *Reagan's Path to Victory* (New York: Free Press, 2004.)

51. The fall of Lucifer, to be precise.

52. Philip Jenkins, "The Next Christianity," *The Atlantic*, Vol. 290, No. 3, October 2002.

53. This phrase is not in fact original to her. It was originally used in a letter to her from the then Italian foreign minister, Antonio Martino, responding to her congratulations on his election. She liked the phrase so much that, with his permission, she used it in the eulogy.

INDEX

Aaron, Benjamin, 69
Abrams, Elliot, 274
Action Committee for Peace and
    Cooperation, 210
Adams, Tom, 219
Afghanistan, 52, 62, 81, 113–14,
    230, 272, 276–77
AFL-CIO, 132, 172–73, 191
Africa, 3, 51
Agca, Mehmet Ali, 66, 67, 76, 79,
    80, 86, 112, 132
The Age of Reason (Hayward), 51
Aksen, Herman, 209, 210, 215
Alexander, Andrew, 22
Allen, Richard V., 91–92, 138, 141,
    171, 176, 229
All-Union Central Council of the
    Trade Unions, 261
al Qaeda, 76, 237
Anderson, Martin, 238, 239
Andreotti, Giulio, 78–79
Andropov, Yuri, 195, 197; Brezh-
    nev's imperial overstretch and,
    228; death of, 229, 232; funeral
    of, 226–27; John Paul II,
    attempted assassination of and,
    77, 80–81; John Paul II as threat
    to Soviet power and, 92, 111;
    Polish problem and, 204–5; Soli-
    darity, birth of and, 118; Solidar-
    ity, Soviet response to and,
    121–22, 128, 132, 133–34;
    Soviet decline and, 232; Soviet
    Third World interventions and,
    124, 201
Angola, 3, 36, 39, 51, 159, 199,
    230, 231, 272
Annan, Noel, 225
Annenberg, Walter, 20–21, 22, 23,
    24
Antall, Josef, 306
Antonov, Sergei, 77, 80
Antrim, HMS, 220
Arbatov, Georgi, 227
Argentina, 96. *See also* Falklands
    War
arms control: alliance diplomacy
    and, 186; Carter administration
    and, 47; Cold War and, 184–86;
    missile diplomacy and, 205–9;
    NATO and, 206, 207, 209, 288;
    "peace movement" and, 206,
    209–17; Reagan, Ronald and,

61, 184, 197–98, 207; SDI and,
    235–47, 266–72, 283–84,
    284–87; Soviet Union and,
    197–98, 228–29, 235–39,
    266–72; Thatcher, Margaret
    and, 207, 208, 215–16; "zero-
    zero option" and, 206–8, 268,
    289. *See also* missile defense
Aron, Raymond, 39, 208
Atlantic Conveyor, 158
Attali, Jacques, 140
Auschwitz, 104
Austin, Hudson, 219

Baader-Meinhof gang, 51
Bahr, Egon, 166
Barricada, 124
Bastian, Gert, 215
The Battle for the Falklands (Hast-
    ings and Jenkins), 144
The Battle of Algiers, 42
Beale, Howard, 43
Belaunde, Fernando, 155
Belgium, 210, 213–14, 215
Beloff, Max, 225
Bence, Gyorgy, 257
Berlin Wall, fall of, 303–4
Bernanke, Ben, 259
Bernardin, Joseph, 240
Bernstein, Carl, 67, 181, 182
Berry, Anthony, 72
Bethell, Tom, 255–56
Bialer, Seweryn, 256
birth control, artificial: Catholic
    Church and, 5, 9, 53; *Humanae
    Vitae* and, 9–12; John Paul II,
    and, 5
Bishop, Maurice, 217–18
Blair, Tony, 332
Blitzer, Wolf, 325, 328
Bogomolov, Oleg, 92, 94
Bolt, Robert, 12
Brandt, Willy, 15
Brezhnev, Leonid, 80, 87–88, 267;
    Carter administration and, 47;
    death of, 198; détente and, 38;
    imperial overstretch of, 227–28;
    John Paul II, attempted assassi-
    nation of and, 78, 80–81; Polish
    problem and, 201; Solidarity,
    birth of and, 115; Solidarity,
    Soviet response to and, 121,
    129, 130, 132, 133; Soviet econ-

omy and, 199; Soviet threat and,
    38, 39; Third World commit-
    ments and, 277
Brezhnev Doctrine, 131, 133
Britain: Anglican-Catholic relations
    and, 164–65; Anglo-Irish agree-
    ment and, 84; economy of, 3;
    Falklands War and, 142–61;
    Grenada invasion and, 217–26;
    John Paul II visit (1982) to,
    163–66; NATO and, 106; oil
    and inflation in, 36; terrorism,
    rise of and, 34–35. *See also*
    Thatcher, Margaret
British Broadcasting Corporation
    (BBC), 104, 237
Brock, Bill, 58
Broder, David, 70
Brogan, Colm, 22, 42
Brokaw, Tom, 184
Brown, Harold, 44
Brown, Irving, 173
Bruguiere, Jean-Louis, 79–80
Brzezinski, Zbigniew, 44, 92, 127,
    171, 172, 176
Buchanan, Pat, 252
Buckley, William F., Jr., 242
Bujak, Zbigniew, 120
Bukovsky, Vladimir, 62, 101–2, 122,
    185, 227–28
Bulgaria, 78, 80
Bush, George H. W., 220, 227, 279,
    300, 304, 313
Butler, Robert, 72, 75, 226

Caddell, Patrick, 49–50
Caldicott, Helen, 241
Callaghan, Jim, 49, 116, 185, 212,
    213; Labour government
    (Britain) and, 55–56, 58–60;
    monetarism and, 59; "peace
    movement" and, 214; Soviet
    Communism and, 106
Cambodia, 27, 36, 51, 272, 277
Cameron, David, 332
Campaign for Nuclear Disarma-
    ment, 210
Campbell, John, 332
The Camp of the Saints (Raspail),
    42–43
Canning, George, 12
Cardenal, Ernesto, 192
CARICOM, 221

Carlos the Jackal, 39, 76, 79, 80
Carlton, David, 218, 222
Carrington, Lord, 112, 145, 149
Carter, James Earl, 61, 108, 110, 237, 280; 1976 presidential election and, 33; 1980 presidential election and, 63; Communism and, 48–49; energy crisis and, 49–50; failures of, 48–52; foreign policy of, 46–47, 51, 113; health care and, 63; human rights reform and, 49; Iran hostage crisis and, 49–50, 62, 112; "malaise" speech (1979) of, 49–50; "peace movement" and, 214; radicalism of, 44, 46; religion and, 44, 46; Soviet invasion of Afghanistan and, 62; Soviet threat and, 49; Thatcher, Margaret and, 113. See also Carter administration
Carter administration: arms control and, 47; character of, 33–34; Cold War and, 47; collapse of, 48–52; defense spending and, 44; foreign policy of, 46–48, 61–62; NWIO and, 45–46; as post-American, 44–48, 61–62; Soviet threat and, 46–48, 47–48, 62.
Casaroli, Agostino, 94, 95, 180, 187, 239; John Paul II, attempted assassination of and, 78; Ostpolitik and, 15–16, 47
Casey, William, 171, 172, 176, 177, 189, 274
Castro, Fidel, 44, 125, 189, 231
Catholic Church: birth control, artificial and, 5, 9, 53; Christian-Marxist dialogues and, 12–19; Communism and, 12–19, 93, 109; democratization of, 8; IRA terrorism and, 109–10; in Latin America, 97–100; Liberaldom and, 4; liberation theology and, 52, 100; Marxism and, 5, 12–23; Reagan Central America policy and, 191–92; sexuality and, 9–12, 96–97; Solidarity and, 120, 131, 188; teaching authority of, 12; Vatican II and, 3, 6–9, 52
Centesimus Annus (John Paul II), 311
Central America: liberation theology and, 177, 180; Marxist guerrilla groups in, 36; Reagan Doctrine in, 272–78; Solidarity and, 122; Soviet interventions in, 177; U.S. policy in, 178

Central Intelligence Agency (CIA), 131, 180, 181, 199
Centre for Policy Studies (Britain), 25
"The Challenge of Peace" (USCCB), 240–42
Channon, Paul, 20
Charles, Eugenia, 219
Chattaway, Christopher, 20
Chebrikov, Viktor, 111, 197, 198
Chernenko, Konstantin, 85; John Paul II threat to Soviet power and, 111; Solidarity and, 118; Soviet decline and, 232–33
Chernyaev, Anatoly, 106, 135, 228; as Andropov's successor, 227; arms control and, 266; "peace movement" and, 211–12; Polish situation and, 199–200; Reykjavik summit and, 266; Soviet decline and, 229, 231–32; Soviet Third World interventions and, 124
China, 3, 51, 127, 160
Christian Democratic Party (Italy), 78
Christianity, Marxism and, 12–19
Christopher, Warren, 123
Churchill, Winston, 52, 106, 160, 222, 323
Clark, William, 176, 184, 185, 239
Clifford, Clark, 299
Club of Rome, 38, 41
Coard, Bernard, 219
Coard, Phyllis, 219
Cockburn, Claud, 218
Cold War: arms control and, 184–86; Carter administration and, 47; Gorbachev, Mikhail and, 290; new front for, 182–88; Reagan, Ronald and, 91, 185, 229, 289; Soviet threat and, 39; Thatcher, Margaret and, 105, 106; United States and, 88; victory in, 229, 283–84, 289
Cold War liberalism, 44
Commager, Henry Steele, 89, 184
Committee of Youth Organizations, 126
Committees for Social Resistance (KOSs), 201
Commonwealth Disaster Management Agency, 173
Communism: Callaghan, Jim and, 106; Carter, James Earl and, 48–49; Carter administration and, 46–48; Catholic Church and, 12–19, 93, 109; cultural resistance to, 17–20, 47, 94, 101, 119; détente and, 4, 62; fall of, 304–8; Helsinki Final

Act and, 47; in Hungary, 291–93; ideological resistance to, 29–30; John Paul II and, 12–19, 53, 55, 84; Ostpolitik and, 4, 15–17, 18, 47, 94, 109; Reagan, Ronald and, 29–30, 87–89, 303–4; religious freedom and, 18; Thatcher, Margaret and, 106–7
Congregation for the Doctrine of the Faith (CDF), 193–94
Connolly, Cyril, 42
Conquest, Robert, 22, 184–85
Conservative Party (Britain). See Tory Party
Conservative Political Center (CPC) (Britain), 21
Cooke, Cardinal, 86
Coolidge, Calvin, 301–02
Cooper, Frank, 112
Cossiga, Francesco, 213, 214
Cracow, Poland, 5, 8–9, 103
Cradock, Sir Percy, 299
Crawford, Cynthia ("Crawfie"), 72, 73
Craxi, Bettino, 216
Crowe, Bill, 286
Crucitti, Francesco, 66
Cuba, 36, 123, 125, 188, 219–20, 284
Cuilapan, Mexico, 98–99
Cywinski, Bogdan, 101
Czechoslovakia, 16, 172, 211, 306–7; Catholic Church in, 18; Polish problem and, 204; Soviet invasion of, 126

Dart, Justin, 27
Davies, Norman, 17
Davis, Mark W., 237
Deaver, Michael, 86, 88
"Decision to Work against the Policies of the Vatican in Relation to Socialist States," 111
decolonization, 3, 40, 45
de Gaulle, Charles, 210
de la Billiere, Peter, 115
Delors, Jacques, 322
Democratic Party, Democrats: McGovernization of, 33, 211; Reagan, Ronald and, 191
DeMuth, Christopher, 259
d'Estaing, Valery Giscard, 126
détente, 4, 30, 38, 40, 62
Deutsche Welle, 104
Dobrynin, Anatoly, 88, 267
Donaldson, Sam, 283
Dozo, Lami, 145
Dubcek, Alexander, 307
Duncan, Silas, 142
Dziwisz, Stanislaw, 66, 67, 117

Eagleburger, Lawrence, 152
East Germany, 16, 172
Economics (Samuelson), 255
Ehrlich, Paul, 40, 41
Einaudi, Luigi, 274
Eisenstein, Sergei, 302
Elizabeth, Queen, 217, 225
El Salvador, 124–25, 178, 180, 188, 189–91, 191–92, 230, 277
Endurance, HMS, 143, 144, 145
Entebbe crisis, 43
Ethiopia, 49, 51, 199, 232
European Community, 105, 167. *See also* European Union (EU)
European Union (EU), 97, 262; agricultural subsidies of, 41; British overpayment to, 105, 106
Exiles (Osborne), 42

Falklands War, 142–61; "Falklands effect" and, 159–61; France and, 150; impact of, 159–61; John Paul II and, 163–65; Latin America and, 154, 161; Operation Goa and, 144; Reagan, Ronald and, 144, 150–51, 152, 153–54, 156, 158, 161; Thatcher, Margaret and, 84, 144–46, 148–53, 155, 156, 157–61; UN and, 150, 158; United States and, 150–57, 158; victory in, 157–61
Fallaci, Oriana, 129
Fearless, 143, 144
feminism, 2–3, 97
Finch, Peter, 43
First Things, 12
Fitzgerald, Frances, 238
Foot, Michael, 156, 160, 213, 216
Ford, Gerald: 1976 presidential election and, 28–31, 33; energy crisis and, 37; government regulation and, 29; Thatcher, Margaret and, 57
Foreign Affairs, 256
Foreign Policy magazine, 46
Fox, Robert, 165
France: Falklands War and, 150; Grenada invasion and, 221; oil and inflation in, 36; "peace movement" in, 210
Friedman, Milton, 22, 266
Frum, David, 36, 39

Galbraith, Evan, 248
Galbraith, John Kenneth, 255
Galtieri, Leopoldo, 145, 147, 153, 155–56
Gdansk, Poland, 116–19
General Belgrano, 154, 155

Geneva arms control talks (1982), 205
Genscher, Hans-Dietrich, 206
Geremek, Bronislaw, 117
Germany, "peace movement" in, 206, 215
Gierek, Edward, 122; John Paul II papal visit to Poland and, 96, 102; John Paul II threat to Soviet power and, 93; Solidarity and, 115–16, 119
glasnost, 84, 135, 182, 294, 305
Glemp, Cardinal, 131, 132–33, 179
Glenamara, Lord. *See* Short, Edward
Gleysteen, Dirk, 19, 20, 22, 25, 26
Gomulka, Wladyslaw, 116
Gorbachev, Mikhail, 159; Afghan war and, 276; arms control and, 206, 283–84, 284–87, 289; Central American guerrilla groups and, 124–25; Cold War and, 290; Geneva summit and, 248–52; *glasnost* and, 84, 182, 294, 305; John Paul II, attempted assassination of and, 78, 78–79, 84; John Paul II and, 308–12; John Paul II threat to Soviet power and, 93, 111; Kennedy, Edward meeting with, 252–54; *perestroika* and, 84, 182, 266, 294, 305, 312; privatization and, 265; Reykjavik summit and, 266–72, 284, 284–87, 289; SDI and, 234, 237–38, 243, 245, 290; Solidarity and, 122; Soviet decline and, 233–34, 257; Soviet economy and, 199; Soviet Third World interventions and, 124–25, 201; Soviet Union, collapse of, 305, 307–8, 312–17, 317–24; Thatcher, Margaret and, 84–85, 233, 243, 245, 293–94, 312–17
Gorbachev, Raisa, 266
Graham, Kay, 138
Greenspan, Alan, 259
Grenada: Cuba and, 219–20; People's Revolutionary Government (PRG) in, 217, 219; Reagan, Ronald and, 217–26; Soviet decline and, 230–32; U.S. invasion of, 217–26, 230–32
Gromov, Boris, 276
Gromyko, Andrei, 133, 198; Gorbachev, Mikhail and, 233; John Paul II threat to Soviet power and, 94–95; "peace movement" and, 211–12; Polish problem and, 202; Reykjavik summit and, 269; SDI and, 242, 269;

Solidarity and, 118, 121–22, 129
Gross, John, 61
GRU (Russian military intelligence), 80

Haig, Al, 88, 170, 176; arms control and, 206–7; Central American policy and, 188–89; Falklands War and, 151, 152, 153–56; John Paul II-Reagan meeting and, 179; nuclear weapons and, 180
Haq, Muhammad Zia-ul-Haq, 276
Harris, Ralph, 22
Hastings, Max, 144
Hattersley, Roy, 19
Havel, Vaclav, 204, 306–7
Hayek, F. A., 22, 260, 266
Hayward, Ron, 211, 212, 213
Hayward, Steven, 51
Healey, Denis, 57, 140
Heath, Edward: Conservative government of, 1, 3; corporate socialism of, 25; economic policy of, 24–25; failure of, 57; Thatcher, Margaret and, 20, 23, 25; union reform and, 58; "U-turn" of, 24–25
Helsinki Final Act, 47
Henderson, Sir Nicholas, 112, 137, 138, 158
Heseltine, Michael, 20, 222
Hill, James, 238
Hinckley, John, 65, 68, 69, 71, 86–87, 89, 132
His Holiness (Bernstein and Politi), 181
Holland, 213–14, 215
Hong Kong, China, 107, 200, 266
Horizon, 42
Horn of Africa, 51, 272
Howe, Geoffrey, 19, 20, 105, 106, 220, 222, 259
Howell, David, 20
Humanae Vitae (Paul VI), 9–12
Hume, Basil, 163, 164, 165
Hungary, 14, 16, 172, 291–93, 305–6
Hunt, Rex, 147

Iliescu, Ion, 317
Imposimato, Ferdinando, 80
INLA, 109
Institute of Economic Affairs, 22
International Monetary Fund (IMF), 56, 139
Intrepid, 143, 144
IRA: terrorism and, 86, 109–10; Thatcher, Margaret, attempted assassination of by, 72, 75
Iran, 3, 37, 45, 272

Iran-Contra affair, 70, 278–81, 285
Iran hostage crisis (1980), 49–50,
    62, 63, 112, 113, 114–15
Ireland, 112; Anglo-Irish agreement
    and, 84; John Paul II visit to,
    109–10; terrorism in, 35, 164
Iron Curtain, 88, 93, 94
Islamic Grey Wolves, 76
Israel, 45; Entebbe crisis and, 43;
    terrorism, rise of, 34–35

Jablonski, Henryk, 102
Jamaica, 219, 230
Jandal, Shafik, 124, 125
Jankowski, Henryk, 117
Japan, 34, 36
Jaruzelski, Wojciech, 115; Polish
    problem and, 201, 202–4; Soli-
    darity and, 122, 128, 130–35,
    166, 187, 295–98
Jay, Peter, 185
Jenkins, Roy, 142
Jenkins, Simon, 144
John Paul I, 53–54, 55
John Paul II: achievements of,
    330–31; Anglican-Catholic
    relations and, 164–65; arms
    control and, 179–80, 239,
    242–43; attempted assassina-
    tion of, 65–66, 66–68, 75–84,
    112, 132; birth control, artifi-
    cial and, 5; British-Vatican rela-
    tions and, 163–66; Centesimus
    Annus of, 311; character of, 1,
    4–5; Church, government of
    and, 7–9; Communism and,
    12–20, 47, 53, 55, 84, 94, 101,
    119; death of, 329–30; ecu-
    menism and, 6–7; election as
    pope of, 53–55; Falklands War
    and, 163–65; Gorbachev,
    Mikhail and, 308–12; Helsinki
    Final Act and, 47; Humanae
    Vitae and, 9–12; influence of, 1;
    IRA terrorism and, 109–10,
    164; Laborem Exercens (On
    Human Work) of, 310, 311;
    liberation theology and,
    97–100, 180, 193–94; Love
    and Responsibility of, 10; Man-
    agua visit of, 192–95; Memory
    and Identity of, 81; Mexico,
    pilgrimage to of, 97–100;
    Nicaragua visit (1983) of, 100;
    orthodoxy of, 5–6, 9, 12, 18,
    53, 55; papal visit to Poland of,
    92, 95–96, 100–105, 108–9;
    Reagan, Ronald and, 179–82;
    Redemptor Hominis of, 94;
    religious freedom and, 6, 7, 18,

84, 94, 293; sexuality, mar-
    riage, and family and, 9–12, 53;
    Slavorum Apostoli of, 204; Sol-
    idarity, birth of and, 117; Soli-
    darity and, 77, 84, 130–31,
    135, 176–81, 188, 295–96; Sol-
    licitudo Rei Socialis (On Social
    Concern) of, 310; "theology of
    the body" of, 96–97; threat to
    Soviet power of, 92–96, 111; as
    too Catholic, 2, 19, 52; UN
    address (1979) of, 110–11; Ut
    Unum Sint of, 6; Vatican II and,
    5, 6–9; visit to Britain (1982)
    of, 163–66
Johnson, Frank, 26, 55–56, 58
Johnson, Paul, 225
Jordan, 34, 35, 150
Joseph, Sir Keith, 19, 24–26
Justice Department, U.S., 34

Kadar, Janos, 291
Kagan, Robert, 274
Kampelman, Max, 283
Kania, Stanislaw, 55, 122, 127,
    130; Solidarity and, 128, 131,
    132
Keeble, Chris, 165
Kelly, Petra, 215
Kennedy, Edward, 108, 197–98;
    Gorbachev, Mikhail meeting
    with, 252–54; Soviet decline
    and, 257
Khmer Rouge, 35, 36
Khomeini, Ayatollah, 49, 278
Kirkland, Lane, 173, 191
Kirkpatrick, Jeanne, 154, 161, 176,
    304
Kissinger, Henry: China and, 3;
    détente and, 29; energy crisis
    and, 37; foreign policy of, 29;
    Reagan, Ronald and, 29;
    Thatcher, Margaret and, 57
Koch, Edward, 110
Koenig, Cardinal, 54
Kohl, Helmut, 214, 216, 314, 323
Kosygin, Alexei, 107
Krauthammer, Charles, 275
Kristol, Irving, 30
Krol, John, 92, 176
Kuklinski, Ryszard, 126–27, 132
Kulikov, Viktor, 134
Kuron, Jacek, 101
Kuusinen, Otto, 227
Kvitsinsky, Yuli, 205, 208

Labedz, Leo, 40
Laborem Exercens (On Human
    Work) (John Paul II), 310, 311

Labour government (Britain): arms
    control and, 215; Callaghan,
    Jim and, 55–56, 58–60; eco-
    nomic policy of, 22; mone-
    tarism and, 56–57; "peace
    movement" and, 213; union
    reform and, 59
Lady Caroline Lamb, 12
Laghi, Piu, 176
Lake, Anthony, 44
The Late Great Planet Earth (Lind-
    sey), 40
Latin America: Catholic Church in,
    97–100; democratization in,
    161; economic structure of, 97;
    Falklands War and, 143, 154,
    161; liberation theology in, 5,
    12–19, 97–100; United States
    and, 161
Lawson, Nigel, 259, 260, 262, 263,
    313
Laxalt, Paul, 30, 31
Leach, Sir Henry, 145–47
Lebanon, 35, 221, 231
Lefebvre, Marcel, 8
Lekachman, Robert, 38
Lenczowski, John, 184, 185
Lenin Steelworks (Poland), 15
Letwin, Shirley Robin, 264
Lewek, Antoni, 203
Lewin, Sir Terence, 157
Lewis, Anthony, 184
Lexington, USS, 142
Liberaldom, 4, 51
liberals, Catholic: John Paul II's
    "theology of the body" and,
    97; Vatican II and, 3, 8
liberation theology: Catholic
    Church and, 52, 100; Central
    America and, 177, 180; Christ-
    ian-Marxist dialogues and, 13,
    100; John Paul II and, 97–100,
    180, 193–94; in Latin America,
    5, 12–19, 97–100
Libya, 226
The Limits to Growth (Club of
    Rome), 38
Lindsey, Hal, 40, 41
Linhard, Richard, 269
Lipset, Seymour Martin, 257
Lipski, Jan Jozef, 101
Lithuania, 93, 272
London Daily Mail, 22
London Daily Telegraph, 22, 26,
    30, 43, 55, 223
London Spectator, 55
London Sunday Times, 198
London Times, 225
Louis, John J., 141

Love and Responsibility (John Paul II), 10
Lovelock, James, 11
Lublin, Poland, 115–16
Luciani, Albino. *See* John Paul I
Lyle, Robbie, 173–75

Macierewicz, Antoni, 101, 127
Macmillan, Brit government, 23
Macrae, Norman, 37
Magee, Patrick, 74, 75
Malvinas. *See* Falklands War
Marcos, Ferdinand, 274
Martin, David, 98
Martino, Antonio, 51
Marx, Karl, 39, 208
Marxism: Catholic Church and, 5, 12–23; Christianity and, 12–19; as doctrine of power, 13–14; *Ostpolitik* and, 13, 15
Matak, Sirik, 35–36
Matlock, Jack, 283
Maulding, Reginald, 19
Mazowiecki, Tadeusz, 117, 298–99
McCarthy, Eugene, 33
McFarlane, Bud, 221, 224, 245, 272, 274, 284
Medium-Term Financial Strategy (MTFS), 260
Meese, Edwin, 138, 239
Melady, Thomas P., 78
Memory and Identity (John Paul II), 81
Menges, Constantine C., 275, 280
Mexico, John Paul II pilgrimage to, 97–98
Michnik, Adam, 17, 305
Milosevic, Slobodan, 292
missile defense: NORAD and, 238–39; nuclear disarmament and, 237–38; SDI, 235–47, 266–72. *See also* arms control
Mitrokhin, Vasili, 79
Mitrokhin Commission, 79–80
Mitterrand, Francois, 140, 150, 166, 221, 248, 267, 271, 323
Mlynar, Zdenek, 307
Mobilization for Survival, 210
monetarism: Callaghan, Jim and, 59; Labour government and, 56–57; of Thatcher, Margaret, 57, 135, 138
Monroe, James, 275
Moro, Aldo, 35
Morris, Edmund, 68, 70, 326, 327
Morrow, Douglas, 238
Mountbatten, Lord Louis, 35, 109
Moynihan, Daniel Patrick, 30, 62, 70, 110–11
Mozambique, 3, 51, 199, 272
Mugabe, Robert, 105

Munich, 76
Munich Olympics (1972), 39
Mutual Assured Destruction (MAD), 238, 243, 244–45

Naimski, Piotr, 101, 102, 103, 127, 134
National Association of Evangelicals, 89, 184
National Endowment for Democracy, 172, 183, 280
National Press Club, 30
National Review, 22, 38, 255, 304
National Security Agency (NSA), 152
National Security Directive (NSDD) 32, 185–86; NSDD 66, 186; NSDD 75, 186
Natta, Alexander, 265
Neave, Airey, 86, 109
Netanyahu, Jonathan, 43
Network, 43
Neuhaus, Richard John, 12
New Jewel Movement, 217
Newsweek, 28, 31
New World Economic Order, 37
New World International Order (NWIO), 45–46
New York Times, 109, 184, 203, 272
Nicaragua, 39, 178, 231; Contras in, 188–92; John Paul II visit to, 100; liberation theology in, 180; Marxist guerrilla groups in, 36; Sandinista government in, 123–24, 188, 277–78; Soviet interventions in, 123–24
Nidal, Abu, 80
Nitze, Paul, 205, 208–9, 268, 269, 283
Nixon, Richard, 2, 33, 48, 237, 267, 275; China and, 3; government regulation and, 29; welfare revolution and, 3
Noonan, Peggy, 247
Nordhaus, William, 256
North, Oliver, 278
North American Aerospace Defense Command (NORAD), 238–39
North Atlantic Treaty Organization (NATO), 112, 127, 135, 314–15; arms control and, 206, 207, 209, 288; Britain and, 106; "dual track" policy of, 140; missile diplomacy and, 205; Operation Able Archer and, 228; "peace movement" and, 213–14; SDI and, 245–46; Solidarity and, 131
No to the Neutron Bomb, 210
Nott, John, 143–44, 146–47

Nowa Huta, Poland, 14–15
Nowak, Jan, 173
"nuclear freeze" movement, 215, 241
nuclear weapons: détente and, 4; John Paul II and, 179–80; John Paul II-Reagan meeting and, 179–80; Mutual Assured Destruction and, 238, 243, 244; Reagan, Ronald and, 32, 63, 179–80

Obando, Miguel, 192
O'Boyle, Cardinal, 11
oil: Carter administration and, 49–50; economic impact of, 36–37; stagflation and, 37; West, decline of and, 36–38
Olivier, Sir Lawrence, 85
The Omen (Lindsey), 41
O'Neill, Tip, 69
Open Society Institute, 173
Operation Able Archer, 228
Operation Goa, 144
Organization of East Caribbean States (OECS), 219, 224
Organization of Petroleum Exporting Countries (OPEC), 34, 36–38, 39
Ortega, Daniel, 190–91, 193
Ortega, Humberto, 123
Osborne, John, 42
Ostpolitik, 13, 109; Communism and, 4, 15–17, 18, 47, 94; Marxism and, 13, 15; Paul VI and, 15–16; in Poland, 16–19; West Germany and, 15; Wyszynski, Stefan and, 16
Ottawa G-7 summit (1981), 139, 140

Pacem in Terris, 204
Palmer, Mark, 272, 273, 274
Parkinson, Cecil, 158
Parr, Jerry, 68, 71
Parsons, Anthony, 150, 158
Paul VI, 95; death of, 52; *Humanae Vitae* and, 9–12; legacy of, 53; *Ostpolitik* and, 15–16
"peace movement," 209–17; arms control and, 206, 215–17; in France, 210; in Germany, 206, 215; Labour government and, 213; NATO and, 213–14; as revolutionary social movement, 210–11; Soviet Union and, 211–12, 216–17; Thatcher, Margaret and, 84, 213–14
Peele, Roger, 86
perestroika, 84, 135, 182, 266, 294, 305, 312

Perle, Richard, 140–41, 151, 206, 257, 268, 269–70
personalism, Christian, 6, 18, 96
Pinkowski, Jozef, 122
Pinochet, Augusto, 45, 274
Pipes, Richard, 173, 184–85, 186
Pius XII, 12–13
Podhoretz, Norman, 30
Poindexter, John, 278, 284
Poland: Catholic Church in, 14–15, 102, 109, 295–96; Communism in, 1, 5, 16–20, 101–2; Gdansk strike in, 116–19; John Paul II papal visit to, 92, 95–96, 100–105, 108–9, 187; martial law imposed on, 163, 166–82; Nazi invasion of, 5; Ostpolitik in, 16–19; Soviet Union collapse and, 171; Thatcher, Margaret visit to, 294–99; U.S. support for, 171–77. See also Solidarity
Polish Communist Party (PORP), 202
Politi, Marco, 67, 181
Ponomarev, Boris, 124, 209, 212, 231
Pontifical Commission on Peace and Justice, 240, 242
Ponto, Jurgen, 35
Popieluszko, Jerzy, 202–3, 293
The Population Bomb (Ehrlich), 40, 41
Portugal, 3, 215
Poszgay, Imre, 306
Powell, Charles, 288
Powell, Colin, 304
Powell, Enoch, 149, 160
Price, Wesley, 68
Primakov, Yevgeny, 201
Program of Economic Recovery, 86
progressives, Catholic: Church, government of and, 7; John Paul II and, 6, 9
Protection of Trading Interests Act, 169
Protestantism: evangelical, 98, 100; Pentecostal, 98
Pryce-Jones, David, 318
Puebla, Mexico, 97–98
Pym, Francis, 25, 149, 153, 155

Radio Free Europe, 104
Radio Martio, 284
Rakhmanin, 121
RAND Corporation, 199
Raspail, Jean, 42–43
Ratzinger, Joseph, 54, 193–94
Reagan, Maureen, 86
Reagan, Nancy, 31, 70, 139, 249, 266

Reagan, Ronald, 48, 137; 1968 presidential nomination and, 2; 1976 presidential nomination and, 28–32; 1980 presidential election and, 62–63; achievements of, 326–28; America, defense of and, 29, 61–62; arms control and, 61, 179–80, 184, 197–98, 207; attempted assassination of, 65–66, 67–71, 82–83, 86–89; as California governor, 1, 27, 27–28; Carter administration and, 61–62; Central American policy of, 178, 188–92; character of, 1, 4–5; Cold War and, 91, 185, 229, 289; Communism and, 303–4; death of, 324–26; defense spending and, 86; détente and, 30; economic policy of, 62–63, 69, 86, 138–39, 257–64; Falklands War and, 144, 150–56, 158, 161; Geneva summit and, 248–52; Gorbachev-Kennedy meeting and, 252–54; Grenada invasion and, 217–26, 230–32; health care and, 63; Helsinki Final Act and, 47; Iran-Contra affair and, 70, 278–81, 285; Iran hostage crisis and, 63; John Paul II and, 179–82; Kissinger, Henry and, 29; military buildup and, 135; missile diplomacy and, 205; Mitterrand, Francois and, 248; Moscow summit (1988) and, 301–3; nuclear pacifism of, 32, 63, 178, 179–80; Poland, support for and, 171–77; religion and, 176; Reykjavik summit and, 266–72, 283–84, 284–87, 289; SDI and, 234, 235–47, 266–72, 290; Solidarity and, 131, 132, 176–81; taxation and, 86, 260–61; terrorism and, 278; Thatcher, Margaret and, 27, 57, 60, 137–38, 139–41, 223–26, 299–301; as too American, 2, 32, 52, 63; Vietnam War and, 61; Westminster speech (1982) of, 88, 182–85, 273
Reagan Doctrine, 186, 187, 188, 272–81; in Central America, 272–78; freedom fighters, support for and, 272–76; Iran-Contra affair and, 278–81
Reaganomics, 69, 138, 261
realpolitik, 187
Reece, Gordon, 85, 185, 219
Reeves, Richard, 70, 272–78, 300
Regan, Donald, 138, 270, 284, 300

religious freedom: Christian humanism and, 7; Communism and, 18; John Paul II, Pope and, 18, 84, 94, 293; Vatican II and, 6, 7
Republican Party, Republicans: 1968 presidential nomination and, 2; Liberaldom and, 4; Rockefeller, Nelson and, 30
Reykjavik summit, 266–72, 283–84, 284–87
Rhodesia, 3, 40, 51, 105–6, 112
Roach, John, 240
Rockefeller, Nelson, 28, 29, 30
Rodman, Peter, 189, 201, 227, 232, 273, 277, 280
Rodriguez, Carlos Rafael, 189
Romania, 231, 317
Ruiz, Henri, 124
Russell, Bertrand, 230

Sadat, Anwar, 35
Safire, William, 304
Samuelson, Paul, 255, 256
Sandinista Front of National Liberation (SFNL), 123–24
Saturday Night Live, 279
Saudi Arabia, 37
Scargill, Arthur, 261–62, 297; "Scargill insurrection" of 1984–85, 23
Schell, Jonathan, 241
Schlesinger, Arthur, Jr., 256
Schlesinger, James, 286
Schmidt, Helmut, 49, 108, 126, 166; arms control and, 206; missile diplomacy and, 205; "peace movement" and, 213
Schotte, Jan, 240
Scoon, Sir Paul, 217, 225
Scowcroft, Brent, 26, 315
SDI. See Strategic Defense Initiative
Second Vatican Council. See Vatican II
Seldon, Arthur, 22
Sestanovich, Steve, 273
sexuality, Catholic Church and, 9–12, 96–97
sexual revolution (1960s), 2–3, 9, 53, 97
SFNL. See Sandinista Front of National Liberation
Shaddick, Ray, 68
Shaw, Bernard, 325
Sheffield, HMS, 154, 155
Shevardnadze, Edward, 269, 289
Short, Edward, 211
Shultz, George, 170, 176, 191, 245, 246, 268, 271, 274–75, 283, 285, 289, 300
Sikorski, Radek, 276, 305
Singapore, 200, 266

Smith, Adam, 266
Smith, Geoffrey, 151, 152, 154, 161, 169, 170, 207, 286
Social Democratic Party (SPD) (West Germany), 126, 142
Solidarity: American labor movement and, 131, 132, 172–73; birth of, 115–20; Brezhnev Doctrine and, 131, 133; Catholic Church and, 131, 188; Central America and, 122; Cold War and Soviet Union and, 120, 122; John Paul II and, 84, 117, 130–31, 135, 188; NATO and, 131; pipeline sanctions and, 167–70; private aid to, 173–75; Reagan, Ronald and, 131, 132; revival of, 295–98; Soviet response to, 120–29, 129–35, 166–82; Thatcher, Margaret and, 131; U.S. support for, 167–71, 180–82; Walesa, Lech and, 116, 119, 120, 129–34, 173, 187
Solzhenitsyn, Alexander, 185, 216
Somalia, 49
Somoza, Anastasio, 123, 192, 273
South Africa, 3, 45
South Korea, 200, 266
Soviet Politburo: John Paul II, attempted assassination of and, 77, 80, 81; Polish problem and, 203; Solidarity and, 121–22, 128–29, 130, 133; Tokyo summit (1979) and, 107
Soviet Union: Afghanistan, invasion of by, 62, 81, 113–14; Afghanistan invasion of, 52; Afghan war and, 276–77; appeasement of, 62; arms control and, 197–98, 205–9, 228–29; British policy toward, 84–85; Catholic Church and, 14; Cold War and, 120, 122; collapse of, 308–12, 312–17; decline of, 198–205, 252–57; Eastern Europe, rule of and, 1; economy of, 135, 199, 255–56; John Paul II, attempted assassination of and, 77–82, 112; John Paul II papal visit to Poland and, 100–105; John Paul II threat to power of, 92–96, 111; "peace movement" and, 211–12, 216–17; Polish problem and, 201–5; SDI and, 235–39; Solidarity and, 115–20, 120–35, 166–82; terrorism and, 39; Thatcher, Margaret and, 113; Thatcher, Margaret visit to, 293–94; Third World interventions of, 36, 39–40, 122–25,

177, 200–201, 276, 305; Walesa, Lech and, 297; West, decline of and, 34, 38–40
Soylent Green, 41
Speakes, Larry, 284
Spielberg, Steven, 76
Springsteen, George S., 26
stagflation, 37, 39
Stalin, Joseph, 210, 318
Stasi (East German intelligence service), 80
State Department, U.S.: arms control and, 207, 208; "dual track" policy and, 140; Grenada invasion and, 221, 222; SDI and, 245
St. John-Stevas, Norman, 19
Stockman, David, 138
Stone, Norman, 22
Strategic Arms Limitation Talks (SALT), 46, 61
Strategic Defense Initiative (SDI), 234; Geneva summit and, 248–52; Gorbachev, Mikhail and, 243, 266–72, 290; John Paul II and, 239, 242–43; MAD and, 238, 243, 244–45; NATO and, 245–46; NORAD and, 238–39; nuclear disarmament and, 246; Reagan, Ronald and, 235–47, 266–72, 290; Reykjavik summit and, 266–72, 284–87; Soviet Union and, 235–39; Thatcher, Margaret and, 236, 239, 243–47, 286–87; USCCB and, 240–42
Supreme Court, U.S., abortion and, 2–3
Survey, 40
Suslov, Mikhail, 118, 133, 212
Switzerland, 34, 34–35

Talbott, Strobe, 256–57
Tebbit, Margaret, 72
Tebbit, Norman, 65, 71, 72
Telchuk, Horst, 314
terrorism: IRA, 109–10; in Ireland, 164; John Paul II, attempted assassination of and, 76–77; Reagan, Ronald and, 278; rise of, 34–35; Soviet threat and, 39; West, decline of and, 34–35
Thatcher, Margaret: achievements of, 331–34; Andropov's funeral and, 226–27; Anglo-Irish agreement and, 84; arms control and, 205–8, 215–16, 286–88; attempted assassination of, 65–66, 71–75, 84–86; as British minister of education, 1, 19–20, 24; British-Vatican relations and, 163–66; Carter, Jimmy

and, 113; as chancellor of the exchequer, 1–2; character of, 1, 4–5; Cold War and, 105, 106; Communism, fall of and, 312–17; Communism and, 106–7; conservatism of, 59; CPC lecture (1968) of, 21–22, 23; defense spending and, 106; "dual track" policy and, 140–41; Eastern European diplomacy of, 291–99; economic policy of, 22, 23–24, 57–58, 84, 105, 106, 135, 138–39, 141–42, 257–64; Falklands War and, 84, 144–46, 148–53, 155–61; foreign policy of, 105, 112; general election manifesto (1970) and, 24; Gorbachev, Mikhail and, 84–85, 233, 243, 293–94, 312–17; Grenada invasion and, 220–22, 223–26, 231; Heath, Edward Conservative government and, 20, 23, 25; Helsinki Final Act and, 47; Iran-Contra scandal and, 280–81; Iranian hostage crisis and, 114–15; IRA terrorism and, 109–10, 164; "Iron Lady" speech of, 27, 106; monetarism of, 57, 135, 138; outspokenness of, 19–20, 22; "peace movement" and, 84, 213–14; Polish problem and, 163, 166–71; as prime minister, 2, 23, 60, 105; public spending and, 105, 106; Reagan, Ronald and, 27, 60, 137–38, 139–41, 223–26, 299–301; religion and, 85–86; Rhodesia problem and, 105–6, 112; "Scargill insurrection" and, 23, 261–62; SDI and, 236, 239, 243–47, 286–87; Solidarity and, 131; taxation and, 58, 106; terrorism and, 114; as too conservative, 2, 21, 26, 52; Toryism of, 21–22; as Tory leader, 23, 26–27; union reform and, 58, 59, 105; United States and, 21, 57; winter of discontent and, 148
Thatcher, Sir Denis, 27, 72, 73, 137, 142, 143
Thatcherism, 21–22, 257–58, 262
"These for Conversation with Representatives of the Polish Leadership," 121
Third World: anti-Communist guerrilla fighters in, 272–75; decolonization and, 3; Marxist guerrilla groups in, 40, 42–43; oil and, 37–38; Soviet interventions in, 36, 39–40, 122–25,

177, 200–201, 276, 305; UN
and, 3, 39; Vietnam War and,
45
Thomas, Hugh, 22, 225
Thompson, E. P., 215
Thurow, Lester, 255
Time magazine, 110, 182, 256,
275, 280, 285
Tokyo summit (1979), 107–9
Tomasek, Frantisek, 93, 204, 306
Tongues of Fire (Martin), 98
Tory Party (Britain): Heath,
Edward and, 1, 3, 24–25; labor
unions and economic policy
and, 3; Liberaldom and, 4;
Thatcher, Margaret and, 20–23,
26; union reform and, 58
totalitarianism, 110
Trafford, Tony, 73
"Truce of 1968," 12
Trudeau, Pierre, 139, 233
Tunney, John, 197, 198

Ukraine, 93, 94, 183
UN Declaration of Human Rights,
93–94
United Nations (UN), 30; China
and, 3; Falklands War and,
150, 158; John Paul II address
(1979) to, 110–11; OPEC oil
price hikes and, 37; Third
World and, 3, 39–40
United States: Cold War and, 88;
Contra funding and, 188–92;
Falklands War and, 150–57,
158; Grenada and, 217–26;
Keynesian revolution in economics in, 3; Latin America
and, 161; "nuclear freeze"
movement in, 215; sexual revolution in, 2–3; social decline in,
34–40; Soviet threat and,
38–40; spirit of enterprise in,
263–64; Thatcher, Margaret
and, 57; Third World anti-
Communist guerrilla fighters
and, 272–75; Vietnam Syn-
drome in, 36, 39, 47; Vietnam
War and, 29, 35–36; welfare
revolution in, 3

UN Security Council, 3
UN Security Council Resolution
502, 150
U.S. Conference of Catholic Bish-
ops (USCCB), 240–42
Ustinov, Dmitriy, 81, 118, 198, 202
Ut Unum Sint (John Paul II), 6

Vance, Cyrus, 44, 50
Vatican II: Catholic Church and, 3,
52; Church, government of
and, 7–9; Cracow, Poland and,
8–9, ecumenism and, 6–7;
implementation of, 6–9; John
Paul II and, 5, 6–9; liberals,
Catholic and, 8; liturgy and, 3;
religious freedom and, 6, 7
Versailles G-7 summit, 168
Vietnam: China and, 51; Commu-
nism in, 107
Vietnam War, 3, 27, 29, 33, 44,
210; Reagan, Ronald and, 61;
Third World and, 45; United
States and, 29, 35–36; West,
decline of and, 34, 35–36
Voice, 103, 104
Voice of America, 104
Voigt, Karsten, 125–26
Volcker, Paul, 186, 259

Wakeham, John, 72, 73
Wakeham, Roberta, 72
Waldheim, Kurt, 43
Walentynowicz, Anna, 116
Walesa, Lech, 116, 117, 119, 120,
129–34, 173, 176, 177, 187,
297
Walker, Peter, 20, 233, 262
Walters, Dick, 248
Walters, Vernon, 171, 177
Warnke, Paul, 46
Warnock, Mary, 332
Warsaw Pact, 38–39, 120, 126,
127, 134, 178, 290
Washington Post, 70, 138, 273
Watergate, 28, 29, 44, 45, 279
Watkins, Jim, 239
Weigel, George, 181, 192, 204,
241; Falklands War and, 156;
Humanae Vitae and, 11; John

Paul II and Communism and,
17; John Paul II and religious
freedom and, 7; John Paul II
and Vatican II and, 8, 9; John
Paul II election and, 92; John
Paul II papal visit to Poland
and, 104; John Paul II threat to
Soviet power and, 95, 111,
112; John Paul II visit to Britain
and, 164
Weinberger, Caspar, 176, 300; arms
control and, 206–7; Falklands
War and, 151, 152, 154;
Grenada invasion and, 221;
military buildup and, 88, 186;
Reykjavik summit and, 268;
SDI and, 235, 243, 245
Welch, Colin, 43
welfare revolution, 3
West: psychological climate in,
40–43; social decline in, 34–40
West Germany, 4, 13, 34–35
Whitelaw, Willie, 26, 114, 153
Wicker, Tom, 184
Williams, Gary, 220
Wilson, Harold, 212
Wojtyla, Karol. *See* John Paul II
Wolf, Charles, Jr., 199
Workers Defense Committee
(KOR), 101, 117, 201
World Bank, 139
World Peace Council, 209, 210
Wyszynski, Stefan, 54; John Paul II
and, 5; Solidarity and, 117,
118, 120, 131; Soviet Commu-
nism and, 16, 17

Yeats, William Butler, 41
Yeltsin, Boris, 289–90, 321, 323–24
Yemen, 272
Yes, Prime Minister, 226

Zagladin, Vadim, 125, 126; Gor-
bachev-Kennedy meeting and,
252–54; John Paul II threat to
Soviet power and, 93
Zakheim, Dov, 151
Zimbabwe, 51, 105. *See also*
Rhodesia